The Dave Given Rock'n'Roll Stars Handbook

The Dave Given Rock 'n' Roll Stars Handbook

Rhythm and Blues Artists and Groups

An Exposition-Banner Book

Exposition Press   Smithtown, New York

First Edition

Library of Congress Catalog Card Number: 79-57513

ISBN 0-682-49577-8

Printed in the United States of America

Preface

The phrase "ROCK'N'ROLL" spells not only excitement but also a vital sense of being young. It is difficult to explain, but Frank Zappa caught something of it when he said, "It was during the Korean War, when I'd listen to black radio stations. That music I enjoyed the best." To musicians, it may mean technic with David Gates describing it as "basic with four chord triplet ballad," and Bob Dylan seeing it as "an extension of twelve bar blues."

In agreement, I carefully chose the artists to fill this handbook (and the matched set of volumes to follow) with a wide range from Doo-Wopp to Rock-A-Billy to Rock as we know it today. To me, Rock'n'Roll can be "Rhythm'n'Blues" pleading or shouting, and much of our contemporary Disco may *not* be so! Each of us, whether we play or listen, may have our own vision and little is gained by attempting dissection of that wonderful sound of which Alan Freed (then deejay in Cleveland) so aptly coined a phrase to challenge us to move with the beat to *"rock* forward on the ball of your foot *and roll* back on your heel" . . . to ROCK AND ROLL!

This handbook, and eventually the matched set of volumes, is intended as an accurate and enjoyable encyclopedic overview of the artists, groups, and recordings (singles) for the daily use of the professional, the devoted fan, the enthusiastic listener, and the young novice entering upon enjoyment of his very first single. It is also a flesh-and-blood document of the men and women who contributed so much to our enjoyment, with a ready-reference discography of the recordings which gave it life and meaning.

This initial work represents part of a lengthy hobby of love reaching from boyhood into manhood and owes much to the personal contribution and encouragement of a real friend, Fred Masotti, of Hamilton, Ontario. In dedicating it to my father and mother I am mindful of the countless parents who, with varied patience and some misgivings, bravely bore the great onslaught of sound in their homes and who, eventually, each in their own way, learned to rock and roll with it!

Last, this book was written for you—the young at heart—that you might not only enjoy "Rock'n'Roll" but enjoy it more abundantly!

The Dave Given Rock 'n' Roll Stars Handbook

♭ ♯ ♪ ♩ 𝅗𝅥

Arthur Alexander

Born in Florence (five miles from Sheffield) Alabama, on May 10, 1940.

Like many other Southern artists, ARTHUR ALEXANDER had his musical beginning in the harmonious sounds of the Church, where his father played his guitar and his mother sang at the services. His talented father played accompaniment to Gospel songs and was popular at Saturday night gigs and so forth. None of Arthur's brothers or sisters became involved in music, although he did claim that one of his sisters could really sing but was not enthused about a singing career.

Arthur Alexander was singing with Gospel groups from as early as sixth grade. He became the youngest member of one youthful group but was permitted to perform only part-time locally and not on out-of-town engagements. The group kept on making music, with little or no opportunity, locally, of ever getting close to a recording studio. Arthur found work as a bellhop in a Sheffield hotel and kept on developing his musical-group activities.

A friend of Arthur's heard about Tom Stafford, a manager in Florence, and soon introduced young Alexander to him. Stafford had written lyrics without music, and soon, together, the pair began putting words to music and laying plans to do something about their songs. Arthur was getting along chording on his guitar and Tom Stafford penned "Sally Sue Brown," which Arthur put to music; they both liked the sound of it. A third individual, Donnie Frith, joined the ambitious music-makers and, being able to play the guitar and piano, soon provided some solid backup music. Arthur Alexander continued creating melodies for Tom Stafford's lyrics, and the group began plans for better things ahead.

Around that time two other enterprising local hopefuls came along, Rick Hall and Billy Shirrill (both then playing with a group called the "Fairlanes," originally out of Hamilton, Alabama), and things began to happen in a small way. Tom Stafford's father owned a drugstore with a large vacant room upstairs, and, equipped with a small family two-track tape recorder, the group set about finishing the area with burlap, egg crates, and so forth, to control sound and begin, in a fashion, to make their own demos.

Along came another piece of seeming good fortune in the person of Henry Bennett, who had written "She Wants To Rock," a song then pleasing, in 1958. Tom Stafford, liking the sound of it, secured a license, and the group was in the music-publishing business. Tom enthusiastically demonstrated a demo of it to SUN RECORDS in Memphis (where Elvis Presley had his start) and a record was cut, but it didn't get anywhere. Tom, still fired up, took their own song "Sally Sue Brown" and caught the interest of Judd Phillips (Sam Phillips's brother) at JUDD RECORDS, but the release never made any big waves.

Undaunted, Arthur Alexander kept on bell-hopping at the hotel while the group began pooling spare cash for greater effort. Rick Hall discovered an old tobacco barn on the outskirts of Muscle Shoals and, again, the group got busy working at it until it was ready for makeshift recording. With an Ampex four-track tape recorder, they were in production! The group, now minus Billy Shirrill, who had left for Nashville to make it on his own, began producing better quality demos, which Arthur Alexander and Rick Hall carried around the studios in Nashville, with little success. Interest was shown in the song itself, but there was no encouragement for the group. Rick Hall, a strong-minded person, remained convinced that one of the demos, "You Better Move On," was a potential hit and that all that was needed was more effort and development!

Barely a month later, Arthur and Rick ran into Noel Ball, deejay at station WMHA in Nashville and A&R man at DOT RECORDS. Noel agreed that the group had something good. Time dragged by, month after month, before the administrators seemed to get on with recording "You Better Move On," but within three months of release in 1962 it hit the Charts. Unfortunately, Noel Ball left DOT RECORDS and the group wandered in the wilderness through SOUND STAGE 7 and MONUMENT to WARNER BROTHERS. Still, success at DOT RECORDS saw production of their fine Rhythm and Blues number "You Better Move On/A Shot Of Rhythm'N'Blues" (DOT 16309), which became a double-sided smash. "Where Have You Been (All My Life)" (DOT 16357) became a follow-up success, and "Anna (Go To Him)" (DOT 16387) was aired internationally by the "Beatles" on their "BEATLEMANIA" album! Arthur Alexander enjoyed six other releases at DOT RECORDS.

Two recording stints at SOUND STAGE 7 (with Noel Ball's friend Fred Foster) saw production of "The Other Woman" (2556), "Show Me The Road" (2572), "Set Me Free" (2619), "Bye Bye Love" (2626), and "Cry Like A Baby" (1652), which became a "Boxtops" hit in 1968. One record was produced at MONUMENT, "I Need You Baby/Spanish Harlem (1060). After three popular recordings at WARNER BROTH-

ERS, including "I'm Coming Home" (7571) and "Lover Please" (7676), Arthur Alexander cut a great version of Steve Alaimo's 1963 hit "Every Day I Have To Cry" (CHECKER 1032) on BUDDAH 492 and followed it with a tribute to Elvis Presley, "Hound Dog Man's Gone Home," on MUSIC MILL 1012. Arthur Alexander also cut "You Better Move On" and "You're Gonna Love Yourself In The Morning," a song written by Donnie Fritts on ABC-DUNHILL Label, but they were never released!

Arthur Alexander went on the road in both the U.S. and the U.K. with great success, cut several popular albums, and gave us his latest single, "Sharing The Night Together" (BUDDAH 522 and 602), a song by Eddie Struzick, BUDDAH's studio manager. Arthur Alexander, having no band of his own, used the studio musicians from Muscle Shoals to Nashville to Memphis and worked with most of them personally at one time or another. George Soule and Al Cartier produced for Arthur Alexander. George, talented in his own right, had one recording of his own ("Get Involved") and wrote the Percy Sledge hit "I'll Be Your Everything." The career of Arthur Alexander, apart from his musical accomplishment and widespread popularity as an entertainer, has to be appreciated as the saga of one man's dream and of a human spirit that refused to let it go!

Discography

AS "JUNE ALEXANDER"

JUDD

1020	SALLY SUE BROWN (1960)/In The Middle Of It All

AS "ARTHUR ALEXANDER"

DOT

16309	YOU BETTER MOVE ON (2-62)/A Shot Of Rhythm And Blues
16357	WHERE HAVE YOU BEEN (ALL MY LIFE) (5-62)/Soldier Of Love
16387	ANNA (GO TO HIM) (10-62)/I Hang My Head And Cry
16425	YOU'RE THE REASON (1-63)/Go Home Girl
16454	I WONDER WHERE YOU ARE TONIGHT (4-63)/Dream Girl
16509	BABY BABY (8-63)/Pretty Girls Everywhere
16554	KEEP GUESSING (11-63)/Where Did Sally Go
16616	BLACK NIGHT (1964)/Ole John Amos
16737	DETROIT CITY (1964)/You Don't Care

SOUND STAGE 7

2556	THE OTHER WOMAN (1-66)/(Baby) For You
2572	SHOW ME THE ROAD (10-66)/Turn Around

MONUMENT

1060 I NEED YOU BABY (1968)/Spanish Harlem

SOUND STAGE 7

2619 SET ME FREE (10-68)/Love's Where Life Begins
2626 BYE BYE LOVE (3-69)/Another Place Another Time
2652 CRY LIKE A BABY (3-70) ["Boxtops" '68 hit. MALA 593]/ Glory Road

WARNER BROTHERS

7571 I'M COMING HOME (3-72)/It Hurts To Want It So Bad
7633 MR. JOHN/You Got Me Knockin'
7676 LOVER PLEASE (2-73)/They'll Do It Every Time

BUDDAH

492 EVERY DAY I HAVE TO CRY (SOME) (9-75)/Everybody Needs Somebody To Love
522 SHARING THE NIGHT TOGETHER (7-76)/She'll Throw Stones At You

MUSIC MILL

1012 HOUND DOG MAN'S GONE HOME (1977) [Tribute to Elvis]/ So Long Baby

BUDDAH

522* SHARING THE NIGHT TOGETHER (11-78) ["Dr. Hook" '78 hit. CAPITOL 4621]/She'll Throw Stones At You

*Also issued on BUDDAH 602.

♭ ♯ ♪ ♩ 𝅗𝅥

J. J. Barnes

Real Name: "James Jay Barnes." Born in Detroit, Michigan, on November 30, 1943.

J. J. BARNES has become a Soul Master of high regard within the United Kingdom. All of his RIC-TIC and GROOVESVILLE sides are much sought after. Rooted in Gospel, Jimmy sang originally with the "Hurricane Travellers." In 1959, he formed his own Gospel choir, the "Halo Gospel Singers."

From the early Sixties he recorded for numerous Detroit labels, but it was not until 1965 and his first RIC-TIC release, "Please Let Me In/I Think I Found A Love" (106), that the R&B market took note of regional success. The follow-up, "Real Humdinger/I Ain't Gonna Do It" (RIC-TIC 110), released in February of the following year, became not only a Chart Smash in the R&B Top-Twenty but established J. J. Barnes as a Soul singer with top ratings. His production work for RIC-TIC and GROOVESVILLE came from "DON DAVIS" (who also did much for the career of the "Dramatics," Johnnie Taylor, Major Lance, Tyrone Davis, and others) and in no uncertain terms made J. J. Barnes recordings *GEMS!*

Some of his other popular Soul entries are "My Love Came Tumbling Down/Won't You Let Me Know" (KABLE 913), "Just One More Time" (MICKAYS 3004), and his GROOVESVILLE hits "Baby Please Come Back Home" (1006) and follow-up "Now That I Got You Back" (1008). Unfortunately, at the end of the Sixties, Don Davis and J. J. Barnes ran into business differences, which separated them, leaving Jimmy to continue alone, seeking for a major break! PERCEPTION Label man Dave Jordan, at the end of 1973, had J. J. Barnes record "You Are Just A Living Doll/Touching You" (PERCEPTION 546).

Discography

J. J. BARNES AND THE "DELL-FI'S"

KABLE

913* MY LOVE CAME TUMBLING DOWN (1961)/Won't You Let Me Know

J. J. BARNES

MICKAYS

3004† JUST ONE MORE TIME (1962)/Hey Child I Love You
3114 THESE ARMS OF LOVE (1962)/Color Green
? LONELY NO MORE (1962-63)/Get A Hold On Yourself
351 TEEN AGE QUEEN (1963)/Some One
353 SO FAR AWAY (1964)/Love Requires Understanding

RING

101 POOR UNFORTUNATE ME (I AIN'T GOT NOBODY) (1964)/She Ain't Ready

JAMES BARNES AND THE "AGENTS"

GOLDEN WORLD

101 FREE AT LAST (GREAT DAY A COMING) (1965)/Free At Last (Great Day A Coming) [Instr.]
102 GOOD AND FUNKY (1965)/The Bomb [by "Funky Four Plus"]

J. J. BARNES

INVASION

1001 MY BABY (ca. 1965)/You're Still My Baby

RIC-TIC

106 PLEASE LET ME IN (11-65)/I Think I Found A Love
110 REAL HUMDINGER (2-66)/I Ain't Gonna Do It
115 DAY TRIPPER (6-66) ["Beatles" tune]/Don't Bring Me Bad News
117 SAY IT (10-66)/Deeper In Love

---

*Also RICH 1005 and MERCURY/SURE 1737 (5-62).
†Also SCEPTER 1266 (10-63).

GROOVESVILLE

1006	BABY PLEASE COME BACK HOME (5-67)/Chains Of Love
1008	NOW THAT I GOT YOU BACK (11-67)/Forgive Me

REVILOT

216	HOLD ON TO IT (2-78)/Now She's Gone
218	SAD DAY A COMING (1968)/I'll Keep Coming Back
222	OUR LOVE IS IN THE POCKET (1968)/All Your Goodies Are Gone [Instr.]
225	SO-CALLED FRIENDS (1969)/Now She's Gone [Instr.]

BUDDAH

120	EVIDENCE (7-69)/I'll Keep Coming Back

VOLT

4027	SNOWFLAKES (11-69)/Got To Get Rid Of You

TOUCH

1000	TO AN EARLY GRAVE/Cloudy Days

LEO

?	SOUL EMOTIONS/Wouldn't It Be A Pleasure

PERCEPTION

546	YOU ARE JUST A LIVING DOLL (12-73)/Touching You

CONTEMPO

7003	HOW LONG (1977)/The Erroll Flynn

♭ ♯ ♪ ♩ 𝅗𝅥

"Beatles"

MEMBERS: *John Winston Lennon,* lead singer, rhythm guitar, harmonica, piano (born Oxford Street Maternity Hospital, Liverpool, October 9, 1940); *James Paul McCartney,* lead singer, guitar, fuzz bass, piano (born Walton Hospital, Liverpool, June 18, 1942); *George Harrison,* vocal, lead guitar, sitar (born 12 Arnold Grove, Wavetree, Liverpool, February 25, 1943); Stuart Sutcliffe, bass guitar (art-student friend of John Lennon—left group in Hamburg, West Germany in 1961—died there following year of brain hemorrhage); Pete Best, drums, organ (joined 1960 and left 1962; replaced by Ringo Starr); *Ringo (Richard Starkey) Starr,* vocal, drums (born 9 Madryn Street, Liverpool, July 7, 1940).

Hometown: Liverpool, England.

The "BEATLES" were the true kingpins of Rock and Roll for almost all of the Sixties. Their original compositions, recordings, and films have become a permanent legend of the music of their time, affecting the entire world of music and the directions of all those who successfully followed them. They represented the meeting of the men and the moment, coming at a time when teenagers did not have any idol in the wake of the great Elvis Presley and when black Rhythm and Blues artists dominated the scene. The "Beatles" became the first white group from Britain to climb U.K. and U.S. Charts. Classical composer Aaron Copland aptly said it: "When people want to re-create the mood of the Sixties they will play 'Beatle' music." Truly the "FAB FOUR," they went from a few deutschmarks a night in 1960 to $304,000 a night in 1962! The phenomenon of the "Beatles" and "Beatlemania" was compared by London's *Daily Telegraph* to the mass hysteria of Adolf Hitler's Nuremberg demonstrations. The *Sunday Times* music critic called the "Beatles" "the greatest composers since Beethoven." They are remembered as the best of the "LIVERPOOL SOUND" and as surpassing all advance record sales with "Can't Buy Me Love" (CAPITOL 5150) at two and a half million, and as being top-billed on the Ed Sullivan show that attracted seventy-three million TV viewers. They also sang "All You Need Is Love" (CAPITOL 5964) on the worldwide *Our World* television show before an estimated viewer audience of over a hundred and fifty million!

John Lennon, while at Quarrybank Grammar School in Liverpool, formed his own skiffle group, the "Quarrymen," with Eric Griffiths (guitar), Pete Shotton (washboards), and Colin Hanson (drums). Johnny Hutch and Tommy Moore also served on drums. George Harrison, at Liverpool Institute, formed his "Rebels." Paul McCartney also attended the Institute. Richard Starkey (Ringo Starr), after school hours, was perfecting his drumming with the Eddie Clayton skiffle group. June 1956 saw the forming nucleus of this famous foursome when sixteen-year-old John Lennon and fourteen-year-old Paul McCartney came together from their different groups at a Rock concert in Woolton Parish Church in Liverpool. Both were fascinated with the guitar and the entire Rock sound, and they spent much time practicing and perfecting arrangements. George Harrison, Paul's friend and only fifteen years of age, joined the "Quarrymen" in 1958, and that year they changed the group's name to "Johnny and the Moondogs." The following year saw the addition of guitarist (bass) Stuart Sutcliffe and another change of name, to "The Silver Beatles." The group had now earned a fair local following, acquired a manager, Allan Williams, enjoyed their first audition through Larry Parnes (U.K. impresario), and headed for Scotland on a two-week engagement tour as backup to Johnny Gentle. John and Paul had now developed a seasoned combination style, having played together as the "Nurk Twins" at one time during 1957. Peter Best, whose mother owned the Liverpool Casbah Club and who had a following of his own, joined the "Silver Beatles" as drummer in 1960 and was influential in having the group name changed to its final form, "The Beatles."

The "Beatles" made their first foreign assignment in Hamburg, West Germany, which had to be cut short because George Harrison was underage! In April 1961, the group did their first recording, "My Bonnie/The Saints" (POLYDOR 24673), as the "Beat Brothers" and featuring Tony Sheridan. They were the resident group at Liverpool's Cavern Club before taking off for their second engagement in Hamburg, where, after a three-month stay, they returned to Liverpool, leaving Stu Sutcliffe behind them. Stu had fallen in love with a pretty German hairdresser, Astrid Kirchherr, and decided to stay in Hamburg and settle down. Incidentally, it was Astrid who gave Stuart the French hairdo and suggested he wear a buttoned, tight-fitting leather jacket, both of which the entire group liked and made famous! That same year, Brian Epstein (local music store owner who had accidentally heard of the "Beatles" and listened to them playing at the Cavern) became their manager, in December. The group had now made quite a musical reputation for themselves at the

Kaiser-Keller and Top Ten Club in Hamburg, while also getting rave notices at the Cavern, and the Indra Club, and an extra big show at Litherland Town Hall in Liverpool.

Brian had the group make demo tapes and made the rounds of the major recording studios, contacting DECCA, PYE, COLUMBIA, HMV, and EMI, but with little initial success. March 1962 saw DECCA Label make possibly the biggest mistake of all when it turned down the demo tapes! The group made a return engagement to Hamburg, where, following the death of Stu Sutcliffe from brain hemorrhage, the group decided to remain with four members rather than five! In the meantime, Brian Epstein had met George Martin and when the "Beatles" returned to Liverpool in June the audition was made, but caused the second casualty for the group when Pete Best and his drumming proved unacceptable. The search for a new drummer settled on Ringo (Richard Starkey) Starr, already making a name for himself with "Rory and the Hurricanes" both in Hamburg and Liverpool. Ringo Starr joined the group in 1962, the same year that DECCA Label (belatedly) released "My Bonnie/The Saints" (DECCA 31382) in the United States, and the "Beatles" appeared with Little Richard, Craig Douglas, and Jet Harris at the Liverpool Empire, October 28! October saw release of "Love Me Do/P.S. I Love You" (PARLOPHONE R-4949), which entered the U.K. Charts by December, when the group made their fourth engagement trip to Hamburg.

1963 took off with a bang in "Please Please Me/Ask Me Why" (PARLOPHONE R-4983), becoming No. 1 on the U.K. Charts. In February, John Lennon, Paul McCartney, Brian Epstein, and Dick James formed their own publishing company, "Northern Music Ltd"; the group made its initial TV appearance and entered upon the first U.K. concert tour with top-billing Helen Shapiro. Three other U.K. concert tours were completed that year, the second with the "Beatles" third in billing to Chris Montez and Tommy Roe, with Gerry and the "Pacemakers" (then top of the Charts with "How Do You Do It"); the third with top-billing Roy Orbison when the first signs of Beatlemania showed up with screaming and rioting incidents; and the fourth with the "Beatles" in top-billing and Beatlemania now a reality. 1963 also saw release of "From Me To You" (PARLOPHONE R-5051), "She Loves You" (PARLOPHONE R-5055), and "I Want To Hold Your Hand" (PARLOPHONE R-5084), all of which were released in the U.S. within a year, the big breakthrough being "I Want To Hold Your Hand." The second record (R-5055) created advance orders of 500,000! "Twist And Shout," an EP release, became No. 1, to be followed by "The Beatles Hits" and an album, "With The Beatles" (advance sales of 250,000, surpassing 200,000 achieved by Elvis Presley's "Blue Hawaii"). "I Want To Hold Your Hand" became No. 1 on the Charts immediately on release, with advance orders of one million!

The group made its first major U.K. spectacular on television, "Sunday Night at the London Palladium," where the theatre was mobbed and the full impact of Beatlemania was felt. The group then toured Sweden and on their return to London were met with the first of the many riotous welcomes that would follow them around the world! The "Beatles" then appeared in the Royal Variety Show before H.M. Queen Elizabeth, the Queen Mother, Princess Margaret, and Lord Snowden. The "Beatles" had now arrived, and this was the beginning of their acceptance in show business. 1963 went out as it came in—with a bang! All releases were now in the Top-Twenty, British fan-club membership had topped 80,000, film plans were well under way, and "The Beatles Christmas Show" in London was a big success!

January 1964 saw "I Want To Hold Your Hand" become No. 83 on U.S. Charts and within days become No. 1. The group had a cool reception in a Paris appearance. "Please Please Me" entered the album Charts, and singles kept booming in the U.S. The "Beatles" embarked on a record-breaking U.S. tour, starting with over 10,000 screaming worshipers meeting them at Kennedy Airport and Beatlemania following them through thirty-one appearances in twenty-four cities. They appeared twice on the Ed Sullivan show to top TV ratings and 50,000 fighting for 700 seats! That summer, the group toured Europe, New Zealand, and Australia, with their biggest reception ever, 300,000, at Adelaide! John Lennon headed the best-seller list with his book *In His Own Write* in the U.K. They released twenty singles, including two in West Germany, several in Canada, and the remainder in the U.K. and U.S. "Can't Buy Me Love" (CAPITOL 5150 and PARLOPHONE R-5114) achieved advance sales of two million! 1964, the group began filming *A Hard Day's Night* and saw it well received at a London premiere, with its title song (CAPITOL 5222) becoming No. 1 and the album in the 20s. Later reports of the U.S. tour show that all attendance, fee and grossing records were surpassed, and the British Prime Minister called the "Beatles" "our best exports." The group said goodbye to 1964 with the release of their tenth consecutive hit, "I Feel Fine" (CAPITOL 5327 and PARLOPHONE R-5200), and their long-playing "Beatles For Sale."

The "Beatles" had now scaled the multicolored heights of all their endeavors, top singles, top LPs and albums, top TV appearances, their own radio series (1963), "Pop Go the Beatles," record-smashing tours around the world, a best-seller in books, and top-ranking films, and were now turning their attention to various commercial enterprises. 1965 saw royal honors come to the group in the award of the MBE (Order of the British Empire), with strong public reaction against it and even protests being heard in the House of Lords after many holders of the MBE returned their awards in disgust.

The second U.S. tour proved another success, topped by New York's

Shea Stadium concert, shattering previous show business receipts records! "We Can Work It Out" (PARLOPHONE R-5389 and CAPITOL 5555) became the tenth consecutive instant No. 1 hit on U.K. Charts.

Ringo Starr married Maureen Cox on February 11, 1965, to carry off the second "Beatle" matrimonial event; John Lennon had married Cynthia Powell on August 23, 1962. It was in 1966 that George Harrison showed his interest in India and Eastern mysticism to the public by his visit there and his playing of the sitar. The preceding year saw the world premiere (with Royal attendance) of the "Beatle" film *Help* at the London Pavilion. John Lennon published his second book, *A Spaniard in the Works*. Brian Epstein had also published *A Cellar Full of Noise*. In May of 1966, the "Beatles" made what was to be their last performance in public at Wembley and recorded their first single in almost two years, "Paperback Writer" (CAPITOL 5651 and PARLOPHONE R-5452), *NOT TO JUMP IMMEDIATELY TO TOP OF U.K. CHARTS!* The world tour of 1966, including Japan, was to be their last appearance in public abroad.

From 1966 on things began to happen differently for the "Beatles." John Lennon made a comment about comparing the popularity of "Beatles" over Christ, which provoked a worldwide furor, and, on August 29, 1966, in San Francisco, they made their final live performance! Release of "Revolver" gave the first public intimation of drug use and the separate appearance of a "Beatle," John Lennon, with Dick Lester in the film *How I Won the War* proved an early indication that all was not well with the group. Increasing technological gadgetry, human circumstances, and even personal differences in ambition now impinged on all group activities. The electronic wizardry of their top-ranking records lured the "Beatles" solely to recording. The move away from live tours and the impact of Transcendental Meditation (Maharishi Mahesh Yogi) on the group further complicated the usefulness and personal interests of manager Brian Epstein. Add to this the alleged use of LSD by both Epstein and the group and we can appreciate the fact of his death by suicide in his Belgravia home during the August bank holiday of 1967. Growing dissatisfaction with NELMS ENTERPRISES (which garnered 25% commission on all recording royalties and did little in return) erupted when Brian Epstein's younger brother, Cliff, was appointed manager.

APPLE, a new corporation, was founded, and a struggle for management developed. Paul McCartney favored Lee Eastman of New York, and the others Allen Klein, also of New York. Klein got the job, and this was the beginning of the end for the "Beatles" as a group. Klein freed the group from the NELMS commitment and took over management and investments. Problems between Paul McCartney and Allen

Klein came to a head during the musical arrangements for "Let It Be" and where once nothing could go wrong for the "Beatles" now nothing seemed to go right. APPLE, which had involved itself in assisting new talent, retail merchandise outlets, promotional products, films, and so forth, suffered considerable financial losses, some of which came through overgenerosity to aspiring young musical hopefuls. Court action legally separated the "Beatles" when Justice Stamp decided that Paul McCartney could leave and then committed "Beatles & Company" to a receiver. The decision was accepted by all! George Harrison had already married Patricia Anne Boyd, but John Lennon's marriage to Cynthia had broken down and he was now associating with the talented Japanese-American star, Yoko Ono, whom he later married. Still later, Paul McCartney married Linda Eastman, and from the breakup of the group the wives were to play a major part in the separate development of the "Beatles"!

A string of wonderful recordings, singles and albums, with films of the group in action, was released prior to and during the dissolution period, including "Yellow Submarine" (CAPITOL U.S. 5715, U.K. R-5493), "Hey Jude" (APPLE U.S. 2276, U.K. R-5722), "Let It Be" (APPLE U.S. 2764, U.K. R-5833), the exploratory epoch-making psychedelic album "Sgt. Pepper's Lonely Hearts Club Band," and the controversial (alleged drug allusion) "A Day In The Life," which suffered a BBC ban and wide U.S. radio rejection. Separation by law became separation by fact, with John and Yoko settling in the United States, Paul and Linda taking up residence in Scotland, and with George and Ringo still working out amicable recording arrangements between film engagements in England.

Though the "Beatles" had ceased to be a group by name, the interlocking musical breakup was slow and extended, with John Lennon, Paul McCartney, George Harrison, and Ringo Starr making, each, their very own music together. "Abbey Road" was their last album together as a group, but the double "White Album" (November 1968) has become a showcase of their individual talents as songwriters (John, Paul, and George), arrangers, performers, and truly great artists. Ringo Starr's songwriting, up until the dissolution of the group, comprised only two songs ("Octopus's Garden" from "Abbey Road," and "Don't Pass Me By" from the "White Album") and even a scene from *Let It Be* shows George Harrison helping him write one of these. Ringo surprised us all, though, in his forthcoming three solo film roles, *Candy, The Magic Christian, Lisztomania,* and we shouldn't forget *The Son of Dracula.* He also gave us two solo albums by the latter part of 1970, one of which was "Sentimental Journey," an album of standards remembered from the Liverpool pubs (with Quincy Jones, Johnny Dankworth, and Elmer Bernstein).

1969 onward saw Johnny Lennon form his "Plastic Ono Band" and leading it with vocals and rhythm guitar, Yoko Ono on wind, Eric Clapton on guitar, Klaus Voormann on bass, and Alan White on drums. In 1970, the group comprised John Lennon, Yoko Ono, Klaus Voormann, and Ringo Starr back on the drums. Paul McCartney had created his new band, "Wings," including himself as lead vocals and bass guitar, ex-"Moody Blues" member from Birmingham Brian Arthur Haynes at lead guitar (a spot filled later by rhythm guitarist Henry McCollough in 1973, by Jimmy McCulloch 1974-78, and Laurence Juber in 1979), Linda McCartney (Paul's wife, born in New York City, September 24, 1942) at the keyboards, and Denny Seiwell, drummer from 1971-73 (replaced by Geoff Britton in 1974 and, later, by Joe English in 1975-78, and by Steve Holly in 1979). George Harrison went on to solo successes on both sides of the Atlantic, scoring with his initial "My Sweet Lord/What Is Life" (APPLE R-5884) in the U.K. and "What Is Life/Apple Scruffs" (APPLE 1828), both early in 1971. These were followed by a series of popular recordings through the Seventies on APPLE, EMI, and DARK HORSE to his latest at printing, "Love Comes To Everyone/Soft Touch" (DARK HORSE 8844), released in May 1979. Ringo Starr, apart from his films and albums, released various popular singles on several labels, beginning with "Beaucoups Of Blues/Coochy Coochy" (APPLE 2969) at the close of 1970 to "Heart On My Sleeve/Who Needs A Heart" (PORTRAIT 670018), with most of his recordings at APPLE, and a few at ATLANTIC and PORTRAIT.

At present, John Lennon and his Ono have settled down to family life on their farm in New York State, while Paul McCartney still likes live performances mostly at small English clubs during the summer months. Ringo Starr has become quite a designer of furniture, and George Harrison—after a small legal hassle (successful) over the similarity of "My Sweet Lord" with "He's So Fine" by the "Chiffons"—goes musically on his way in Los Angeles, a good friend of Eric Clapton and now an avid racing car fan.

Discography

AS "BEAT BROTHERS"

POLYDOR (U.K.)

24673* MY BONNIE (1-62) [Feat. Tony Sheridan]/The Saints (When The Saints Go Marching In)

---

*Released in U.S. on DECCA 31382 (4-62).

POLYDOR (GERMANY)

52-025	RUBY BABY (1962)/What'd I Say
52-185†	NICK NACK HULLY GULLY (1962)/Latermen Hully Gully

AS "BEATLES"

PARLOPHONE (U.K.)

R-4949	LOVE ME DO (10-62) [Feat. Paul]/P.S. I Love You [Feat. Paul]
R-4983	PLEASE PLEASE ME (1-63)/Ask Me Why
R-5015	FROM ME TO YOU (4-63)/Thank You Girl
R-5055	SHE LOVES YOU (8-63)/I'll Get You
R-5084	I WANT TO HOLD YOUR HAND (11-63)/This Boy

VEE JAY (U.S.)

498‡	PLEASE PLEASE ME (3-63) [Feat. John]/Ask Me Why [Feat. John]
522**	FROM ME TO YOU (5-63) [John and Paul]/Thank You Girl [John and Paul]

SWAN

4152	SHE LOVES YOU (9-63, 2-64) [John and Paul]/I'll Get You [John and Paul]

CAPITOL (U.S. and CANADA)

5112	I WANT TO HOLD YOUR HAND (1-64) [Feat. John]/I Saw Her Standing There [Feat. Paul]

MGM

13213	MY BONNIE (2-64)/The Saints (When The Saints Go Marching In)

CAPITOL

72133	ROLL OVER BEETHOVEN (12-63) [Feat. George]/Please Mister Postman [Feat. John]
72144	ALL MY LOVING (3-64) [Feat. Paul]/This Boy [John, Paul, and George]

Above two records released only in Canada.

---

†Released in U.S. on MGM 13201 (64).
‡Labeled "Beatles."
**In Canada, CAPITOL 72101.

TOLLIE (U.S.)

9001 TWIST AND SHOUT (3-64) [Feat. John]/There's A Place [John and Paul]
Above was released in Canada on CAPITOL 72146.

CAPITOL (U.S.)

6065 ROLL OVER BEETHOVEN (3-64) [Chuck Berry '56 hit. CHESS 1626]/Misery [Feat. John]

CAPITOL (U.S.)—PARLOPHONE (U.K.) R-5114

5150 CAN'T BUY ME LOVE (3-64) [Feat. Paul]/You Can't Do That [Feat. John]

VEE JAY

581 PLEASE PLEASE ME (2-64)/From Me To You
Above not released in Canada.
587 DO YOU WANT TO KNOW A SECRET (3-64) [Feat. George] [Billy J. Kramer '63 hit. LIBERTY 55586]/Thank You Girl
Above was released in Canada on CAPITOL 72159.

TOLLIE (U.S.)

9008 LOVE ME DO (4-64)/P.S. I Love You

LABELED AS "BEATLES"

MGM (U.S.)

13227 WHY (4-64) [Feat. Tony Sheridan]/Cry For A Shadow [Instr. by George and John]
Above was released in U.K. on POLYDOR 52-275 and labeled "Tony Sheridan & Beat Brothers."

ODEON (GERMANY)

22671 KOMM GIB MIR DEINE HAND (I WANT TO HOLD YOUR HAND)/Sie Liebt Dich (She Loves You)

LABELED AS "DIE BEATLES"

SWAN (U.S.)

4182 SIE LIEBT DICH (5-64) [John and Paul]/I'll Get You [John and Paul]
Above was released in Canada on CAPITOL 72125.

AS "BEATLES"

ATCO (U.S.)

6302 SWEET GEORGIA BROWN (9-64) [Feat. Tony Sheridan]/ Take Out Some Insurance On Me Baby* [Feat. Tony Sheridan]

ATCO

6308 AIN'T SHE SWEET (7-64) [Feat. John]/Nobody Child [Feat. Tony Sheridan]

POLYDOR (U.K.)

NH 52-317 AIN'T SHE SWEET (5-64) [Feat. John]/If You Love Me Baby [Feat. Tony Sheridan]

PARLOPHONE (U.K.)

R-5160 A HARD DAY'S NIGHT (7-64)/Things We Said Today [Feat. Paul]

CAPITOL

5222 A HARD DAY'S NIGHT (7-64) [John and Paul]/I Should Have Known Better [Feat. John]
5235 AND I LOVE HER (7-64) [Feat. Paul]/If I Fell [John and Paul]
5234 I'LL CRY INSTEAD (8-64) [Feat. John]/I'm Happy Just To Dance With You [Feat. George]
5255 MATCHBOX (9-64) [Feat. Ringo]/Slow Down [Feat. John]

CAPITOL (U.S.)—PARLOPHONE (U.K.) R-5200 (11-64)

5327 I FEEL FINE (12-64) [Feat. John]/She's A Woman [Feat. Paul]
5371 EIGHT DAYS A WEEK (2-65) [Feat. John]/I Don't Want To Spoil The Party [Feat. John]

AS PETE BEST

CAMEO

391 KANSAS CITY (4-65) [Feat. John]/Boys [Feat. Ringo]

*Above was also called "If You Love Me Baby" in U.K.

AS "BEATLES"

CAPITOL (U.S.)—PARLOPHONE (U.K.) R-5265 (4-65)

5407 TICKET TO RIDE (4-65) [Feat. John]/Yes It Is [John, Paul, and George]

CAPITOL (U.S.)—PARLOPHONE (U.K.) R-5305 (7-65)

5476 HELP (8-65) [Feat. John]/I'm Down [Feat. Paul]

CAPITOL

5498 YESTERDAY (9-65) [Feat. Paul]/Act Naturally [Feat. Ringo]

CAPITOL (U.S.)—PARLOPHONE (U.K.) R-5389 (12-65)

5555 WE CAN WORK IT OUT (12-65) [Feat. Paul]/Day Tripper [Paul and John]

5587 NOWHERE MAN (3-66) [Feat. John]/What Goes On (In Your Heart) [Feat. Ringo]

CAPITOL (U.S.)—PARLOPHONE (U.K.) R-5452 (6-66)

5651 PAPERBACK WRITER (6-66) [Feat. Paul]/Rain [Feat. John]

CAPITOL (U.S.)—PARLOPHONE (U.K.) R-5493 (8-66)

5715 YELLOW SUBMARINE (8-66) [Feat. Ringo/Elenor Rigby [Feat. Paul]

CAPITOL (U.S.)—PARLOPHONE (U.K.) R-5570 (2-67)

5810 PENNY LANE (2-67) [Feat. Paul]/Strawberry Fields Forever [Feat. John]

CAPITOL (U.S.)—CAPITOL (U.K.) R-5620 (7-67)

5964 ALL YOU NEED IS LOVE (7-67) [Feat. John]/Baby You're A Rich Man [John and Paul]

CAPITOL (U.S.)—CAPITOL (U.K.) R-5655 (11-67)

2056 HELLO GOODBYE (12-67) [Feat. Paul]/I Am The Walrus [Feat. John]

CAPITOL (U.S.)—CAPITOL (U.K.) R-5675 (3-68)

2138 LADY MADONNA (3-68) [Feat. Paul]/The Inner Light [Feat. George]

APPLE (U.S.)—APPLE (U.K.) R-5722 (8-68)

2276 HEY JUDE (9-68) [Feat. Paul]/Revolution [Feat. John]

AS "BEATLES"

APPLE (U.S.)—APPLE (U.K.) R-5777 (4-69)

2490 GET BACK (5-69) [Feat. Paul] [W. Billy Preston on organ]/ Don't Let Me Down [Feat. John]

APPLE (U.S.)—APPLE (U.K.) R-5786 (6-69)

2531 BALLAD OF JOHN & YOKO (6-69) [Feat. John]/Old Brown Shoe [Feat. George]

JOHN LENNON/"PLASTIC ONO BAND"

APPLE (U.S.)—APPLE (U.K.) 13 (7-69)

1809 GIVE PEACE A CHANCE (7-69) [Written by Leon Russell and Bonnie Bramlett]/Remember Love

AS "BEATLES"

APPLE (U.S.)—APPLE (U.K.) R-5814 (10-69)

2654 COME TOGETHER (10-69) [Feat. John]/Something [Feat. George]

JOHN LENNON/"PLASTIC ONO BAND"

APPLE (U.S.)—APPLE (U.K.) 1001 (11-69)

1813 COLD TURKEY (11-69)/Don't Worry Kyoko

APPLE (U.S.)—APPLE (U.K.) 1003 (2-70)

1818 INSTANT KARMA (WE ALL SHINE ON) (2-70)/Who Has Seen The Wind

AS "BEATLES"

APPLE (U.S.)—APPLE (U.K.) R-5833 (3-70)

2764 LET IT BE (3-70) [Feat. Paul]/You Know My Name (Look Up My Number) [John and Paul]

APPLE (U.S.)

2832 THE LONG AND WINDING ROAD (5-70) [Feat. Paul]/For You Blue [Feat. George]

RINGO STARR

2969 BEAUCOUPS OF BLUES (11-70)/Coochy Coochy

GEORGE HARRISON

2995 MY SWEET LORD (11-70)/Isn't It A Pity

JOHN LENNON/"PLASTIC ONO BAND"

1827 MOTHER (1-71)/Why

GEORGE HARRISON

APPLE (U.K.)

R-5884 MY SWEET LORD (1-71)/What Is Life?

APPLE (U.S.)

1828 WHAT IS LIFE? (2-71)/Apple Scruffs

PAUL McCARTNEY

APPLE (U.S.)—APPLE (U.K.) R-5889 (2-71)

1829 ANOTHER DAY (3-71)/Oh Woman, Oh Why?

JOHN LENNON/"PLASTIC ONO BAND"

APPLE (U.K.)

R-5892 POWER TO THE PEOPLE (3-71)/Open Your Box

APPLE (U.S.)

1830 POWER TO THE PEOPLE (4-71)/Touch Me

RINGO STARR

APPLE (U.S.)—APPLE (U.K.) R-5898 (4-71)

1831 IT DON'T COME EASY (4-71)/Early 1970

JOHN LENNON/"ELASTIC OZ BAND (PLASTIC ONO BAND)"

APPLE (U.S.)—APPLE (U.K.) 36

1835 GOD SAVE US (7-71)/Do The Oz

GEORGE HARRISON

APPLE (U.S.)—APPLE (U.K.) R-5912 (7-71)

1836 BANGLA DESH (8-71)/Deep Blue

PAUL & LINDA McCARTNEY

APPLE (U.S.)

1837 UNCLE ALBERT/ADMIRAL HALSEY (8-71)/Too Many People

APPLE (U.K.)

R-5914 BACK SEAT OF MY CAR (8-71)/Heart Of The Country

JOHN LENNON/"PLASTIC ONO BAND"

APPLE (U.S.)

1840 IMAGINE (10-71)/It's So Hard

YOKO ONO/"PLASTIC ONO BAND"

1839 MRS. LENNON (11-71)/Midsummer New York

JOHN & YOKO/"PLASTIC ONO BAND"

APPLE (U.S.)—APPLE (U.K.) R-5970

1842 HAPPY XMAS (WAR IS OVER) (12-71)/Listen The Snow Is Falling

PAUL McCARTNEY/"WINGS"

APPLE (U.S.)—APPLE (U.K.) R-5936 (2-72)

1847 GIVE IRELAND BACK TO THE IRISH (3-72)/Give Ireland Back To The Irish [Instr.]

JOHN LENNON/"PLASTIC ONO BAND" [W. "ELEPHANT'S MEMORY"]

APPLE (U.S.)

1848 WOMAN IS THE NIGGER OF THE WORLD (5-72)/Sisters O Sisters

RINGO STARR

APPLE (U.S.)—APPLE (U.K.) R-5944 (3-72)

1849 BACK OFF BOOGALOO (4-72)/Blindman

PAUL McCARTNEY/"WINGS"

APPLE (U.S.)—APPLE (U.K.) R-5949 (5-72)

1851 MARY HAD A LITTLE LAMB (6-72)/Little Woman Love

YOKO ONO/"PLASTIC ONO BAND"

APPLE (U.S.)

1853 NOW OR NEVER (11-72)/Move On Fast

PAUL McCARTNEY/"WINGS"

APPLE (U.S.)—APPLE (U.K.) R-5973

1857 HI HI HI (12-72)/C Moon

APPLE (U.S.)—APPLE (U.K.) R-5985 (3-73)

1861 MY LOVE (4-73)/The Mess

GEORGE HARRISON

APPLE (U.S.)—APPLE (U.K.) R-5988

1862 GIVE ME LOVE (GIVE ME PEACE ON EARTH) (5-73)/ Miss O'Dell

PAUL McCARTNEY/"WINGS"

APPLE (U.S.)—APPLE (U.K.) R-5987 (6-73)

1863 LIVE AND LET DIE (7-73)/I Lie Around

RINGO STARR

APPLE (U.S.)—APPLE (U.K.) R-5992

1865 PHOTOGRAPH (10-73)/Down And Out

YOKO ONO

APPLE (U.S.)

1867 WOMAN POWER (9-73)/Men, Men, Men

APPLE (U.K.)

48 RUN RUN RUN (11-73)/Men, Men, Men

JOHN LENNON/"PLASTIC ONO BAND"

APPLE (U.S.)—APPLE (U.K.) R-5994

1868 MIND GAMES (11-73)/Meat City

PAUL McCARTNEY/"WINGS"

APPLE (U.S.)—APPLE (U.K.) R-5993 (11-73)

1869 HELEN WHEELS (11-73)/Country Dreamer

RINGO STARR

APPLE (U.S.)—APPLE (U.K.) R-5995 (2-74)

1870 YOU'RE SIXTEEN (12-73) [Johnny Burnette '60 hit. LIBERTY 55285]/Devil Woman

PAUL McCARTNEY/"WINGS"

APPLE (U.S.)—APPLE (U.K.) R-5996

1871 JET (2-74)/Mamunia [in U.S.]: Let Me Roll It [in Canada]

RINGO STARR

APPLE (U.S.)

1872 OH MY MY (3-74)/Step Lightly

PAUL McCARTNEY/"WINGS"

1873 BAND ON THE RUN (4-74)/Nineteen Hundred And Eighty Five

APPLE (U.K.)

R-5997 BAND ON THE RUN (6-74)/Zoo Gang

JOHN LENNON/"PLASTIC ONO NUCLEAR BAND"

APPLE (U.S.)—APPLE (U.K.) R-5998 (10-74)

1874 WHATEVER GETS YOU THRU THE NIGHT (9-74)/Beefy Jerky [W. Little Big Horns, Booker Table, and "Maitre D's"]

PAUL McCARTNEY/"WINGS"

APPLE (U.S.)—APPLE (U.K.) R-5999 (10-74)

1875 JUNIOR'S FARM (11-74)/Sally G

RINGO STARR

APPLE (U.S.)—APPLE (U.K.) R-6000

1876 ONLY YOU (11-74) ["Platters" '55 hit. MERCURY 70633]/ Call Me

GEORGE HARRISON

APPLE (U.S.)

1877 DARK HORSE (11-74)/I Don't Care Anymore

JOHN LENNON

APPLE (U.S.)—APPLE (U.K.) R-6003 (1-75)

1878 #9 DREAM (12-74)/What You Got

GEORGE HARRISON

APPLE (U.S.)—APPLE (U.K.) R-6002 (12-74)

1879 DING DONG, DING DONG (1-75)/Hari's On Tour (Express)

APPLE (U.K.)

R-6001 DARK HORSE (2-75)/Hari's On Tour (Express)

RINGO STARR

APPLE (U.S.)

1880 NO NO SONG (2-75) [Written by Hoyt Axton]/Snookeroo

APPLE (U.K.)

R-6004 SNOOKEROO (2-75)/Oo-Wee

JOHN LENNON

APPLE (U.S.)—APPLE (U.K.) R-6005 (4-75)

1881 STAND BY ME (3-75) [Ben E. King '61 hit. ATCO 6194]/ Move Over Ms L

PAUL McCARTNEY/"WINGS"

CAPITOL (U.S.)—APPLE (U.K.) R-6006

4091 LISTEN TO WHAT THE MAN SAID (5-75)/Love In Song

RINGO STARR

APPLE (U.S.)

1882 IT'S ALL DOWN TO GOODNIGHT VIENNA (6-75)/Oo-Wee
Ringo Starr sang with Keith Moon (of the "Who") on single "Solid Gold" (TRACK 40387).
John Lennon was featured on Elton John's '75 song "I Saw Her Standing There" (MCA 40364).

GEORGE HARRISON

EMI (APPLE Subsidiary)

1884 YOU (9-75)/World Of Stone

JOHN LENNON

APPLE (U.K.)

R-6009 IMAGINE (10-75)/Working Class Hero

"WINGS"

CAPITOL (U.S.)—APPLE (U.K.) R-6008

4145 YOU GAVE ME THE ANSWER (11-75)/Letting Go

CAPITOL (U.S.)—CAPITOL (U.K.) R-6010

4175 VENUS AND MARS ROCK SHOW (12-75)/Magneto And Titanium Man

GEORGE HARRISON

EMI (U.S.)—CAPITOL (U.K.) R-6012

1885 THIS GUITAR (2-76)/Māya Love

"WINGS"

CAPITOL

4256 SILLY LOVE SONGS (4-76)/Cook Of The House

"BEATLES"

4274 GOT TO GET YOU INTO MY LIFE (6-76) [Feat. Paul]/Helter Skelter [Feat. Paul]

"WINGS"

4293 LET 'EM IN (7-76)/Beware My Love

RINGO STARR

ATLANTIC

3361 A DOSE OF ROCK'N'ROLL (10-76)/Cryin'

"BEATLES"

CAPITOL

4347 OB-LA-DI, OB-LA-DA (11-76) [Feat. Paul]/Julia [Feat. Paul]

GEORGE HARRISON

DARK HORSE

8294 THIS SONG (11-76)/Learning How To Love You

RINGO STARR

ATLANTIC

3371 HEY BABY (12-76) [Bruce Channel '62 hit. SMASH 1731]/ Lady Gaye

GEORGE HARRISON

DARK HORSE

8313 CRACKERBOX PALACE (1-77)/Learning How To Love You

"WINGS"

CAPITOL

4385 MAYBE I'M AMAZED (2-77)/Soily

"SUZY & THE RED STRIPES" [LINDA McCARTNEY]

EPIC

50403 SEASIDE WOMAN (6-77)/B-Side Of Seaside

RINGO STARR

ATLANTIC

3429 WINGS (9-77)/Just A Dream

3412 DROWNING IN THE SEA OF LOVE (11-77) [Long Version] [Joe Simon '71 hit. SPRING 120]/Drowning In The Sea Of Love [Short Version]

"WINGS"

CAPITOL

1869 COUNTRY DREAMER (11-77)/Helen Wheels
4504 GIRL'S SCHOOL (12-77)/Mull Of Kintyre
4559 WITH A LITTLE LUCK (3-78)/Backwards Traveller/Cuff Link

RINGO STARR

PORTRAIT

670015 LIPSTICK TRACES (ON A CIGARETTE) (5-78) [Benny Spellman '62 hit. MINIT 644; "O'Jays" '65 hit. IMPERIAL 66102]/Old Time Relovin'

"WINGS"

CAPITOL

4594 I'VE HAD ENOUGH (6-78)/Deliver Your Children

RINGO STARR

PORTRAIT

670018 HEART ON MY SLEEVE (7-78)/Who Needs A Heart

"WINGS"

CAPITOL

4625 LONDON TOWN (8-78)/I'm Carrying

"BEATLES"

4612 SGT. PEPPER'S LONELY HEARTS CLUB BAND/WITH A LITTLE HELP FROM MY FRIENDS (10-78)/A Day In The Life

GEORGE HARRISON

DARK HORSE

8763 BLOW AWAY (3-79)/Soft-hearted Hana

"WINGS"

COLUMBIA

3-10939 GOODNIGHT TONIGHT (3-79)/Daytime Nightime Suffering

GEORGE HARRISON

DARK HORSE

8844 LOVE COMES TO EVERYONE (5-79)/Soft Touch

"WINGS"

COLUMBIA

3-11020 GETTING CLOSER (6-79)/Spin It On
1-11070 ARROW THROUGH ME (8-79)/Old Siam, Sir

PAUL McCARTNEY

COLUMBIA

1-11162 WONDERFUL CHRISTMASTIME (12-79)/Rudolph the Red-Nosed Reggae

Jesse Belvin

Born in Texarkana, Arkansas, on December 15, 1933. Died by accidental death in Little Rock, Arkansas, on February 6, 1960.

JESSE BELVIN made song a many-splendored thing, and his rich vocal style, best suited for the ballad, endeared him to millions of music lovers. His "Goodnight My Love" (MODERN 1005) is monumentally that kind of song that remained Alan Freed's fit conclusion to his show on New York's WINS radio. It was R&R hit man Alan Freed who was responsible for Jesse Belvin coming to New York and recording for RCA in 1958 (Jesse, in turn, brought Jimmy Norman and the "Chargers" to RCA).

Jesse Belvin, ever a friendly, warm-hearted person, began singing early in a church choir, at the age of seven. He was reared in Los Angeles and, there, attended Jefferson High and Compton Junior College, where he joined with "Big Jay" McNeely to blossom quickly into a full-fledged band singer. During the early Fifties, Jesse Belvin enlisted in the U.S. Army, where, after training at Fort Ord, he went on to serve with NATO forces in Germany. On discharge, Jesse became session man behind the "Feathers," background for the "Capris," the "Hollywood Flames," and later the "Shields" and the "Chargers." In 1953, Jesse Belvin recorded "Dream Girl" (SPECIALTY 447), a duet with Marvin Phillips. (Marvin, later, became part of that popular duet team "Marvin & Johnny" of "Cherry Pie" fame.)

Jesse Belvin's two hits came under an experimental group, the "Cliques" (pronounced "Clicks") and with his good friend—and later CLASS hit-maker—Eugene Church. These were "Girl Of My Dreams" (MODERN 987) and "My Desire" (MODERN 995). Jesse was the songwriter who helped West Coast artists. The "Penguins' " hit "Earth Angel," although credited to him in some articles, was, in fact, written by group member and leader, Curtis Williams. "Goodnight My Love" (MODERN 1005) became a standard and was revived many times by artists and groups after 1956: the "Fleetwoods," the "4-Seasons," Ben. F. King, Paul Anka, the "Duprees" and Lenny Welch, to name just a few. Jesse Belvin gave a beautiful rendition of the Sam Cooke hit "(I Love You) For Sentimental Reasons" (KENT 326).

Some of Jesse Belvin's other noted hit entries are "Funny" (RCA 7387) and "Guess Who" (RCA 7469); the latter was written by Jesse's wife, Jo-Ann, and it was dedicated to Jesse himself. (This was revived in the late Sixties by Rudy Winters.) Possibly two of Jesse Belvin's most outstanding favorites were album cuts: "(I'm Afraid) The Masquerade Is Over" and his memorable "My Last Goodbye." His tragic end occurred in Little Rock, Arkansas, where Jesse (and his wife), allegedly in a bit of car racing with Jackie Wilson, sustained a head-on collision, which caused the death of Jesse and his wife, Jo-Ann. Truly a sad conclusion to the career of a highly talented performer, whom many of us remember as the "Beloved Jesse Belvin."

Discography

AS "4 DOTS AND A DASH"

IMPERIAL

5115 DON'T CRY BABY (1951) [Feat. Big Jay McNeely]/All That Wine Is Gone

JRM

003 GOING AWAY BABY (1951) [W. Sonny Harper, Blues]/No Lovin' Woman Blues

RECORDED IN HOLLYWOOD

120 DREAM GIRL (1951)/Hang Your Tears Out To Dry

IMPERIAL

5164 I'LL NEVER LOVE AGAIN (1952) [Feat. Jesse Belvin]/Let's Do It

AS "FEATHERS"

RECORDED IN HOLLYWOOD

412 LOVE SONG (1952) [Reissued on CANDLELITE 472]/Love Comes Tumbling Down
1056 DEAR HEART (1952)/Betty My Darling

SPECIALTY

435 CONFESSIN' BLUES (1952)/Baby Don't Go

AS "JESSE AND MARVIN"

447 DREAM GIRL (1953)/Daddy Loves Baby

AS "FEATHERS"

550 GONE (1955)/One Little Blessing
559 WHERE'S MY GIRL (1955)/Love Love Of My Life

AS "SHEIKS"

FEDERAL

12237 SO FINE/Sentimental Heart

MONEY

208 I'M ONLY A FOOL (1956)/Trouble And Misery

AS "CAPRIS" [W. Red Callender Orch. Feat. Jesse Belvin]

CASH

1056 BEWARE (1956)/Dry Your Eyes

AS "CLIQUES"

MODERN

987 GIRL OF MY DREAMS (5-56)/I Wanna Know Why
995 MY DESIRE (4-56)/I'm In Love With A Girl

JESSE BELVIN

1005 GOODNIGHT MY LOVE (11-56)/Let Me Love You Tonight
1013 SEÑORITA (4-57)/I Need You So
1015 DON'T CLOSE THE DOOR (TO HAPPINESS) (5-57)/By My Side
1020 SAD AND LONESOME (8-57)/I'm Not Free
1025 YOU SEND ME (11-57)/Summertime

1027 JUST YOU SAY HELLO (11-57)/My Satellite [With the "Spacemakers"]

KENT

326 (I LOVE YOU) FOR SENTIMENTAL REASONS (1958) [Sam Cooke '57 hit. KEEN 4002]/Señorita

CLASS

267 DEEP IN MY HEART (1958)/I'm Confessin'

AS "SHARPTONES"

ALADDIN

3431 SUGAR DOLL (1958)/Let Me Dream

AS "CHARGERS" [Produced and arranged by Shorty Rogers]

RCA

7301 OLD MACDONALD (1958) [Feat. Jesse Belvin]/Dandilyon

JESSE BELVIN

7310 VOLARE (1958)/Ever Since We Met

AS "CAPRIS" [BLACK WEST COAST GROUP]

TENDER

518 ENDLESS LOVE (1-59)/Beware

JESSE BELVIN

RCA

7387 FUNNY (1-59)/Pledging My Love

AS "CHARGERS" [Produced and arranged by Shorty Rogers]

7417 HERE IN MY HEART (2-59) [Feat. Jesse Belvin]/The Counterfeiter

JESSE BELVIN

RCA

7469 GUESS WHO (4-59)/My Girl Is Just Enough Woman For Me

KNIGHT

2021 LITTLE DARLING (4-59)/Deacon Dan Tucker

RCA

7543 HERE'S A HEART (1959)/It Could've Been Worse
7596 GIVE ME LOVE (1959)/I'll Never Be Lonely Again
7675 THE DOOR IS ALWAYS OPEN (1960)/Something Happens To Me

IMPACT

LOOKING FOR LOVE

JAMIE

1145 GOODNIGHT MY LOVE (1-60)/I Want You With Me Christmas

♭ ♯ ♪ ♩ 𝅗𝅥

Brook Benton

Real Name: "Benjamin Franklin Peay." Born in Camden, South Carolina, on September 19, 1931.

It was BROOK BENTON'S relaxed velvet-toned voice with enormous personality appeal on record that helped him to sell twenty-five million discs! A rich, flowing style, full of creative versatility, led his fans to dub him with the popular phrase "Babbling Brook." Much of his hit success is credited to the songwriting of Clyde Otis (MERCURY's A&R executive, whom he met in 1958, and who signed Brook), his own inimitable quality style, and to Belford Hendricks, who also arranged his music. The combined early written contributions of Brook Benton and Clyde Otis were "Looking Back" and "Nothing In The World," both hits for Nat King Cole; "A Lover's Question" for Clyde McPhatter; "In A Dream" and "Everything" for Roy Hamilton, and "The Stroll" for the "Diamonds." The songwriting trio, Brooks, Otis and Hendricks, produced Brook Benton's first three hits of 1959: "It's Just A Matter Of Time," "Endlessly," and "Thank You Pretty Baby." This was the beginning of Brook's four-year Chart action!

Brook Benton lived most of his childhood in Lugoff, South Carolina, where he first sang in the choir of the Efuces Methodist Church. During his Jackson High School years, he sang with the "Camden Jubilee Singers" while also working as a milk delivery boy. At seventeen, Brook moved to New York, where, to make ends meet, he drove a delivery truck for a garment center. He joined Bill Langford's Spiritual quartet (the Langfordaires"), the "Golden Gate Quartet," and finally in 1951 became a member of the "Jerusalem Stars," which also included Bill Pinkney (Bill Massey, James Green, Jimmy Griffin). Between 1953 and 1957, Brook Benton's backup came from the group the "Sandmen" (OKEH, EPIC, and VIK). Brook's first minor solo hit success came with the 1958 entry "A Million Miles From Nowhere" (VIK 0311). It was not until "It's Just A Matter Of Time" (MERCURY 71394, 1959) that he struck a No. 1 record on R&B and Pop Charts. The following year, Brook Benton and Dinah Washington scored with two soulful duets, "Baby (You've Got What It Takes)" and "A Rockin' Good Way."

Brook Benton recorded many beautiful ballads: "So Many Times," "The Ties That Bind/Hither And Thither And You," "Kiddio," "It's Just A House (Without You)," and "Hotel Happiness/Still Waters Run Deep." Other notables were the popular "Boll Weavil Song," uptempo rocker "Hit Record," and the two last hits for MERCURY in 1963, "I Got What I Wanted" and "My True Confession" (that was produced by Shelly Singleton and arranged by Bill Justis).

Recording with RCA and REPRISE, Brook, sadly enough, failed to score a national hit, but with ATLANTIC's subsidiary, COTILLION, in 1970, he recorded a Tony Joe White song, "Rainy Night In Georgia," which proved itself a Soul favorite! This showed that Brook Benton still had the winning ingredients. He remains an active nightclub performer, an executive in New York, and, there, with his wife and children, remains persistent at recording.

Discography

AS "SANDMEN"

Benjamin Peay, lead; Walter Springer, second tenor; Thurman Haynes, baritone; Adriel McDonald, bass.

OKEH

7052 SOMEBODY TO LOVE (2-55)/When I Grow Too Old To Dream
7058 THE KENTUCKIAN SONG (6-55) [From the movie *The Kentuckian*]/Ooh
7065 SOME OF MY BEST FRIENDS (10-55)/Bring Me Love

BROOK BENTON

EPIC

9177 LOVE MADE ME YOUR FOOL (11-56)/Give Me A Sign
9199 THE WALL (1957)/All My Love Belongs To You

VIK

0285 COME ON BE NICE (1957) [W. "Sandmen"]/Wanna Do Everything For You
0311 A MILLION MILES FROM NOWHERE (3-58)/Devoted
0325 BECAUSE YOU LOVE ME (1958)/Crimolie Skirt

MERCURY

71394 IT'S JUST A MATTER OF TIME (2-59)/Hurtin' Inside
71443 ENDLESSLY (4-59)/So Close

71478 THANK YOU PRETTY BABY (7-59)/With All Of My Heart
71512 SO MANY WAYS (10-59)/I Want You Forever
71554 THIS TIME OF THE YEAR (WHEN CHRISTMAS IS NEAR) (12-59)/Nothing In The World (Could Make Me Love You More Than I Do)
71558 HOW MANY TIMES (1960)/This Time Of The Year

BROOK BENTON AND DINAH WASHINGTON

71565 BABY (YOU'VE GOT WHAT IT TAKES) (1-60)/I DO

BROOK BENTON

71566 THE TIES THAT BIND (4-60)/Hither And Thither and Yon

BROOK BENTON AND DINAH WASHINGTON

71629 A ROCKIN' GOOD WAY (5-60)/I Believe

BROOK BENTON

71652 KIDDIO (8-60)/The Same One
71722 FOOLS RUSH IN (WHERE ANGELS FEAR TO TREAD) (11-60)/Someday You'll Want Me To Want You
71730 MERRY CHRISTMAS—HAPPY NEW YEAR (12-60)/This Time Of The Year
71766 IT'S JUST A HOUSE (WITHOUT YOU) (2-61)/If You Have No Real Objection
71774 THINK TWICE (2-61)/For My Baby
71820 THE BOLL WEEVIL SONG (5-61) [Orig. a Tex Ritter song, 1953]/Your Eyes
71859 FRANKIE AND JOHNNY (8-61)/It's Just A House (Without You)
71903 REVENGE (11-61)/Really, Really
71912 SHADRACK (1-62)/Lost Penny
71925 WALK ON THE WILD SIDE (2-62)/Somewhere In The Used To Be
71962 HIT RECORD (5-62)/Thanks To The Fool
72024 LIE TO ME (8-62)/With The Touch Of Your Hand
72055 HOTEL HAPPINESS (11-62)/Still Waters Run Deep
72099 I GOT WHAT I WANTED (I LOST WHAT I HAD) (3-63)/Dearer Than Life
72135 MY TRUE CONFESSION (6-63)/Tender Years
72177 TWO TICKETS TO PARADISE (9-63)/Don't Hate Me
72207 STOP FOOLIN' (12-63) [W. Damito Jo]/Baby, You've Got It Made

72214 THIS TIME OF YEAR (12-63)/You're All I Want For Christmas
72230 GOING GOING GONE (1-64)/After Midnight
72266 TOO LATE TO TURN BACK NOW (5-64)/Another Cup Of Coffee
72303 A HOUSE IS NOT A HOME (7-64)/Come On Back
72333 LUMBERJACK (10-64)/Don't Do What I Did
72365 DO IT RIGHT (12-64)/Please Please Make It Easy
72398 THE SPECIAL YEARS (1965)/Where There's A Will
72446 LOVE ME NOW (7-65)/Sleepin' At The Fcot Of The Bed

RCA

47-8693 MOTHER NATURE, FATHER TIME (11-65)/You're Mine (And I Love You)
47-8879 BREAK HER HEART (7-66)/In The Evening By The Moonlight
47-8944 THE ROACH SONG (10-66)/Where Does A Man Go To Cry?
47-9031 OUR FIRST CHRISTMAS TOGETHER (12-66)/Silent Night
47-9096 ALL MY LOVE BELONGS TO YOU (4-67)/Wake Up
47-9105 KEEP THE FAITH, BABY (2-67)/Going To Soulsville

REPRISE

0611 LAURA (WHAT'S HE GOT THAT I AIN'T GOT) (8-67)/You're The Reason I'm Living
0649 GLORY OF LOVE/Weakness In A Man
0676 INSTEAD OF LOVIN' YOU/Lonely Street

COTILLION

44007 DO YOUR OWN THING (10-68)/I Just Don't Know What To Do With Myself
44031 TOUCH 'EM WITH LOVE (4-69)/She Knows What To Do For Me
44034 NOTHING CAN TAKE THE PLACE OF YOU (7-69) [Toussaint McCall '67 hit. RON 3]/Woman Without Love
44057 RAINY NIGHT IN GEORGIA (1-70)/Where Do I Go From Here
44072 A LITTLE BIT OF SOAP (4-70) ["Jarmels" '61 hit. LAURIE 3097]/My Way
44078 DON'T IT MAKE YOU WANT TO GO HOME (6-70) [Joe South '69 hit. CAPITOL 2592]/I've Gotta Be Me
44093 SHOES (12-70)/Let Me Fix It
44110 HEAVEN HELP US ALL (4-71) [Stevie Wonder '70 hit. TAMLA 54200]/Whoever Finds This (I Love You)

BROOK BENTON WITH "DIXIE FLYERS"

44119 TAKE A LOOK AT YOUR HANDS (6-71)/If You Think God Is Dead
44130 PLEASE SEND ME SOMEONE TO LOVE (9-71) [Percy Mayfield classic!]/Black Child Can't Smile

44138	A BLACK CHILD CAN'T SMILE (11-71)/If You Think God Is Dead
44141	LET US GET TOGETHER WITH THE LORD (12-71)/Soul Santa
44152	MOVIN' DAY (5-72)/Poor Make Believer

MGM

14440	IF YOU'VE GOT THE TIME/You Take Me Home Honey
2006-301	SWEET MEMORIES (7-73)/If You've Got The Time

CONFIDENCE

69	LAY LADY LAY/South Carolina

BRUT

810	LAY LADY LAY (12-73)/Touch Of Class
813	ALL THAT LOVE WENT TO WASTE
816	SOUTH CAROLINA (4-74)

BROOK BENTON

STAX

0231	I KEEP THINKING OF MYSELF (1975)/Winds Of Change

ALL PLATINUM

2364	CAN'T TAKE MY EYES OFF OF YOU (1976)/Weekend With Feather
4146-311*	BARTENDER (1976)/Taxi
-315*	MY FUNNY VALENTINE (1977)/You Were Gone

OLDE WORLD

1100	MAKIN' LOVE IS GOOD FOR YOU (1-78)/Better Times
1107	SOFT (8-78)/Glow Love

*British releases.

♭ ♯ ♪ ♩ 𝅗𝅥

"Blue Notes"

ORIGINAL MEMBERS (JOSIE through to 1969 UNI; total sixteen members): *Harold Melvin* (lead singer, piano, music arranger, group manager); *Bernard Wilson* (baritone); *Jesse Gillis, Jr.* (first tenor—replaced by John Atkins, lead singer); *Roosevelt Broder* (tenor—replaced by Hughie Owens and Richard Anthony, lead singers); *Franklin Peaker* (bass—replaced by Lawrence "Larry" Brown, bass).

MEMBERS 1972-1975 (DASH through PHILADELPHIA-INTERNATIONAL): *Theodore "Teddy" Pendergrass* (lead singer); *Harold Melvin* (first tenor); *Bernard Wilson* (choreographer, arranger, and baritone); *Lloyd Parks* (first tenor—replaced by Jerry Cummings, lead singer); *Hubert Yarbrough* (first tenor).

POST-1975 (ABC releases): *David Ebo* (lead singer); *Dwight Johnson* (bass); *Harold Melvin* (first tenor and business manager); *Bill Spratley* (tenor); *Ollie Woodson* (tenor).

Hometown: Philadelphia, Pennsylvania.

The "BLUE NOTES" were the originators of the "Beat Concerto" production/strings techniques used in New York during the early Sixties, notably in the classics "My Hero" (VAL-UE 213), "She Is Mine (INSTANT ACTION 101), and "Blue Star" (20TH CENTURY 1213). The group was rooted in Doo-Wopp and during the mid-Sixties leaned strongly toward Soul in their recordings, particularly in what became a Northern Soul favorite in Britain, entitled "Get Out (And Let Me Cry)" (LANDA 703), which was backed by that memorable and soulful "You May Not Love Me." Harold Melvin and the original "Blue Notes" were a truly classy, beautifully polished group. They started in 1954 as school chums just having a musical good time. They went to New York City and recorded the standard "If You Love Me (. . . If The Sea Should Suddenly Run Dry, etc.)" (JOSIE 800). In 1960, they recorded that lovely ballad "My Hero" (VAL-UE 213) for Doc Bagby's label and $500, but with poor sales response. The "Blue Notes" went on the Chittlin' Circuit, with bowties and all formal attire, which kept their hopes up! It was the 1960s star Martha Reeves who introduced the group to the William Morris Agency, from where they went on to become a top nightclub act.

"Teddy" Pendergrass joined the "Blue Notes" in 1970 as a replacement for John Atkins. Pendergrass was an ordained minister and had played drums with a James Brown Band (not *the* James Brown) and with the "Cadillacs" group. He was an outstanding dancer as well as a tremendous hoarse Gospel vocal delivery much in the manner of the "Dells' " lead singer, Marvin Junior. Along with "Teddy" Pendergrass, the "Blue Notes" had a strong falsetto singer in Lloyd Parks (a former member of the "Epsilons" of 1970 fame—"The Echo," STAX 0021). The recording "I Miss You (PHIL-INT. 3516) introduced Lloyd's falsetto shrill contribution with "Teddy" Pendergrass's intense commanding performance and Harold Melvin, as first tenor, pleading and talking a creative atmosphere! A fabulous record, indeed, which highlighted a singer who has made it as far as stardom, and money can prove it, but his thoughts musically reflect sadness in the loss of his one love and his little boy! A desperate and classic last effort possibly to reach "his woman" through the hearing of his plea. The follow-up, the outward and visual pride in song, was "If You Don't Know Me By Now" (PHIL-INT. 3520), a two-million seller! A talented dramatic expression of one man's love so simple to see that there need be little doubt in her mind concerning it.

All of the "Blue Notes' " PHILADELPHIA-INTERNATIONAL releases are masterpieces produced by Leon Huff, Kenny Gamble, and Harold Melvin (Leon played piano on "I Miss You"—PHIL-INT. 3516). "The Love I Lost" (PHIL-INT. 3533) is a Disco party favorite, "Satisfaction Guaranteed (Or Take Your Love Back)" (PHIL-INT. 3543) is a dance hit, and "Where Are All My Friends" (PHIL-INT. 3552) has gut feeling! During 1975, the "Blue Notes" gave us a Disco smash, "Bad Luck" (PHIL-INT. 3562), "Hope That We Can Be Together Soon" (PHIL-INT. 3569), a beautiful duet with Sharon Paige, and that inspirational "Wake Up Everybody" (PHIL-INT. 3579), followed by yet another super dance record, "Tell The World How I Feel About 'Cha Baby" (PHIL-INT. 3588).

Sad to relate, such a success story came to an abrupt end! Late in 1975, Harold Melvin filed a "breach of contract" suit against Wilson, Brown, Parks, and Pendergrass for $624,000. Harold Melvin claimed to be the exclusive manager of the "Blue Notes," and the other four members of the group had acquired another manager, Buddy Nolan. The ensuing personal disagreements led to a dissolving of the ever-popular and highly successful group, with "Teddy" Pendergrass remaining with

PHILADELPHIA-INTERNATIONAL as solo star and Harold Melvin forming a new group and signing with the ABC label, and both continued on their own successful ways.

Discography

AS "BLUE NOTES"

JOSIE

800 IF YOU LOVE ME (5-56)/There's Something In Your Eyes, Elouise
814 WITH THIS PEN (1-57) [Feat. Todd Randall]/Letters
823 THE RETRIBUTION BLUES (8-57)/Wagon Wheels
IMPORTANT NOTE: *The "Blue Notes" who recorded for RAMA [W. Joe Loco], BLUECO, DOT, and BROOKE III are a different group!*

3 SONS

103 W-P-L-J (1958) ["4 Deuces" '55 tune. MUSIC CITY 790]/ While I'm Away

GAMUT

100 MY HEART CRIES FOR YOU (1959)/Shrimp Boats Are Coming

TICO

1063 CHARLOTTE AMALIE/Make A Box

INSTANT ACTION

101 SHE IS MINE (1960)/The Letter

VAL-UE

213 MY HERO (10-60)/A Good Woman
215 OH HOLY NIGHT (12-60)/Winter Wonderland

20TH CENTURY

1213 BLUE STAR (4-61)/Pucker Your Lips

PORT

70021 IF YOU LOVE ME (1961)/There's Something In Your Eyes, Elouise

RED TOP

135 MY HERO (1963)/A Good Woman

RENOWN

108 TIME WILL TELL (1963) [Feat. Hughie Owens]/I'm Going Home

LANDA

703 GET OUT (1-61) [Feat. John Atkins]/You May Not Love Me

SWAN

4257 THE BOSTON MONKEY (1966) [Feat. Richard Anthony]
This was a deejay one-sided promo.

AS "THE BLUE NOTES"

ARCTIC

135 WHAT CAN A MAN DO (1967) [Feat. Harold Melvin]/Go Away

UNI

55132 NEVER GONNA LEAVE YOU (1969)/Hot Chills And Cold Thrills

AS "HAROLD MELVIN & THE BLUE NOTES"

DASH

5005 NEVER GONNA LEAVE YOU (1972)/Hot Chills, Cold Thrills & Fever

PHILADELPHIA-INTERNATIONAL, CBS

3516 I MISS YOU (7-72)/I Miss You [Part 2]
3520 IF YOU DON'T KNOW ME BY NOW (9-72)/Let Me Into Your World
3525 YESTERDAY I HAD THE BLUES (3-73)/Ebony Woman
3533 THE LOVE I LOST (9-73)/The Love I Lost [Part 2]
3543 SATISFACTION GUARANTEED (OR TAKE YOUR LOVE BACK (4-74)/I'm Weak For You
2441 I'M COMING HOME TOMORROW (6-74)/I'm Coming Home Tomorrow [Part 2]
3552 WHERE ARE ALL MY FRIENDS (11-74)/Let It Be You
3562 BAD LUCK (3-75)/Bad Luck [Part 2]

3569 HOPE THAT WE CAN BE TOGETHER SOON (7-75) [W. Sharon Paige]/Be For Real

3579 WAKE UP EVERYBODY (11-75)/Wake Up Everybody [Part 2]

3588 TELL THE WORLD HOW I FEEL ABOUT 'CHA BABY (4-76)/You Know How To Make Me Feel So Good

ABC

12240 REACH FOR THE WORLD (2-77) [Feat. David Ebo]/Stay Together [W. Sharon Paige]

TEDDY PENDERGRASS SOLO

PHILADELPHIA-INTERNATIONAL

3622 I DON'T LOVE YOU ANYMORE (5-77)/Somebody Told Me

AS "HAROLD MELVIN & THE BLUE NOTES"

ABC

12268 AFTER YOU LOVE ME, WHY DO YOU LEAVE ME (5-77) [W. Sharon Paige]/Big Singing Star

FEATURING PHILADELPHIA-INTERNATIONAL ALL-STARS: LOU RAWLS; BILLY PAUL; ARCHIE BELL; TEDDY PENDERGRASS; "O'JAYS"; DEE DEE SHARP GAMBLE.

PHILADELPHIA-INTERNATIONAL

3627 LET'S CLEAN UP THE GHETTO (6-77) [Vocal]/Let's Clean Up The Ghetto [Instr. by the MFSB]

TEDDY PENDERGRASS SOLO

34390 THE WHOLE TOWN'S LAUGHING AT ME (9-77)/The More I Get, The More I Want

AS "HAROLD MELVIN AND THE BLUE NOTES"

ABC

12327 BABY, YOU GOT MY NOSE OPEN (1-78)/Try To Live A Day

TEDDY PENDERGRASS

COLUMBIA

5-83648	CLOSE THE DOOR (5-78)/Get Up, Get Down, Get Funky, Get Loose
5-83657*	ONLY YOU (10-78)/It Don't Hurt Now

AS "HAROLD MELVIN & THE BLUE NOTES"

ABC

12366	NOW IS THE TIME (10-78)/Power Of Love

TEDDY PENDERGRASS

PHILADELPHIA-INTERNATIONAL

8-3669	LIFE IS A SONG WORTH SINGING (2-79)/Cold, Cold World
8-3696	TURN OFF THE LIGHTS (6-79)/If You Know Like I Know
9-3717	COME GO WITH ME (8-79)
9-3733	SHOUT AND SCREAM (12-79)

AS "HAROLD MELVIN & THE BLUE NOTES"

SOURCE

41156	PRAYIN' (12-79)/Praying [Instr.]

*Also on PHIL-INT 460.

♭ ♯ ♪ ♩ 𝅗𝅥

James Brown

Real Name: "James Brown." Born in Pulaski, Tennessee, on May 3, 1928.

JAMES BROWN sings his songs with raw emotionalism and with unflagging personal power. Staying with his roots in Blues and Gospel, he hasn't altered his style, like so many others, for the mainstream buying market. "SOUL BROTHER NUMBER ONE," as he is most aptly called, he shouts, pleads moaningly, and screams to his audiences for an average of three hundred personal performances a year.

As the hardest-working man in the business, James Brown gave wide help and support throughout the impoverished ghetto areas of America. His J.B.E. (James Brown Enterprises) is a corporate body active in these areas, providing job opportunities, salaries, and so forth, toward black-owned businesses. Here is a black ghetto boy with a dream who knew poverty and the inside of a reform school after his one and only serious scuffle with the law and who made his way back. He often shined shoes on the steps of radio station WRDW in Augusta, Georgia, for pennies, to own it one day and to own two million dollars of Long Island, some one hundred apartment buildings, and a chain of restaurants! As a youngster, he had danced for loose change thrown by GIs at Fort Gordon. Reared in the South Carolina hills bordering Georgia, he first made music on a 10¢ Jew's harp given him by his father, and learned to play the organ, the drums, and the bass guitar while being reared by his father and an aunt.

Any one of several sporting careers might have developed for this enterprising youth out of his athletic prowess, because he had some boxing for about three years, and showed promise for baseball and football, though for the latter he was handicapped by size, but there was no question of the fact that he was "with it" in music! "Music," says James Brown, "became a necessity. It was my only way out of poverty, out of the ghetto."

James Brown first sang with the "Cremona Combo," then later formed the "3 Swanees," comprising Bobby Byrd, Johnny Terry, and himself

(Bobby Byrd and James Brown had met and sung together at Augusta Baptist Church). The mushrooming success of the "Five Royales" (from Winston-Salem) and Little Richard (from Macon) inspired the new group to head for Macon and hoped-for opportunity. Little Richard had now reached national prominence but had developed problems with his manager, Clint Brantley, who, now in search of new challenge, turned his attention to the struggling new group. They had by this time become known as the "Famous Flames" (after Charles Brown's "Three Blazers") and shortly broadened out to include Nashville Knox, Sylvester Keel, and Nafloyd Scott as regular guitarist.

Opportunity came knocking in 1956, when Ralph Bass, producer and talent scout for KING RECORDS out of Cincinnati, heard James Brown's dubbing of "Please, Please, Please," an original! Clint Brantley drove down to Macon, signed the group, and rushed them back to KING Studios for the recording of "Please, Please, Please" (FEDERAL 12258) and early release. KING RECORDS, formed by Syd Nathan in 1954 as a race label, had achieved considerable success in Rhythm and Blues, and so on, and gave us stars like Billy Ward and the "Dominoes" and Hank Ballard and the "Midnighters."

For a period of eighteen months after the initial success came diminishing returns, though James Brown's releases were exceptional: "I Feel That Old Feeling Coming On" (FEDERAL 12264), "No, No, No, No"/ "Hold My Baby's Hand" (FEDERAL 12277), "Let's Make It" (FEDERAL 12289), "I Won't Plead No More"/"Chonnie-On-Chon (Havin' A Rock'n'Roll Party)" (FEDERAL 12290), "Love Or A Game" (FEDERAL 12295), "You're Mine, You're Mine" (FEDERAL 12300). Each had that unique Rock and Roll treatment in the good old Fifties sound!

By 1958, a crisis had loomed for James Brown and the "Famous Flames," with the original members becoming discouraged and leaving for more stable livelihoods. New members were Bill Holdings, Louis Madison, Guitar Gable, John Faire or Bobby Roach, Madison (or Lucas) Gonder (piano), Baroy Scott, and another member simply designated "J. W." Louis Madison was vocal and organizer. For James Brown and his reconstituted "Famous Flames" it was still a struggle for survival! He had written most of his material out of a personal dependence on a blend of Church and popular acts around him and was now feeling a need for change. It was then that James Brown recorded his first "outsider" compositions, such as "Begging, Begging" (FEDERAL 12316) and "That Dood It" (FEDERAL 12311), both written by Toombs & Dixon and completely different from anything that he had previously done.

Great pressure was being exerted by Syd Nathan and KING RECORDS, with even the threat that they might drop the group, but James Brown answered the ultimatum with his next recording (in New York, for the first time) and produced a big one, "Try Me" (FEDERAL

12337), which, he still claims, was the turning point in his great career. From 1959 to 1961, James Brown produced twelve hits in succession while completely departing from and surpassing his earlier style. Some of this success grew out of a growing experience and concentrated management control achieved on his personal appearances (now nearing 300 per year) with a permanent six-piece band now widely acclaimed as the "J.B.'s." (The "James Browns" consisted of Lee Diamond, tenor sax; and Charles Connors, drums—both from Little Charles's "Upsetters.") In 1959, the "J.B.'s" consisted of J. C. Adams, tenor sax; Bobby Roach, guitar; Fats Gonder, guitar; Bernard Odum, base; and Nat Kendricks, drums, and the "Famous Flames" backup. This earned experience was added to the recordings, and thus "THE JAMES BROWN SOUND WAS BORN"! The "Famous Flames" now included Johnny Terry, Bill Holdings, "J. W." (background vocal), Clifford Scott (tenor sax), George Dorsey, Ernie Hayes, Lucas Gonder or Gene Redd, Kenny Burrell, Bobby Roach, David "Panama" Francis (drums), and Gene Redd handling the arrangements.

Some of James Brown's most beautiful and stimulating recordings during this period were "I've Got To Change" (FEDERAL 12352), "Good Good Loving" (FEDERAL 12361), "I'll Go Crazy" (FEDERAL 12369), "Think" (FEDERAL 12370), "This Old Heart" (FEDERAL 12378), "The Bells" (KING 5423), and "Bewildered" (KING 5442).

James Brown, with his big band punch rhythms, Afro-Cuban and Puerto Rican soul sounds, appealed strongly to blacks, but his image, sounds, effects, and message were not as readily accepted by the vaster white enthusiasts. "James Brown's Soul Revue" went rolling on to break all box office records! He became one of the greatest showmen in the Soul World and a great businessman. As James Brown aptly said of himself, "I'm 20% showman, talent and 80% businessman." Proof is in the fact that, from a one-time baseball pitcher (who sustained an injured leg) with an undersize handicap, he went on to apply his very athletic gyrations and his restless energetic nature to music and song. James Brown has been called the last of the great vaudeville entertainers because of his revue-style personal performances, with complete supporting acts, including singers, dancers, and comedians, rolled into a colorful entertainment package breaking all box office records. He is also one of the truly great independents who still produces his own image, sound, effects, and message.

James Brown hits continued for KING: "I Don't Mind" (KING 5466), "Lost Someone" (KING 5573), "Night Train" (KING 5614), "Shout And Shimmy" (KING 5657), "Mashed Potatoes U.S.A." (KING 5672), and "Prisoner Of Love" (KING 5739). The pressures of growth began to be felt. James Brown, realizing that his present contractual arrangements could hinder his expanding horizons, had attempted on occasion to break loose. He and Bert Bart started their own label, TRY ME RECORDS (distributed by KING), featuring "Johnny & Bill" (two of the "Famous Flames"), Tammi Montgomery (later Tammi Terrell on MOTOWN), and the "Poets." He also formed his own production company, FAIR DEAL, with releases through SMASH RECORDS (a division of the nationwide Mercury Corporation) out of Chicago, but this dynamic venture, which involved one vocal album and two singles, was interrupted by court injunctions and legal wrangling. "Out Of Sight" (SMASH 1919) was the first of a kind to sell in large quantities to white enthusiasts, based on compulsive dance riffs behind James Brown singing easily remembered taglines, with a distinct shift from vocal harmony to heavy band rhythm accompaniment.

Into the mid-Sixties, James Brown was making a powerful impact on a broader, more lucrative market: "Papa's Got A Brand New Bag" (KING 5999), "I Got You (I Feel Good)" (KING 6015), and it was evident that a whole new turning point in "The James Brown Story" was happening! His Chart success and hits increased in rapid proportion, and with them many Soul entries, more notably: "It's A Man's World" (KING 6035), "Money Won't Change You" (KING 6048), "Don't Be A Drop-Out" (KING 6056), "Bring It Up" (KING 6071), "Let Yourself Go" (KING 6100), "Cold Sweat" (KING 6110), "There Was A Time" (KING 6144), and the popular "I Got The Feeling" (KING 6155).

The tremendous influence of James Brown was demonstrated on the eve of Dr. Martin Luther King's tragic death, when, at the request of the mayor of Boston, he appeared on local television to counteract rising violence. The President of the United States acclaimed James Brown as the man responsible for preventing riots! James Brown then recorded "America Is My Home" (KING 6112), a fine record, "I Guess I'll Have To Cry, Cry, Cry" (KING 6141), "Say It Loud—I'm Black & I'm Proud" (KING 6187), and the magnificent "Goodbye My Love" (KING 6198), highlighting the end of yet another period and the beginning of a New Sound for James Brown.

In 1969, James Brown was named "The Number One Male R&B Artist" by *Cashbox,* a popular music industry publication, and during that year he produced such hits as "Tit For Tat (Ain't No Taking Back)" (KING 6204), "Give It Up Or Turnit-A Loose" (KING 6213), "I Don't Want Nobody To Give Me Nothing (Open The Door, I'll Get It Myself)" (KING 6224), and the introduction of the "Popcorn" dance craze! The Seventies saw James Brown forming the group the "New Dapps," with the two Collins brothers, Phelps (guitar) and William (bass), who eventually went on to form their own group, the "House Guests." The "J.B.'s" also left to record independently. James Brown carried on producing hits: "It's A New Day" (KING 6292), "Get Up (I Feel Like Being A Sex Machine)" (KING 6318), "Super Bad" (KING 6329), followed by a sincere personal venture, "King Heroin" (POLYDOR 14116), to combat drugs among American youth, in 1972, and another hit, "Papa Don't Take No Mess" (POLYDOR 14255). Two of James Brown's "Tribute Records" that deserve attention are his "I Need Your Love So Bad" (POLYDOR 14268) to Little Willie John, and "Love Me Tender" (POLYDOR 14460) to Elvis!

James Brown became personally involved in the promotion of several protégés, such as "Macao (Parker) & All King's Men," Lyn Collins, and Sweet Charles (whom he publicly described as having "the potential to become a super superstar"). James Brown also provided soundtracks for *Black Caesar* and *Slaughter's Big Rip-Off* both in 1973, and starred in the film *Come to the Table.*

It is worth mentioning that two of James Brown's "J.B.'s" band directors, Nat Jones and later Alfred Lewis, deserve credit for shaping the particular Sounds of James Brown! James Brown will carry on and live on in some of his well-earned musical titles that stuck with the Man and the Sound: "King of The One-Nighter," "King James," "Godfather Of Soul," Minister of the New New Super Heavy Funk," "The Creator," "The King of Soul," and, of course, "MISTER DYNAMITE"!

Discography

JAMES BROWN

FEDERAL

12258	PLEASE, PLEASE, PLEASE (3-56)/Why Do You Do Me?
12264	I FEEL THAT OLD FEELING COMING ON (5-56)/I Don't Know
12277	NO, NO, NO, NO (8-56)/Hold My Baby's Hand
12289	LET'S MAKE IT (9-56)/Just Won't Do Right
12290	I WON'T PLEAD NO MORE (10-56)/Chonnie-On-Chon
12292	GONNA TRY (2-57)/Can't Be The Same (Always) [Duet with Bobby Byrd]
12295	MESSING WITH THE BLUES (5-57)/Love Or A Game
12300	YOU'RE MINE, YOU'RE MINE (6-57)/I Walked Alone
12311	THAT DOOD IT (11-57)/Baby Cries Over The Ocean
12316	THAT'S WHEN I LOST MY HEART (2-58)/Begging, Begging
12337	TRY ME (10-58)/Tell Me What I Did Wrong
12348	I WANT YOU SO BAD (3-59)/There Must Be A Reason
12352	I'VE GOT TO CHANGE (5-59)/It Hurts To Tell You
12361	GOOD, GOOD, LOVING (9-59)/Don't Let It Happen To Me
12364	GOT TO CRY (11-59)/It Was You
12369	I'LL GO CRAZY (2-60)/I Know It's True (I Found Someone)

AS "NAT KENDRICKS & THE SWANS" (JAMES BROWN'S BACKUP BAND)

DADE

1804 DO THE MASHED POTATOES (2-60)/Do The Mashed Potatoes

JAMES BROWN

FEDERAL

12370 THINK (4-60) ["Five Royales" '57 hit. KING 5053]/You've Got The Power [Duet with Bea Ford]
12378 THIS OLD HEART (8-60)/Wonder When You're Coming Home

KING

5423 THE BELLS (10-60) ["Dominoes" '53 hit. FEDERAL 12114]/And I Do What I Want
5438 HOLD IT [Instr.] (12-60)/The Scratch [Feat. J. C. Davis, tenor sax]
5442 BEWILDERED (2-61)/If You Want Me
5466 I DON'T MIND (5-61)/Love Don't Love Nobody
5485 STICKY-SUDS [Instr.] (4-61)/Sticky-Suds [Part 2]
5519 CROSS FIRING (6-61)/Night Flying [Instr.]
5524 BABY, YOU'RE RIGHT (8-61) [The Answer to Joe Tex's "You Keep Her"]/I'll Never Let You Go
5547 I LOVE YOU, YES I DO (9-61)/Just You And Me, Darling
5573 LOST SOMEONE (12-61)/Cross Firing [Instr.]
5614 NIGHT TRAIN (3-62)/Why Does Everything Happen To Me
5657 SHOUT AND SHIMMY (6-62)/Come Over Here
5672 MASHED POTATOES U.S.A. (10-62) [Instr.]/You Don't Have To Go
5701 THREE HEARTS IN A TANGLE (12-62)/I've Got Money
5710 EVERY BEAT OF MY HEART (2-62) [Instr.]/Like A Baby
5739 PRISONER OF LOVE (4-63)/Choo-Choo Locomotion [Instr.]
5767 THESE FOOLISH THINGS (7-63)/(Can You) Feel It [Part 1] [Instr.]
5803 SIGNED, SEALED AND DELIVERED (9-63)/Waiting In Vain
5829 I'VE GOT TO CHANGE (11-63)/The Bells
5842 OH BABY DON'T YOU WEEP (1-64)/Oh Baby Don't You Weep [Part 2]
5853 IN THE WEE WEE HOURS (OF THE NITE) (2-64)/Please, Please, Please

SMASH

1898 CALEDONIA (4-64)/Evil [Instr.]
1908 THINGS I USED TO DO (6-64)/Out Of The Blue

KING

5876 HOW LONG DARLING (6-64)/Again
5899 SO LONG (6-64)/Dancin' Little Thing

SMASH

1919 OUT OF SIGHT (7-64)/Maybe The Last Time

KING

6032 TELL ME WHAT YOU'RE GONNA DO (8-64)/I Don't Care
5956 FINE OLD FOXY SELF (11-64)/Medley: Found Someone; Why Do You Do Me
5968 HAVE MERCY BABY (2-65)/Just Won't Do Right

SMASH

1975 WHO'S AFRAID OF VIRGINIA WOLFE? (3-65)/Devil's Hideaway [Instr.]
1989 I GOT YOU (1965)/Only You [WITHDRAWN]

KING

5999 PAPA'S GOT A BRAND NEW BAG (7-65)/Papa's Got A Brand New Bag [Part 2]

SMASH

2008 TRY ME (8-65)/Papa's Got A Brand New Bag

KING

6015 I GOT YOU (I FEEL GOOD) (11-65)/I Can't Help It (I Just Do, Do, Do)
6020 LOST SOMEONE (1-66)/I'll Go Crazy

SMASH

2028 NEW BREED (2-66)/New Breed [Part 2]

KING

6025 AIN'T THAT A GROOVE (3-66)/Ain't That A Groove [Part 2]
6029 PRISONER OF LOVE (3-66)/I've Got To Change
6032 COME OVER HERE (3-66)/Tell Me What You're Gonna Do
6035 IT'S A MAN'S MAN'S WORLD (4-66)/Is It Yes Or Is It No

SMASH

2042 JAMES BROWN'S BOO-GA-LOO (6-66)/Lost In A Mood

KING

6048 MONEY WON'T CHANGE YOU (7-66)/Money Won't Change You [Part 2]

SMASH

2064 OUR DAY WILL COME (10-66)/Let's Go Get Stoned

KING

6056 DON'T BE A DROP-OUT (10-66)/Tell Me That You Love Me
6064 CHRISTMAS SONG (11-66)/Christmas Song [Part 2]
6065 SWEET LITTLE BABY BOY (JESUS) (12-66)/Sweet Little Baby Boy (Jesus) [Part 2]
6071 BRING IT UP (1-67)/Nobody Knows
6086 KANSAS CITY (3-67)/Stone Fox [Instr.]

AS "JAMES BROWN & VICKI ANDERSON"

6091 THINK (1967)/Nobody Cares (Only by Vicki Anderson)

JAMES BROWN

SMASH

2093 JIMMY MACK (5-67)/What Do You Like

KING

6100 LET YOURSELF GO (5-67)/Good Rockin' Tonight

BETHLEHEM

3089 YOURS AND MINE [Instr.] (6-67)/I Love You Porgy

KING

6110 COLD SWEAT (7-67)/Cold Sweat [Part 2]

AS "JAMES BROWN & VICKI ANDERSON"

6111 IT WON'T BE ME (1967)/Mona Lisa [WITHDRAWN]

JAMES BROWN

6122 GET IT TOGETHER (10-67)/Get It Together [Part 2]
6133 FUNKY SOUL #1 [Instr.] (1967)/The Soul of J.B.

6141 JUST PLAIN FUNK (1967)/I'll Have To Cry
6144 I CAN'T STAND MYSELF (WHEN YOU TOUCH ME) (12-67)/There Was A Time
6151 YOU'VE GOT TO CHANGE YOUR MIND (2-68) [Duet with Bobby Byrd]/I'll Lose My Mind [By Bobby Byrd]
6155 I GOT THE FEELING (3-68)/If I Ruled The World
6159 MAYBE GOOD, MAYBE BAD [Instr.] (1968)/Maybe Good, Maybe Bad [Part 2]
6112 AMERICA IS MY HOME (5-68)/America Is My Home [Part 2]
6164 SHHHHH (FOR A LITTLE WHILE) (4-68)/Here I Go
6166 LICKING STICK—LICKING STICK (5-68)/Licking Stick—Licking Stick [Part 2]
6141 I GUESS I'LL HAVE TO CRY, CRY, CRY (7-68)/I Guess I'll Have To Cry, Cry, Cry [Part 2]
6187 SAY IT LOUD (I'M BLACK AND I'M PROUD) (9-68)/Say It Loud (I'm Black And I'm Proud) [Part 2]
6198 GOODBYE MY LOVE (11-68)/Shades Of Brown [Instr.]
6203 YOU KNOW IT (12-68)/Santa Claus Goes Straight To The Ghetto
6204 TIT FOR TAT (AIN'T NO TAKING BACK) (12-68)/ Believers Shall Enjoy (Non-Believers Shall Suffer)
6205 LET'S UNITE THE WORLD AT CHRISTMAS (12-68)/In The Middle
6213 GIVE IT UP OR TURNIT-A LOOSE (1-69)/I'll Lose My Mind
6216 "STEVE SOUL" A TALK WITH THE NEWS (2-69) [CUT OUT]/Shades Of Brown

AS "JAMES BROWN & MARVA WHITNEY"

6218 YOU'VE GOT TO HAVE A JOB (2-69)

JAMES BROWN

6222 SOUL PRIDE [Instr.] (3-69)/Soul Pride [Part 2]
6223* YOU'VE GOT TO HAVE A MOTHER FOR ME (4-69)/ You've Got To Have A Mother For Me [Part 2]
6224 I DON'T WANT NOBODY TO GIVE ME NOTHING (OPEN THE DOOR, I'LL GET IT MYSELF) (4-69)/I Don't Want Nobody To Give Me Nothing (Open The Door, I'll Get It Myself) [Part 2]
6235 THE LITTLE GROOVE MAKER [Issued with three flips and each was withdrawn]/(1) The Little Groove Maker [Part 2]; (2) Any Day Now; (3) I'm Shook
6240 THE POPCORN (5-69)/The Chicken
6245 MOTHER POPCORN (YOU GOT TO HAVE A MOTHER FOR ME) (6-69)/Mother Popcorn (You Got To Have A Mother For Me) [Part 2]

---

*UNISSUED.

6250 LOWDOWN POPCORN [Instr.] (8-69)/Top Of The Stack
6258 WORLD (9-69)/World [Part 2]
6255 LET A MAN COME IN AND DO THE POPCORN (10-69)/ Let A Man Come In And Do The Popcorn [Part 2]
6275 LET A MAN COME IN AND DO THE POPCORN (12-69)/ Gittin' A Little Hipper [Part 2] [Instr.]
6277 IT'S CHRISTMAS TIME (11-69)/It's Christmas Time [Part 2]
6280 AIN'T IT FUNKY NOW (11-69)/Ain't It Funky Now [Part 2]
6292 IT'S A NEW DAY (2-70)/Georgia On My Mind
6290 FUNKY DRUMMER (3-70)/Funky Drummer [Part 2]

AS "JAMES BROWN & VICKI ANDERSON"

6293 LET IT BE ME (4-70)/No More Heartaches, No More Tears (by Vicki Anderson)

JAMES BROWN

6310 BROTHER RAPP (5-70)/Brother Rapp [Part 2]
6318 GET UP (I FEEL LIKE BEING A SEX MACHINE) (7-70)/ Get Up (I Feel Like Being A Sex Machine) [Part 2]

BETHLEHEM

3098 A MAN HAS TO GO TO THE CROSSROADS (8-70)/The Drunk

KING

6329 SUPER BAD (10-70)/Super Bad [Part 2]

AS "MACEO & ALL THE KING'S MEN"

HOUSE OF FOX

1 GOTTA GET 'CHA (11-70)

KING

6334 HEY AMERICA (12-70)/Hey America [Part 2]
6340 SANTA CLAUS IS DEFINITELY HERE TO STAY (12-70)/ Santa Claus Is Definitely Here To Stay [Instr.] [Part 2]
6347 GET UP, GET INTO IT, GET INVOLVED (12-70)/Get Up, Get Into It, Get Involved [Part 2]
6366 SPINNING WHEEL (2-71)/Spinning Wheel [Part 2]
6368 SOUL POWER (2-71)/Soul Power [Part 2]
6363 I CRIED (5-71)/World [Part 2]

PEOPLE

2500 ESCAPE-ISM (6-71) Escape-ism [Part 2]
2501 HOT PANTS (SHE GOT TO USE WHAT SHE GOT TO GET WHAT SHE WANTS (7-71)/Hot Pants (She Got To Use What She Got To Get What She Wants [Part 2]

JAMES BROWN

POLYDOR

14088 MAKE IT FUNKY (8-71)/Make It Funky [Part 2]
14098 MY PART/MAKE IT FUNKY [Part 3] (10-71)/My Part/Make It Funky
14100 I'M A GREEDY MAN (11-71)/I'm A Greedy Man [Part 2]

AS "FRED WESLEY & THE J.B.'s"

PEOPLE

602 GIMME SOME MORE (1-72)/Rabbit Got The Gun

JAMES BROWN

KING

6359 TALKING LOUD & SAYING NOTHING (2-72)/Talking Loud & Saying Nothing [Part 2]

PEOPLE

14116 KING HEROIN (3-72)/Theme From King Heroin
14125 THERE IT IS (5-72)/There It Is [Part 2]
14129 HONKY TONK (6-72)/Honky Tonk [Part 2]
14139 (GET ON THE) GOOD FOOT (8-72)/(Get On The) Good Foot [Part 2]

AS "FRED WESLEY & THE J.B.'s"

614 BACK STABBERS (1972)/J. B. Shout

JAMES BROWN

14153 I GOT A BAG OF MY OWN (11-72)/Public Enemy #1 [Part 1]
14157 WHAT MY BABY NEEDS NOW IS A LITTLE LOVIN' (12-72) [W. Lyn Collins]/This Guy—This Girl's In Love
14161 SANTA CLAUS GOES STRAIGHT TO THE GHETTO (12-72)/Sweet Little Baby Boy (Jesus)

14162 I GOT ANTS IN MY PANTS (1-73)/I Got Ants In My Pants [Part 2]
14168 DOWN AND OUT IN NEW YORK CITY (3-73)/Mama's Dead

"FRED WESLEY & THE J.B.'S"

621 DOIN' IT TO DEATH (6-73)/Everybody Got Soul

JAMES BROWN

POLYDOR

14194 SEXY, SEXY, SEXY (8-73)/Slaughter's Theme
14210 STONED TO THE BONE (12-73)/Stoned To The Bone (Some More)
14223 THE PAYBACK (3-74)/The Payback [Part 2]
14244 MY THANG (6-74)/Public Enemy #1 [Part 1]
14255 PAPA DON'T TAKE NO MESS (8-74)/Papa Don't Take No Mess [Part 2]

"FRED WESLEY & THE J.B.'S"

PEOPLE

643 ROCKIN' FUNKY WATERGATE (9-74)/Rockin' Funky Watergate [Part 2]

JAMES BROWN

POLYDOR

14258 FUNKY PRESIDENT (PEOPLE IT'S BAD) (11-74)/Coldblooded
14268 REALITY (2-75)/I Need Your Love So Bad [Little Willie John '56 hit. KING 4841]
14270 SEX MACHINE (5-75)/Sex Machine [Part 2]
14281 HUSTLE!!! (DEAD ON IT) (7-75)/Dead On It [Part 2]
14295 SUPERBAD, SUPERSLICK (10-75)/Superbad, Superslick [Part 2]
14301 HOT (I NEED TO BE LOVED, LOVED, LOVED, LOVED) (1-76)/Superbad, Superslick
14303 DOOLEY'S JUNKYARD DOGS (2-76)/Dooley's Junkyard Dogs [Part 2]
14304 (I LOVE YOU) FOR SENTIMENTAL REASONS (3-76)/Goodnight My Love
14326 GET UP OFFA THAT THING (6-76)/Release The Pressure

"FRED WESLEY & THE J.B.'S"

PEOPLE

655 IT'S THE J.B.'s MONAURAL (1976)/It's The J.B.'s Monaural [Part 2]
663 ALL ABOARD THE FUNKY SOUL TRAIN (3-76)/Thank You For Lettin' Me Be Myself

JAMES BROWN

POLYDOR

14354 I REFUSE TO LOSE (10-76)/Home Again
14360 BODY HEAT (12-76)/Body Heat [Part 2]
14388 KISS IN '77 (5-77)/Woman '77

AS "JAMES BROWN & J.B.'S"

14409 GIVE ME SOME SKIN (8-77)/People Wake Up And Live

"FRED WESLEY & THE HORNY HORNS"

ATLANTIC

3408 UP FOR THE DOWN STROKE (8-77)/When In Doubt—Vamp!

JAMES BROWN

POLYDOR

14433 TAKE ME HIGHER AND GROOVE ME (11-77)/Summertime [W. Martha High]
14438 IF YOU DON'T GIVE A DOGGONE ABOUT IT (12-77)/People Who Criticize
14460 LOVE ME TENDER (3-78) [Tribute to Elvis!]/Have A Happy Day [W. the "New J.B.'s"]
14465 EYESIGHT (4-78)/I Never, Never, Never Will Forget
14487 THE SPANK (6-78)/Love Me Tender
14512 NATURE (10-78)/Nature [Part 2]
14522 FOR GOODNESS SAKES, LOOK AT THOSE CAKES (12-78)/For Goodness Sakes, Look At Those Cakes [Part 2]
14540 SOMEONE TO TALK TO (3-79)/Someone To Talk To [Part 2]
14557 IT'S TOO FUNKY IN HERE (5-79)/Are We Really Dancing?

"J.B.'S"

DRIVE

6277 ROCK GROOVE MACHINE (8-79)/Rock Groove Machine [Part 2]

JAMES BROWN

POLYDOR

2005 STAR GENERATION (9-79)/Women Are Something Else
2034 THE ORIGINAL DISCO MAN (11-79)/
2054 REGRETS (1-80)/

♭ ♯ ♪ ♩ 𝅗𝅥

Dee Clark

Real Name: "Delecta Clark." Born in Blythsville, Arkansas, on December 7, 1938.

DEE CLARK proved to be one of those R&R artists who could put everything they had into a song. With his soulful, yet joyful, manner Dee Clark could sing and climb up to a high-pitched climax with love for a particular girl! Not only was his rendering truly sweet but he had the remarkable ability of being able to sing with at least six different voices (like New Orleans's Clarence Henry).

Dee Clark was one of six children, having two brothers and three sisters, and was named Delecta after his mother. The family moved to Chicago, where Dee attended Farren and Calhoun grammar schools and where he began singing Gospel. It was during 1952 that Dee Clark founded the "Hambone Kids," which comprised Sammy Grier, Ronnie Strong, and himself. They recorded "Hambone" (OKEH 6862).

During 1955, Dee Clark began singing with the group the "Goldentones," and, after winning a talent show, discovery came through Herb "Cool Gent" Kent, a local disc jockey. After the group's audition at VEE JAY's studios and signing, came "This Is The Night" (VEE JAY 173) and "You Know" (VEE JAY 207), with Dee Clark as vocalist. Dee was also vocalist with the "Delegates," a group comprising Johnny Carter (later with the "Flamingos" and "Dells"), Teddy Long, John McCall, and Douglas Brown. One of their recordings was "Convention" (VEE JAY 212).

It was with FALCON (a subsidiary of VEE JAY) that Dee Clark made his first solo effort, but it was not until his national hit "Nobody But You" (ABNER 1019) that things began to happen for him. There, he joined Little Richard's band the "Upsetters" and, during 1959, recorded hits "Just Keep It Up" (ABNER 1026), "Hey Little Girl" (ABNER 1029), and a Doris Troy composition, "How About That" (ABNER 1032), which was backed by a Dee Clark classic, "Blues Get Off My Shoulder."

While touring the Southern states, Dee Clark joined with the Phil

Upchurch combo, which became his backup group. Dee wrote this band's hit "You Can't Sit Down" (BOYD label), which was recorded in 1961. Dee Clark then recorded "Raindrops" (VEE JAY 383), his own composition and a million-seller, that same year! During his VEE JAY contract, Dee Clark continued to record Little Richard's styled rockers "Dance On Little Girl" (VEE JAY 443) and that delightful well-arranged "Shook Up Over You" (VEE JAY 487).

Dee Clark's "I'm Going Home" (CONSTELLATION 108) produced a compelling Soul potential, and his "Hot Potato" (CONSTELLATION 165) proved to be another exciting disc. Dee Clark recorded on several labels, UNITED ARTISTS, WAND and WARNER BROTHERS, throughout the Sixties and Seventies. Dee then moved to Los Angeles and was signed by CHELSEA. His last hit was "Ride The Wild Horse" (CHELSEA 3025) in Disco fashion, which was produced by Kenny Nolan of "I Like Dreamin' " fame.

Discography

AS "HAMBONE KIDS" [W. "RED SAUNDERS ORCHESTRA"]

OKEH

6862 HAMBONE (3-52)/Boot 'Em Up
6884 ZEBEL, ZEBEL (8-52)/La Raspa

AS "GOLDEN TONES" [Pre-"KOOL GENTS"]

JAY DEE

806 ONE PRETTY BABY (1955)/The Meaning Of Love

"Kool Gents": Dee Clark, lead; John McCall, first tenor; Doug Brown, second tenor; Teddy Long, baritone and second tenor; John Carter, bass.

AS "KOOL GENTS"

VEE JAY

173 THIS IS THE NIGHT (1-56) [Feat. John McCall]/Do Ya Do [Feat. Teddy Long]
207 YOU KNOW (8-56) [Feat. John McCall]/I Just Can't Help Myself [Feat. John McCall and Dee Clark]

BETHLEHEM

3061 COME TO ME/Picture On The Wall

AS "DELEGATES"

VEE JAY

212 THE CONVENTION (9-56)/Jay's Rock [Big Jay McNeely]
243 MOTHER'S SON (1957) [Feat. Dee Clark]/I'm Gonna Be Glad [Feat. John McCall]

DEE CLARK

FALCON

1002 GLORIA (6-57) [W. "Kool Gents"]/Kangaroo Hop
1005 24 BOY FRIENDS (10-57)/Seven Nights
1009 OH LITTLE GIRL (5-58)/Wondering

DEE CLARK [W. "RILEY HAMPTON ORCHESTRA"]

ABNER

1019 (I DON'T WANT) NOBODY BUT YOU (12-58)/When I Call You
1026 JUST KEEP IT UP (5-59)/Whispering Grass

DEE CLARK

1029 HEY LITTLE GIRL (8-59) [Backup Little Richard's "Upsetters"]/If It Wasn't For Love
1032 HOW ABOUT THAT (12-57)/Blues Get Off My Shoulder [Bobby Parker's '55 tune. VEE JAY 279]
1037 AT MY FRONT DOOR (3-60) ["Eldorados" '55 hit. VEE JAY 147]/Ching-A-Ling

VEE JAY

355 YOU'RE LOOKING GOOD (8-60)/Gloria
372 YOUR FRIENDS (2-61)/Because I Love You
383 RAINDROPS (5-61)/Want To Love You
394 GOTUS DELLUVIA (8-61) [W. Al Smith]/Livin' With Vivian
409 YOU'RE TELLING OUR SECRETS (10-61)/Don't Walk Away From Me
428 YOU ARE LIKE THE WIND (12-61)/Drums In My Heart
443 DANCE ON LITTLE GIRL (4-62)/Fever
462 I'M GOING BACK TO SCHOOL (10-62)/Nobody But You

487 SHOOK UP OVER YOU (2-63)/I'm A Soldier Boy
532 HOW IS HE TREATING YOU? (7-63)/The Jones Brothers
548 WALKING MY DOG (10-63)/Nobody But Me

CONSTELLATION

108 CROSSFIRE TIME (11-63)/I'm Going Home
113 IT'S RAINING (3-64)/That's My Girl
132 HEARTBREAK (9-64)/Warm Summer Breezes
142 IN MY APARTMENT (2-65)/I Ain't Gonna Be Your Fool
147 T.C.B. (5-65)/It's Impossible
165 HOT POTATO (11-65)/I Don't Need (Nobody Like You)
193 I'M GOING HOME (8-66)/Old Fashioned Love

WAND

1177 NOBODY BUT YOU (1968)/Nobody But You [Part 2]

UNITED ARTISTS

50759 YOU CAN MAKE ME FEEL GOOD (4-71)/Old Time Religion

COLUMBIA

4-44200 LOST GIRL (1971)/In These Very Tender Moments

WARNER BROTHERS

7720 HAPPY MAN (7-73)/Raindrops

CHELSEA

3025* RIDE THE WILD HORSE [Vocal] (7-75)/Ride The Wild Horse [Instr.]

*Produced by Kenny Nolan of "I Like Dreamin' " fame.

Sam Cooke

Real Name: "Sam Cook." Born in Clarksdale, Mississippi, on January 2, 1931. Died in Los Angeles, California, on December 10, 1964.

SAM COOKE, "Mr. Soul," was a major contributor toward bridging the gap between Gospel and Soul. Sam had a particularly elegant manner and handsome appearance, besides having an astute business instinct. He had a vocal smoothness and uniqueness in leaping an octave, plus a happy and optimistic element of yodel phrasing (la la la la ti ta . . . and others), which became his recording trademark. His business associate, co-writer, and co-producer was James W. Alexander (former manager of the "Pilgrim Travellers"), and it was he who helped inspire Sam's career, while Rene Hall did much of the arranging. Sam Cooke and J. W. Alexander formed the Gospel rooting S.A.R. label in 1961 (named after Sam and Alexander), and through it Sam discovered the talents of many artists, such as the "Sims Twins" ("Sooth Me"), Johnnie Taylor ("Rome Wasn't Built In A Day/Never Never"), Johnny Morisette ("Meet Me At The Twistin' Place"), and the "Valentinos' " Bobby Womack ("Looking For A Love," "It's All Over Now"). With the forming of the DERBY label, in 1963, Sam introduced two new stars, Mel Carter and Billy Preston.

Sam was one of six children of the Reverend and Mrs. Charles Cook, and shortly after his birth the family moved to Chicago's South Side, where his father became preacher with the Christ Holiness Church. It was there that Sam, from the age of nine, sang in the choir. Sam then joined with his brother and two sisters to form a Gospel group, the "Singing Children." During his schooldays at Wendell Phillips High he joined the "Highway Q.C.'s," named after the Highway Baptist Church. It was from there that Sam went to become the lead singer with the most prominent gospel group, the "Soul Stirrers," replacing Robert H. Harris, an artist after whom Sam Cooke developed his style. Sam toured with the group, retaining close ties with the Reverend Cecil L. Franklin, whose daughter, Aretha, was singing in the choir at that time. Here his stay lasted until 1956, and it was during this period that Sam Cooke wrote "Be With Me Jesus," "I Have A Friend Above All Others," "Jesus Wash All My Troubles Away" and "That's Heaven To Me," which was recorded in the Seventies by Bobby Womack. Sam was credited with writing several early Gospel standards that he sang, notably SPECIALTY 802, 878, 896, and 907.

In 1957, under the pseudonym "Dale Cooke," Sam Cooke recorded the beautiful and passionate "Lovable" for Art Rupe's SPECIALTY label (596). Word leaked out that "Dale Cooke" was really Sam Cooke and "Soul Stirrers" dismissed Sam! A song, "You Send Me," which was written by Sam's brother, was turned down by SPECIALTY label. Bumps Blackwell, A&R man and Sam's manager, brought the song to band leader Bob Keen (who owned KEEN as well as DEL-FI labels) and it was released as a single. The record sold 2.5 million copies! SPECIALTY came back with a similar "I'll Come Running Back To You," with Sam Cooke playing the guitar!—and it (SPECIALTY 619) too sold a million! Riding high on hits "(I Love You) For Sentimental Reasons" (KEEN 400), "Win Your Love For Me" (2006) and "Love You Most Of All/ Blue Moon" (2008), Sam Cooke with J. W. Alexander formed the KAGS Publishing Company. The first hit was "Everybody Likes To Cha Cha Cha," in which Sam credited his second wife, Barbara Campbell, as the writer. Sam Cooke had two unfortunate incidents, both car accidents. In the first, at Fresno, California, he lost his first wife, Delores, who was killed. In the second, while Sam was touring in Arkansas, his valet-driver was killed, while entertainer Lou Rawls suffered a concussion and Sam very nearly lost one of his eyes!

While recording with KEEN label during 1959 and 1960, Sam Cooke produced the hits "Only Sixteen" (a Sixties Terry Black hit and, again, popularized in the Seventies by "Dr. Hook and His Medicine Band"), "There I've Said It Again" (written by the New York Brill Building team Paul Evans and Barry Mann; popularized in 1963 by Bobby Vinton), "Wonderful World" (written by Lou Adler and Herb Alpert; popularized in 1965 by "Herman's Hermits" and, during the Seventies, by Johnny Nash and also by James Taylor/Paul Simon). A dispute arose between Sam Cooke and KEEN label, with Sam suing because of insufficient royalties and winning his case with KEEN, allegedly facing bankruptcy. KAGS rights were purchased by Sam and, in turn, sold to RCA for $15,000.

Sam worked with Hugo and Luigi, producers at RCA, and during the early Sixties he recorded many Pop-oriented favorites: "Chain Gang" (written along with L. C. Cooke and revived in the Seventies by Jimmy Croce), "Cupid" (popularized by Johnny Nash and "Tony Orlando & Dawn"), "Twistin' The Night Away" (a Seventies hit by Rod Stewart), "Bring It On Home To Me/Havin' A Party" (duets with Lou Rawls, and recorded by many other artists), and then "Another Saturday Night" (a Seventies revival hit by Cat Stevens).

Sam Cooke was later dubbed "The Father of Soul" because he inspired and influenced so many later stars. "Baby, Baby, Baby" with the classic "Send Me Some Lovin' ": these two gems, one side uptempo roller and the other with Sam's soulful pleading, are excellent examples of his diversity. "Little Red Rooster" (old howlin' wolfblues classic, featuring Billy Preston, organ, and Ray Charles, piano, in session) and his outstanding Rock and Roll classic "(Ain't That) Good News" (8299) had real Chart appeal!

Tragedy struck Sam Cooke at the height of his career, after a performance at a Los Angeles night spot, wherein he encountered a bizarre and still clouded set of circumstances, resulting in his being shot to death. The court evidence submitted regarding an apparent misunderstanding, struggle, and shooting, which took place at a local roadside motel, led to a verdict of "justified homicide" and an acquittal.

Strangely enough, the release recording that followed Sam Cooke's death was "Shake" (covered by Otis Redding), and the classic "A Change Is Gonna Come" marked a sad and tragic ending! His widowed wife, Barbara Campbell (they had two children), later married Bobby Womack.

Discography

SAM COOKE WITH THE "SOUL STIRRERS" (Gospel Recordings)

1951-56 Lineup: Sam Cooke, Paul Foster, R. B. Robinson, S. Roy Crain, T. L. Buster, and Jesse L. Farley.

AS "SOUL STIRRERS"

SPECIALTY

802 JESUS GAVE ME WATER [Feat. Sam Cooke]/Peace In The Valley
845 JESUS PAID THE DEBT/Blessed Be The Name Of The Lord
851 HE'LL WELCOME ME [Feat. Sam Cooke and Paul Foster]/End Of My Journey
859 HE'S MY FRIEND UNTIL THE END [Feat. Sam Cooke]/Come And Go To That Land [Feat. Sam Cooke and Paul Foster]
868 ANY DAY NOW/Jesus, I'll Never Forget

878 NEARER TO THEE [Feat. Sam Cooke]/Be With Me Jesus [Feat. Sam Cooke and Paul Foster]
882 I'M SO GLAD (TROUBLE DON'T LAST ALWAYS) [Feat. Sam Cooke and Paul Foster]/One More River
892 WONDERFUL [Feat. Sam Cooke]/Farther Along
896 TOUCH THE HEM OF HIS GARMENT [Feat. Sam Cooke]/ Jesus, Wash Away My Troubles
902 PILGRIM OF SORROW [Feat. Sam Cooke]/In A Few More Days
907 WERE YOU THERE (WHEN THEY CRUCIFIED MY LORD? [Feat. Sam Cooke]/Sinner, Run To Jesus

AS "DALE COOKE"

596 LOVABLE (1957)/Forever

SAM COOKE

KEEN

4013 YOU SEND ME (10-57)/Summertime

SPECIALTY

619 I'LL COME RUNNING BACK TO YOU (12-57)/Forever

KEEN

4002 (I LOVE YOU) FOR SENTIMENTAL REASONS (12-57)/ Desire Me
4009 LONELY ISLAND (3-58)/You Were Made For Me
2005 ALL OF MY LIFE (1958)/Stealing Kisses
2006 WIN YOUR LOVE FOR ME (8-58)/(Love Song from) Houseboat
2008 LOVE YOU MOST OF ALL (11-58)/Blue Moon

SPECIALTY

627 I DON'T WANT TO CRY (1958)/That's All I Need To Know
667 I NEED YOU NOW (1959)/Happy In Love

KEEN

2018 EVERYBODY LIKES TO CHA CHA CHA (3-59)/Little Things To Do

KEEN

2022	ONLY SIXTEEN (6-59)/Let's Go Steady Again
2101	SUMMERTIME (1959)/Summertime [Part 2]
2105	THERE I'VE SAID IT AGAIN (11-59)/One Hour Ahead Of The Posse
2111	'T-AIN'T NOBODY'S BIZNESS (1960)/No One
2112	WONDERFUL WORLD (5-60)/Along The Navajo Trail
2117	WITH YOU (1960)/I Thank God
2118	STEAL AWAY (1960)/So Glamorous [W. the "Stars"—white group]
2122	MARY MARY LOU (1960)/Eee-Yi-Ee-Yi-Oh

RCA

7701	TEENAGE SONATA (3-60)/If You Were The Only Girl
7730	YOU UNDERSTAND ME (4-60)/I Belong To Your Heart
7783	CHAIN GANG (8-60)/I Fall In Love Every Day
7816	SAD MOOD (12-60)/Love Me
7853	THAT'S IT, I QUIT, I'M MOVIN' ON (3-61)/What Did You Say?
7883	CUPID (6-61)/Farewell My Love
7927	FEEL IT (10-61)/It's All Right

SAR

122	JUST FOR YOU (1961)/Made For Me

RCA

7983	TWISTIN' THE NIGHT AWAY (2-62)/One More Time
8036	BRING IT ON HOME TO ME (5-62) [W. Lou Rawls]/Having A Party [W. Lou Rawls]
8088	NOTHING CAN CHANGE THIS LOVE (9-62)/Somebody Have Mercy [W. Lou Rawls]
8129	SEND ME SOME LOVIN' (1-63) [Little Richard '57 hit. SPECIALTY 598]/Baby, Baby, Baby
8164	ANOTHER SATURDAY NIGHT (4-63)/Love Will Find The Way
8215	FRANKIE AND JOHNNY (7-63)/Cool Train
8247	LITTLE RED ROOSTER (10-63) [W. Billy Preston, organ; Ray Charles, piano]/You Gotta Move
8299	(AIN'T THAT) GOOD NEWS (6-64)/Basin Street Blues
8368	GOOD TIMES (1964)/Tennesee Waltz
8426	COUSIN OF MINE (9-64)/That's Where It's At
8486	SHAKE (1-65)/A Change Is Gonna Come
8539	IT'S GOT THE WHOLE WORLD SHAKIN' (4-65)/(Somebody) Else My Troublin' Mind
8586	WHEN A BOY FALLS IN LOVE (6-65) [Mel Carter '63 hit. DERBY 1003]/The Piper
8631	SUGAR DUMPLING (7-65)/Bridge Of Tears
8751	FEEL IT (1965)/It's All Right
8803	LET'S GO STEADY AGAIN (4-66)/Trouble Blues
8934	MEET ME AT MARY'S PLACE (9-66)/If I Had A Hammer

SAM COOKE AND THE "SOUL STIRRERS"

SPECIALTY

921 MUST JESUS BEAR THE CROSS ALONE (1971)/Last Mile Of The Way
928 CHRIST IS ALL (6-71)/Just Another Day

SAM COOKE

CHERIE

4501 DARLING I NEED YOU NOW (1971)/Win Your Love For Me

♭ ♯ ♪ ♩ 𝅗𝅥

Bobby Darin

Real Name: "Walden Robert Cassoto." Born May 14, 1936, in The Bronx, New York City. Died December 20, 1973, in Los Angeles, California.

BOBBY DARIN, throughout a lengthy career, had that inimitable gift of ensuring adult acceptance with his well-adapted showmanship and personal charisma that were the delight of audiences of all age groups. His recording development jumped from early rockabilly DECCA releases to Rock and Roll New Orleans-style ATCO selling releases, into the sophisticated writing approach of the Sixties "cabaret" and on into the later Sixties folk-style CAPITOL releases, and finally blending with Rhythm and Blues. This was not a fragmentation of himself but rather a cohesive growth in entertainment personality that became the great Bobby Darin. The name "Bobby Darin" was chosen from a telephone book.

Through all of this Bobby was plagued with a heart problem—a legacy of rheumatic fever at the age of eight—but he went on giving of his very best because he "knew there were millions who loved and treasured his recordings" and he became that one person recording solo who could motivate his own beat Rock and Roll!

Bobby Darin's aggressiveness stemmed from his early years of struggle in the Bronx section of New York City, where he was born Walden Robert Cassoto, and where his father (whom he described as a small-time gangster) died before Bobby's birth, thus leaving the mother, daughter, and baby son on welfare. They were the beginning of tough years. Bobby was not only aggressive but bright, and graduated with honors from Bronx High School, winning a scholarship to Hunter College, where he chose Drama. During those years Bobby learned to play the piano, vibraphone, guitar, and drums.

Bobby, then, met Don Kirshner (who later headed Screen Gems Music and also worked at the N.Y.C. Brill Building with Pops songwriters Carole King, Gerry Goffin, Ellie Greenwich and Jeff Barry, and who also launched the "Monkees'" success and the "Archies"). Bobby and Don wrote and sang radio commercials for the local radio station. Together, they wrote a song, "My First Love," of which George Scheck (then manager of Connie Francis) took a demo to DECCA RECORDS, and this led to a contract for Bobby Darin. In March of 1956, Bobby Darin made a guest appearance on television with Tommy Dorsey and, that same year, gave us several initial records, including his excellent "Silly Willy" (DECCA 29922 and 30737). Unfortunately, immediate disagreement arose between DECCA and the enthused, headstrong young artist over objectives and choice of material and they parted company.

Don Kirshner then brought Bobby Darin to Ahmet Ertegun, president of ATLANTIC RECORDS, where he soon made his debut with "(I Found A) Million Dollar Baby" (ATCO 6092). Later, from a song idea inspired by the mother of "Murray the K" (a local deejay), Bobby recorded "Splish Splash" (ATCO 6116), which became a smash hit! Other hits followed, among which were "Queen Of The Hop" (ATCO 6127), "Dream Lover" (ATCO 6140), which was backed by the "Cues" (the group that gave us the 1955 disc "Burn The Candle" on CAPITOL 3245), and the great Bobby Darin "No. 1 Hit of 1959"—"Mack The Knife" (ATCO 6147).

Bobby Darin soon became an outstanding performer and national sensation, singing many times at the Copacabana and in the films *Pepe, Too Late Blues, Come September, Hell Is for Heroes, Point Blank,* and with Sandra Dee in *If a Man Answers*. Bobby, a clean-cut, good-looking young performer, went on recording, to give us, among others, "Clementine" (ATCO 6161), "Artificial Flowers" (ATCO 6179), "Nature Boy" (ATCO 6196), "Multiplication" (ATCO 6214), and "Things" ATCO 6229). In 1960, Bobby Darin married the blonde actress Sandra Dee and won an Oscar as the Best Supporting Actor for his role in *Captain Newman, M.D.* In 1962, he went to CAPITOL RECORDS and gave us the beautiful hit "18 Yellow Roses" (CAPITOL 4970).

Special mention should be made of the following Folk Rock entries: "If I Were A Carpenter" (ATLANTIC 2350), which was written by Folk Rock singer Tim Harden, and "The Girl That Stood Beside Me/ Reason To Believe" (ATLANTIC 2365), with flip-side written by Tim Harden, who also wrote the 1971 release "Simple Song Of Freedom" (MOTOWN 1193). His other hits were "Lovin' You" (ATLANTIC 2376), "The Lady Came From Baltimore" (ATLANTIC 2395), "Darling Be Home Soon" (ATLANTIC 2420), "Long Line Rider" (DIRECTION 350), and "Melodee" (MOTOWN 1183). Bobby and Sandra were divorced in 1967.

Alas! Bobby Darin's song ended on December 11, 1973, when he entered Cedars of Lebanon Hospital in Los Angeles, California, for an examination that showed that one of the artificial valves (inserted into the heart in 1971) was not functioning properly. He underwent a six-hour open-heart surgical operation but, shortly after midnight, Thursday,

December 20, Bobby Darin was pronounced dead. The brashly ambitious Bobby Darin once vowed publicly that he would be a legend before he was twenty-five. At thirty-seven, he was indeed a legend!

Discography

BOBBY DARIN

DECCA

29883 ROCK ISLAND LINE (4-56) [W. "Jaybirds"] [Lonnie Donegan '56 hit. LONDON 1650]/Timber
29922 SILLY WILLY (6-56) [W. "Jaybirds"]/Blue-Eyed Mermaid
30031 HEAR THEM BELLS (9-56)/The Greatest Builder
30225 DEALER IN DREAMS (3-57)/Help Me
30737 SILLY WILLY (8-57)/Dealer In Dreams

ATCO

6092 MILLION DOLLAR BABY (7-57)/Talk To Me
6103 DON'T CALL MY NAME (12-57)/Pretty Baby
6109 JUST IN CASE YOU CHANGE YOUR MIND (3-58)/So Mean
6116 SPLISH SPLASH (6-58)/Judy, Don't Be Moody

AS "RINKY DINKS—FEAT. BOBBY DARIN"

6121 EARLY IN THE MORNING (7-58) [Buddy Holly '58 hit. CORAL 62006]/Now We're One
Above sides originally as "Ding Dongs Feat. Bobby Darin," BRUNSWICK 55073.
6128 MIGHTY MIGHTY MAN (11-58)/You're Mine

BOBBY DARIN

6127 QUEEN OF THE HOP (10-58)/Lost Love
6133 PLAIN JANE (2-59)/While I'm Gone
6140 DREAM LOVER (4-59)/Bullmoose
6147 MACK THE KNIFE (8-59) [A Kurt Weill song from *The Threepenny Opera*]/Was There A Call For Me
6158 BEYOND THE SEA (1-60)/That's The Way Love Is
6161 CLEMENTINE (3-60)/Tall Story
6167 (WON'T YOU COME HOME) BILL BAILEY (5-60)/I'll Be There
6173 BEACHCOMBER (9-60) [Instr.]/Autumn Blues [Bobby Darin at piano]
6179 ARTIFICIAL FLOWERS (10-60)/Somebody To Love
6183 CHILD OF GOD (12-60)/Christmas Auld Lang Syne

6188 (UP A) LAZY RIVER (2-61)/Oo-Ee-Train
6196 NATURE BOY (5-61) [Nat King Cole '48 hit. CAPITOL 15054]/Look For My True Love
6200 COME SEPTEMBER (7-61) [Instr.]/Walk Back To Me
6206 YOU MUST HAVE BEEN A BEAUTIFUL BABY (9-61)/Sorrow Tomorrow
6211 O COME ALL YE FAITHFUL (11-61)/Ave Maria
6214 MULTIPLICATION (12-61)/Irresistible You [Bobby Peterson '60 hit. V-TONE 214]
6221 WHAT'D I SAY (3-62)/What'd I Say [Part 2]
6229 THINGS (7-62)/Jailor Bring Me Water
6236 BABY FACE (9-62)/You Know How

CAPITOL

4837 IF A MAN ANSWERS (10-62)/A True, True Love

ATCO

6244 I FOUND A NEW BABY (12-62)/Keep A Walkin'

CAPITOL

4897 YOU'RE THE REASON (I'M LIVING) (1-63) [Bobby Edwards '61 hit. CREST 1075]/Now You're Gone
4970 18 YELLOW ROSES (5-63)/Not For Me
5019 TREAT MY BABY GOOD (8-63)/Down So Long
5079 BE MAD LITTLE GIRL (11-63)/Since You've Been Away
5126 I WONDER WHO'S KISSING HER NOW (3-64)/As Long As I'm Singing

ATCO

6297 MILORD (6-64)/Golden Earrings
6316 SWING LOW, SWEET CHARIOT (9-64)/Similau
6334 HARDHEARTED HANNAH (12-64)/Minnie The Moocher

CAPITOL

5257 THE THINGS IN THIS HOUSE (10-64)/Wait By The Water
5359 HELLO DOLLY (2-65)/Golden Earrings
5399 VENICE BLUE (4-65)/World Without End
5443 WHEN I GET HOME (6-65)/Lonely Road
5481 THAT FUNNY FEELING (9-65)/Gyp The Cat

ATLANTIC

2305 WE DIDN'T ASK TO BE BROUGHT HERE (10-65)/Funny What Love Can Do
2317 SILVER DOLLAR (2-66)/The Breaking Point
2329 MAME (4-66)/Walking In The Shadow Of Love
2341 MERCI CHERI (6-66)/Who's Afraid Of Virginia Wolfe?
2350 IF I WERE A CARPENTER (9-66)/Rainin'

2365 THE GIRL THAT STOOD BESIDE ME (12-66)/Reason To Believe
2376 LOVIN' YOU (1-67)/Amy
2395 THE LADY CAME FROM BALTIMORE (4-67)/I Am
2420 DARLING BE HOME SOON (7-67) ["Lovin' Spoonful" '67 hit. KAMA SUTRA 220]/Hello Sunshine
2433 SHE KNOWS (9-67)/Talk To The Animals

CAPITOL

2354 SALLY (1-69)

DIRECTION

350 LONG LINE RIDER (2-69)/Change
351 ME AND MR. HOHNER (5-69)/Song For A Dollar
352 DISTRACTIONS (8-69)/Jive

DIRECTION (4000 SERIES)

4000 (9 TO 5) JIVE'S ALIVE (10-69)/Sugar Man
4001 BABY MAYE (12-69)/Sweet Reason
4002 MAYBE WE CAN GET IT TOGETHER (3-70)/Rx-Pyro

MOTOWN

1183 MELODEE (5-71)/Someday We'll Be Together
1193 I'LL BE YOUR BABY TONIGHT (1971)/Simple Song Of Freedom
1203 SAIL ALONG (7-72)/Hardheaded Woman
1212 AVERAGE PEOPLE (11-72)/Something In Her Love
1217 HAPPY (Love Theme from *Lady Sings the Blues*) (12-72)/Something In Her Love

♭ ♯ ♪ ♩ 𝅗𝅥

"Delfonics"

MEMBERS: *William Hart* (lead singer) born in Washington, D.C., January 17, 1945; (brother) *Wilbert Hart,* born in Philadelphia, Pennsylvania, October 19, 1947; *Randy Cain,* born in Philadelphia, Pennsylvania, May 2, 1942 (replaced by Major Harris, born in Richmond, Virginia, February 9, 1947, who was also replaced in late 1973 by Bruce Peterson).

Hometown: Philadelphia, Pennsylvania.

This "sweet sexy soul" trio was truly one of the major factors in the creation of the "Philadelphia Sound." The "DELFONICS," a pure, classy falsetto harmony group, began as a quartet back in 1965 and was known then as the "Four Gents," and Stan Watson (who later formed BELL'S PHILLY GROVE label) took a personal interest in the group. A name change was suggested, and from that of the two groups "Orphonics" and "Del Vikings" came the name "Delfonics." William Hart, original member but now with the "Veltones," was inspired by the singing style of Little Anthony ("Imperials"), and from there the "Delfonics" developed their own sound.

The group's all-time classic is "La La (Means I Love You)" (PHILLY GROVE 150), which was beautifully written, arranged, and produced by Thom Bell, who played keyboards and tympanies on that session. Also on that disc were Ronnie Baker (bass), Norman Harris (guitar), Roland Chambers (guitar), Vince Montana (vibes), and Earl Young (later "Trammps' " bass lead singer) on drums. Their hits continued with "I'm Sorry" (PHILLY GROVE 151), "Break Your Promise" (PHILLY GROVE 152), "Ready Or Not Here I Come (Can't Hide From Love)" (PHILLY GROVE 154), on through to "Didn't I (Blow Your Mind This Time)" (PHILLY GROVE 161), an emotional pulsating performance that hit the Top-Ten Chart in 1971.

Major Harris—former member of the "Jarmels," of "Little Bit Of Soap" fame, and singer with the "Teenagers," the "Impacts," the "Tarmels," and "Nenette Turner Rebellion," helped complement the group sound. Major Harris had a successful solo career through the mid-Seventies, with exceptional ballad treatment of "Love Won't Let Me Wait" (ATLANTIC 3248). The "Delfonics" have continued making their own distinctive sounds through the Seventies, but have never quite reached their late-Sixties sales impact.

Discography

AS "DELFONICS"

CAMEO

472 YOU'VE BEEN UNTRUE (1966)/I Was There

PHILLY GROVE

150 LA LA (MEANS I LOVE YOU) (2-68)/Can't Get Over Losing You
151 I'M SORRY (8-68)/You're Gone

MOON SHOT

6703 HE DON'T REALLY LOVE YOU (5-68)/Without You

PHILLY GROVE

152 BREAK YOUR PROMISE (8-68)/Alfie
154 READY OR NOT HERE I COME (12-68)/Somebody Loves You
156 FUNNY FEELING (6-69)/My New Love
157 YOU GOT YOURS & I'LL GET MINE (8-69)/Loving Him
161 DIDN'T I (BLOW YOUR MIND THIS TIME) (1-70)/Down Is Up, Up Is Down
162 TRYING TO MAKE A FOOL OF ME (6-70)/Baby I Love You
163 WHEN YOU GET RIGHT DOWN TO IT (9-70)/I Gave To You
166 HEY! LOVE (6-71)/Over & Over
169 WALK RIGHT UP TO THE SUN (10-71)/Round And Round
172 TELL ME THIS IS A DREAM (6-72)/I'm A Man
174 THINK IT OVER (12-72)/I'm A Man
176 I DON'T WANT TO MAKE YOU WAIT (6-73)/Baby I Miss You
177 ALFIE (9-73)/Start All Over Again
182 I TOLD YOU SO (1-74)/Seventeen And In Love
184 LYING TO MYSELF (6-74)/Hey Babe

AS "MAJOR HARRIS BOOGIE BLUES BAND"

ATLANTIC

3217	EACH MORNING I WAKE UP (11-74)/Just A Thing To Do
3248	LOVE WON'T LET ME WAIT (4-75)/After Loving You
3321	JEALOUSY (4-76)/Tynisa
3336	IT'S GOT TO BE MAGIC (6-76)/Just A Thing That I Do

WMOT

4002	LAID BACK LOVE (11-76)/This Is What You Mean To Me

AS "DELFONICS"

ARISTA

0308	DON'T THROW IT ALL AWAY (4-78)/I Don't Care What People Say

♭ ♯ ♪ ♩ 𝅗𝅥

"Dells"

MEMBERS: *"El Rays"* (Sextet): Johnny Funches, lead tenor; Marvin Junior, first tenor; Lucius McGill, tenor (quit group in 1954); Verne Allison, tenor; Mike McGill, baritone; Chuck Barksdale, bass.

"The Dells" (Quintet): Johnny Funches (1955-60), lead tenor; Marvin Junior (1960 to date), lead tenor; Johnny Carter, first tenor (formerly with "Flamingos," replaced Johnny Funches in 1962); Chuck Barksdale, bass; Mike McGill, baritone; Verne Allison, second tenor.

Hometown: Harvey, Illinois.

The "DELLS" have always had their very own personal and masterful touch in singing a song. Each performance is a rare blend of distinction and versatility behind one of the most powerful and controlled awesome lead singers in the Soul World, Marvin Junior! Here is a veteran quintet that has more than survived for well over twenty-five years, most capable of singing Doo-Wopp, standards, occasionally Gospel, Rhythm and Blues to Disco, and the popular hits of the day. Talent and perseverence are the two major factors that have made the "Dells" Chicago's No. 1 Soul group.

The group's roots go back to singing while attending Thornton High School in Harvey, a suburb of Chicago, Illinois, their hometown, out of which they still operate. Several of the members sang Gospel in church and it was in 1954, then formed as the "El Rays" (which means "The Kings"), that they recorded a regional hit, "Darling I Know" (CHECKER 794), for the CHESS subsidiary label. It was shortly after this period that the group, now known as the "Dells," came into contact with Harvey Fuqua and the "Moonglows" (of 1954 "Sincerely" fame: CHESS 1581). It was there and then that the "Dells" learned to sing five-part harmony while rehearsing with each of the "Moonglow" members. The group then signed a contract with Vivian Carter's VEE JAY label, where they recorded two moderate hits, "Tell The World" (VEE JAY 134) and "Dreams Of Contentment" (VEE JAY 166), but a third, "Oh! What A Night" (VEE JAY 204), proved to be a smash hit, selling over a million copies. The lyrics for "Oh! What A Night" were written by Johnny Funches and Marvin Junior while both were reminiscing over a party held the previous night. Since then, it has become a Rhythm and Blues classic and certainly the "Dells' " biggest hit!

Several VEE JAY recordings worth mentioning since then are "Why Do You Have To Go" (VEE JAY 236), "A Distant Love" (VEE JAY 251), "Pain In My Heart" (VEE JAY 258), and "I'm Calling" (VEE JAY 292). Late in 1958, the group became involved in an automobile accident on the Ohio Turnpike but, fortunately, none of the quintet was killed. After this sudden tragedy, the group might have quit or backed off a bit, but their togetherness prompted still more nightclub appearances and, in due time, the signing of a contract with the CHESS subsidiary label, ARGO. One hit in 1962, "Bossa Nova Bird" (ARGO 5428), led toward a major change in personnel. Johnny Funches left the group, to be replaced by Johnny Carter, former member of the "Flamingos." During 1963, the "Dells" backed up Barbara Lewis on her hit "Hello Stranger" (ATLANTIC 2182).

The "Dells" really started happening during 1967. They then hit the Charts with the beautiful "O-O I Love You" (CADET 5574), followed by the hits "There Is" (CADET 5590), "Wear It On Our Face" (CADET 5599), and that spectacular hit "Stay In My Corner" (CADET 5612). Actually, each and every record since then is a standard, and when you listen to the "Dells" sound, with its classy, sophisticated harmony, there is little doubt of their own polished treatment! The hits kept coming: "Does Anybody Know I'm Here" (CADET 5631), "I Can Sing A Rainbow/Love Is Blue" (CADET 5641), the updated version of "Oh! What A Night" (CADET 5649), and the Oldies updated versions for "Nadine" (CADET 5667), "Long Lonely Nights" (CADET 5672), and "Glory Of Love" (CADET 5679).

The "Dells" rolled on with the times and truly kept their sound both refreshing and original. Thus it was Bobby Miller to Charles Stepney production, then to the famed Detroit producer Don Davis (who helped the "Parliaments," the "Dramatics," Johnny Taylor, and so on) to when the "Dells" struck their 1973 giant hit with "Give Your Baby A Standing Ovation" (CADET 5696). The following releases by the group during the Seventies mark most exceptionally what the "Dells" truly are: "The Love We Had (Stays On My Mind)" (CADET 5683), "I Miss You" (CADET 5700), "I Wish It Was Me You Loved" (CADET 5702), "Bring Back The Love Of Yesterday" (CADET 5703), "We Got To Get Our Thing Together" (MERCURY 73723), "Betcha Never Been Loved (Like

This Before)" (MERCURY 73901), and "(You Bring Out) The Best In Me" (ABC 12440). A great group that has given so much and for so many. They deserve a long standing ovation, the Mighty, Mighty "Dells"!

Discography

AS "THE EL RAYS"

CHECKER

794 DARLING I KNOW (6-54)/Christine

AS "THE DELLS"

VEE JAY

134 TELL THE WORLD (4-55)/Blues At Three [. . . "Count Morris"]
166 DREAMS OF CONTENTMENT (12-55)/Zing Zing Zing
204 OH! WHAT A NITE (8-56)/Jo Jo
230 MOVIN' ON (12-56)/I Wanna Go Home
236 WHY DO YOU HAVE TO GO (2-57)/Dance, Dance, Dance
251 A DISTANT LOVE (6-57)/O Bop She Bop Cubop Cubop
258 PAIN IN MY HEART (8-57)/Time Makes You Change
274 WHAT YOU SAY BABY (3-58)/The Springer
292 JEEPERS CREEPERS (8-58)/I'm Calling
300 WEDDING DAY (11-58)/My Best Girl
324 DRY YOUR TEARS (9-59)/(Baby) Open Up Your Heart
338 OH! WHAT A NITE (12-59)/I Wanna Go Home
376 HOLD ON TO WHAT YOU'VE GOT (2-61)/Swingin' Teens

ARGO

5414 GOD BLESS THE CHILD (5-62)/I'm Going Home
5428 BOSSA NOVA BIRD (10-62)/Eternally
5442 HI DIDDLEY DEE DUM DUM (6-63)/If It Ain't One Thing, It's Another
5456 GOODBYE, MARY-ANN (10-63)/After You

VEE JAY

595 SHY GUY (5-64)/What Do We Prove
615 OH WHAT A GOOD NITE (8-64)/Wait 'Til Tomorrow
674 STAY IN MY CORNER (4-64) [Orig. slow version]/It's Not Unusual
712 HEY SUGAR (DON'T GET SERIOUS) (12-65)/Poor Little Boy

CADET

5538 THINKIN' ABOUT YOU (8-66)/The Change We Go Through (For Love)
5551 OVER AGAIN (12-66)/Run For Cover

AS "THE DELLS AND JO ANN GARRETT"

CHESS

1992 I'M SO AFRAID (1967)/You Can't Come In

AS "THE DELLS"

CADET

5563 INSPIRATION (5-67)/You Belong To Someone Else
5574 O—O, I LOVE YOU (11-67)/There Is
5590 THERE IS (1-68)/Show Me (Baby)
5599 WEAR IT ON OUR FACE (4-68)/Please Don't Change Me Now
5612 STAY IN MY CORNER (6-68)/Love Is So Simple
5621 ALWAYS TOGETHER (10-68)/I Want My Momma
5631 DOES ANYBODY KNOW I'M HERE (12-68)/Make Sure
5636 HALLWAYS OF MY MIND (3-69)/I Can't Do Enough
5641 I CAN'T SING A RAINBOW/LOVE IS BLUE (5-69)/ Hallelujah Baby
5649 OH! WHAT A NIGHT (8-69)/Believe Me
5658 (SITTIN' ON THE) DOCK OF THE BAY (11-69) [Otis Redding '68 hit. VOLT 157]/When I'm In Your Arms
5663 OH WHAT A DAY (1-70)/The Change We Go Through
5667 OPEN UP MY HEART (4-70)/Nadine [Orig. "Coronets" hit. CHESS 1549]
5672 LONG LONELY NIGHTS (7-70) [Lee Andrews/Hearts '57 hit. CHESS 1665]/Little Understanding
5679 GLORY OF LOVE (2-71) ["5 Keys" '51 hit. ALADDIN 3099]/ Whiter Shade Of Pale [British "Procol Harem" '67 hit, DERAM 7507]
5683 THE LOVE WE HAD (STAYS ON MY MIND) (8-71)/ Freedom Means
5689 IT'S ALL UP TO YOU (2-72)/Oh My Dear
5691 WALK ON BY (8-72)/This Guy's In Love With You
5694 I'D RATHER BE WITH YOU (12-72)/Just As Long As We're In Love
5696 GIVE YOUR BABY A STANDING OVATION (4-73)/Closer
5698 MY PRETENDING DAYS ARE OVER (10-73)/Let's Make It Last
5700 I MISS YOU (1-74)/Don't Make Me A Storyteller
5702 (OH) I WISH IT WAS ME YOU LOVED (7-74)/Two Together Is Better Than One

CADET

5703 LEARNING TO LOVE YOU WAS EASY (IT'S SO HARD TRYING TO GET OVER YOU)* (9-74)/Bring Back The Love Of Yesterday [Written by Willie Schofield, formerly of the "Falcons"]

5707 YOU'RE THE GREATEST (5-75)/Glory Of Love

AS "THE DELLS" WITH "DRAMATICS"

5710 LOVE IS MISSING FROM OUR LIVES (7-75)/I'm In Love

AS "THE DELLS"

5711 WE GOT TO GET OUR THING TOGETHER (10-75)/The Power Of Love

MERCURY

73723 WE GOT TO GET OUR THING TOGETHER (11-75)/ Reminiscing

73759 POWER OF LOVE (2-76)/Gotta Get Home To My Baby

73809 SLOW MOTION (6-76)/Ain't No Black & White In Music

73842 NO WAY BACK (9-76)/Too Late For Love

73909 OUR LOVE (5-77)/Could It Be

73901 BETCHA NEVER BEEN LOVED (LIKE THIS BEFORE) (8-77)/Get On Down

73977 PRIVATE PROPERTY (1-78)/Teaser

TM

101 SUPER WOMAN (7-78) [Also on ABC 12386]/My Life Is So Wonderful (When You're Around)

ABC

12422 I WANNA TESTIFY (11-78) ["Parliaments" '67 hit. REVILOT 207]/Drowning For Your Love

12440 (YOU BRING OUT) THE BEST IN ME (1-79)/Wrapped Up Tight

MCA

8703 THOUGHT I COULD (7-79)/Plastic People [also on MCA 41051]

*Above also has flip "Sweeter As The Days Go By."

♭ ♯ ♪ ♩ 𝅗𝅥

Bo Diddley

Adopted Name: "Ellas McDaniels" (his parents' name being Bates), born in McComb, Mississippi, on December 30, 1928.

BO DIDDLEY was among the first of the Rhythm and Blues artists to experiment with the effects of a heavily amplified guitar. He actually popularized the offbeat electronic riffs into what could be termed a funky back-beat or "basic bottom" beat. It was with a hypnotic jungle rhythm that Bo Diddley recorded his hit classics "Bo Diddley/I'm A Man" (CHECKER 814), "Diddley Daddy" (CHECKER 819), "Pretty Thing" (CHECKER 827), and "Who Do You Love" (CHECKER 842).

Bo Diddley was reared in a strict Baptist tradition when his family moved to Chicago, received his classical violin lessons from music director Professor O. W. Frederick, and played in the Ebenezer Baptist Congress Band. Shortly after, he studied trombone at the Foster Vocational School. At age ten, he got his first guitar as a Christmas present and joined the rhythm trio the "Langley Avenue Jive Cats," which included Jerome Green (maracas) and Frank Kirkland (drums). Bo Diddley and Earl Hooker (it was Earl's brother, Bluesman John Lee Hooker, who inspired Bo to play the guitar) went to the same high school, and it was there that Bo Diddley, Earl Hooker, and another buddy, Billy Boy Arnold, took an interest in music.

Bo Diddley worked as a stone-truck driver besides making his way playing the guitar and performing as an amateur boxer. In fact, the name "Bo Diddley" came from his boxing days! The "Langley Avenue Jive Cats," which now included Billy Boy Arnold (harmonica) and Jody Williams (guitar), went on to perform professionally at Chicago's 708 Club, and it was from there that Bo Diddley made demo tapes. Not everything was going smoothly for Bo Diddley on the domestic scene, where his first wife maliciously smashed his guitar, but Bo managed to save the power unit, acquire another guitar, and went forward to still better things.

Inspired by other Bluesmen Muddy Waters and Howlin' Wolf, Leonard and Phil Chess saw promise in Bo Diddley. Bo's song called "Uncle John" was renamed "Bo Diddley," and on the session they used Otis Spann on the piano. Alan Freed, WINS Radio, New York, plugged the song and it became a hit. It was Dr. Tommy Small, local New York deejay, who featured Bo Diddley on a Rhythm and Blues show at the Apollo Theater in 1955. Bo Diddley remained an innovator and recorded many dance hits between 1955 and 1962. Many of these were in good fun with humorous implications: "Say Man" (CHECKER 931), "Road Runner" (CHECKER 942), "Pills (Or Love's Labor Lost)" (CHECKER 985) and even his 1962 hit "You Can't Judge A Book By Its Cover" (CHECKER 1019). Most of his records were his own compositions and were backed by Jerome Green (maracas) and Bo's own half-sister, Normigene Woffard, known as "The Duchess," on rhythm guitar. In the late Sixties, Bo Diddley lost both of them; Jerome Green left for a day job and "The Duchess" to raise a family!

The Rock and Roll world has always admired Bo Diddley through his Rock and Roll years, when he recorded such favorites as "Crackin' Up" (CHECKER 924) and "She's Alright" (CHECKER 936), through his British tour with the Everly Brothers, Little Richard, and the "Rolling Stones" right to his Seventies movies *Let the Good Times Roll* and *Keep on Rockin'*. Each and every musician owes a lot of gratitude to Bo Diddley, because Bo has been a highly influential artist, along with Chuck Berry, Ronny Hawkins and the "Band," and the whole British Rock scene! Bo Diddley now lives in Los Lunas, New Mexico, from where he travels frequently on Rock and Roll revival shows.

Discography

BO DIDDLEY

CHECKER

814 BO DIDDLEY (5-55)/I'm A Man
819 DIDDLEY DADDY (7-55)/She's Fine, She's Mine
827 PRETTY THING (10-55)/Bring It To Jerome
832 DIDDY WAH DIDDY (3-56)/(I'm) Looking For A Woman
842 WHO DO YOU LOVE (9-56)/I'm Bad
850 COPS & ROBBERS (1-57)/Down Home Special
860 HEY BO DIDDLEY (5-57)/Mona (I Need You Baby)
878 SAY BOSS MAN (1-58)/Before You Accuse Me
896 HUSH YOUR MOUTH (8-58)/Dearest Darling
907 WILLIE AND LITTLE (11-58)/Bo Meets The Monster
914 I'M SORRY (3-59)/Oh Yea
924 CRACKIN' UP (7-59)/The Great Grandfather
931 SAY MAN (9-59)/Clock Strikes 12

936 SHE'S ALRIGHT (11-59)/Say Man, Back Again
942 ROAD RUNNER (3-60)/My Story
951 WALKIN' AND TALKIN' (7-60)/Crawdad
965 (BO DIDDLEY'S A) GUN SLINGER (11-60)/Signifying Blues
976 NOT GUILTY (5-61)/Aztec
985 PILLS (OR LOVE'S LABOR LOST) (12-61)/Call Me
1019 YOU CAN'T JUDGE A BOOK BY THE COVER (8-62)/I Can Tell
1045 GREATEST LOVER IN THE WORLD (1963)/Surfer's Love Call
1083 MAMA KEEP YOUR BIG MOUTH SHUT (1964)/Jo-Ann

AS "BO DIDDLEY & CHUCK BERRY"

1089 CHUCK'S BEAT (1964)/Bo's Beat

BO DIDDLEY

1098 HEY GOOD LOOKIN' (1964)/You Ain't Bad (As You Claim To Be)
1123 500 PERCENT MORE MAN (10-65)/Let The Kids Dance
1142 WE'RE GONNA GET MARRIED (6-66)/Do The Frog
1158 OOH BABY (1-67)/Back To School [Also on CHESS 15167]
1168 WRECKIN' MY LOVE LIFE (5-67) [Also on CHECKER 15545 with flip "Boo-Ga-Loo Before You Go"]/Boogaloo Baby
1200 ANOTHER SUGAR DADDY (6-68)/I'm High Again
1213 BO DIDDLEY 1969 (1-69)/Soul Train
1238 SHAPE I'M IN (3-71)/Polluted

CHESS

2117 I SAID SHUT UP WOMAN (8-71)/I Love You More Than You'll Ever Know
2129 BO DIDDLEY—IT IS (7-72)/Inflation
2134 HUSBAND IN LAW (11-72)/Bo Jam

RCA

10618 NOT FADE AWAY (5-76)/Drag On

♭ ♯ ♪ ♩ 𝅗𝅥

"Dramatics"

MEMBERS (originals for WINGATE and SPORT labels): Larry Reed (lead singer, replaced by Willie Howard in 1968); Bob Davis (replaced by Willie Ford in 1968); Ron Banks; Larry Demps; Elbert Wilkins.

VOLT Label Group: Ron Banks (lead first tenor), born May 10, 1951; Larry "L. J." Reynolds (lead first & second tenor), born January 27, 1950; Larry Demps (lead baritone), born February 23, 1949; Willie Ford (lead bass), born July 10, 1950; Lenny Mayes (lead second tenor), born April 5, 1950.

Hometown: Detroit, Michigan.

The "DRAMATICS," a young, multitalented quintet, had a unique group characteristic in that each member could sing lead! Though with their own polished distinguished style, they somewhat resembled the "Dells," their idols, with whom they recorded an album. The group began in the early Sixties, concentrating on the Motown super groups and had a debut on the ED WINGATE label. Interestingly enough, the first record was incorrectly credited to the "Dynamics" instead of the "Dramatics." The "Dramatics" cut the first moderate Soul hit, "All Because Of You," on another Detroit label, SPORT (101). WINGATE and SPORT sides were produced by Richard Morris.

While performing at local nightclubs and on the Chittlin' Circuit, the "Dramatics" signed with the VOLT (STAX) label and there, with a couple of one-million sells, "Whatcha See Is Whatcha Get" (VOLT 4058) and "In The Rain" (VOLT 4075), the group got national attention. The group Chart action on "Toast To The Fool" (VOLT 4082), "Hey You! Get Off My Mountain" (VOLT 4090), and "Fell For You" (VOLT 4099), and later "Highway To Heaven" (VOLT 4108) set the trend for a successful album with the "Dells," of which "Door To Your Heart" was their first CADET release. The VOLT (STAX) sides were produced by Don Davis.

The "Dramatics" then recorded a soulful 1975 disc of little action, "Feel It" (MAINSTREAM 5571) that showed real professional approach. A beautiful JOYRIDE album followed, featuring 1976 releases: "Be My Girl," and the lovely "I Can't Get Over You." Disco was now the "in" sound, and, like so many other groups, the "Dramatics" had a follow-up album, aptly entitled "DRAMATICS," highlighting "Shake It Well," which mentioned American cities and the music they loved to dance to. "Why Do You Want to Do Me Wrong" (ABC 12429) is a Disco favorite!

Discography

AS "DRAMATICS"

WINGATE

018 BINGO! (1966)/Somewhere
022 INKY DINKY WANG DANG DOO (1966)/Baby I Need You

SPORT

101 ALL BECAUSE OF YOU (6-67)/If You Haven't Got Love

VOLT

4058 WHATCHA SEE IS WHATCHA GET (7-71) [Feat. Willie Howard]/Thankful For Your Love
4071 GET UP AND GET DOWN (GET OFF YOUR SEAT) (12-71)/Fall In Love, Lady Love
4075 IN THE RAIN (2-72) [Feat. Willie Howard]/(Gimme Some) Good Soul Music
4082 TOAST TO THE FOOL (8-72)/Your Love Is Strange
4090 HEY YOU! GET OFF MY MOUNTAIN (5-73)/The Devil Is Dope
4099 FELL FOR YOU (10-73)/Now You Got Me Loving You
4108 HIGHWAY TO HEAVEN (8-74)/I Made Myself Lonely

CADET

5704 DOOR TO YOUR HEART (8-74)/Choosing Up To You
5706 TUNE UP (12-74)/Don't Make Me No Promises

ABC

12090 ME AND MRS. JONES (5-75) [Billy Paul '72 hit. PHIL-INT 73521]/I Cried All The Way Home

CADET

5710 LOVE IS MISSING FROM OUR LIVES (7-75) [W. "Dells"]/ I'm In Love

MAINSTREAM

5571 FEEL IT (9-75)/No Rebate On Love

AS "RON BANKS & DRAMATICS"

ABC

12125 (I'M GOING BY) THE STARS IN YOUR EYES (8-75)/ Trying To Get Over Losing You

AS "DRAMATICS"

12150 YOU'RE FOOLING YOU (12-75)/I'll Make It So Good
12180 I WAS THE LIFE OF THE PARTY (4-76)/Treat Me Like A Man
I WAS THE LIFE OF THE PARTY (5-76)/Things Are Changing
12220 FINGER FEVER (10-76)/Say The Word
12235 BE MY GIRL (12-76)/Richest Man Alive
12258 I CAN'T GET OVER YOU (4-77)/Sundown Is Coming
12299 SHAKE IT WELL (8-77)/That Heaven Kind Of Feeling
12331 OCEANS OF THOUGHTS AND DREAMS (2-78)/Come Inside

By WEE GEE (Willie Howard's Solo)

JUPAR

533 YOU'VE BEEN A PART OF ME (4-78)/You've Been A Part Of Me [Part 2]

AS "DRAMATICS"

ABC

12372 STOP THE WEEPING (7-78)/California Sunshine
12400 DO WHAT YOU WANT TO (8-78) [Daryl Hall-John Oates Composition]/Jane
12429 WHY DO YOU WANT TO DO ME WRONG (11-78)/Yo' Love (Can Only Bring Me Happiness)

MCA

41017 I JUST WANNA DANCE WITH YOU (4-79)/I've Got A Schoolboy Crush On You
8737 THAT'S MY FAVORITE SONG (7-79)

"Earth, Wind and Fire"

ORIGINAL MEMBERS: Maurice White (lead vocals, Kalimba, drums), born December 19, 1941; Verdine White (vocals, bass, percussion), born July 25, 1951; Wade Flemons (from Coffeyville, Kansas); Don Whitehead; Jacob Ben Israel; Clint Washington; Michael Bill; Leslie Drayton; Alex Thomas; and female member.

1971: Maurice White; Verdine White; Phillip Bailey (vocals, congas), born May 8, 1951, from "Stoval Sisters Band"; Larry Dunn (Lawrence Dunhill) (organ, moog synthesizer), born June 19, 1953; Alan McKay (guitar, sitar, percussion), born February 2, 1948, from "Watts 103rd St. Rhythm Band"; Ralph Johnson (drums, percussion), born July 4, 1951, from the "Nite-Liters"; Andrew Woolfolk (soprano, sax, flute), born October 11, 1950; Jessica Cleaves (drums, percussion), born 1948, from "Friends Of Distinction" and replaced in 1973 by Fred White (brother of Maurice and Verdine), born January 13, 1955.

Others (1973): Roland Bautista; Ronald Wayne Laws.

Hometown: Chicago, Illinois.

The group "EARTH, WIND AND FIRE" emerged as a distinct musical phenomenon with a universal message at a critical time in the early Seventies. With its own unique fusion of Jazz, Rhythm and Blues, Rock and Pop, it met the anti-Rock anger head-on and contributed much in calming public fears, both psychological and political, over the raucous, hard-driving, ear-splitting crescendo pouring out of San Francisco. This positive-minded and highly talented group was the forefront of a counter-revolution of sorts that saw the deafening impact of Rock being absorbed into a more mature and intricate musical rendition. Artificial barriers began to give way before the fervor and intensity of those late-Sixties artists maturing into a more meaningful and sophisticated art form. Music itself was transformed almost in one decade by the influx of exciting jazz artists, such as Maurice White himself, and black music was finding its lofty perch on white charts, and Country sounds were being heard on northern airwaves.

Here, we rightfully acknowledge "Earth, Wind and Fire"—aptly described by their own contemporaries as "the hottest group around today"—as a positive dynamic force that crossed over all barriers in the highly complex world of modern music. To understand where these nine talented young men are coming from, one has only to sit still and listen to the superb material that makes up their lyrics: "Devotion" (COLUMBIA 3-10026), "Keep Your Head To The Sky" (COLUMBIA 4-45953), "Shining Star" (COLUMBIA 3-10090), "That's The Way Of The World" (COLUMBIA 3-10172), "Getaway" (COLUMBIA 3-10373), and "Saturday Nite" (COLUMBIA 3-10439). Add to this that unquestionable quality of fiery sound, colorful choreography with imaginative excellence, and a well-articulated message readily understood by all those present, and we easily understand why "Earth, Wind and Fire" literally turn to gold and platinum everything they happen to touch and now rank as the most successful stage and recording act of all time!

Maurice White, the live pulsating core of the group, was born in the cradle of music itself, Memphis, Tennessee. There, he claims to have received most of his "root" training coming up through the Church and the music-laden streets of his famous hometown, and rubbing shoulders with Isaac Hayes, David Porter, Booker T. Jones, and others emerging to fame from STAX label. Everybody then was caught up with the big sound of Rock, but Maurice was fascinated with the intricacies of jazz and other exciting possibilities in music. His father, a doctor, had hopes that Maurice would follow in his footsteps, and he did start out in the study of medicine, but after only a year he heard the pied pipers with their new sounds and he liked what he heard.

In Chicago, when barely eighteen, Maurice White sought out good music teachers and studied at the Conservatory there, while developing his talent as part of a jazz gig, playing drums, four nights weekly. This exposure brought Maurice a studio gig with the CHESS label of Leonard Chess, where "he played everything and on everybody's records for the company." It was while there that he met Ramsey Lewis, who, at that time, had Isaac Young and Red Holt in trio, with both in the process of departure. At Ramsey's request and with the opportunity of still greater experience, Maurice White with Cleveland Eaton joined as trio replacements (for Young and Holt, who then soon became known as "The Young Holt Unlimited") and stayed over 1965-67 to make ten albums (CHESS label) before leaving in January of 1970. During the latter part of the Sixties, Maurice McAllister featured as lead singer with the "Radiants," an R&B group on CHESS, and as part of the "Maurice and Mac" duet representing eleven records with the "Radiants" 1962-68 and four records (three on CHECKER and one on CHESS) as a duet from 1968-71.

Over that same period Maurice White had made several interesting visits to the Orient and had studied there under two masters, achieving a total change of purpose and life that was to influence his thinking and his music ever after. These 1968-69 visits, coupled with extensive travel and study (religion and philosophy), brought Maurice White to a decision about his life's mission and his music! His first group venture was the "Salty Peppers" and their cutting of a record for CAPITOL. Then Maurice White relocated in California and turned his attention to a protracted dream of his own (something that lasted across four years) to form a special kind of group, and "Earth, Wind and Fire" was born! The group made three singles for WARNER BROTHERS, with only "Love Is Life/This World Today" (WARNER BROTHERS 7492) proving a minor success and both albums meeting poor response in spite of wide promotion.

Dissastisfaction with the W.B. contract, in that there was little understanding of what the group was aiming at musically, not being straight Rhythm and Blues, prompted managers Bob Cavello and Joe Ruffalo to approach Clive Davis of COLUMBIA RECORDS. Clive was delighted with what he heard, bought the group's contract and first album from WARNER BROTHERS for $100,000, and produced the first "Earth, Wind and Fire" album, to sales in excess of three hundred thousand (as compared with sales on both albums out of WARNER BROTHERS for only eighty thousands!). The second album was certified GOLD and sold over six hundred and fifty thousand, to be followed by yet a third and another GOLD shortly after release, making "Earth, Wind and Fire" a major new group early in 1974.

Ramsey Lewis joined the group in the cutting of two singles in 1974-75: "Hot Dawgit" (COLUMBIA 3-10056) and "Sun Goddess" (COLUMBIA 3-10103), and these were followed by a steady stream of smash hits: "Serpentine Fire" (COLUMBIA 3-10625), an infectious and stimulating record with enormous disco appeal, "Fantasy" (COLUMBIA 3-10688), "Got To Get You Into My Life" (COLUMBIA 3-10686), "September" (COLUMBIA 3-10854), "Wonderland" (COLUMBIA 3-10956), done in May 1979 with the female group the "Emotions," with the same spontaneous, winning "Earth, Wind and Fire" sound, and the latest, "After The Love Has Gone" (COLUMBIA 3-11033), rounding out nineteen splendid recordings, with a fair sprinkling of gold and platinum ratings. Incidentally, the word *serpentine* (pronounced "ser-pen-teen") comes from a form of yoga in India and means the magic fluid in the spine, the actual energy that runs from the gonads into the brain, a process that is reactivated every twenty-nine and a half days!

1974 saw creation of their own KALIMBA PRODUCTIONS, a name suggested by Ralph Johnson after Maurice White's own instrument. Here, Maurice produced for the "Emotions," Deniece Williams, and an album for D. J. Rogers, the Rhythm and Blues shouter. Verdine handled the "Pockets" in the same way, and Larry Dunn co-produced an album for Ramsey Lewis. Though laboring under a heavy and constantly busy schedule, Maurice White and his "Earth, Wind and Fire" group maintain an intimate, family-type of relationship with strong spiritual values that respect their talented individualities. There can be little doubt that "Earth, Wind and Fire," with its powerful message, musical content, and infectious rhythm will go on to shake the music world outside the continental United States and everyone will appreciate that unique sound years ahead of its time!

Discography

WADE FLEMONS [Original Member of Group]

VEE JAY

295 HERE I STAND (11-58)/My Baby Likes To Rock
309 HOLD ME CLOSE (1-59)/You'll Remain Forever
321 SLOW MOTION (8-59)/Walking By The River
335 WHAT'S HAPPENING (12-59)/Goodnight, It's Time To Go
344 EASY LOVIN' (5-60)/Woops Now
368 AIN'T THAT LOVIN' YOU BABY (12-60)/I'll Come Runnin'
377 AT THE PARTY (4-61)/Devil In Your Soul
389 PLEASE SEND ME SOMEONE TO LOVE (9-61)/Keep On Loving Me
427 HALF A LOVE (1-62)/Welcome Stranger
471 I HOPE, I THINK, I WISH (11-62) [Conway Twitty's '62 hit. MGM 13112]/Ain't These Tears?
533 THAT TIME OF YEAR (6-63)/I Came Running
578 WATCH OVER HER (1-64)/When It Rains It Pours [W. "Four Seasons"]

"RADIANTS" [Feat. MAURICE McALLISTER]

CHESS

1832 FATHER KNOWS BEST (10-62)/One Day I'll Show You
1849 PLEASE DON'T LEAVE ME (3-63)/Heartbreak Society
1872 I'M IN LOVE (10-63)/Shy Guy

1887 NOBLE THE BARGAIN MAN (3-64)/I Gotta Dance To Keep My Baby
1904 VOICE YOUR CHOICE (1-65)/If I Only Had You
1925 IT AIN'T NO BAD THING (5-65)/I Got A Girl
1939 WHOLE LOT OF WOMAN (9-65)/Tomorrow

"RADIANTS"

CHESS

1954 I WANT TO THANK YOU BABY (4-66)/Baby You've Got It
1986 FEEL KIND OF BAD (4-67)/Anything You Do Is Alright
2021 THE CLOWN IS CLEVER (12-67)/Don't Take Your Love (From Me)
2037 HOLD ON (4-68)/I'm Glad I'm The Loser

"MAURICE AND MAC"

CHECKER

1197 YOU LEFT THE WATER RUNNING (5-68)/You're The One
1206 LEAN ON ME (10-68)/Why Don't You Try Me

"RADIANTS"

CHESS

2066 CHOO CHOO (1-69)/Ida Mae Foster

"MAURICE AND MAC"

CHECKER

1218 LAY IT ON ME (3-69)/What Am I Gonna Do

"RADIANTS"

CHESS

2078 BOOK OF LOVE (9-69)/Another Mule Is Kicking In Your Stall
2083 I'M SO GLAD I'M THE LOSER (11-69)/Shadow Of A Doubt

TWINLIGHT

153 MY SUNSHINE GIRL (1970)/Don't Want To Face The Truth

"MAURICE AND MAC"

CHESS

2102 YOU CAN'T SAY I DIDN'T TRY (2-71)/Lay It On Me

"EARTH, WIND AND FIRE"

WARNER BROTHERS

7480 FAN THE FIRE (5-71)
7492 LOVE IS LIFE (7-71)/The World Today
7549 I THINK ABOUT LOVIN' YOU (2-72)/C'Mon Children

COLUMBIA

4-45747 MOM (12-72)/Power
4-45800 WHERE HAVE ALL THE FLOWERS GONE (4-73)/Time Is On Your Side
4-45953 KEEP YOUR HEAD TO THE SKY (11-73)/Build Your Nest
4-46070 KALIMBA STORY (7-74)/Tee Nine Chee Bit
3-10026 DEVOTION (10-74)/Fair But So Uncool

RAMSEY LEWIS AND "EARTH, WIND AND FIRE"

3-10056 HOT DAWGIT (11-74)/Tambura

"EARTH, WIND AND FIRE"

3-10090 SHINING STAR (2-75)/Yearnin' & Learnin'

RAMSEY LEWIS AND "EARTH, WIND AND FIRE"

3-10103 SUN GODDESS (3-75)/Jungle Strut

"EARTH, WIND AND FIRE"

3-10172 THAT'S THE WAY OF THE WORLD (7-75)/Africano
3-10251 SING A SONG (1975)/Sing A Song [Instr.]
3-10309 CAN'T HIDE LOVE (3-76)/Gratitude

3-10373	GETAWAY (7-76)/Getaway [Instr.]
3-10439	SATURDAY NITE (11-76)/Departure
3-10492	ON YOUR FACE (3-77)/Biyo
3-10625	SERPENTINE FIRE (10-77)/Serpentine Fire [Instr.]
3-10688	FANTASY (2-78)/Runnin'
3-10786	GOT TO GET YOU INTO MY LIFE (7-78) ["Beatles" '76 hit. CAPITOL 4274]/I'll Write A Song For You
3-10854	SEPTEMBER (11-78)/Love's Holiday

"EARTH, WIND AND FIRE" AND "EMOTIONS"

3-10956	BOOGIE WONDERLAND (5-79)/Boogie Wonderland [Instr.]

"EARTH, WIND AND FIRE"

3-11033	AFTER THE LOVE HAS GONE (7-79)/Rock That!
1-11093	IN THE STONE (10-79)/You and I
1-11165	STAR (12-79)/You and I

♭ ♯ ♪ ♩ 𝅗𝅥

Tommy Edwards

Born in Richmond, Virginia, on February 17, 1922.
Died in Richmond, Virginia, on October 22, 1969.

TOMMY EDWARDS produced a warm, sincere style of love song that reflected in a personal way those happy times during the late Fifties when he was at the height of his success. He had a manner of rendition similar to that of the great, gentle Nat King Cole.

Tommy Edwards's career started very early, from the age of nine in show business and, in his teens during the Forties, he sang and played the piano on his own radio show. In 1946, he wrote "That Chick's Too Young To Fry" for bandleader Louis Jordan, which was recorded in April of 1953 by the "Prisonaires" (SUN), and also "Trust Me" (KING 4656), a 1953 song for the group the "Swallows"!

Although Tommy Edwards enjoyed little initial success at the time of his early MGM releases "Morning Side Of The Mountain" (MGM 10989) and "It's All In The Game," (MGM 11035) each, later, became Chart classics as new releases in 1958 and 1959! "It's All In The Game" was from an old song, "Melody in 'A' Major," which was originally written back in 1912 by General Gates Dawes, who became Vice-President of the United States under Calvin Coolidge, 1925-29.

Other notable favorites that reflected Tommy Edwards's immense appeal were "A Fool Such As I" (MGM 11395), "That's All" (MGM 11604), "Love Is A Sacred Thing" (MGM 12248), "Please Love Me Forever" (MGM 12688), "Love Is All We Need" MGM 12722), "It's Only The Good Times (I Remember)" (MGM 12794), and "I Really Don't Want To Know" (MGM 12890). Tommy Edwards's songs were generally sung with a gentle friendly vocal treatment!

Discography

AS "TOMMY EDWARDS TRIO"

TOP

1158 THAT'S WORRYIN' ME (1949)/Venus Is

TOMMY EDWARDS

NATIONAL

7079 JUST LOVE, MY SWEET (1949)/HELP! HELP!

COLUMBIA

38950 COWBOY RHUMBA (1950)/How High The Moon

MGM

10884 ONCE THERE LIVED A FOOL (1950)/Friends Of Johnny's
10921 OPERETTA (1950)/Gypsy Heart
10973 BEGGAR IN LOVE (1951)/I'll Never Know Why
10989 MORNING SIDE OF THE MOUNTAIN (3-51)/F'r Instance
11035 IT'S ALL IN THE GAME (7-51)/All Over Again
11077 SOLITAIRE (10-51)/My Concerto
11097 CHRISTMAS IS FOR CHILDREN (12-51)/Kris Kringle
11134 PLEASE MISTER SUN (5-52)/Where I May Live With My Love
11170 FORGIVE ME (8-52)/The Bridge
11209 MY GIRL (1952)/Piano, Bass And Drums
11268 EASY TO SAY (1953)/The Greatest Sinner Of Them All
11326 YOU WIN AGAIN (1953) [Hank Williams '53 hit. MGM 11318]/Sinner Or Saint
11395 A FOOL SUCH AS I (1953)/I Can't Love Another
11465 AU REVOIR (1953)/I Lived When I Met You
11485 TAKE THESE CHAINS FROM MY HEART (1954)/Paging Mr. Jackson
11541 THE LOVER'S WALTZ (1954)/Baby, Baby, Baby
11582 BLUEBIRD (1954)/So Little Time
11604 THAT'S ALL (10-54)/Secret Love
11624 IT'S CHRISTMAS ONCE AGAIN (12-54)/Everyday Is Christmas
11668 THERE WAS A TIME (1955)/Wall Of Ice
11718 WITHIN MY HEART (1955)/The Joker
11763 LINGER IN MY ARMS (1955)/If You Would Love Me Again
11821 I HAVE THAT KIND OF HEART (1953)/You Walk By
11932 SERENADE TO A FOOL (1956)/It Could Have Been Me
11993 WELCOME TO MY HEART (1956)/Spring Never Came Around This Year
12054 A TEARDROP ON A ROSE (1956)/To Those Who Wait
12095 MY SWEETHEART, MY BEST FRIEND AND I (1956)/Baby Let Me
12248 LOVE IS A SACRED THING (1957)/There Must Be A Way To Your Heart
12342 THE DAY THAT I LOST YOU (1957)/My Ship
12514 WE'RE NOT CHILDREN ANYMORE (1958)/Anyplace, Anytime
12688 IT'S ALL IN THE GAME (8-58)/Please Love Me Forever
12722 LOVE IS ALL WE NEED (11-58)/Mr. Music Man
12757 PLEASE MISTER SUN (2-59)/The Morning Side Of The Mountain

MGM

12794 MY MELANCHOLY BABY (5-59)/It's Only The Good Times (I Remember)
12814 I'VE BEEN THERE (8-59)/I Looked At Heaven (And You Looked Back At Me)
12837 HONESTLY AND TRULY (11-59)/(New In) The Ways Of Love
12871 DON'T FENCE ME IN (2-60)/I'm Building Castles Again
12890 I REALLY DON'T WANT TO KNOW (5-60)/Unloved
12916 IT'S NOT THE END OF EVERYTHING (10-60)/Blue Heartaches
12959 AS YOU DESIRE ME (1961)/Susie Wong
12981 ONE AND TWENTY (1961)/Vaya Con Dios (May God Be With You)
13002 THE GOLDEN CHAIN (1961)/That's The Way With Love
13032 I'M SO LONESOME I COULD CRY (1961) [Hank Williams '49 hit. MGM 10560]/My Heart Would Know
13057 TABLES ARE TURNING (1962)/I'll Cry You Out Of My Heart
13100 TONIGHT I WON'T BE THERE (1962)/Please Don't Tell Me
13128 SOMETIMES YOU WIN, SOMETIMES YOU LOSE (1963)/May I
13172 COUNTRY BOY (1963)/Love Is Best Of All
13317 YOU WIN AGAIN (1964)/Take These Chains From My Heart

MUSICOR

1159 I MUST BE DOING SOMETHING WRONG (2-66)/I Cried I Cried

♭ ♯ ♪ ♩ 𝅗𝅥

"Eighth Day"

MEMBERS *(Black)*: Melvin Davis, lead singer, drums; Tony Newton, bass guitar; Michael Anthony, guitar; Carole Stallings, electric violin and vocals; Anita Sherman, vibes, tambourine and vocals.

MEMBERS *(White)*: Bruce Nazarian, guitar and organ (later joined "Brownsville Station"); Jerry Paul, congas and percussion; Lynn Harter, vocals.

Hometown: Detroit, Michigan.

The "EIGHTH DAY" group were session musicians who achieved popular Soul attention during 1971 with the hits "She's Not Just Another Woman" (INVICTUS 9087), a Top-Ten Chart entry, and "You've Got To Crawl (Before You Walk)" (INVICTUS 9098). Lead vocalist Melvin Davis gave us one of the great Rhythm and Blues ballads in the pleasing and pulsating "I'm Worried" (INVICTUS 9115 & INVICTUS 1259), a truly remarkable performance from a veteran singer.

The group originally started during the mid-Sixties after Melvin Davis had sung with the "Nite Sounds" for FORTUNE label. It was after their recording of several Pop-oriented items, "Hey Boy! (This Girl's In Love With You)" (KAPP 862), "Raining Sunshine" (KAPP 894), and the lovely "Building With A Steeple" (KAPP 916), that Brian Holland, Lamont Dozier, and Eddie Holland took an interest in the "Eighth Day." Holland-Dozier-Holland, in their direction of material and production development of an outstanding group, obtained Tony Newton from MOTOWN. Tony Newton played bass guitar for Smokey Robinson and the "Miracles" and soon became an important contributor to the "Eighth Day." Thus, from a Pop vein of KAPP label, the "Eighth Day" became a top Soul act through Holland-Dozier-Holland and INVICTUS label!

Discography

AS "MELVIN DAVIS & NITE SOUNDS"

FORTUNE

551 PLAYBOY (DON'T YOU PLAY IN SCHOOL) (1962)/I Won't Be Your Fool
552 HARLEM GIRL (1962)/The Roll

AS "EIGHTH DAY"

KAPP

862 HEY BOY! (THIS GIRL'S IN LOVE WITH YOU) (11-67)/ A Million Lights

MELVIN DAVIS

MALA

590 SAVE IT (2-68)/This Love Was Meant To Be

AS "EIGHTH DAY"

KAPP

894 RAINING SUNSHINE (3-68)/That Good Old-Fashioned Way
916 BUILDING WITH A STEEPLE (7-68)/Glory

MELVIN DAVIS

MALA

12009 LOVE BUG GOT A BEAR HUG (7-68)/Faith

AS "EIGHTH DAY"

INVICTUS

9087 SHE'S NOT JUST ANOTHER WOMAN (5-71)/I Can't Fool Myself
9098 YOU'VE GOT TO CRAWL (BEFORE YOU WALK) (9-71)/ It's Instrumental To Be Free
9107 IF I COULD SEE THE LIGHT (1-72)/I

MELVIN DAVIS

9115 I'M WORRIED (3-72)/Just As Long

AS "EIGHTH DAY"

9117 EENY-MEENY-MINY-MO (THREE'S A CROWD) (3-72)/ Rocks On My Head
9124 I GOTTA GO HOME (6-72)/Good Book

GRT

901 HEAR THE GRASS GROW/Bring Your Love Back

MELVIN DAVIS

INVICTUS

1259 I'M WORRIED (1-74)/You Made Me Over

♭ ♯ ♪ ♩ 𝅗𝅥

"Five Satins"

MEMBERS:

"Scarlets": Fred Parris (lead vocal); Silvester "Sy" Hopkins; Nat Mosley; Al Denby; Bill Powers.

"5 Satins" (on STANDORD 100): Fred Parris (lead vocal); Jim Freeman (bass); Lewis Peeples (tenor); Eddie Martin; Stanley Dorch.

"5 Satins" (on STANDORD 200): Fred Parris; Jim Freeman; Eddie Martin; Jesse Murphy (piano).

"5 Satins" (on EMBER 1005): Al Denby; Fred Parris (lead vocal); Jim Freeman; Eddie Martin; Jesse Murphy (piano).

"5 Satins" (while Fred Parris was in U.S. Army): Bill Baker (lead vocal); Jim Freeman; Tommy Kilebrew; Jesse Murphy (piano).

Reformed *"Scarlets"* (KLIK 7905), *"5 Satins", "New Yorkers":* Fred Parris (lead vocal); Richie Freeman (tenor); Wes Forbes (second tenor); "Sy" Hopkins (bass); Lewis Peeples (harmony).

"5 Satins" (70s): Fred Parris (lead vocal); Corky Rogers (bass); Jimmy Curtis (baritone); Richie Freeman (tenor); Jerry Jackson (tenor).

As *"Black Satin":* Fred Parris (lead vocal); Richie Freeman; Jimmy Curtis; Nate Marshall.

Hometown: New Haven, Connecticut.

"In The Still Of The Night (I'll Remember)" (EMBER 1005) is acknowledged as one of the best R&B ballads of all time and is now a black harmony standard, with sales in excess of fourteen million! It came "humming" to Fred Parris very early one morning—during basic training at Philadelphia after the drafting of Fred and members of his "Scarlets" into the U.S. Army—and something precious of those encompassing silences was later recorded in a basement of a New Haven church.

The "Scarlets" sang together professionally during 1953 at Hill House High School. Fred Parris had written "Dear One" and "I've Lost" (a/b RED ROBIN 128), and these were brought to Dan Robinson, the brother of Bobby Robinson, RED ROBIN owner. Although each of the "Scarlets' " four releases, "Dear One/I've Lost" (RED ROBIN 128), "Love Doll/ Darling I'm Yours" (RED ROBIN 133), "Cry Baby/True Love" (RED ROBIN 135), and "Kiss Me/Indian Fever" (RED ROBIN 138), sold well regionally, it was at a time when R&B was being sought by black enthusiasts and therefore had a smaller market. Between times while on military duty in Texas and Philadelphia and his weekend trips home to New Haven, Fred Parris formed the original "Five Satins." He was encouraged to record for STANDORD by the owner, and hence the lovely "All Mine" (STANDORD 100) with music and the original "In The Still Of The Night (I'll Remember)" (STANDORD 200), which, of course, was later leased to the EMBER label (1005) in 1956.

Bill Baker and the newly formed "Five Satins" (while Fred Parris and the original members were in U.S. Army) recorded "(I'm In Love With A) Wonderful Girl" (EMBER 1008) and "To The Aisle" (EMBER 1019), which was written by Billy Don Smith and became a nationwide hit for 1957; "Our Anniversary" (EMBER 1025), and, lastly, that beautiful ballad "Love With No Love In Return" (EMBER 1028). After Fred Parris returned from his military duties in Japan he reformed the original "Scarlets" and recorded one of his own compositions, "She's Gone (With The Wind)" (KLIK 7905). This same group under Fred became the "Five Satins" and recorded "A Night To Remember" (EMBER 1038), "When Your Love Comes Along" (FIRST 104, distributed by EMBER), "Shadows" (EMBER 1056), and "I'll Be Seeing You" (EMBER 1061). It was a dispute over EMBER label's alleged poor promotion of the regional hit "Shadows" (EMBER 1056) that caused the "Five Satins" to leave that label.

The group went on to record for the WALL label, after a couple of recordings for CUB, but as the "New Yorkers," in 1961. Without a national hit the group decided to return to New Haven so that the members might continue their livelihood, and there Wes Forbes remained to work in a rehabilitation center. 1969 came with the Rock and Roll revival shows, and the "Five Satins" became stars all over again. They were so well received that they were given a major part in the Rock and Roll film *Let the Good Times Roll* in 1973. Throughout the Seventies the "Five Satins" became a nightclub spectacular and a highly professional act that could always bring a sophisticated and personal warmth, no matter what sort of audience there was!

Discography

AS "SCARLETS" [Featuring FRED PARRIS]

RED ROBIN

128 DEAR ONE (2-54)/I've Lost
133 LOVE DOLL (7-54)/Darling I'm Yours
135 CRY BABY (11-54)/True Love
138 KISS ME (5-55)/Indian Fever

AS "FIVE SATINS"

STANDORD

100 ALL MINE (1-56)/Rosemarie
200 IN THE STILL OF THE NIGHT (I'LL REMEMBER) (4-56)/ Jones Girl

EMBER

1005 IN THE STILL OF THE NIGHT (I'LL REMEMBER) (6-56)/ Jones Girl
1008 (I'M IN LOVE WITH A) WONDERFUL GIRL (10-56)/ Weeping Willow
1014 OH HAPPY DAY (3-57)/Our Love Is Forever
1019 TO THE AISLE (6-57)/Wish I Had My Baby
[Above release issued also as "Bill Baker & Five Satins."]
1025 OUR ANNIVERSARY (10-57)/Pretty Girl
1028 A MILLION TO ONE (2-58)/Love With No Love In Return

AS "FRED PARRIS & SCARLETS"

KLIK

7905 SHE'S GONE (WITH THE WIND) (2-58)/The Voice

AS "FIVE SATINS"

EMBER

1038 A NIGHT TO REMEMBER (7-58)/Señorita Lolita

FIRST (**Distributed by EMBER**)

104 WHEN YOUR LOVE COMES ALONG (5-59)/Skippity Doo

AS "FREDDIE AND LOU" (FRED PARRIS AND LEWIS PEEPLES)

THUNDER

2150 YOU'LL BE MINE TONIGHT (1959)/Rosalie

AS "WILDWOODS"

CAPRICE

101 WHEN THE SWALLOWS COME BACK TO CAPISTRANO (8-59)/Heart Of Mine
[Above release also on CAPRICE 102.]

AS "FIVE SATINS"

EMBER

1056 SHADOWS (10-59)/Toni My Love

AS "SCARLETS" (The AL DENBY Group)

FURY

1036 TRULY YOURS (1960)/East Of The Sun

AS "FIVE SATINS"

EMBER

1061 I'LL BE SEEING YOU (4-60)/A Night Like This

CUB

9071 YOUR MEMORY (6-60)/I Didn't Know
9077 THESE FOOLISH THINGS (8-60)/A Beggar With A Dream

EMBER

1066 THE TIME (11-60)/Candlelight

CUB

9099 GOLDEN EARRINGS (2-61)/Can I Come Over Tonight

EMBER

1070 WISHING RING (4-61)/Tell Me Dear

AS "NEW YORKERS"

WALL

547 MISS FINE (5-61)/(At Night) Dream A Little Dream
548 TEARS IN MY EYES (5-61)/A Little Bit

AS "CHEROKEES" (Featuring FRED PARRIS)

UNITED ARTISTS

367 MY HEAVENLY ANGEL (10-61)/Bed Bug

AS "FIVE SATINS"

368 TILL THE END (10-61)/On A Lover's Island

TIME MACHINE

570 NO ONE KNOWS (1962)/Wonder Why [Never Released!]
571 LONELY HEARTS (1962)/The Masquerade Is Over

CHANCELLOR

1110 (I'M AFRAID) THE MASQUERADE IS OVER (5-62) ["Harptones" '57 hit. RAMA 214]/Raining In My Heart
1121 DOWNTOWN (8-62)/Do You Remember

TIMES SQUARE

4 ALL MINE (1-63)/Rosemarie

WARNER BROTHERS

5367 REMEMBER ME (6-63)/Kangaroo

AS "FRED PARRIS & SCARLETS"

EVENT

4287 DEAR ONE/I've Lost

CANDLELITE

411 SHE'S GONE (WITH THE WIND)/(Somewhere) A Voice Is Calling

AS "FIVE SATINS"

ROULETTE

4563 AIN'T GONNA DANCE (5-64)/You Can Count On Me

SAMMY

103 NO ONE KNOWS (1964) [W. Dick Arnold]/Musical Chairs [Instr.]

TIMES SQUARE

21 PARADISE ON EARTH (1965)/Monkey Business [By "Pharotones"]

AS "FRED PARRIS & THE RESTLESS HEARTS"

CHECKER

1108 WALK A LITTLE FASTER (5-65)/No Use In Crying

ATCO

6439 BRING IT HOME TO DADDY (9-66)/Land Of Broken Hearts

GREEN SEA

107 I'LL BE HANGIN' ON (2-67)/I Can Really Satisfy
106 BLUSHING BRIDE (7-67)/Giving My Love To You

MAMA SADIE

1001 IN THE STILL OF THE NIGHT (I'LL REMEMBER) (1967) [Instr.]/Heck No

"FREDDIE PARIS" (Spelled with only one "R")

RCA

9232 TAKE ME AS I AM (6-67)/It's O.K. To Cry Now
9358 FACE IT BOY, IT'S OVER (11-67)/Little Things Can Make A Woman Cry
9571 THERE SHE GOES (7-68)/Young Hearts, Young Hands

AS "BILL BAKER & FIVE SATINS"

MUSICTONE

119 TEENAGE TRIANGLE/Why Did Summer Have To End
1108 TO THE AISLE/Just To Be Near You

AS "FIVE SATINS"

NIGHTRAIN

901 ALL MINE (1970) [With added music]/The Voice

"FRED PARIS"

BIRTH

101 DARK AT THE TOP OF MY HEART [A demo that was never released]

AS "FIVE SATINS"

RCA

74-0478 DARK AT THE TOP OF MY HEART (6-71)/Summer In New York (Wander With The Wind)

KIRSHNER (Owned by Don Kirshner)

4251 VERY PRECIOUS OLDIES (WELCOME BACK HOME) (9-73)/You Are Love

4252 TWO DIFFERENT WORLDS (6-74)/Love Is Such A Beautiful Thing

KLIK

1020 I LOVE YOU SO ["5 Satins"]/Story To You ["Nutmegs"]

AS "BLACK SATIN"

BUDDAH

477 EVERYBODY STAND AND CLAP YOUR HANDS (9-75) [For The Entertainer]/Hey There Pretty Lady

452 TEARS, TEARS, TEARS* [Originally written by Fred Parris; Ben E. King '67 hit, ATCO 6472]/Tears, Tears, Tears [Part 2]

*U.K. release.

♭♯♪♩𝅗𝅥

Aretha Franklin

Born in Memphis, Tennessee, on March 25, 1942.

ARETHA FRANKLIN is SOUL! The Reverend James Cleveland, Gospel shouter and the family friend who taught Aretha to play the piano, once stated, "Aretha is Soul—she has never left the Church and what you hear on her famous recordings is only an outward expression of what she feels deep inside." From her earthy Gospel roots at the age of twelve, when she toured and sang with her father's evangelistic choir, Aretha was considered early to be the artistic heir of the great Mahalia Jackson.

Her phenomenal success story, since joining ATLANTIC RECORDS, has proved that everything Aretha Franklin touches turns to gold, earning her twenty solid gold singles, ten Grammy awards, a million album sales, and a tremendous European concert tour! Little wonder her adoring fans have long since acclaimed her "LADY SOUL," while the critics have gone on to describe her as the best natural singer since Billy Holiday.

Aretha was born one of five children to the Reverend Cecil L. and Barbara Franklin in that Mecca of Music, Memphis! Shortly after, the family moved to Buffalo, where she suffered the two abiding tragedies of her life before she was ten, in the departure of her mother from the home and, within four years, in 1952, the news of her mother's death. The family then moved to Detroit, where her father, now a well-known fiery Gospel preacher and recorder of over fifty-two volumes of sermons on CHESS RECORDS, assumed the rectorship of the affluent middle-class New Bethel Baptist Church on the outside edge of the ghetto, and where Aretha first sang in the choir. There the tender-aged Aretha, in the home of a popular and very busy father, was cared for by family friends Frances Steadman and Marion Williams, both members of "The Clara Ward Singers." Clara Ward, herself, became the earliest inspiration of the budding young Gospel singer!

At eighteen years of age Aretha Franklin, then an accomplished Church singer in her own right, ventured onto the recording scene, where she recorded religious numbers for JVB (owned by Joseph Von Battle) and CHECKER (a CHESS subsidiary). That same year, encouraged by Major "Mule" Holly (bassist for pianist Teddy Wilson), she went to New York to audition for COLUMBIA's John Hammond with her demo "Today I Sing The Blues."

It was Della Reese who introduced Aretha Franklin to Ted White, who was to become her business manager and then her husband. With COLUMBIA RECORDS, Aretha enjoyed some isolated success on the charts with "Won't Be Long" (41923), "Rock-A-Bye Your Baby With A Dixie Melody" (42167), and "Try A Little Tenderness" (42520). The label brought in Clyde Otis, who had a successful songwriting hit background with Brook Benton, and the result was a moderate Aretha Franklin hit, "Running Out Of Fools" (COLUMBIA 43113). Happy in the early years of her marriage, Aretha gave birth to four boys.

Jerry Wexler, ATLANTIC's vice-president and producer, recognized the singing potential of Aretha Franklin in her COLUMBIA recordings and, late in 1966, had Ahmet Ertegun (president of the label) secure her contract! It was Wexler's decision, along with Arif Mardin (Turkish co-producer, arranger, and music director) and Tom Dowd, to have Aretha Franklin record out of "Fame Studios," Muscle Shoals, Alabama, and backed her there with the best rhythm section in the entire business, Spooner Oldham at the piano, Tom Coghill and Jimmy Johnson on guitars, the familiar team of Jackson, Love and Chalmers on horns, and Roger Hawkins on the drums! It was then that everything Aretha Franklin touched in song actually turned to GOLD.

Aretha recorded a series of top hits, including "I Never Loved A Man (The Way I Love You)" (ATLANTIC 2386), a beautiful rendition of a Ronnie Shannon tune with exquisite keyboard sound and relaxed, dignified singing. Other hits followed: "Respect" (ATLANTIC 2403), "Baby I Love You" (ATLANTIC 2427), "A Natural Woman" (ATLANTIC 2441), which was written by Carole King, the double-sided smash release "(Sweet, Sweet Baby) Since You've Been Gone/Ain't No Way" (ATLANTIC 2486), "Think" (ATLANTIC 2518), and "The House That Jack Built" (ATLANTIC 2546).

These were tremendously busy and hard-driving years, aptly described by Aretha herself: "We lived in a suitcase. We were on the road ninety percent of the time and those years took their toll." They brought divorce and real heartbreak to Aretha Franklin!

Fatigued and distressed of heart, Aretha tried to retreat from public life, and it was only the loyalty and continuing concern of her close friends that prevented a worsening of a real tragedy. Here, truly, was a great professional artist with none of that glossy veneer of show business or the often phony glamour of top stardom! Aretha's voice became a shrill, trembling scream sensation, soaring and swooping, richly and deeply tinged with real emotion and pain! Here, we had Aretha Franklin with brains, voice, and heart.

Aretha Franklin's hits of the Seventies included "Rock Steady" (ATLANTIC 2838), "Day Dreaming" (ATLANTIC 2866), "Master of Eyes (The Deepness Of His Eyes)" (ATLANTIC 2941) "Angel" (ATLANTIC 2969), "Until You Come Back" (ATLANTIC 2995), "I'm In Love" (ATLANTIC 2999), "Ain't Nothing Like The Real Thing" (ATLANTIC 3200), and "Without Love" (ATLANTIC 3224). The sun broke through late in the Seventies, and Aretha Franklin, on April 11, 1978, married Glynn Turman, with her father performing the ceremony in his Detroit church. Aretha's sisters, Erma and Carolyn, both made recordings during the Sixties. Erma was most successful with two chart entries, "Big Boss Man" and "Piece Of My Heart."

Discography

ARETHA FRANKLIN

JVB

74	NEVER GROW OLD (1956)/You Grow Closer

CHECKER

861	NEVER GROW OLD (1957)/You Grow Closer
941*	PRECIOUS LORD (3-60)/Precious Lord [Part 2]

COLUMBIA

41793	TODAY I SING THE BLUES (11-60)/Love Is The Only Thing [Duet with Paul Owerns]
41923	WON'T BE LONG [W. Ray Bryant Combo] (3-61)/Right Now [W. Ray Bryant Combo]
41985	ARE YOU SURE (4-61)/Maybe I'm A Fool
42167	ROCK-A-BYE YOUR BABY WITH A DIXIE MELODY (10-61)/Operation Heartbreak
42266	I SURRENDER DEAR (2-62)/Rough Lover (It's A Heartbreakin')
42456	DON'T CRY BABY (7-62)/Without The One You Love
42520	TRY A LITTLE TENDERNESS (9-62)/Just For A Thrill
42625	TROUBLE IN MIND (12-62)/God Bless The Child
42796	SAY IT ISN'T SO (4-63)/Here's Where I Came In (Here's Where I Walk Out)
42874	SKYLARK (10-63)/You've Got Her
42933	KISSIN' BY THE MISTLETOE (12-63)/Johnny
43009	SOULVILLE (5-64)/Evil Gal Blues

*Also released on JVB 75.

43113 RUNNIN' OUT OF FOOLS (9-64)/It's Just A Matter Of Time
43177 THE CHRISTMAS STORY (12-74)/Winter Wonderland
43203 CAN'T YOU JUST SEE ME (1-65)/Little Miss Raggedy Ann
43241 ONE STEP AHEAD (5-65)/I Can't Wait Until I See My Baby's Face
43333 NO NO (I'M LOSING YOU) (7-65)/Sweet Bitter Love
43442 THERE IS NO GREATER LOVE (11-65)/You Made Me Love You
43515 HANDS OFF (6-66)/Tighten Up Your Tie, Button Up Your Jacket (Make It For The Door)
43637 SWANEE (7-66)/You Made Me Love You
43827 CRY LIKE A BABY (10-66)/Follow Your Heart
44181 LEE CROSS (6-67)/Until You Were Gone
44270 TAKE A LOOK (9-67)/Follow Your Heart
44381 MOCKINGBIRD (12-67) [Duet with Nate Nelson]/A Mother's Love
44441 SOULVILLE (2-68)/If Ever I Would Leave You
44851 JIM (5-69)/Friendly Persuasion
44951 TODAY I SING THE BLUES (9-69)/Love Is The Only Thing

ATLANTIC

2386 I NEVER LOVED A MAN (THE WAY I LOVE YOU) (3-67)/ Do Right Woman, Do Right Man
2403 RESPECT (4-67) [Otis Redding '65 hit. VOLT 128]/Dr. Feel Good
2427 BABY I LOVE YOU (7-67)/Going Down Slow [W. King Curtis]
2441 A NATURAL WOMAN (9-67)/Baby, Baby, Baby
2464 CHAIN OF FOOLS (12-67)/Prove It
2486 (SWEET SWEET BABY) SINCE YOU'VE BEEN GONE (3-68)/Ain't No Way
2518 THINK (5-68)/You Send Me
2546 THE HOUSE THAT JACK BUILT (8-68)/I Say A Little Prayer
2574 SEE SAW (11-68) [Don Covay and "Good Timers" '65 hit. ATLANTIC 2301]/My Song
2603 THE WEIGHT (2-69) ["Band" '68 hit. CAPITOL 2269]/ Tracks Of My Tears
2619 I CAN'T SEE MYSELF LEAVING YOU (4-69)/Gentle On My Mind
2650 SHARE YOUR LOVE WITH ME (8-69) [Bobby Bland '64 hit. DUKE 377]/Pledging My Love/The Clock [Medley]
2683 ELEANOR RIGBY (11-69) ["Beatles" '66 hit. CAPITOL 5715]/ It Ain't Fair
2706 CALL ME (2-70)/Son Of A Preacher Man
2731 THRILL IS GONE (5-70) [B. B. King hit. BLUESWAY 61032]/ Spirit In The Dark
2751 LET IT BE (9-70) ["Beatles" '70 hit. APPLE 2764]/Don't Play That Song
2772 BORDER SONG (HOLY MOSES)* (11-70) [Elton John '70 hit]/You & Me

---

**Backup:* Chuck Rainey (bass), Cornell Dupree (guitar), Billy Preston (organ), King Curtis (tenor sax), and Ray Lucas (drums).

2787 YOU'RE ALL I NEED TO GET BY (11-71) ["Marvin & Tammi" '68 hit. TAMLA 54169]/Pullin'
2796 BRIDGE OVER TROUBLED WATER (4-71) ["Simon & Garfunkel" '70 hit. COLUMBIA 45079]/Brand New Me†
2817 SPANISH HARLEM (7-71) [With Dr. John at organ]/Lean On Me
2838 ROCK STEADY (11-71)/Oh Me, Oh My†
2866 DAY DREAMING (3-72)/I've Been Loving You Too Long
2883 ALL THE KING'S HORSES (6-72)/April Fools
2901 WHOLY HOLY (9-72) [W. "James Cleveland & Southern California Community Choir"]/Give Yourself To Jesus
2941 MASTER OF EYES (2-73)/Moody's Mood Of Love
2969 ANGEL (7-73)/Sister From Texas
2995 UNTIL YOU COME BACK TO ME (11-73)/If You Don't Think
2999 I'M IN LOVE (4-74) [Wilson Pickett '67 hit. ATLANTIC 2448]/Oh Baby
3200 AIN'T NOTHING LIKE THE REAL THING (9-74) ["Marvin & Tammi" '68 hit. TAMLA 54163]/Eight Days On The Road
3224 WITHOUT LOVE (11-74)/Don't Go Breaking My Heart
3249 WITH EVERYTHING I FEEL IN ME (1-75)/Sing It Again—Say It Again
3289 MR. D.J. (5 FOR THE D.J.) (9-75)/As Long As You Are There
3311 YOU (12-75)/Without You
3326 SOMETHING HE CAN FEEL (5-76)/Loving You Baby
3358 JUMP (10-76)/Hooked On Your Love
3373 LOOK INTO YOUR HEART (1-77)/Rock With Me
3393 BREAK IT TO ME GENTLY (3-77)/Meadows Of Springtime
3418 WHEN I THINK OF YOU (8-77)/Touch Me
3468 ALMIGHTY FIRE (WOMAN OF THE FUTURE) (4-78)/I'm Your Speed
3495 MORE THAN JUST A JOY (9-78)/This You Can Believe
3605 LADIES ONLY (8-79)
3632 HALF A LOVE (11-79)

†Backup on "Brand New Me" and "Oh Me, Oh My": Eric Gale (guitar and bass), Hugh McCracken (guitar), Donny Hathaway (organ), and Al Jackson (drums).

♭ ♯ ♪ ♩ 𝅗𝅥

Marvin Gaye

Real Name: "Marvin Pentz Gay, Jr." Born in Washington, D.C., on April 2, 1939.

MARVIN GAYE is a psychological soul-searching vocalist and multi-talented individual on piano, guitar, and drums, besides being a composer-producer with a fascinating interchange of singing styles over a period of two decades with the MOTOWN label. Marvin's roots are in Gospel, from where he sang "Journey To The Sky" at a special Kentucky church convention. He was one of a family of four, two boys and two girls, to the Reverend and Mrs. Marvin Gay, Sr., and was raised in the lower black section of Washington, D.C. He played guitar and sang with brother Frankie an inspiring song, "His Eye Is On The Sparrow" (which was released much later, in 1968, as a single by Marvin on MOTOWN 1128 and proved a classic performance).

While attending Cardoza High School, Marvin Gaye sang with the "Rainbows," a Washington group that recorded a 1955 hit, "Mary Lee" (RED ROBIN 134), but Marvin had not joined them until late in 1956 and sang only at record hops and on tour, but nothing recorded. Three of the group members, James "Sally" Nolan, Reese Palmer and Chester Simmons, joined with Marvin Gaye to form the "Marquees," who not only recorded a 1957 hit, "Wyatt Earp" (OKEH 7096), but also backed Bo Diddley on "I'm Sorry" (CHECKER 914). This group actually became the "Moonglows," upon Harvey Fuqua's permission, and also included Chuck Barksdale (noted "Dells" member). Marvin Gaye was the featured vocalist on "Mama Loocie" (CHESS 1738).

Harvey Fuqua, lead singer and leader, became influential both as a friend and business associate of Marvin for many years to come. Harvey went to MOTOWN as arranger-producer executive and brought Marvin Gaye with him. It was while at a 1960 party that Berry Gordy, Jr., heard Marvin, and from there Marvin, for about two years, became session drummer for the "Miracles." Harvey Fuqua married Berry Gordy's sister Gwen, while Marvin married the younger sister, Anna, in 1961. This highly talented combination entered upon a friendly working undertaking that soon proved itself the beginning of the MOTOWN success story.

William Stevenson was co-writer and producer for Marvin's first three hits: "Stubborn Kind Of Fellow" (TAMLA 54068), backed by the "Vandellas," and proving to be a break for Martha Reeves; "Hitch Hike" (TAMLA 54075), with a Southern R&B flavoring and funky dance appeal; and "Pride And Joy" (TAMLA 54079), which Marvin Gaye dedicated to his wife, Anna!

Then came Marvin Gaye's solo efforts: "Can I Get A Witness" (TAMLA 54087), "You're A Wonderful One" (TAMLA 54093), "Baby Don't Do It" (TAMLA 54101), and "How Sweet It Is (To Be Loved By You)" (TAMLA 54107), all of which were Holland-Dozier-Holland compositions, with Brian Holland and Lamont Dozier handling production. "Can I Get A Witness" was a Gospel Rocker (which was later popularized by Lee Michaels, A&M 1303); "Baby Don't Do It" was recorded by "Small Faces," and Marvin's classic "How Sweet It Is (To Be Loved By You)" proved to be a later hit for James Taylor (WARNER BROTHERS 8109) in 1975.

Marvin Gaye, with his handsome, debonair appearance and soft tenor vocal, was also ideally suited for duets. William Stevenson produced an album with Marvin Gaye and Mary Wells together, from which came Marvin's single "Once Upon A Time/What's The Matter With You Baby" (MOTOWN 1057). Around the same time Marvin Gaye struck "Try It Baby" (TAMLA 54095), which was written and produced by Berry Gordy. Marvin then made duets with Kim Weston: "What Good Am I Without You" (TAMLA 54104) and their hit "It Takes Two (To Make A Dream Come True)" (TAMLA 54141); both written and produced by William Stevenson. (Kim Weston later married Mickey Stevenson and, together, in the Seventies, owned the MIKIM label). This duet period was a departure of sorts from Marvin Gaye's inimitable style solos and might have created a confidence problem if it had not been for "Smokey" Robinson.

"Smokey" Robinson—a major writer, producer, and lead singer (the "Miracles") influenced Marvin Gaye toward a more distinctive Motown sound, and Marvin rendered appealing discs: "I'll Be Doggone" (TAMLA 54112), "Ain't That Peculiar" (TAMLA 54122), "One More Heartache" (TAMLA 54129), and "Take This Heart Of Mine" (TAMLA 54132); each written and produced by "Smokey" Robinson! At that time, Marvin also gave us "Pretty Little Baby" (TAMLA 54117), which was written and produced by Clarence Paul (who had done much in creating Stevie Wonder). Now very much in the "4 TOPS" idiom, and again from the song writing of Holland-Dozier-Holland, Marvin Gaye gave us "Little Darling (I Need You)" (TAMLA 54138) and "Your Unchanging Love" (TAMLA 54153).

Early in 1967 came Tammi Terrell (ex-wife of boxer Ernie Terrell) to join voices with Marvin Gaye in a highly successful duet story that ended in tragedy and left a sadness that affected Marvin's life and career. During this highlight period, Marvin Gaye and Tammi Terrell rendered "Ain't No Mountain High Enough" (TAMLA 54149), "Your Precious Love" (TAMLA 54156), "Ain't Nothing Like The Real Thing" (TAMLA 54163), "You're All I Need To Get By" (TAMLA 54169), and others; all beautiful songs written by Nick Ashford and Valerie Simpson (who went on to a distinguished singing career of their own). The Marvin and Tammi duet "If I Could Build My Whole World Around You" (TAMLA 54161) was written by Johnny Bristol, Harvey Fuqua, and Vernon Bullock. Each of these songs was a work of art and was sung with inspiration. But behind all this a tragedy was evolving. Tammi Terrell had undergone a series of operations for brain tumor at a Philadelphia hospital, and, on March 16, 1970, while in dual performance at William and Mary College, she collapsed and died in Marvin Gaye's arms!

During the late Sixties, Marvin contributed several Chart entries: "You" (TAMLA 54160), written and produced by Ivy Hunter and, much in the "4 TOPS" style, "Chained" (TAMLA 54170); written and produced by Frank Wilson. Along with these, Norman Whitfield (who created a sound for the "Temptations," "Undisputed Truth," and "Rose Royce") made a tremendous contribution writing and producing for Marvin Gaye: "I Heard It Through The Grapevine" (TAMLA 54176), written along with Barrett Strong (1960 hit-maker of "Money" ANNA IIII), becoming a No. 1 hit nationally and 2.5 million seller, and an all-time classic for Marvin; "Too Busy Thinking About My Baby" (TAMLA 54181), "That's The Way Love Is" (TAMLA 54185), "How Can I Forget/Gonna Give Her All The Love I've Got" (TAMLA 54190), and "The End Of Our Road" (TAMLA 54195), Marvin Gaye's Tribute to Tammi!

In the Seventies, Marvin Gaye (Mr. Perfectionist himself) showed his real self and class: "What's Goin' On" (TAMLA 54201), "Mercy Mercy Me" (TAMLA 54207), "Inner City Blues" (TAMLA 54109), marking a trend toward God and Marvin's distinctive freedom of expression, now with his own production expertise. Anna separated from Marvin in 1972 and, in March 1975, filed for divorce. In the meantime, Marvin Gaye, in 1973, recorded another big hit, "Let's Get It On" (TAMLA 54234), and followed through with another series of duet singles with Diana Ross, a major hit, "My Mistake (Was To Love You)" (MOTOWN 1269), and others. Marvin Gaye then entered upon a self-imposed exile from live performances, and his last recording success came with a Disco-oriented "Got To Give It Up" (TAMLA 54280). A truly remarkable career that can be fondly remembered while listening to that album song "Save The Children," Marvin Gaye's plea to the world. A truly great artist with a truly great delivery!

Discography

WITH THE "MOONGLOWS"

CHESS

1738 UNEMPLOYMENT (10-59) [Feat. Harvey Fuqua]/Mama Loocie [Feat. Marvin Gaye]

MARVIN GAYE

TAMLA

54041 LET YOUR CONSCIENCE BE YOUR GUIDE (5-61)/Never Let You Go
54055 SANDMAN (1-62)/I'm Yours, You're Mine
54063 A SOLDIER'S PLEA (5-62) [With "Love-Tones"]/Taking My Time
54068 STUBBORN KIND OF FELLOW (10-68) [With "Vandellas"]/ It Hurts Me Too
54075 HITCH HIKE (1-63)/Hello There Angel
54079 PRIDE AND JOY (5-63)/One Of These Days
54087 CAN I GET A WITNESS (10-63)/I'm Crazy 'Bout My Baby
54093 YOU'RE A WONDERFUL ONE (3-64)/When I'm Alone, I Cry

MARVIN GAYE AND MARY WELLS

MOTOWN

1057 ONCE UPON A TIME (5-64)/What's The Matter With You Baby

MARVIN GAYE

TAMLA

54095 TRY IT BABY (6-64)/If My Heart Could Sing
54101 BABY DON'T YOU DO IT (9-64)/Walk On The Wild Side

MARVIN GAYE AND KIM WESTON

54104 WHAT GOOD AM I WITHOUT YOU (10-64)/I Want You 'Round

MARVIN GAYE

54107 HOW SWEET IT IS (TO BE LOVED BY YOU) (12-64)/Forever
54112 I'LL BE DOGGONE (3-65)/You've Been A Long Time Coming
54117 PRETTY LITTLE BABY (7-65)/Now That You've Won Me
54122 AIN'T THAT PECULIAR (10-65)/She's Got To Be Real
54129 ONE MORE HEARTACHE (2-66)/When I Had Your Love
54132 TAKE THIS HEART OF MINE (5-66)/Need Your Lovin', Want You Back
54138 LITTLE DARLING (I NEED YOU) (8-66)/Hey Diddle Diddle

MARVIN GAYE AND KIM WESTON

54141 IT TAKES TWO (1-67)/It's Got To Be A Miracle

MARVIN GAYE AND TAMMI TERRELL

54149 AIN'T NO MOUNTAIN HIGH ENOUGH (5-67)/Give A Little Love

MARVIN GAYE

54153 YOUR UNCHANGING LOVE (7-67)/I'll Take Care Of You

MARVIN GAYE AND TAMMI TERRELL

54156 YOUR PRECIOUS LOVE (9-67)/Hold Me Oh My Darling

MARVIN GAYE

54160 YOU (1-68)/Change What You Can

MARVIN GAYE AND TAMMI TERRELL

54161 IF I COULD BUILD MY WHOLE WORLD AROUND YOU (12-67)/If This World Were Mine
54163 AIN'T NOTHING LIKE THE REAL THING (4-68)/Little Ole Boy, Little Ole Girl
54169 YOU'RE ALL I NEED TO GET BY (7-68)/Two Can Have A Party

MARVIN GAYE

MOTOWN

1128 HIS EYE IS ON THE SPARROW (9-68)/Just a Closer Walk With You [Gladys Knight and the "Pips"]

TAMLA

54170 CHAINED (9-68)/At Last

MARVIN GAYE AND TAMMI TERRELL

54173 KEEP ON LOVIN' ME HONEY (10-68)/You Ain't Livin' Till You're Lovin'

MARVIN GAYE

54176 I HEARD IT THROUGH THE GRAPEVINE (11-68) [Gladys Knight and the "Pips" '67 hit. SOUL 35039]/You're What's Happening

MARVIN GAYE AND TAMMI TERRELL

54179 GOOD LOVIN' AIN'T EASY TO COME BY (2-69)/Satisfied Feeling

MARVIN GAYE

54181 TOO BUSY THINKING ABOUT MY BABY (4-69)/Wherever I Lay My Hat (That's My Home)

54185 THAT'S THE WAY LOVE IS (8-69)/Gonna Keep On Tryin'

MARVIN GAYE AND TAMMI TERRELL

54187 WHAT YOU GAVE ME (11-69)/How You Gonna Keep It

MARVIN GAYE

54190 HOW CAN I FORGET (1-70)/Gonna Give Her All The Love I've Got

54195 END OF OUR ROAD (6-70)/Me And My Lonely Room

54201 WHAT'S GOIN' ON (2-71)/God Is Love
54207 MERCY, MERCY ME (THE ECOLOGY) (7-71)/Sad Tomorrows
54209 INNER CITY BLUES (MAKE ME WANNA HOLLER) (10-71)/Wholly Holy
54221 YOU'RE THE MAN (5-72)/You're The Man [Part 2]
54228 TROUBLE MAN (12-72)/Don't Mess With Mr "T"
54234 LET'S GET IT ON (7-73)/I Wish It Would Rain

MARVIN GAYE AND DIANA ROSS

MOTOWN

1280 YOU'RE A SPECIAL PART OF ME (10-73)/I'm Falling In Love With You

MARVIN GAYE

TAMLA

54241 COME GET TO THIS (11-73)/Distant Lovers
54244 YOU SURE LOVE TO BALL (1-74)/Just To Keep You Satisfied

MARVIN GAYE AND DIANA ROSS

MOTOWN

1269 MY MISTAKE (WAS TO LOVE YOU) (2-74)/Include Me In Your Life
1296 DON'T KNOCK MY LOVE (7-74) [Wilson Picket '71 hit. ATLANTIC 2797]/Just Say, Just Say

MARVIN GAYE

TAMLA

54253 DISTANT LOVERS (9-74)/Trouble Man
54264 I WANT YOU (4-76)/I Want You [Instr.]
54273 AFTER THE DANCE (8-76)/Feel All My Love Inside
54280 GOT TO GIVE IT UP (4-77)/Got To Give It Up [Part 2]

DIANA ROSS, MARVIN GAYE, SMOKEY ROBINSON, AND STEVIE WONDER

MOTOWN

1455 POPS WE LOVE YOU (1-79) [Vocal]/Pops We Love You [Instr.]

MARVIN GAYE

TAMLA

54298 A FUNKY SPACE REINCARNATION (2-79) [Part 2]/[Part 1]
54305 EGO TRIPPING OUT (10-79)/Ego Tripping Out [Instr.]

Al Green

Born in Forest City, Arkansas, on April 13, 1946.

AL GREEN, the "Prince of Soul," is a remarkably talented stylist who has the recognizable Soul charisma. His distinctive and exciting falsetto vocals could be directed toward the sweet love ballad or the demanded high-pitched shrill. Al Green had everything: youth, elegance, sexuality, and experience in his having sung on the Chittlin' Circuit, touring the South and the Midwest during the Sixties.

Al was born into the Gospel-rooted family of Robert and Cora Green in Forest City, Arkansas, and when he was nine he moved with his family to Grand Rapids, Michigan, in 1955. Five years later, in 1960, Al Green made his singing debut with the recording "Girl I Love/Never Had A Chance" (FARGO 1004). During his high school days, Al sang with his brothers, Robert, William and Walter, in a Gospel group, the "Green Brothers."

In 1964, Al Green formed the group the "Creations," which included Gene Mason, Curtis Rogers, and Palmer James. Palmer James formed the ZODIAC label and, during 1967, the "Creations" recorded "Footsteps" (ZODIAC 21005), a Gospel-flavored entry!

Al Green, for a time, sang with the "Soul Mates" group, which comprised Al's brother, Robert, and his friend Lee Virgins. Palmer Jones and Curtis Rogers formed HOT LINE MUSIC JOURNAL label, and Al Green and the "Soul Mates" recorded "Back Up Train" (HOT LINE MUSIC JOURNAL 15000). Unfortunately for Al, he was not able to follow it up and it became an isolated hit.

A series of events then happened that had a lasting effect on Al Green's career. In 1969, Joe Cuoghi at HI RECORDS died and was replaced by one of the most distinguished of producers, Willie Mitchell, who, very shortly, as head man of that label, discovered Al Green while he was performing at a Midland, Texas, nightclub. Willie Mitchell, a seasoned musician with many funky instrumental classics to his credit, started working as A&R man with each and every one of Al Green's hits from 1969 through 1977, until Al Green started his own music studio, where he handled his own production and produced for others. When he was with HI label he was backed by Willie Mitchell's band, which comprised Mabon Hodges (guitar), Charles Hodges (organ), Leroy Hodges (bass), and Howard Grimes (drums). Al Green's biggest hits with HI were "Tired Of Being Alone" (HI 2194), "Let's Stay Together" (HI 2202), "Look What You Done For Me" (HI 2211), "Call Me (Come Back Home)" (HI 2235), "I'm Still In Love With You" (HI 2216), "You Ought To Be With Me" (HI 2227), "Here I Am (Come And Take Me)" (HI 2247) and "Sha La La" (HI 2274), each having a top-Chart appeal! On October 18, 1973, mishap came to Al Green when his back was scalded by boiled grits and he had to be hospitalized. The woman responsible, Mary Woodson, committed suicide.

His later recordings are all beautiful and include the dynamic and thrilling "Keep Me Crying" (HI 2319) and the enjoyable "I Tried To Tell Myself" (HI 2322), "Love & Happiness" (HI 2324), and the record that was his debut as writer/producer, "Belle" (CREAM 77505). Apart from his exciting musical career, Al Green continues to serve in yet a higher calling as a minister of the Gospel with his own congregation!

Discography

AL GREEN

FARGO

1004 GIRL I LOVE (1960)/Never Had A Chance

AS "CREATIONS"

ZODIAC

21005 FOOTSTEPS (9-67)/A Dream

AS "AL GREENE & SOUL MATES"

HOT LINE MUSIC JOURNAL

15000 BACK UP TRAIN (12-67)/Don't Leave Me
15001 DON'T HURT ME NO MORE (5-68)/Get Yourself Together
15002 LOVER'S HOLIDAY (10-68)/I'll Be Good To You

AL GREEN

HI

2159 I WANT TO HOLD YOUR HAND (5-69) ["Beatles" '64 hit. CAPITOL 5112]/What Am I Gonna Do With Myself
2164 ONE WOMAN (9-69)/Tomorrow's Dreams
2172 YOU SAY IT (1-70)/Gotta Find A New World
2177 RIGHT NOW, RIGHT NOW (6-70)/All Because (I'm A Foolish One)
2182 I CAN'T GET NEXT TO YOU (10-70) ["Temptations" '69 hit. GORDY 7093]/Ride Sally Ride
2188 DRIVIN' WHEEL (1971) [Junior Parker '61 hit. DUKE 335]/True Love
2194 TIRED OF BEING ALONE (7-71)/Get Back Baby
2202 LET'S STAY TOGETHER (12-71)/Tomorrow's Dreams
2211 LOOK WHAT YOU DONE FOR ME (3-72)/La-La For You
2216 I'M STILL IN LOVE WITH YOU (7-72)/Old Time Lovin'

BELL

258 GUILTY (9-72)/Let Me Help You

HI

2227 YOU OUGHT TO BE WITH ME (10-72)/What Is This Feeling
2235 CALL ME (COME BACK HOME) (2-73)/What A Wonderful Thing Love Is
2247 HERE I AM (COME AND TAKE ME) (7-73)/I'm Glad You're Mine
2257 LIVIN' FOR YOU (12-73)/It Ain't No Fun To Me
2262 LET'S GET MARRIED (3-74)/So Good To Be Here
2274 SHA-LA-LA (MAKE ME HAPPY) (9-74)/School Days
2282 L-O-V-E (LOVE) (3-75)/I Wish You Were Here
2288 OH ME, OH MY (DREAMS IN MY ARMS) (7-75)/Strong As Death (Sweet As Love)
2300 FULL OF LOVE (11-75)/Could I Be The One
2306 LET IT SHINE (5-76)/There's No Way
2319 KEEP ME CRYIN' (11-76)/There Is Love
2322 I TRIED TO TELL MYSELF (2-77)/Something
2324 LOVE & HAPPINESS (8-77) [Also on LONDON DISC 3006]/Glory Glory

HI (Distributed by CREAM)

77505 BELLE (10-77)/Chariots Of Fire
78511 I FEEL GOOD (3-78)/Feels Like Summer
78522 TO SIR WITH LOVE (12-78)/Wait Here

AS "ERNEST JACKSON" (AL GREEN)

STONE

001 LOVE AND HAPPINESS (4-73)/Hogwash
202 JOY AND AFFECTION (10-73)/

♭ ♯ ♪ ♩ 𝅗𝅥

"Bill Haley and the Comets"

MEMBERS: Bill Haley (William John Clifton Haley, Jr.), guitar, born July 6, 1925, at Highland Park, Detroit, Michigan; Rudy Pompelli, sax, born 1928, died February 5, 1976; Alex Rex (Al Pompelli, brother of Rudy), bass; John Grande, accordion and piano; Francis Beecher, Spanish guitar; Don Raymond (Ralph Jones), drums; Billy Williamson, steel guitar.

Hometown: Chester, Pennsylvania.

"BILL HALEY AND THE COMETS" were the first white group to bring us the new sound of Rock and Roll from 1951 to today, with their recordings "Rocket 88" (HOLIDAY 105), a cover of the "Jackie Brenston and Delta Cats" '51 R&B disc (CHESS 2632), and "Rock The Joint" (ESSEX 303), their hit with a driving dance-band beat and appeal that became a Rock and Roll standard. They performed as "Bill Haley & Saddlemen" during that Rockabilly early era with Dave Miller's subsidiary (of ESSEX) label HOLIDAY and as "Bill Haley and Comets" on his Philadelphia ESSEX label, which led to a more popular sound in the 1953 hits "Crazy, Man, Crazy" (ESSEX 321) and "Live It Up" (ESSEX 332). It was with a friend, the late Danny Cedarone, that Bill Haley wrote the song "Rock-A-Beatin' Boogie," which was recorded by the "Esquire Boys," the Treniers," and, later, Johnny Maddox, but it was the "Bill Haley and the Comets' " version with pronounced word phrase "Rock, rock rock everybody roll, roll roll everybody" that inspired Alan Freed, then disc jockey with WJW in Cleveland, Ohio, to coin the phrase Rock and Roll."

It was after signing a contract with DECCA, thanks to manager Dave Myers, that Bill Haley—with his famous "kiss curl," Gibson guitar, and immense personal appeal—became a star! The group recorded their first of many hits, "Shake, Rattle And Roll" (DECCA 29204), which was written by Jesse Stone (alias Charles Calhoun), who was pianist with the early "Drifters" sessions, and the song was originally a '54 R&B hit by Joe Turner (ATLANTIC 1026). In 1955, Bill Haley and his "Comets" recorded their all-time standard, "Rock Around The Clock" (DECCA 29124), which has since then sold more singles than any other Rock and Roll—TWENTY-THREE MILLION! The song was written by Max C. Freedman and Jimmy De Knight (real name James Myers) and originally recorded by Sonny Dae. This song was also featured as title track for the '55 film *Blackboard Jungle.*

It was in 1955 that Bill Haley and the "Comets" recorded their third and final million seller, "See You Later Alligator" (DECCA 29791), a catchy tune that was originally written and recorded by Robert Guidry (alias Bobby Charles) on CHESS 1609. The group had now become a Rock and Roll trademark, a popular nightclub attraction, and part of the late Sixties Rock and Roll revival, which certainly started a whole new interest in the roots of that sound!

Bill Haley was born on July 6, 1925, at Highland Park, a suburb of Detroit, Michigan. He has Indian blood on his father's side. At seven years of age, his family moved to Booth Corner, a suburb of Philadelphia, where they operated a farm. Young Bill Haley (his full name was William John Clifton Haley, Jr.) was musically influenced in Country and Western; his father played the banjo and mandolin, while his mother played the organ at their Baptist church. Bill took to playing the guitar and at thirteen years of age traveled with a Country group, the "Down Homers." At nineteen, Bill became Country disc jockey and music director for the small radio station WPWA in Chester, Pennsylvania, at which time he formed a hillbilly band, "The Four Aces Of Western Swing," and recorded his first record, "Candy Kisses," in 1949. "Yodelling Bill" Haley was also disc jockey at WSJN in Bridgeport, New Jersey, in 1945.

Bill Haley married his blonde sweetheart of his high school days in 1953 around the same time his band act, with the great saxophone of Rudy Pompelli, was creating so much excitement wherever they performed. "Razzle Dazzle" and "Rip It Up" were two early stage favorites! In the Sixties the group was overshadowed by the "Beatles," but Bill Haley starred in a 1957 film, *Don't Knock the Rock.* After the sudden death of Rudy Pompelli, that popular man with the sax, in 1976, both British and American fans were saddened, and this seemed to become the fitting end to the group.

Discography

AS "BILL HALEY & HIS FOUR ACES OF WESTERN SWING"

COWBOY

1202 CANDY KISSES (3-49)/Tennessee Border
1700 FOUR LEAF CLOVER BLUES (1950)/Too Many Parties
1701 MY SWEET LITTLE GIRL FROM NEVADA (9-50)/My Palomino And I

CENTER

STAND UP AND BE COUNTED/Loveless Blues

AS "BILL HALEY AND SADDLEMEN"

KEYSTONE

5101 DEAL ME A HAND (3-50)/Ten Gallon Stetson
5102 SUSAN VAN DUSEN (8-50)/I'm Not To Blame

AS "BILL HALEY'S SADDLEMEN"

ATLANTIC—(HILLBILLY SERIES)

727* WHY DO I CRY OVER YOU (11-50)/Gonna Dry Every Tear With A Kiss

AS "BILL HALEY & SADDLEMEN"

HOLIDAY

105 ROCKET 88 (5-51)/Tearstains On My Heart
108 GREEN TREE BOOGIE (9-51)/Deep Down In My Heart

AS "BILL HALEY & LORETTA (DUET) WITH SADDLEMEN"

110 PRETTY BABY (11-51) ['50 R&B tune by "Griffin Brothers"]/ I'm Crying ["Memphis Slim" tune original]

---

*ATLANTIC 727 record was released on ATLANTIC MELODISCS Subsidiary 2752 in Britain.

AS "BILL HALEY & SADDLEMEN"

111 A YEAR AGO THIS CHRISTMAS (12-51)/Don't Want To Be Alone This Christmas
113 JUKEBOX CANNONBALL (2-52)/Sundown Boogie

AS "BILL HALEY AND COMETS"

ESSEX

303 ROCK THE JOINT (5-52) [Jimmy Preston '49 tune. GOTHAM]/Ivy Heart
305 ROCKING CHAIR ON THE MOON (8-52)/Dance With The Dolly (With A Hole In Her Stocking)
310 STOP BEATIN' AROUND THE MULBERRY BUSH (12-52)/Real Rock Drive
321 CRAZY, MAN, CRAZY (5-53)/Whatcha Gonna Do
327 PAT-A-CAKE (9-53)/Fractured
332 LIVE IT UP (2-54)/Farewell, So Long, Goodbye
340 I'LL BE TRUE (6-54)/Ten Little Indians
348 STRAIGHT JACKET (10-54)/Chattanooga Choo Choo
374 JUKEBOX CANNONBALL (3-55)/Sundown Boogie
381 ROCKET 88/Green Tree Boogie
399 ROCK THE JOINT/Farewell, So Long, Goodbye

TRANS WORLD

718 YES INDEED/Real Rock Drive

DECCA

29124 ROCK AROUND THE CLOCK (4-54) [Jimmy DeKnight tune. PEAK 105]/Thirteen Women (And Only One Man In Town)
29204 SHAKE, RATTLE AND ROLL (7-54)/A. B. C. Boogie
29317 DIM, DIM THE LIGHTS (10-54)/Happy Baby
29418 MAMBO ROCK (2-55)/Birth Of The Boogie
29552 RAZZLE-DAZZLE (7-55)/Two Hound Dogs
29713 BURN THAT CANDLE (10-55)/Rock-A-Beatin' Boogie
29791 SEE YOU LATER ALLIGATOR (12-55)/The Paper Boy
29870 R-O-C-K (3-56)/The Saints' Rock And Roll
29948 HOT DOG BUDDY BUDDY (6-56)/Rockin' Through The Rye
30082 RIP IT UP (8-56)/Teenager's Mother (Are You Right?)
30085 RUDY'S ROCK (10-56)/Blue Comet Blues
30148 DON'T KNOCK THE ROCK (1-57)/Choo Choo Ch'Boogie
30214 FORTY CUPS OF COFFEE (3-57)/Hook, Line And Sinker
30314 (YOU HIT THE WRONG NOTE) BILLY GOAT 6-57)/Rockin' Rollin' Rover
30394 THE DIPSY DOODLE (9-57)/Miss You
30461 ROCK THE JOINT (1-58)/How Many (Broken Hearts)?
30530 MARY, MARY LOU (3-58)/It's A Sin
30592 SKINNY MINNIE (4-58)/Sway With Me
30681 LEAN JEAN (8-58)/Don't Nobody Move

30741	CHIQUITA LINDA (UN POQUITO DE TU AMOR?) (11-58)/Whoa Mabel
30781	B. B. BETTY (2-59)/Corrine, Corrina
30844	I GOT A WOMAN (5-59)/Charmaine
30873	A FOOL SUCH AS I (7-59)/Where'd You Go Last Night?
30926	CALDONIA (9-59)/Shaky
30956	JOEY'S SONG (10-59)/Ooh! Look-A-There, Ain't She Pretty
31030	SKOKIAAN (A SOUTH AFRICAN SONG) (1-60)/Puerto Rican Peddlar
31080	STRICTLY INSTRUMENTAL (5-60)/(Put Another Nickel In) Music, Music, Music!
31650	THE GREEN DOOR (8-64)/Yeah! She's Evil

WARNER BROTHERS

5145	CANDY KISSES (3-60)/Tamiami
5154	CHICK SAFARI (6-60)/Hawk
5171	SO RIGHT TONIGHT (9-60)/Let The Good Times Roll, Creole
5228	FLIP FLOP & FLY (7-61)/Honky Tonk

GONE

5111	THE SPANISH TWIST (9-61)/My Kind Of Woman
5116	RIVIERA (11-61)/War Paint

APT

25081	BURN THAT CANDLE (1965)/Stop, Look, And Listen
25087	HALEY A GO GO (1965)/Tongue-Tied Tony

NEWTOWN

5013	TENOR MAN (1963)/Up Goes My Love
5014	MIDNIGHT IN WASHINGTON (1963)/White Parakeet
5024	DANCE AROUND THE CLOCK (1964)/What Can I Say After I Say I'm Sorry

NICETOWN

5025	TANDY (1964)/You Call Everybody Darling

LOGO

7005	YAKETY SAX/Boot's Blues [By Boots Randolph]

KASEY

7006	A. B. C. BOOGIE/[Flip *not* by Bill Haley]

ORFEON

1047	FLORIDA TWIST/Negra Consentida
1195	PUE DE PAPAS/Anoche

UNITED ARTISTS

50483 THAT'S HOW I GOT TO MEMPHIS (2-69)/Ain't Love Funny Ha Ha Ha

JANUS

162 A LITTLE PIECE AT A TIME (11-71)/Travelling Band

MGM

14688 KOHOUTEK (1-74)/Tony's Theme

ARZEE

4677 WITHIN THIS BROKEN HEART OF MINE (10-77)/Yodel Your Blues Away

AS "JODIMARS" [Members of Bill Haley's "Comets"]

CAPITOL

3285 LET'S ROCK (1955)/Now Dig This

AS "KINGSMEN" [Instrumentals, Members of Bill Haley's "Comets"]

EAST WEST

115 WEEKEND (8-58)/Better Believe It
120 THE CAT WALK (1958)/Conga Rock

AS "LIFEGUARDS" [Members of Bill Haley's "Comets"]

ABC PARAMOUNT

10021 EVERYBODY OUT 'A THE POOL (1959)/Teenage Tango

DR

69 EVERYBODY OUT 'A THE POOL (1965)/Teenage Tango

♭ ♯ ♪ ♩ 𝅗𝅥

Ronnie Hawkins and the "Hawks"

Ronnie Hawkins was born in Huntsville, Arkansas, on January 10, 1935.

"Hawks" (1952): Initially, an all-black backup group to Ronnie Hawkins, forced to disband by strong public racial prejudice at that time. Rebirth in 1958, as an all-white quartet (including Ronnie Hawkins), achieved good regional following. 1959-63 saw almost total change of personnel as backup group to Ronnie Hawkins, achieving national and international recognition for their recordings. In 1963, Ronnie Hawkins and the "Hawks" mutually parted company, each to solo in their "own" type of music. The "Hawks" went on to become "Canadian Squires," "Levon & the Hawks" and, finally, "The Band."

"Hawks" Quartet (1958): Ronnie Hawkins, lead vocal; Jimmy Luke (Jimmy Paul Paulman), lead guitar; Will "Pop" Jones, piano; Levon Helm, drums.

"The Hawks" Backup (1959-63): James G. Evans, bass guitar (replaced in 1961 by Robbie Robertson, then bass guitar); Fred Cash, lead guitar; Jerry Penfound, sax (replaced in 1962 by Garth Hudson, organ, sax and accordion); Levon Helm, drums.

Others: Fred Carter, lead guitar; Dominic Troiano, guitar; John Till, lead guitar; Bob Boucher, bass; Gordy Fleming, piano; David Lewis, drums.

"Hawks" to "The Band" (1963-): Levon Helm, music director, vocals, drums (born in Marvell, Arkansas, on May 26, 1943); Jaime "Robbie" Robertson, songwriter, lead guitar (born in Toronto, Canada, on July 5, 1944); Richard "Beak" Manuel, piano (born in Stratford, Canada, April 3, 1944); Rick Danko, country fiddle, mandolin, bass (born in Simcoe, Canada,

on December 9, 1943); Garth Hudson, keyboards, sax, accordion (born in London, Canada, August 2, 1942).

RONNIE HAWKINS, known over the years as "Rompin', stompin' Ronnie Hawkins," is one of the true hot rock'n'rollers who refused to stop rocking! He, initially, began singing Rockabilly and Rhythm and Blues, but always with the intention of spreading the word and developing other stars to do it. It was Ronnie Hawkins who blazed the way for Conway Twitty, David Clayton Thomas, Robbie Lane, "Crowbar" and his own backup group the "Hawks" who later, in 1968, became best known as "The Band"!

Ronnie Hawkins was born in Huntsville, Arkansas, but the family moved early across the state to Fayetteville, and it was there that young Ronnie first sang in the church choir and went on to excel in physical training in high school and at the University of Arkansas. In 1952, Ronnie Hawkins formed his first "Hawks," an all-black group, only to go nowhere with it because of the then-existing racial prejudice. Ronnie turned to earning a living as best he could, whether it be pumping gas or laboring on a local construction site, while making some nightclub appearances around Memphis in 1956.

With the emergence of "King" Elvis, and the great Rock and Roll backwash he created, Ronnie Hawkins reformed the "Hawks" in 1958 (as a quartet, including himself as lead singer) and moved boldly into the famed and highly competitive Memphis circuit of SUN/PHILLIPS INT. rock stars! The group made good regionally in live performances, and many demo tapes were cut for various recording companies but were "lost" in that prolific Rock and Roll talent shuffle. A disc was actually cut for one label and was never released! Ronnie Hawkins and the "Hawks" had "arrived," with Ronnie now one of the best drawing attractions regionally, but, strangely enough, no discs were forthcoming.

In the meantime, Ronnie Hawkins answered to national service and joined the U.S. Army artillery unit at Fort Sill, Oklahoma. The versatile country boy, an excellent rifleman since his boyhood, was honorably released after six months' service and thus returned to his popular wild act with super-backflips, solid stompin', and his very own "camel walk" dance.

1958 saw Ronnie Hawkins and the group, on Conway Twitty's suggestion, head north to Canada, where they played a first club date (two weeks) at the Golden Rail in Hamilton, Ontario. The quartet then recorded a wild version of "Hey Bo Diddley" (QUALITY 6218), and, though this was only moderately successful on the market, they went on to cut "Forty Days" (ROULETTE 4154), "Mary Lou" (ROULETTE 4177), and "Love Me Like You Can" (ROULETTE 4209), which he composed himself. "Hey Bo Diddley" was eventually to become Ronnie Hawkins's theme song!

With Ronnie Hawkins's third version of the "Hawks," the finest of them all, the hits had now become regular (though selling much better in Canada and the Southern states than in the rest of the U.S.), giving us "The Ballad of Caryl Chessman" (ROULETTE 4231), "Ruby Baby" (ROULETTE 4249), "Summertime" (ROULETTE 4267), "Cold Cold Heart" (ROULETTE 4311), a Hank Williams Country classic, and "There's A Screw Loose" (ROULETTE 4502), among others. Nor should we overlook that great Rockabilly album and favorite "ODESSA"! Again, in the meantime, Ronnie Hawkins had completed a successful live tour of the United Kingdom (and appeared on ITV's Jack Good's *Boy Meets Girl* TV show and others out of Manchester), enjoyed appearing in Paris, France, and had a terrific coast-to-coast tour across Canada!

It was following these events that we saw the final changes to Ronnie Hawkins and his "Hawks," with the coming of Robbie Robertson, who became lead guitar, Richard "Beak" Manuel to the keyboard, Rick Danko with his bass, country fiddle and mandolin, and classic musician of them all, Garth Hudson, to share the keyboards and saxophone at times with other members of the group! Ronnie Hawkins had already appeared at the famous New York City club the Round Table, where he not only introduced his $600 black suede suit but also his "Twist" routine.

Things were happening to Levon Helm and the other "Hawks," who had now donned all-white suits with long glossy lapels and, with this, appeared a decided preference for a change of direction in their music. This brought about an amicable arrangement late in 1963, where Levon Helm (the sole remaining Arkansan) and the "Hawks" split with Ronnie Hawkins and went their own solo way! In 1964, Ronnie Hawkins formed his own recording HAWK label and released his first disc, "Got My Mojo Working/Let The Good Time Roll" (HAWK 102), followed by "Bluebirds Over The Mountain" (HAWK 106), and the "Rolling Stones" tune "Little Red Rooster" (HAWK 107). On these, Ronnie Hawkins used a young Canadian group, the "Disciples," on the first recording, but, because they remained with him for only about four months, he had to form a completely new group, none other than his fourth version of the "Hawks"! The group comprised John Till, lead guitar; Bob Boucher, baby bass; Gordy "Mainline" Fleming, keyboards; Dave Lewis, drums. The group stuck together and Ronnie Hawkins's second release, "Bluebirds Over The Mountain," proved a big hit, reaching No. 4 on Canada's CHUM Charts, though the group did not back Ronnie on that recording. The lead guitarist was ex-"Hawk" Fred Carter!

Levon Helm and his fellow "Hawks" cut a record for the APEX label, "Uh-Uh-Uh/Leave Me Alone" (76964), calling themselves "The Canadian Squires." They also recorded two other discs for ATCO label,

"The Stones I Throw/He Don't Love You" (6383) and "Go Go Lisa/He Don't Love You" (6625), which was not released until 1968! On these, the signature was "Levon & The Hawks." The group finally settled on the title "The Band" and went on to record, for CAPITOL label, "The Weight" (2269), "Up On Cripple Creek" (2635), "Rag Mama Rag" (2705), and the Chuck Willis 1958 hit "(I Don't Want To) Hang Up My Rock And Roll Shoes" (3500) among others. Levon Helm eventually took off to form his own group, "The RCO All-Stars," comprising Levon Helm, vocal and drums; Steve Cropper, guitar; Scotty Edwards, bass; and Barry Beckett, keyboards. They cut one record for the ABC label, "Milk Cow Boogie/Blues So Bad" (12336).

"The Band" went on to give us "Out Of The Blue/The Well" (WARNER BROTHERS 8592). Levon Helm gave us a record of his own, "Ain't No Way To Forget You" (ABC 12416), and Rick Danko (of "The Band") released a couple of his own: "What A Town (ARISTA 0306) and "Java Blues" (ARISTA 0320). "The Band," under the shrewd guidance of Levon Helm, saw yeoman service as backup to the great Bob Dylan (almost immediately after they had "almost" latched on as Sonny Boy Williamson's backup not too long before his death!).

Ronnie Hawkins, now thoroughly acclimatized in Canada, where he was now unquestionably the leading artist, went merrily on his live tours, recording hits, and got himself an exciting home-base establishment in downtown Toronto! There, Ronnie, partly owns Le Coq D'Or, the first teenage nightclub, in Canada and spends most of his working nights playing amid a beautiful historic-like Viking setting of a long Viking ship bar, great shields and swords, and so forth. Added to this are his two bountiful farms back in Arkansas and another flourishing club down there, called "Rockwood," his famous Rolls-Royce and nine other whopping cars, and one need not wonder long why Ronnie Hawkins can look so contented as he looks out of the great window of his executive offices above his now famous "Hawks Nest" and murmurs something of his personal philosophy in the words "Live fast, love hard, die young and leave a Beautiful Memory."

Discography

AS "RONNIE HAWKINS QUARTET"

QUALITY (Released in Canada)

6218 HEY BO DIDDLEY (9-58)/Love Me Like You Can

RONNIE HAWKINS

ROULETTE

5154 FORTY DAYS (6-59)/One Of These Days
4177 MARY LOU (8-59) [Young Jessie (of "Flairs") '55 hit. MODERN 961]/Need Your Lovin'

AS "ROCKIN' RONALD & THE REBELS"

ORCHID

5005 KANSAS CITY (1959) [Wilbert Harrison '59 hit. FURY 1023]/Cuttin' Out

END

1043 KANSAS CITY (10-59)/Cuttin' Out

RONNIE HAWKINS

ROULETTE

4209 SOUTHERN LOVE (1-60)/Love Me Like You Can
4228 LONELY HOURS (4-60)/Clara
4231 BALLAD OF CARYL CHESSMAN (7-60)/Death Of Floyd Collins
4249 RUBY BABY (1-61) ["Drifters" '53 hit. ATLANTIC 1089]/Hay Ride
4267 SUMMERTIME (7-61) [Sam Cooke '57 hit. KEEN 34013]/Mister And Mississippi
4311 COLD COLD HEART (2-62) [Hank Williams' Country Classic]/Nobody's Lonesome For Me
4400 COME LOVE (7-62)/I Feel Good
4483 BO DIDDLEY (4-63)/Who Do You Love
4502 THERE'S A SCREW LOOSE (8-63)/High Blood Pressure

"DAVID ROCKINGHAM TRIO" [Feat. "ROBBIE" ROBERTSON, Guitar]

JUBILEE

913 DAWN (11-63)/That's All

JOSIE

917 WITH MIDNIGHT/Bee Dee
922 JO-DE-VIE/Soulful Chant

AS "CANADIAN SQUIRES" ["HAWKS"]

APEX

76964 UH-UH-UH (1964)/Leave Me Alone [Also on Ware 6002]

RONNIE HAWKINS

HAWK

102 I GOT MY MOJO WORKIN' (8-64) [Backed by Robbie Lane's "Disciples"]/Let The Good Times Roll
106 BLUEBIRDS OVER THE MOUNTAIN (1-65) [Ersel Hickey '58 hit. EPIC 9263]/Diddley Diddley Daddy
107 LITTLE RED ROOSTER (4-65) ["Rolling Stones" tune]/Goin' To The River

AS "LEVON (HELM) & THE HAWKS"

ATCO

6383 THE STONES I THROW (6-65)/He Don't Love You
6625 GO GO LIZA JANE (Released 1968)/He Don't Love You

RONNIE HAWKINS

YORKVILLE

40516 HOME FROM THE FOREST (12-67)/Bitter Green
40519 REASON TO BELIEVE (4-68)/Mary Jane

AS "THE BAND"

Robbie Robertson (vocals, lead guitar); Garth Hudson (vocals, organ); Richard Manuel (vocals, piano); Rick Danko (vocals, bass); Levon Helm (vocals, drums).

CAPITOL

2269 THE WEIGHT (8-68)/I Shall Be Released

RONNIE HAWKINS

HAWK

301 MATCHBOX (10-69) [Carl Perkins '57 hit. SUN 261]/Little Bird

AS "THE BAND"

CAPITOL

2635 UP ON CRIPPLE CREEK (11-69)/The Night They Drove Old Dixie Down

RONNIE HAWKINS

COTILLION

44060 DOWN IN THE VALLEY (1-70) ["Clovers" '57 hit. ATLANTIC 1152]/Matchbox

AS "THE BAND"

CAPITOL

2705 RAG MAMA RAG (2-70)/The Unfaithful Servant

RONNIE HAWKINS

COTILLION

44067 BITTER GREEN (5-70) [Gordon Lightfoot '68 hit. UNITED ARTISTS 50,447]/Forty Days
44076 LITTLE BIRD (10-70)/One More Night

AS "THE BAND"

CAPITOL

2870 TIME TO KILL (10-70)/The Shape I'm In

RONNIE HAWKINS

HAWK

1205-01 PATRICIA (3-71)/Black Sheep Boy

AS "THE BAND"

CAPITOL

3199 LIFE IS A CARNIVAL (10-71)/The Moon Struck One
3249 WHEN I PAINT MY MASTERPIECE (1-72)/Where Do We Go From Here
6188 UP ON CRIPPLE CREEK (1972)/The Night They Drove Old Dixie Down

RONNIE HAWKINS

MONUMENT

ZS7-1 CORA MAE (9-72)/Diddley Diddley Daddy

AS "THE BAND"

CAPITOL

3433 DON'T DO IT (9-72)/Rag Mama Rag
3500 (I DON'T WANT TO) HANG UP MY ROCK AND ROLL SHOES (12-72) [Chuck Willis '58 hit. ATLANTIC 1179]/ Caledonia Mission

RONNIE HAWKINS

MONUMENT

8548 CORA MAE (5-73)/Lawdy Miss Clawdy
8561 LONESOME TOWN (9-73)/Kinky
8573 BO DIDDLEY (12-73)/Lonely Hours

AS "THE BAND"

CAPITOL

3758 AIN'T GOT NO HOME (12-73) [Clarence Henry '56 hit. ARGO 5259]/Get Up Jake
3828 THIRD MAN THEME (3-74)/W. S. Walcott Medicine Show

BOB DYLAN & "THE BAND"

ASYLUM

11043 MOST LIKELY YOU'LL GO YOUR WAY (AND I'LL GO MINE) (8-74)/Stage Freight [by "The Band"]

RONNIE HAWKINS

POLYDOR

2065-303 LADY CAME FROM BALTIMORE (1976) [Bobby Darin '67 hit. ATLANTIC 2395]/Will The Circle Be Unbroken

AS "THE BAND"

CAPITOL

4230 OPHELIA (3-76)/Hobo Jungle
4316 TWILIGHT (8-76)/Acadian Driftwood
4361 GEORGIA ON MY MIND (11-76)/The Night They Drove Old Dixie Down
6246 AIN'T GOT NO HOME (1977)/Don't Do It

LEVON HELM & "THE RCO ALL-STARS"

Levon Helm (vocals, drums); Barry Beckett (keyboards); Steve Cropper (guitar); Scott Edwards (bass).

ABC

12336 MILK COW BOOGIE (2-78)/Blues So Bad

AS "THE BAND"

WARNER BROTHERS

8592 OUT OF THE BLUE (5-78)/The Well

LEVON HELM

ABC

12416 AIN'T NO WAY TO FORGET YOU (11-78)

RICK DANKO [From "THE BAND"] SOLO

ARISTA

0306 WHAT A TOWN
0320 JAVA BLUES

♭ ♯ ♪ ♩ 𝅗𝅥

Buddy Holly

Real Name: Charles Hardin Holley. Born in Lubbock, Texas, on September 7, 1936. Died in plane crash, with J. P. "Big Bopper" Richardson and Ritchie Valens, near Mason City, Iowa, on February 3, 1959.

The sounds of BUDDY HOLLY and his chirpin' "Crickets" are beloved music indeed to many fans throughout the world. His million-sellers, "Peggy Sue/Everyday" (CORAL 61885), "It Doesn't Matter Anymore [Paul Anka's composition]/Raining In My Heart" (CORAL 62074), the latter a Boudleaux & Felice Bryant composition, and the "Crickets' " own "That'll Be The Day/I'm Lookin' For Someone To Love" (BRUNSWICK 55009), "Oh Boy!/Not Fade Away" (BRUNSWICK 55035), and "Maybe Baby/Tell Me How" (BRUNSWICK 55053), all reflected a happy and fun-loving young spirit. Buddy Holly, in his writing and singing of songs, imparted a unique, hesitant, nervous, hiccuping style that was youthful and refreshing, besides being reminiscent of the good old Rock and Roll of the Fifties. Buddy was most effective with his "chord" lead guitar, his accentuated beat and rhythmic pattern effecting a combination of rhythm and lead guitar. Buddy Holly's voice, integrated into this steady rhythmic beat, was delightfully complemented by the drumming of Jerry Allison.

Buddy Holly was born the youngest of four musically talented children of Lawrence and Ella Holley. His older brother, Lawrence, was versatile at the violin and guitar, while the younger brother, Travis, played the accordion, piano, and guitar. His sister, Patricia, no doubt was also musically inclined. Buddy was encouraged from his earliest years to play the violin. At the age of eight, accompanied by his brother, Lawrence, Buddy played and sang "Down The River Of Memories" at a country fair talent show and earned a prize of five dollars!

It was during his schooling at J. T. Hutchinson Junior High that Buddy met Bob Montgomery (who played a guitar). With another schoolfriend, Larry Welborn (who played bass), and with Buddy himself playing a guitar, they formed a musical trio. The group, inspired by

Hank Williams and others, played Country-Western swing, Bluegrass, gospel, and Rhythm and Blues. During those same years, Buddy also sang with two mixed choirs, the "Choralaires" and the "Westernaires," besides his attendance at the family's fundamentalist Baptist church.

The group got a break on the local radio station, KDAV, through the owner, Dave Stone, where they performed on a weekly half-hour basis under the heading "The Buddy and Bob Show." A great event happened then for young Buddy Holly when Elvis Presley (on one of his tours through the South) came to Lubbock and Buddy had the pleasure of meeting him, but, unfortunately, he never had the opportunity of appearing or touring with Elvis. Still, in the fall of 1955 and when only nineteen, Buddy and his friends started off on a big Country show that featured "Bill Haley and the Comets," Johnny Cash, Floyd Cramer, and others. It was the Nashville talent scout for that show, Eddie Crandall, who contacted KDAV's Dave Stone to encourage Buddy Holly to make demos!

Buddy had graduated now and, besides owning a Gibson acoustic guitar, had acquired his famous fender Stratocaster guitar, along with a brand-new Oldsmobile (from his parents). He organized a new group, the "Three Tunes," comprising Jerry Allison with his drums (born in Hillsboro, Texas, August 31, 1939), Sonny Curtis and his guitar (born in Meadow, Texas, May 9, 1937), and another Texan, Don Guess, bass. They drove together to Nashville and auditioned for DECCA. Problems arose there because DECCA was a Country-oriented label and maintained a closed mind on Rock and Roll, with the result that only Country was tolerated. The "Three Tunes" recorded "Blue Days—Black Nights" with the flip-side "Love Me" (DECCA 29854) backed by Grady Martin (guitar). The studio backup band with Boots Randolph and Grady Martin was used on most of the other four singles, and this was highly unsatisfactory for Buddy Holly and the "Three Tunes." Buddy and the group went on a tour with Hank Thompson.

It was while in Clovis, New Mexico, that producer and musician Norman Petty saw the possibilities in Buddy Holly. In 1957, Buddy Holly formed his famous chirpin' "Crickets" comprising Jerry Allison (drums), Niki Sullivan (rhythm guitar), and Joe B. Mauldin (bass). Norman Petty had hopes of introducing Buddy Holly and the "Crickets" with "That'll Be The Day" on the ROULETTE label but was unsuccessful, because that label was enjoying success with Buddy Knox and Jimmy Bowen. Bob Thiele of Peer-Southern Publishing Company in New York heard the demo of "That'll Be The Day," liked it, and suggested that Buddy Holly and the "Crickets" record on separate labels, but decision problems developed between Norman Petty, Buddy Holly, and the "Crickets" almost immediately after mutual agreement to do this, resulting in confusion, disillusionment, and separation. Niki Sullivan left the group after "Maybe Baby" (BRUNSWICK 55053) and it was not until 1959 that Tommy Allsup replaced him. In the meantime, following Bob Thiele's advice, Buddy Holly and the "Crickets" recorded "That'll Be The Day/ I'm Lookin' For Someone To Love" (BRUNSWICK 55009) and other hits, such as "Think It Over" (BRUNSWICK 55072) and "It's So Easy (To Fall In Love)" (BRUNSWICK 55094).

Buddy Holly and the "Crickets" recorded quite a few hits, some of which were released before and after his accidental death, and including some of his favorites (besides the million-sellers previously mentioned): "I'm Gonna Love You Too/Listen To Me" (CORAL 61947), with "I'm Gonna Love You Too" being also popularized by the "Hullaballos" in 1965 and by Terry Jacks in 1973; "Rave On/Take Your Time" (CORAL 61985), "Heartbeat/Well . . . All Right" (CORAL 62051), with "Heartbeat" popularized by "Freddie & Dreamers" and "Herman's Hermits; "Peggy Sue Got Married/Crying, Waiting, Hoping" (CORAL 62134); "True Love Ways" (CORAL 62210), which was popularized by "Peter and Gordon" in 1965, and the excellent disc "Reminiscing" (CORAL 62329), with King Curtis on the sax.

The "Crickets" had many unforgettable recordings with and without Buddy Holly, including (besides the hits previously mentioned), "Love's Made A Fool Of You" (BRUNSWICK 55124), popularized by "Bobby Fuller Four" (which also recorded a big hit, "I Fought The Law," a composition of Sonny Curtis), "When You Ask About Love" (BRUNSWICK 55153), and also that fine entry, "More Than I Can Say" (CORAL 62198). Jerry Allison, who married the real Peggy Sue of the songs, made records under his middle name, Ivan, backed by Buddy Holly on his guitar, and Jerry Allison also backed Johnny Burnette on his hit "Dreamin' " in 1960! Jerry Allison and Sonny Curtis also backed up Eric Clapton on his album.

The "Crickets" have had a long and distinguished career both in sessions and records. Some of their later members were Earl Sinks from Odessa, Texas; Jerry Naylor, who was born in Stephenville, Texas, on March 6, 1939; pianist Glen D. Hardin, who was born in Wellington, Texas, on April 18, 1938; Buzz Cason (see Discography information); and Steve Krikorian; and they were backed by Glen Campbell (guitar) and Leon Russell (piano) in the Sixties.

In 1958, twenty-two-year-old Buddy Holly married his Puerto Rican sweetheart, Maria Elena Santiago, and the happy couple moved to New York City. Buddy Holly joined the touring "Nation's Top Rock'n'Roll Artists," which included J. P. "Big Bopper" Richardson (real name, Jape Richardson, a Beaumont, Texas, disc jockey) of "Chantilly Lace" fame; seventeen-year-old Ritchie Valens (real name, Ritchie Valenzuela, born in Los Angeles, California) of "Donna" fame, along with "Dion & Belmonts," Waylon Jennings, and others.

The big tragedy came suddenly and unexpectedly very late on the evening of February 3, 1958, at the close of another wonderful performance of the tour at the Surf Ballroom, Mason City, Iowa, with the entire group very happy but extremely tired. Everybody dreaded the long bus trip to Fargo, and someone suggested hiring a plane so that they could get there early and have a good rest before the next show. One group agreed to the idea, comprising Buddy Holly, Ritchie Valens and "Big Bopper" Richardson, and Mr. and Mrs. Carrol Anderson (who operate the Surf Ballroom) volunteered to drive the happy group out to Dwyer Flying Service's hangar outside of Mason City, where they joined pilot Roger Peterson and the waiting Beechcraft Bonanza.

The Andersons stood around and waved goodbye as they took off into the thirty-five-mile-per-hour wind and quickening snowfall. The plane crashed not too far away from Mason City and all of these young talented people were found dead in or around the wreckage. Well, we shall remember them just as Don McLean sings in "American Pie": "IT WAS THIS DAY THE MUSIC DIED."

Discography

BUDDY HOLLY AND THE "CRICKETS"
(Shown Individually and Collectively)

SONNY CURTIS

CORAL

60954 SOMEDAY YOU'RE GONNA BE SORRY (1954)/Forever Yours
61023 NO MORE TEARS (1954)/Best Way To Hold A Girl

BUDDY HOLLY and "THREE TUNES"

DECCA

29854 BLUE DAYS—BLACK NIGHTS (4-56)/Love Me [W. Grady Martin, rhythm guitar]
30166* MODERN DON JUAN (12-56)/You Are My One Desire

*Studio band backup from Boots Randolph, sax; Grady Martin, guitar.

CORAL

61852 WORDS OF LOVE (7-57)/Mailman, Bring Me No More Blues

"CRICKETS"

BRUNSWICK

55009 THAT'LL BE THE DAY (8-57)/I'm Lookin' For Someone To Love

BUDDY HOLLY (Backed by "THREE TUNES")

DECCA

30434 THAT'LL BE THE DAY (9-57)/Rock Around With Ollie Vee

BUDDY HOLLY

CORAL

61885 PEGGY SUE (10-57)/Everyday

"CRICKETS"

BRUNSWICK

55035 OH BOY! (11-57)/Not Fade Away

BUDDY HOLLY (Backed by "THREE TUNES")

DECCA

30543 YOU ARE MY ONE DESIRE (1-58)/Love

BUDDY HOLLY

CORAL

61947 I'M GONNA LOVE YOU TOO (2-58)/Listen To Me

"CRICKETS"

BRUNSWICK

55053 MAYBE BABY (2-58)/Tell Me How

NIKI SULLIVAN

DOT

15751 IT'S ALL OVER (4-58)/Three Steps To Heaven

BUDDY HOLLY

CORAL

61985 RAVE ON (5-58)/Take Your Time

BUDDY HOLLY (Backed by "THREE TUNES")

DECCA

30650 TING-A-LING (6-58)/Girl On My Mind

"CRICKETS"

BRUNSWICK

55072 THINK IT OVER (7-58)/Fool's Paradise

BUDDY HOLLY

CORAL

62006 EARLY IN THE MORNING (8-58) [Bobby Darin and "Rinky Dinks" '58 hit. ATCO 6121]/Now We're One

SONNY CURTIS

DOT

15754 WRONG AGAIN (1958)/Laughing Stock
15799 PRETTY GIRL (9-58)/Willa Mae Jones

IVAN (JERRY ALLISON)

CORAL

62017 OH YOU BEAUTIFUL DOLL (9-58)/Real Wild Child

"CRICKETS"

BRUNSWICK

55094 IT'S SO EASY (TO FALL IN LOVE) (9-58)/Lonesome Tears

BUDDY HOLLY

CORAL

62051 HEARTBEAT (1-59)/Well . . . All Right

"CRICKETS" (WITHOUT BUDDY HOLLY)

BRUNSWICK

55124 LOVE'S MADE A FOOL OF YOU (2-59)/Someone, Someone

BUDDY HOLLY

CORAL

62074 IT DOESN'T MATTER ANYMORE (2-59)/Raining In My Heart

IVAN (JERRY ALLISON)

62081 FRANKIE FRANKENSTEIN (3-59)/That'll Be Alright

BUDDY HOLLY

62134 PEGGY SUE GOT MARRIED (7-59)/Crying, Waiting, Hoping

"CRICKETS"

BRUNSWICK

55153 WHEN YOU ASK ABOUT LOVE (10-59)/Deborah

CORAL

62198 MORE THAN I CAN SAY (1960)/Baby My Heart

SONNY CURTIS

62207 TALK ABOUT MY BABY (5-60)/The Red-Headed Stranger

BUDDY HOLLY

62210 TRUE LOVE WAYS (6-60)/That Makes It Tough
62238 DON'T CHA KNOW (1960)/Peggy Sue Got Married
62283 (Canadian) YOU'RE SO SQUARE (1961) [Elvis tune "(You're So Square) Baby, I Don't Care"]/Valley Of Tears

"CRICKETS"

LIBERTY

55385 HE'S OLD ENOUGH TO KNOW BETTER (11-61)/I'm Feeling Better
55441 DON'T EVER CHANGE (4-62)/I'm Not A Bad Guy [Feat. Glen Campbell on guitar]

BUDDY HOLLY

CORAL

62329 REMINISCING (9-62)/Wait Till The Sun Shines, Nellie

"CRICKETS"

LIBERTY

55492 PARISIAN GIRL (10-62)/I Believe In You
55495 LITTLE HOLLYWOOD GIRL (12-62)/Parisian Girl
55540 MY LITTLE GIRL (4-63)/Teardrops Fall Like Rain

BUDDY HOLLY

CORAL

62352 TRUE LOVE WAYS (4-63)/Bo Diddley

"CRICKETS"

LIBERTY

55603 APRIL AVENUE (8-63)/Don't Say You Love Me

BUDDY HOLLY

CORAL

62369 WISHING (9-63)/Brown-Eyed Handsome Man

SONNY CURTIS

DIMENSION

1017 SO USED TO LOVING YOU (1963)/Last Song I'm Ever Gonna Sing

BUDDY HOLLY

CORAL

62390 ROCK AROUND WITH OLLIE VEE (1-64)/I'm Gonna Love You Too

"CRICKETS"

LIBERTY

55660 LONELY AVENUE (1-64)/You Can't Be In-Between
55668 PLEASE PLEASE ME (2-64)/From Me To You [Both "Beatles" hits]

SONNY CURTIS

DIMENSION

1024 A BEATLE I WANT TO BE (1964)/So Used To Loving You

BUDDY HOLLY

CORAL

62407 NOT FADE AWAY (1964)/Maybe Baby

"CRICKETS"

LIBERTY

55696 LA BAMBA (5-64)/All Over You
55742 I THINK I'VE CAUGHT THE BLUES (11-64)/We Gotta Get Together

JERRY ALLISON & "CRICKETS"

55767 EVERYBODY'S GOT A LITTLE PROBLEM (2-65)/Now Hear

BUDDY HOLLY

CORAL

62448 WHAT TO DO (3-65)/Slippin' And Slidin'

SONNY CURTIS (SOLOS)

VIVA

602 MY WAY OF LIFE (7-66)/Last Call
607 DESTINY'S CHILD (3-67)/The Collector
617 I WANNA GO BUMMIN' AROUND (10-67)/Gypsy Man
626 ATLANTA GEORGIA STRAY (11-68)/Day Drinker
630 THE STRAIGHT LIFE (1969)/How Little Men Care
634 DAY GIG (1969)/Holiday For Clowns
636 GIRL OF THE NORTH (1969)/Hung Up In Your Eyes

"CRICKETS"

MUSIC FACTORY

415 MILLION DOLLAR MOVIE (1968)/A Million Miles Away

BUDDY HOLLY

CORAL

62554 RAVE ON (7-68)/Early In The Morning
62558 LOVE IS STRANGE (3-69) [Mickey & Sylvia '56 hit. GROOVE 0175]/You Are The One
62618 I'M LOOKIN' FOR SOMEONE TO LOVE (1969)/That'll Be The Day

"CRICKETS"

BARNABY

2061 TRUE LOVE WAYS (3-72)/Rockin' '50's Drummer

MGM

14541 WASN'T IT NICE IN NEW YORK CITY (5-73)/Hayride

"BUDDY HOLLY & THE CRICKETS"

MCA

60000 I'M LOOKIN' FOR SOMEONE TO LOVE/That'll Be The Day
60004 EVERYDAY/Peggy Sue
40905 IT DOESN'T MATTER ANYMORE (5-78)/Peggy Sue

NIKI SULLIVAN (ADDITIONAL SOLOS)

JUBILEE

5441 I CRY ALL THE TIME [Niki and Gene Evans]/Then Came The Fall [The "Hollyhawks"]

JOLIE

074 DO THE DIVE [Ronnie Fuller with Niki Sullivan on guitar]
075 IT REALLY DOESN'T MATTER/You Better Get A Move On

BUZZ CASON (ONE OF "CRICKETS"): Discography from the Beginning
BUZZ CASON WITH "CASUALS"

NU-SOUND

101* HELP ME (1957)/My Love Song For You

DOT

TILL YOU COME BACK TO ME (1957)/Hello Love

GROUP AS "(ORIGINAL) CASUALS"

BACK BEAT

503 SO TOUGH (1958)/I Love My Darling

---

*Released on DOT 15557.

(WITH GROUP) "STATUES" [Feat. Buzz Cason as "GARY MILES"]

LIBERTY

55245 BLUE VELVET (4-60)/Keep The Hall Light Burning

As Alias "GARY MILES"

55261 LOOK FOR A STAR (6-60) [Deane Hawley '60 hit. DORE 554]/Afraid Of Love

As Alias "GARY MILLS"

IMPERIAL

5674* LOOK FOR A STAR (6-60)

(WITH GROUP) "STATUES"

LIBERTY

55279 DREAM GIRL (9-60)/Wishing Well
55292 WHITE CHRISTMAS (12-60)/Jeanie With The Light Brown Hair
55363 THE COMMANDMENTS OF LOVE (1961)/Love At First Sight

As Alias "GARY MILES"

55596 CANDY (8-63)/Do The Bug
55714 ECSTASY (6-64)/Here Goes A Fool

(BUZZ CASON in) "BUZZ AND BUCKY"

AMY

924 TIGER A-GO GO (1965)/Bay City

---

*The record had much success in Britain on TOP RANK label, and was featured in the horror movie *Circus of Horrors*.

BUZZ CASON

WARNER BROTHERS

5663 WHERE WAS LOVE (10-65)/Endless Circle

MONUMENT

938 COME TO ME (1966)/The Good Side Of June
954 WATERMELON (1967)/Good Humor Man

(BUZZ CASON in) "BUZZ AND TRACI"

ELF

90005 MY GIRL, MY GIRL (1967)/Where's My Baby

BUZZ CASON

90026 TONIGHT (2-69)/Debbie And Cherry
90032 NASHVILLE IN THE SUMMER (1969)/Adam and Eve
90036 FUNKY STREET BAND (PLAY IT LOUDER)/Adam And Eve

MEGA

615-0029 TURNING YOUR BACK ON ME/Bilpie

CAPRICE

1002 TEXAS/Heavy Dudes And Heartaches
1974 RACE DRIVIN' MAN/Come Back
2001 RAPID ROY (THE STOCK CAR BOY)/Radial Racer

BERRY HILL

080 THE DEVIL'S TRIANGLE

JANUS

258 PLACES/No Place For A Lady

JERRY NAYLOR (ONE OF "CRICKETS")

SKYLA

1118 STOP YOUR CRYING ('62)/You're Thirteen
1123 JUDEE MALONE ('62)/I'm Tired

MELODYLAND

6012 HE'LL HAVE TO GO (1975)/Once Again

Luther Ingram

Real Name: "Luther Thomas Ingram." Born in Jackson, Tennessee, on November 30, 1944.

LUTHER INGRAM recorded his biggest hit in 1972, with his dramatic million-selling ballad "(If Loving You Is Wrong) I Don't Want To Be Right" (KOKO 2111). He has recorded many Soul gems for the KOKO label (a subsidiary of STAX label), with his first hit being "My Honey And Me" (KOKO 2104). It was Johnny Baylor himself, KOKO label owner, who took note of Luther's ability in New York City in 1964 and remembered him when he formed that label in 1967. Luther Ingram was signed and ever since has become KOKO's biggest hit-maker!

Luther Ingram had his roots in Gospel singing with his three brothers, and it was really producers Jerry Leiber and Mike Stoller who brought him to SMASH label, from whence Luther recorded the 1965 disc "I Was A Spy (For the FBI)/Foxy Devil" (SMASH 2019). "Foxy Devil" was a very catchy uptempo item. Another much sought-after collectible Soul entry was "Exus Trek" (HIB 698).

Several of Luther Ingram's releases during the 1970s deserve honorable mention: "Ain't That Loving You (For More Reasons Than One)" (KOKO 2105) [also popularized in 1972 by Isaac Hayes and David Porter (ENTERPRISE 9049)]; "Be Good To Me Baby" (KOKO 2107); "I'll Love You Until The End" (KOKO 2108); and a real top-notch soulful classic, "Ain't Good For Nothing (But Loving You)" (KOKO 700 Series 721).

Luther Ingram was originally a studio singer who developed a unique style much in the polished fashion of the late Sam Cooke. He was featured in the film *Watts Tax,* as well as having his composition "Respect Yourself" recorded by the "Staple Singers," and his lesser-known "Help Me Love" was recorded by Isaac Hayes.

Discography

LUTHER INGRAM & THE G-MEN

SMASH

2019	I WAS A SPY (FOR THE FBI) (1965)/Foxy Devil

LUTHER INGRAM

DECCA

3179	YOU NEVER MISS YOUR WATER (1965) (William Bell '62 hit. STAX 116)/Ain't That Nice

HIB

698	IF IT'S ALL THE SAME TO YOU, BABE (2-67)/Exus Trek

KOKO

2101	LOOKING FOR A NEW LOVE (1-69)/You Can Depend On Me
2102	PITY FOR THE LONELY (5-69)/Looking For A New Love
2103	PUTTIN' GAME DOWN (1969)/Since You Don't Want Me
2104	MY HONEY AND ME (12-69)/I Can't Stop
2105	AIN'T THAT LOVING YOU (FOR MORE REASONS THAN ONE) (5-70)/Home Don't Seem Like Home
2106	TO THE OTHER MAN (10-70)/I'll Just Call You Honey
2107	BE GOOD TO ME BABY (5-71)/Since You Don't Want Me
2108	I'LL LOVE YOU UNTIL THE END (11-71)/Ghetto Train
2110	MISSING YOU (2-72)/You Were Made For Me
2111	(IF LOVING YOU IS WRONG) I DON'T WANT TO BE RIGHT (5-72)/Puttin' Game Down
2113	I'LL BE YOUR SHELTER (IN TIME OF STORM) (11-72)/I Can't Stop
2115	ALWAYS (4-73)/Help Me Love
2116	LOVE AIN'T GONNA RUN ME AWAY (7-73)/To The Other Man

KOKO (700 Series)

721	AIN'T GOOD FOR NOTHING (BUT LOVING YOU) (7-76)/These Are The Things
724	LET'S STEAL AWAY TO THE HIDEAWAY (4-77)/I've Got Your Love In My Life
725	I LIKE THE FEELING (8-77)/I'm Gonna Be The Best Thing
728	DO YOU LOVE SOMEBODY (12-77)/How I Miss My Baby
731	GET TO ME (5-78)

♭♯♪♩𝅗𝅥

"Intruders"

MEMBERS: Samuel "Little Sonny" Brown (lead singer 1961-70; replaced by Bobby Starr, who was born in Baltimore, Maryland, January 19, 1937); Eugene "Bird" Daughtry, born in Kingston, North Carolina, October 29, 1939; Robert "Big Sonny" Edwards, born in Philadelphia, Pennsylvania, February 22, 1947; Phil Terry, born in Philadelphia, Pennsylvania, November 1, 1943.

Hometown: Philadelphia, Pennsylvania.

The "INTRUDERS" were initially a street-singing Doo-Wopp quintet performing at local dances until their discovery by Michael Gowen and, because of their talent, being signed under contract as the "Four Intruders" to GOWEN label. Their first record, "Come Home Soon" (GOWEN 1401), became a regional No. 1 smash and lasted for a couple of months on the Charts. Group manager Leroy Lovette (who, in the early Sixties, produced for "Patti & the Emblems" and also developed Leon Huff in production and session techniques), guided the "Intruders' " career and produced their 1964 release "But You Belong To Me" (MUSIC VOICE 504).

When Leon Huff and Kenny Gamble formed EXCEL label, the "Intruders" were introduced to that label with "Gonna Be Strong" (EXCEL 101). This proved another Philly hit, and EXCEL label became the GAMBLE label! Gamble and Huff formed their own working production company with their first experimental group, the "Intruders." This led to several Soul releases: "(We'll Be) United" (GAMBLE 201), "Devil With An Angel's Smile" (GAMBLE 203), "It Must Be Love" (GAMBLE 204), "Together" (GAMBLE 205), "Baby, I'm Lonely" (GAMBLE 209), and on toward the "Intruders' " first million-seller in that beautiful sophisticated uptempo classic "Cowboys To Girls" (GAMBLE 214)! This was the introduction to the "PHILADELPHIA SOUND" that would highlight a very successful Seventies period not only for the "Intruders" but also for other groups—the "O'Jays," the "Blue Notes," the "Ebonys," and "Archie Bell & Drells," and so on—all with that same winning production and arrangement hit formula used by Leon Huff and Kenny Gamble!

The "Intruders" kept Chart action alive with "(Love Is Like A) Baseball Game" (GAMBLE 217), "Slow Drag" (GAMBLE 221), and numerous releases until the TOP-TEN OLDIES Revival hit "When We Get Married" (GAMBLE 4004). That same year "Little Sonny" Brown left the group to get married, but returned in 1971 to be featured on two singles, "Pray For Me" (GAMBLE 4014) and "I Bet He Don't Love You (Like I Love You)" (GAMBLE 4016), and then left again to engage in a solo career. Bobby Starr, with intro "I'm Girl Scoutin' " (GAMBLE 4009) and lead singing vocals of distinctive beauty, went on to a highly successful group climax with these Disco-paced winners: "(Win, Place Or Show) She's A Winner" (PHIL-INT. 2212), that fabulous release "I'll Always Love My Mama" (PHIL-INT. 2506), and, lastly, "I Wanna Know Your Name" (PHIL-INT. 2508). The "Intruders" have always remained a top-notch harmony group, with that special high-pitched falsetto vocal excitement!

Discography

AS "FOUR INTRUDERS"

GOWEN

1401 COME HOME SOON (1961)/I'm Sold On You
1404 THIS IS MY SONG (1962)/My Baby

AS "INTRUDERS"

MUSIC VOICE

504 BUT YOU BELONG TO ME (1964)/Smart Too Late

EXCEL

101 GONNA BE STRONG (1965)/All The Time

GAMBLE

201 (WE'LL BE) UNITED (7-66) ["Lovenotes" '57 tune. HOLIDAY 2605]/Up And Down The Ladder
203 DEVIL WITH AN ANGEL'S SMILE (10-66)/A Book For The Broken Hearted
204 IT MUST BE LOVE (1-67)/(You'd Better) Check Yourself
205 TOGETHER (4-67)/Up And Down The Ladder

209 BABY, I'M LONELY (9-67)/A Love That's Real
214 COWBOYS TO GIRLS (3-68)/Turn The Hands of Time
217 (LOVE IS LIKE A) BASEBALL GAME (7-68)/Friends No More
221 SLOW DRAG (11-68)/So Glad I'm Yours
223 GIVE HER A TRANSPLANT (2-69)/Girls, Girls, Girls
225 ME TARZAN, YOU JANE (5-69)/(Who's Your) Favorite Candidate
231 LOLLIPOP (I LIKE YOU) (6-69)/Don't Give It Away
235 SAD GIRL (9-69)/Let's Go Downtown
240 EVERY DAY IS A HOLIDAY (12-69) ["Hollywood Saxons" '63 hit. 20th CENTURY 312]/Old Love
4001 TENDER (WAS THE LOVE WE KNEW) (4-70)/By The Time I Get To Phoenix
4004 WHEN WE GET MARRIED (6-70) ["Dreamlovers" '61 hit. HERITAGE 102]/(Love Doctor) Doctor, Doctor
4007 THIS IS MY LOVE SONG (10-70)/Let Me In Your Mind
4009 I'M GIRL SCOUTIN' (2-71)/Wonder What Kind Of Bag She's In
4014 PRAY FOR ME (6-71)/Best Days Of My Life
4016 I BET HE DON'T LOVE YOU (LIKE I LOVE YOU) (9-71)/Do You Remember Yesterday
4019 MEMORIES ARE HERE TO STAY (1972) [Also GAMBLE 672]/(Win, Place Or Show) She's A Winner

PHILADELPHIA INTERNATIONAL—CBS

2212 (WIN, PLACE OR SHOW) SHE'S A WINNER (8-72) [Also PHIL-INT. 2501]/Memories Are Here To Stay
2506 I'LL ALWAYS LOVE MY MAMA (5-73)/I'll Always Love My Mama [Part 2]
2508 I WANNA KNOW YOUR NAME (10-73)/Hang On In There

"LITTLE SONNY" SOLO

ENTERPRISE

9092 MY WOMAN IS GOOD TO ME (3-74)/It's Hard Goin' Up

"INTRUDERS"

GAMBLE

5751 I WANNA KNOW YOUR NAME (1974)/I'll Always Love My Mama

T.S.O.P.—EPIC

8-4758 A NICE GIRL LIKE YOU (10-74)/To Be Happy Is The Real Thing
8-4766 RAINY DAYS AND MONDAYS (5-75) ["Carpenters" '71 hit. A&M 1260]/Be On Time
8-4771 ENERGY OF LOVE (10-75)/Plain Ol' Fashioned Girl

Syl Johnson

Real Name: "Sylvester Thompson." Born in Holly Springs, Mississippi, on July 1, 1939.

SYL JOHNSON is not only a soulful master of song with his own strong following in Chicago, but he is also a superstar throughout his native South. An active guitarist, writer of lyrics and music, he also produced top Soul artists and works such as Otis Clay (ONE-DER-FUL), "Dynamic Tints" (TWINIGHT), Tyrone Davis (DAKAR), "The Notations" (TWINIGHT), Simtec & Wylie's "Do It Like Mama" (SHAMA 4003), and "Plain And Simple Girl/Hey Cloud" (COTILLION 44098) for Garland Green. A natural product of that musical country, within thirty-five miles of Memphis, Syl Johnson grew up early listening to the sound of his grandfather's music (organ, guitar, and harmonica), who, Syl claimed, "played the harmonica as good as Little Walter!" Both he and his brother Jimmy ("The Deacon") learned to strum on Matt "Guitar" Murphy's guitar, and it was Jimmy who gave us "Don't Slam The Door [Parts 1 & 2]" (MAGNIM 719). Syl also produced for the "Radiants" and played guitar on sessions. Through his fascination with his musical father and Little Walter, Syl Johnson also learned to master the harmonica.

When Syl Johnson was around eight years of age the family moved to Chicago, where he and his brothers, Mac and Jimmy, eventually "jammed" with Magic Sam, Eddie Boyd, Elmore James, Big Boy Arnold, and Junior Wells. Magic Sam lived next door to the Thompsons, and it was there, at a time when Sam was only playing hillbilly and ragtime music, that young Syl Johnson introduced him to fingering of the Blues. Syl himself claims his first engagement was with Shaky Joe, the harmonica player (where he played with Big Boy Arnold and Junior Wells), but his "first real gig" was with Eddie Boyd, where he fitted in with his guitar. Then Syl played with Elmore James and recorded with him. Syl Johnson enjoyed singing Rock and Roll after the style of his two idols, Jackie Wilson and Little Richard, to play his guitar or harmonica, up until the coming of his big Soul revue backup band!

In 1960, Syl Johnson recorded his first record, "Teardrops/They Who Have Love" (FEDERAL 12358), for the KING subsidiary label, both songs written by Howard Scott and produced by Ralph Bass with Lefty Baker on guitar, but with little success. Syl had moderate regional success with "I Got Love" (FEDERAL 12374) and "I Resign From Your Love" (FEDERAL 12454). After his stint with the FEDERAL label, Syl Johnson got his chance as producer with Ronnie Roker, Rennie Roker, and "Magnificent Montague" (Nathaniel Montague, who ran some forty U.S. stations and was a very influential man) and their TAG LTD. label by producing his first recording, the Soul Rocker "Straight Love—No Chaser" (TAG X-1), a great sound!

Rodney Jones (deejay at Station WVON, Chicago) introduced Syl Johnson to TWINIGHT label, where Paul Glass (distributor of TWINIGHT and BUCKINGHAM labels), U.S.A. label owner, had him make several releases for subsidiary TWILIGHT (later TWINIGHT) label. There, Syl Johnson had his biggest hit with "Come On Sock It To Me" (TWILIGHT 100), which was written by Jo Armstead, with music by Syl himself, and featuring Wayne Bennett, Bobby Bland's old guitarist; the flip side "Try Me" was arranged by Fontella Bass, who gave us the 1965 hit "Rescue Me" (CHECKER 1120). Another Soul favorite, "Different Strokes," (TWILIGHT 103), originally written by John Zachery, was accompanied by Freddy Robinson (of Seventies "Black Fox" fame), (WORLD PACIFIC JAZZ 88155) and Bryce Roberts on guitar. Both of these Soul records became classics!

Syl Johnson then co-wrote (with Carl Smith) "Dresses Too Short" (TWINIGHT 110) and produced "Don't Give It Away" (TWINIGHT 118); the flip-side "Going To The Shack," written by Graham Watts, was produced by Jimmy (Syl's brother) and both sides arranged by Jerry Wilson. Then came the exceptional black-appealing "Is It Because I'm Black" (TWINIGHT 125), arranged by Syl, with Jimmy Jones on guitar, and backed by the "Pieces of Peace" band. His "One Way Ticket To Nowhere" (TWINIGHT 134) was written by Johnny Moore (of the "Drifters") and the flip-side "Kiss By Kiss" was written by Bernard Reed (of the "Chi-Lites") and arranged by the late Donny Hathaway. Syl then recorded "Annie Got Hot Pants Power [Parts 1 & 2]" (TWINIGHT 151), which brought an unknown songwriter, Earl Randall, to the fore, who eventually wrote one of Syl Johnson's biggest hits, "Anyway The Wind Blows" (HI 2229).

It was in 1969 that Willie Mitchell (who took over HI RECORDS after death of Joe Cuoghi) heard and liked the performance of Syl Johnson at Chicago's Burning Spear and at the old Club Delisa. Syl expressed happiness with this label, where Willie and James Mitchell not only handle the arrangement but James keeps playing baritone on all recordings and Willie (now stopped playing) is engineer and A&R man. It was here that Syl Johnson found his true groove with "Back For A Taste Of Yor Love" (HI 2250), "Take You Home (To See

Mama)" (HI 2275), and the great-sounding "Take Me To The River" (HI 2285).

Syl Johnson is still an underrated artist with tremendous natural talent who is yet to be fully appreciated, striving to give a sound in beat with his times. His sound, though Bluesy, is not really Blues but has an uptempo thing all of its own and something different. The Southland is still Syl Johnson's best market because they know who he is, understand his music, and appreciate him! His "Mystery Lady" (HI 79529) is one of the exceptional disco records and sounds of today.

Discography

SYL JOHNSON

FEDERAL

12358	TEARDROPS (1960)/They Who Have Love
12374	I GOT LOVE (1960)/Lonely Man
12435	GOTTA MAKE HER MINE (1961)/I've Got To Find My Baby
12454	I RESIGN FROM YOUR LOVE (1962)/Little Sally Walker
12474	WELL OH WELL (1963)/I Wanna Know
12476	I'M LOOKING FOR MY BABY (1963)/Please

TMP-TING

115	FALLING IN LOVE AGAIN (1965)/I've Got To Get Over You

TAG LTD.

X-1	STRAIGHT LOVE—NO CHASER (1966)/Surrounded

TWILIGHT

100	COME ON SOCK IT TO ME (7-67)/Try Me
103	DIFFERENT STROKES (9-67)/Sorry 'Bout Dat

TWINIGHT

106	ODE TO A SOUL MAN (1968)/I'll Take Those Skinny Legs
108	I FEEL AN URGE (1968) [W. Jackie Ross]/Try Me
110	DRESSES TOO SHORT (11-68)/I Can Take Care Of Business
116	I CAN TAKE CARE OF HOMEWORK (3-69)/Take Me Back
118	DON'T GIVE IT AWAY (7-69)/Going To The Shack
125	IS IT BECAUSE I'M BLACK (11-79)/Let Them Hang High
129	CONCRETE RESERVATION (2-70)/Together Forever
134	ONE WAY TICKET TO NOWHERE (6-70)/Kiss By Kiss
144	WE DO IT TOGETHER (1-71)/Thank You Baby

149 GET READY (4-71) ["Temptations" '66 hit. GORDY 7049]/Some Kind Of Thing
151 ANNIE GOT HOT PANTS POWER (9-71)/Annie Got Hot Pants Power [Part 2]

HI

2201 THE LOVE YOU LEFT BEHIND (11-71)/Anyone But You

TWINIGHT

155 THAT'S WHY (1-72) [Jackie Wilson '59 hit. BRUNSWICK 55121]/Everybody Needs Love

HI

2208 THE LOVE YOU LEFT BEHIND (1-72)/Anyone But You
2215 I WANNA SATISFY YOUR EVERY NEED (6-72)/Age Ain't Nothing But A Number
2229 WE DID IT (12-72)/Anyway The Wind Blows
2250 BACK FOR A TASTE OF YOUR LOVE (9-73)/Wind, Blow Her Back My Way
2260 ANYONE BUT YOU (1974)/I'm Yours
2269 LET YOURSELF GO (8-74)/Please Don't Give Up On Me
2275 TAKE YOU HOME (TO SEE MAMA) (11-74)/I Hear The Love Chimes
2285 TAKE ME TO THE RIVER (6-75)/Could I Be Falling In Love
2295 I ONLY HAVE LOVE (1975)/Come On Home
2304 STARBRIGHT, STARLITE (1976)/That's Just My Luck
2308 'BOUT TO MAKE ME LEAVE HOME (1976)/It Ain't Easy

SHAMA

1235 GOODIE-GOODIE-GOOD TIMES (6-77)

HI

78507 FONK YOU (12-77)/That Wiggle
78517 STAND BY ME (8-78) [Ben E. King '61 hit. ATCO 6194]
79529 MYSTERY LADY (3-79)/Let's Dance For Love

♭♯♪♩𝅗𝅥

Ben E. King

Real Name: "Benjamin Earl Nelson." **Born in Henderson, North Carolina, on September 23, 1938.**

The amiable Mr. BEN E. KING has been singing professionally since his twentieth year, 1958. Over that time he has gone from a teen baritone to almost a bass voice in the Seventies, but he has always delivered that smooth cool soulful note with an overlapping effect, much like an artist in the process of developing a masterpiece. He was reared in Henderson, North Carolina, until the age of eleven, when his family moved to New York City. There, his father opened a luncheonette in Harlem, where Ben worked as a youngster and sang. It was in 1956 that Lover Patterson discovered Ben's singing ability and asked him to join his black harmony group, the "5 Crowns." Ben E. King left Seward Park High School before graduation to replace James Clark on the recording of "Popcorn Willie" (CARAVAN 15609). The group, later, dropped "5" from the title, to become simply the "Crowns" on "Kiss And Make Up" (R&B 6901).

In 1959, George Treadwell (manager of the "Drifters") brought the "Crowns" to become the newly formed "Drifters," and soon Jerry Wexler and ATLANTIC label assigned producers Jerry Leiber and Mike Stoller to work with the group. It was Jerry Wexler who decided to go with Ben E. King as lead vocal on the very first recording, "There Goes My Baby" (ATLANTIC 2025), principally because in having written the song Ben could best relate to the "Latin-beat concerto rhythm," and this became a giant hit for the "Drifters" and was acclaimed as the first major Rhythm and Blues group recording to incorporate strings in the background.

ATLANTIC RECORDS had a distinct way of using many different musicians for nearly every session, and its use of the "Drifters" was no exception on the following recordings featuring Ben E. King: "Dance With Me" (ATLANTIC 2040), "This Magic Moment" (ATLANTIC 2050), "Lonely Winds" (ATLANTIC 2062), "Save The Last Dance For Me" (ATLANTIC 2071), "I Count The Tears" (ATLANTIC 2087), and "Sometimes I Wonder" (ATLANTIC 2051), which was released later in 1962. Both "Save The Last Dance For Me" and "I Count The Tears" were written by Doc Pomus and Mort Shuman. "Save The Last Dance For Me" introduced "THE WALL OF SOUND" produced by ATLANTIC with A&R man (and session guitarist) at the time, Phil Spector.

Ben E. King left the "Drifters" in May 1960 to pursue a solo career with his debut "Brace Yourself" (ATCO 6166), which was followed by the Top-Ten national hit "Spanish Harlem" (ATCO 6185), a Leiber/Spector composition and produced by Phil Spector. It was beautifully sung by Ben E. King and greatly enhanced by that Latin-rhythm sound! His "Stand By Me" (ATCO 6194) became and remains a standard, and it seems every big recording artist aspires to do a cover version of a Ben E. King hit, with "Spanish Harlem" being covered by Aretha Franklin, Freddie Scott and others, while "Stand By Me" was covered by Spyder Turner, Ruffin Brothers, John Lennon, Cassius Clay, and so on.

The lovely "Amor" (ATCO 6203), "Don't Play That Song (You Lied)" (ATCO 6222), and "I (Who Have Nothing)" (ATCO 6267) were three of Ben E. King's early hits. The second of these was written by Ben's wife, Betty, and the third sold a million copies for Tom Jones (PARROT 40051) in 1970. Several other notable entries of Ben E. King include "That's When It Hurts" (ATCO 6288), "Goodnight My Love" (ATCO 6390), "What Is Soul" (ATCO 6454), "Tears, Tears, Tears" (ATCO 6472), "Katherine" (ATCO 6493), and the 1975 hit "Supernatural Thing" (ATLANTIC 3241). Many of Ben E. King's compositions were co-written with Bob Gallo, e.g., "What Is Soul" (ATCO 6454). Tony Silvester (of the group "Main Ingredient") and Bert de Coteaux produced a fantastic job on "Supernatural Thing."

In the late Seventies, ATLANTIC label decided to put Ben E. King with the "Average White Band" and it proved to be a winning combination, giving us "Get It Up (For Love)" (ATLANTIC 3402), "A Star In The Ghetto" (ATLANTIC 3427), and "A Fool For You Anyway" (ATLANTIC 3444), with the second of these an extended Disco play and terrific dance favorite. Ben E. King lives today in Teaneck, New Jersey, with Betty, his wife, and family, and performs at R&R revivals and nightclubs in the U.S., Canada, Britain, and Europe.

Discography

AS "5 CROWNS"

Wilbur "Yonkie Paul" Pharr, lead vocal;
Ben E. King, baritone; Nicky Clark, tenor;
Doc Green, bass.

CARAVAN

15609 POPCORN WILLIE (1957)/I Can't Pretend [A & B. Feat. Wilbur Pharr]

AS "CROWNS"

James Clark, lead vocal; Charlie Thomas, lead vocal;
Ben E. King, baritone; Doc Green, bass;
Ellsberry Hobbs, bass.

R & B

6901 KISS AND MAKE UP (1958) [Feat. Charlie Thomas]/I'll Forget About You [Feat. James Clark]

AS "DRIFTERS"

Ben E. King, lead vocal; Charlie Thomas, tenor;
Ellsberry Hobbs, bass; Doc Green, baritone; and
Reggie Kimber, guitar.

ATLANTIC

2025 THERE GOES MY BABY (6-59)/Oh My Love [A&B. Feat. Ben E. King]
[*The above recording had also King Curtis on tenor sax.*]

Ben E. King, lead tenor; Johnny Lee Williams, lead tenor;
Charlie Thomas, tenor; Ellsberry Hobbs, bass;
Billy Davis (Abdul Samad), guitar.

[*Above personnel also on "Save The Last Dance For Me" and "I Count The Tears."*]

2040 (IF YOU CRY) TRUE LOVE, TRUE LOVE (10-59) [Feat. Johnny Lee Williams]/Dance With Me [Feat. Ben E. King]

2050 THIS MAGIC MOMENT (2-60) [Feat. Ben E. King]/Baltimore [Feat. Charlie Thomas]

2062 LONELY WINDS (5-60) [Feat. Ben E. King]/Hey Señorita [Feat. Charlie Thomas]
[*"Baltimore" and "Hey Señorita" were recorded at an earlier 1959 session.*]

AS LAVERN BAKER & BEN E. KING

2067 A HELP-EACH OTHER ROMANCE (8-60)/How Often

AS "DRIFTERS"

2071 SAVE THE LAST DANCE FOR ME (9-60)/Nobody But Me [A&B. Feat. Ben E. King]

BEN E. KING

ATCO

6166 BRACE YOURSELF (9-60)/Show Me The Way

AS "DRIFTERS"

ATLANTIC

2087 I COUNT THE TEARS (12-60) [Feat. Ben E. King]/Suddenly There's A Valley [A Bobby Hendricks/Bill Pinkney duet]
["Suddenly There's A Valley" by Bobby Hendricks/Bill Pinkney recorded 1958.]

BEN E. KING

ATCO

6185 SPANISH HARLEM (1-61)/First Taste Of Love
6194 STAND BY ME (5-61)/On The Horizon
6203 AMOR (8-61)/Souvenir Of Mexico
6207 HERE COMES THE NIGHT (10-61)/Young Boy Blues
6215 ECSTASY (2-62)/Yes
6222 DON'T PLAY THAT SONG (YOU LIED) (4-62)/The Hermit Of Misty Mountain

AS "DRIFTERS"

ATLANTIC

2151 SOMETIMES I WONDER (7-62) [Feat. Ben E. King]/Jackpot [Feat. Rudy Lewis]
["Sometimes I Wonder" was recorded in '60 session of "This Magic Moment" and "Save The Last Dance For Me."]

BEN E. KING

ATCO

6231 TOO BAD (8-62)/My Heart Cries For You
6237 I'M STANDING BY (10-62)/Walking In The Footsteps Of A Fool
6246 TELL DADDY (12-62)/Auf Weidersehn, My Dear
6256 HOW CAN I FORGET (3-63) [Jimmy Holiday '63 hit. EVEREST 2022]/Gloria Gloria
6267 I (WHO HAVE NOTHING) (6-63)/The Beginning Of Time
6275 I COULD HAVE DANCED ALL NIGHT (11-63)/Gypsy
6284 WHAT NOW MY LOVE (2-64)/Groovin'

6288 THAT'S WHEN IT HURTS (4-64)/Around The Corner
6315 IT'S ALL OVER (9-64)/Let The Water Run Down
6328 SEVEN LETTERS (12-64)/River Of Tears
6343 THE RECORD (BABY I LOVE YOU) (4-65)/The Way You Shake It
6357 SHE'S GONE AGAIN (9-65)/Not Now (I'll Tell You When)
6390 GOODNIGHT MY LOVE (1-66) [Jesse Belvin '56 hit. MODERN 1005]/I Can't Break The News To Myself
6413 SO MUCH IN LOVE (5-66)/Don't Drive Me Away
6431 I SWEAR BY STARS ABOVE (9-66)/Get In A Hurry
6454 WHAT IS SOUL? (1-67)/They Don't Give Medals To Yesterday's Heroes
6472 TEARS, TEARS, TEARS (4-67) [Written by Fred Parris, "5 Satins"]/A Man Without A Dream
6493 KATHERINE (6-67)/Teeny Weeny Little Bit
6527 DON'T TAKE YOUR SWEET LOVE AWAY (11-67)/She Knows What To Do For Me

AS "DEE DEE SHARP & BEN E. KING"

6557 WE GOT A THING GOING ON (4-68)/What'cha Gonna Do About It

BEN E. KING

6571 DON'T TAKE YOUR LOVE FROM ME (5-68)/She Knows What To Do For Me

AS "THE SOUL CLAN"

Ben E. King; Otis Redding; Johnny Taylor;
Arthur Conley; Percy Sledge.

ATLANTIC

2530 SOUL MEETING (7-68)/That's How It Feels

BEN E. KING

ATCO

6591 IT'S AMAZING (10-68)/Where's The Girl
6637 TIL I CAN'T TAKE IT ANYMORE (1-69)/It Ain't Fair
6666 HEY LITTLE ONE (5-69)/When You Love Someone

MAXWELL

800 GOODBYE MY OLD GAL (12-69)/I Can't Take It Like A Man
8800 MEDLEY: IN THE MIDNIGHT HOUR; LAY LADY LADY (8-71)

MANDALA (Distributed by STARDAY/KING)

2512	TAKE ME TO THE PILOT (8-72) [Written by Elton John and Bernie Taupin]/I Guess It's Goodbye
2513	INTO THE MYSTIC (3-73) [Written by Van Morrison]/White Moon
2518	SPREAD MYSELF AROUND (1973)/Travelin' Woman

ATLANTIC

3241	SUPERNATURAL THING (2-75)/Supernatural Thing [Part 2]
3274	DO IT IN THE NAME OF LOVE (6-75)/Imagination
3308	I HAVE A LOVE (1-76)/We Got Love
3337	I BETCHA DIDN'T KNOW THAT (6-76)/Smooth Sailing
3358	SOMEBODY'S KNOCKING (12-76)/One More Time

AWB ("AVERAGE WHITE BAND") AND BEN E. KING

3402	GET IT UP (FOR LOVE) (6-77)/Keepin' It To Yourself
3427	A STAR IN THE GHETTO (9-77)/What Is Soul
3444	FOOL FOR YOU ANYWAY (12-77)/The Message

BEN E. KING

3494	TIPPIN' (8-78)/I See The Light
3535	SPOILED (11-78)/Fly Away (To My Wonderland)

♭ ♯ ♪ ♩ 𝅗𝅥

Jerry Lee Lewis

Born in Ferriday, Louisiana, on September 29, 1935.

"Born feet first and rockin' ever since" is a valid self-expressed description of JERRY LEE 'KILLER" LEWIS, who may be the top white Rhythm and Blues Country shouter not only of the Restless Fifties but of all time. Measured by any standard of performance Jerry Lee Lewis is big, dynamic, and explosive—a guy who earned and spent a million, and who was pilloried almost into oblivion by media and public vagaries of indignation, only to fight his way back over the old Nashville musical-wagon trail. A born traveling man—known to have covered 275 one-night stands and 150,000 miles in one year—Jerry Lee Lewis loved the road, the noise of the gusty people who awaited his coming and every gut-catching note from his big music box. He is still, to millions of loyal fans, the wildly acclaimed "hillbillah boyah" with the eruptible lethal power to blast the evening wide open!

His sound has the familiarities of Little Brother Montgomery, Huey "Piano" Smith, Pete Johnson, "Little Richard" Penniman, Ellsworth Liggett, and others, and when caught up in the mimicking "madness" of Jerry Lee Lewis at the keyboard one has to wonder at the words of his title song, "Who's Gonna Play This Old Piano (When I'm Gone)" (MERCURY 73328). Jerry, never a shrinking violet, sees himself as one of the greatest stylists of them all and rated as fourth behind the famous Al Jolson, Jimmie Rodgers, and Hank Williams.

Jerry Lee Lewis was born in Louisiana, where he grew up, near Ferriday, in a small frame house on three acres of land. His father, Elmo Lewis, struggled to live by doing odd-job carpentry, while Mamie, his mother, eked out the family income from her backyard garden patch. Though the family knew poverty, they still enjoyed the home comforts of religion and music. Jerry Lee, together with his two younger sisters (Linda Gail and Frankie Jean), sang alongside both parents in the local Assembly of God Church choir, where Elmo would double at the piano and Jerry Lee add bar-chord rhythm on a guitar. Mamie Lewis saw musical promise in the boy, with decided preference for the piano, and encouraged Elmo to mortgage the little home so that an old Stack upright model might be installed in the living room.

Jerry Lee took to the ivoried keyboard like a duck to water and, playing by ear, taught himself all he ever knew about the piano. Between times, he strummed on his father's guitar to the wonderful radio sounds of "Grand Ole Opry" and the R&B stations. He also enjoyed exposure to the live contemporary music scene at Haney's Big House (a local well-known black nightclub) where while selling his newspapers Jerry Lee saw and heard the exciting Ray Charles, B. B. King, Bobby Blue Bland, Albert King, and many others when they came to town.

Further economic tragedy came when the family lost the homestead through foreclosure of the mortgage, and the thirteen-year-old Jerry Lee ventured on the nightclub scene in Natchez, just over the Mississippi state line, where at "The Wagon Wheel" he became stand-in pianist to blind Paul Whitehead (when Paul played the accordion) and performed four times weekly at the Blue Cat for $6 per night. The eighteen-mile round trip proved too much for Jerry Lee's schooling and this ambitious early venture had to be abandoned. 1952 found Jerry Lee Lewis, now seventeen, playing at the Hilltop Club, getting rave notice on station WNAT, already married (the first of five, or was it eight?), and hoping for a divorce.

After further attempts at schooling and even a stint at Bible College (where he was ejected in disfavor over his musical treatment of a hallowed hymn), Jerry Lee Lewis made an unsuccessful audition bid with "Louisiana Hayride" in Shreveport and a hungry three weeks in Nashville hounding producers for a break, only to latch-on in an upstairs speakeasy (for Country star Roy Hall), where he met imbibing Ernie Tubb, Webb Pierce, and Jimmy Dickens, who often tipped the young hopeful just to play some more! His fascination with the piano in many auditions meant rejections for Jerry Lee Lewis because, apart from the black boogie-woogie pianists, all the rising R&R artists were guitarists.

In 1956, Jerry Lee Lewis cut his own version of Gene Autry's "You're The Only Star In My Blue Heaven" for Sam Phillips of SUN STUDIO, and it was while there that he received his early influence of boogie-woogie and blues keyboard styles. Even before his first hits, "Crazy Arms" (SUN 259) a Ray Price C&W tune, "A Whole Lot Of Shakin' Goin' On" (SUN 267) (which John Lennon of the "Beatles" called the best rock song ever written and which led to revival of some Jerry Lee Lewis classics in his "Roots" album), "Great Ball Of Fire" (SUN 281) and others, Jerry Lee Lewis was on tour doing a string of big dates with Johnny Cash. Incidentally, it was "A Whole Lot Of Shakin' Goin' On" (SUN 267) that introduced the frenetic full-tilt lunacy of Jerry Lee Lewis to the world. His insinuating sexuality with his outrageous blond mane and wide crazy eyes (like a man in an advanced state of delirium tremens) met with mixed reactions from Country deejays and it was not until Jerry Lee Lewis came across nationally on the Steve Allen TV show that his frantic singing style and hypermimicked "madness' struck gold!

The big debacle came shortly after his marriage to Myra Gail, reputedly his second cousin and only thirteen years of age, and on the occasion of his concert tour of Britain. Though this might not have been too outlandish in large areas of the Southern states, it created much indignation and bedlam in London when Jerry Lee Lewis introduced his "Little Queenie" before the press. The public uproar forced the Home Secretary to cut the tour entirely and Jerry Lee Lewis, never a humble soul at the best times, further aggravated the already delicate situation by arrogantly confronting the media and the public, both overseas and at home. Even his forthcoming releases reflected some of his arrogance, such as "The Return Of Jerry Lewis" (SUN 301), "Let's Talk About Us" (SUN 330), "How's My Ex Treating You" (PHILLIPS-INT. 379), "She Even Woke Me Up To Say Goodbye" (SMASH 2244), "She Was My Baby" (SMASH 1906), "If I Had To Do It All Over" (SMASH 2053), "She Still Come Around (To Love What's Left Of Me)" (SMASH 2186), "When He Walks On You (Like You Have Walked On Me)" (MERCURY 73227), and, of course, "What'd I Say" (PHILLIPS-INT. 356). Some of Jerry Lee Lewis's sex-drenched lyrics and his reckless defiance influenced the "Rolling Stones," particularly his song "Down The Line" (SUN 288).

Jerry Lee Lewis continued to be seen on the Charts, especially his 1961 version of "What'd I Say" (PHILLIPS-INT. 356), but the star of the twenty-three-year-old artist who had sold twenty-five million records was in decline through angry media, deejay, and public reaction. Feeling dissatisfied and badly let down, Jerry Lee Lewis left Sam Phillips and his labels to sign with MERCURY and its subsidiary label, SMASH. He also returned to his Country roots but as a tremendous and highly innovative performer who quickly scorned the other brightly polished Nashville sound. "Another Place, Another Time" (SMASH 2146) gave us a smooth piano style and bluesy backup with violin.

Jerry Lee Lewis's appearance at the 1967 Rock and Roll Revival Show, which was held in Toronto, Canada, seemed to be the turning point on his way back up the Charts. Since then, Jerry Lee Lewis has continued to be heard loud and beautifully through the Seventies on MERCURY, SMASH, SUN, and ELEKTRA labels. He has had his moment of frustrating defeat but also his moments of joy, when he introduced his young sister, Linda Gail, both on the stage and on wax. And on "Save The Last Dance For Me" (SUN 1139), with Elvis Presley. Jerry Lee Lewis also had personal tragedy, with one of his young sons drowning in the swimming pool when only three, and another son, a bright young teenager, dying suddenly in the wreckage of his car.

Discography

JERRY LEE LEWIS

SUN

259	CRAZY ARMS (12-56) [Ray Price C&W tune. COLUMBIA 21510]/End Of The Road
267	WHOLE LOT OF SHAKIN' GOIN' ON (4-57)/It'll Be Me
281	GREAT BALLS OF FIRE (11-57)/You Win Again
288	BREATHLESS (2-58)/Down The Line
296	HIGH SCHOOL CONFIDENTIAL (5-58)/Fools Like Me
301	LEWIS BOOGIE (7-58)/The Return Of Jerry Lewis [Narration: George & Lewis]
303	BREAK-UP (8-58)/I'll Make It All Up To You [W. Charlie Rich, piano]
312	I'LL SAIL MY SHIP ALONE (11-58) [Moon Mulligan '50 tune. KING 830]/It Hurts Me So
317	BIG BLON' BABY (2-59)/Lovin' Up A Storm
324	THE BALLAD OF BILLY JOE (6-59)/Let's Talk About Us
330	LITTLE QUEENIE (9-59)/I Could Never Be Ashamed Of You
337	BABY BABY BYE BYE (3-60)/Old Black Joe

AS "THE HAWK"

PHILLIPS-INT.

3559	IN THE MOOD (5-60)/I Get The Blues When It Rains

JERRY LEE LEWIS

SUN

344	HANG UP MY ROCK AND ROLL SHOES (8-60) [Chuck Willis '58 hit. ATLANTIC 1179]/John Henry
352	WHEN I GET PAID (11-60)/Love Made A Fool Of Me
356	WHAT'D I SAY (2-61) [Ray Charles '59 hit. ATLANTIC 2031]/Livin' Lovin' Wreck
364	IT WON'T HAPPEN TO ME (6-61)/Cold Cold Heart
367	SAVE THE LAST DANCE FOR ME (9-61) ["Drifters" '60 hit. ATLANTIC 2071]/As Long As I Live
371	BONNIE B (11-61)/Money
394	I'VE BEEN TWISTIN' (1-62)/Ramblin' Rose
379	SWEET LITTLE SIXTEEN (7-62) [Chuck Berry '58 hit. CHESS 1683]/How's My Ex Treating You
382	GOOD GOLLY MISS MOLLY (11-62) [Little Richard's '58 hit. SPECIALTY 624]/I Can't Trust You
384	TEENAGE LETTER (4-63) (4-63) [W. Linda Gail Lewis]/ Seasons Of My Heart

SMASH

1856 PEN AND PAPER (11-63)/Hit The Road Jack
1886 I'M ON FIRE (4-64)/Bread And Butter Man
1906 SHE WAS MY BABY (7-64)/He Said He'd Dig For Me
1930 HIGH HEEL SNEAKERS (11-64) [Tommy Tucker '64 hit. CHECKER 1067]/You Went Back On Your Word

SUN

396 CARRY ME BACK TO OLD VIRGINIA (3-65)/I Know What It Means

SMASH

1992 ROCKIN' PNEUMONIA AND THE BOOGIE WOOGIE FLU (6-65) [Huey "Piano" Smith and "Clowns" '57 hit. ACE 530]/This Must Be The Place
2006 BABY (YOU'VE GOT WHAT IT TAKES) (10-65) [W. Linda Gail Lewis]/Green Green Grass Of Home
2027 WHAT A HECK OF A MESS! (3-66)/Sticks'N'Stones
2053 MEMPHIS BEAT (9-66)/If I Had To Do It All Over
2103 HOLDIN' ON (6-67)/It's A Hang Up Baby
2122 TURN ON YOUR LOVE LIGHT (11-67) [Bobby Bland '61 hit. DUKE 344]/Shotgun Man
2146 ANOTHER PLACE, ANOTHER TIME (3-68)/I'm Walking The Floor Over You
2164 WHAT'S MADE MILWAUKEE FAMOUS (HAS MADE A LOSER OUT OF ME) (7-68)/All The Good Is Gone
2186 SHE STILL COMES AROUND (10-68)/Slipping Around
2202 LET'S TALK ABOUT US (1-69)/To Make Love Sweeter For You
2220 DON'T LET ME CROSS OVER (4-69) [W. Linda Gail Lewis]/We Live In Two Different Worlds
2224 ONE HAS MY NAME (6-69)/I Can't Stop Loving You

SUN

1101 INVITATION TO YOUR PARTY (8-69)/I Could Never Be Ashamed Of You

SMASH

2244 SHE EVEN WOKE ME UP TO SAY GOODBYE (9-69)/Echoes

SUN

1107 ONE MINUTE PAST ETERNITY (10-69)/Frankie And Johnny

SMASH

2254 ROLL OVER BEETHOVEN (12-69) [W. Linda Gail Lewis]/Secret Places

2257 ONCE MORE WITH FEELING (2-70)/You Went Out Of Your Way

SUN

1115 CAN'T SEEM TO SAY GOODBYE (4-70)/Goodnight Irene

MERCURY

73099 THERE MUST BE MORE TO LOVE THAN THIS (8-70)/ Home Away From Home

SUN

1119 WAITING FOR A TRAIN (ALL AROUND THE WATER TANK) (11-70)/Big Legged Woman

MERCURY

73155 I CAN'T HAVE A MERRY CHRISTMAS WITHOUT YOU (12-70)/In Loving Memories

73192 TOUCHING HOME (3-71)/Woman, Woman (Get Out Of Our Way)

SUN

1125 LOVE ON BROADWAY (6-71)/Matchbox

MERCURY

73227 WHEN HE WALKS ON YOU (LIKE YOU HAVE WALKED ON ME) (7-71)/Foolish Kind Of Man

73248 ME AND BOBBIE McGEE (11-71) [Gordon Lightfoot '70 hit. REPRISE 0926]/Would You Take Another Chance On Me

SUN

1128 I CAN'T TRUST ME IN YOUR ARMS ANYMORE (2-72)/ Your Loving Ways

MERCURY

73273 CHANTILLY LACE (3-72) ["Big Bopper" '58 hit. MERCURY 71343]/Think About It Darlin'

73296 TURN ON YOUR LOVE LIGHT (6-72)/Lonely Weekends

73303 HANDWRITING ON THE WALL (8-72)/Me And Jesus

73328 WHO'S GONNA PLAY THIS OLD PIANO (WHEN I'M GONE) (10-72)/No Honky Tonks In Heaven

73361 NO MORE HANGING ON (2-73)/Mercy Of A Letter

SUN

1130 I CAN'T TRUST ME IN YOUR ARMS ANYMORE (4-73)/ Good Rockin' Tonight

MERCURY

73374 DRINKING WINE SPO-DEE O'DEE (4-73) [Sticks McGee '49 hit. ATLANTIC 873]/Rock And Roll Melody
73405 NO HEADSTONE ON MY GRAVE (7-73)/Jack Daniel's Number 7
73423 SOMETIMES A MEMORY AIN'T ENOUGH (10-73)/Think I Need To Pray
73452 I'M LEFT, YOU'RE RIGHT, SHE'S GONE (2-74) [Elvis Presley '55 hit. SUN 217]/I've Fallen To The Bottom
73462 JUST A LITTLE BIT (4-74)/Meat Man
73491 TELL TALE SIGNS (6-74)/Cold, Cold Morning Light
73618 HE CAN'T FILL MY SHOES (11-74)/Tomorrow's Taking My Baby Away
73661 I CAN STILL HEAR THE MUSIC IN THE RESTROOM (2-75)/Remember Me (I'm The One Who Loves You)
73685 BOOGIE WOOGIE COUNTRY MAN (6-75)/I'm Still Jealous Of You
73729 A DAMN GOOD COUNTRY SONG (1975)/When I Take My Vacation In Heaven
73763 DON'T BOOGIE WOOGIE (1976)/That Kind Of Fool
73822 JERRY LEE'S ROCK AND ROLL REVIVAL SHOW (1976)/ Let's Put It Back Together Again
73872 THE CLOSEST THING TO YOU (1976)/You Belong To Me
55011 MIDDLE AGE CRAZY (11-76)/Georgia On My Mind
55021 COME ON IN (3-78)/Who's Sorry Now
55028 I'LL FIND IT WHERE I CAN (6-78)/Don't Let The Stars Get In Your Eyes

SUN

1139 SAVE THE LAST DANCE FOR ME (12-78) [W. Elvis Presley]/ Am I To Be The One [W. Charlie Rich]
1141 COLD, COLD HEART (3-79)/Hello Josephine

ELEKTRA

46030 ROCKIN' MY LIFE AWAY (4-79)/I Wish I Was Eighteen Again
46067 WHO WILL THE NEXT FOOL BE (7-79) [Charlie Rich '70 hit. SUN 1110]
46591 WHEN TWO WORLDS COLLIDE (1-80)/RITA MAY

♭ ♯ ♪ ♩ 𝅗𝅥

Little Richard

Real Name: "Richard Wayne Penniman." Born in Macon, Georgia, on December 5, 1932.

LITTLE RICHARD, "THE GEORGIA PEACH," *is* ROCK AND ROLL! He gave R&R its meaning, its depth, and in so doing he inspired the careers of other great artists that followed: James Brown, Elvis, Gene Vincent, Jerry Lee Lewis, and Joe Tex, just to name a few. The elegance of his glistening robes and jewelry, combined with his exciting technique of singing and screaming through rapid-fire phrasing with spontaneous pounding on the old keyboard, gave Little Richard the unquestionable stamp of real showmanship!

He was born the third oldest in a family of fourteen children and, though he was reared in comparative poverty, his father, a printer by trade, gave the family a good upbringing according to his Seventh Day Adventist faith. While barely in his teens, Richard sang and danced for pennies advertising herb tonics with Doctor Hudson's Travelling Medicine Show and with Sugarfoot Sam's Medicine Circus. In 1950, he won first prize competing at an Atlanta theater and became a part of the B. Brown Band. Richard was very fond of Wynonie Harris, Roy Brown, and other Blues artists and sang Louis Jordan tunes.

Richard had his audition opportunity with RCA CAMDEN through the cooperation of SAVOY label artist, Billy Wright, and a local disc jockey, Zenas Sears, but though he cut eight bluesy sides during 1951-52 none of these made any big impact. Little Richard formed the "Tempo Toppers," comprising Jimmie Swan, Barry Gilmour, Billy Brooks, and Raymond Taylor. The group was duly signed by the Houston-based PEACOCK label and, while there, recorded Little Richard's best pre-SPECIALTY effort, a rocker, "Little Richard Boogie," with Johnny Otis on vibes, but this was not released until 1956 (PEACOCK 1658). Things were still going rough for Richard and he returned to his hometown, Macon, Georgia, to wash dishes at the Greyhound bus terminal.

Dame Fortune smiled on February 14, 1955, when SPECIALTY's A&R Otis "Bumps" Blackwell played a tape of two Gospel songs submitted by Richard and Art Rupe (SPECIALTY owner)—who happened to be on the lookout for "another Ray Charles"—listened and saw the light of a new star. He bought Little Richard's contract for only $600! Little Richard, who since late 1954 had been playing out of New Orleans clubs, formed a new group, the "Upsetters," with Clifford Burks (tenor sax); Grady Gaines (tenor sax); Wilbert Smith (tenor sax); Ossie Robinson (bass); Nathaniel Douglas (guitar); Charles Connor (drums); and others, Larry Lennear, Milt. Hopkins, Lee Diamond, Oliver Bush, and Chico Booth. A local songwriter, Dorothy LaBostrie, cleared up the lyrics on a song called "Tutti Frutti" with its famous intro "A Wop Bop Alu Bop A Lop Bam Boo," and when recorded (SPECIALTY 561) it became a million-seller! The backup was by the finest session musicians New Orleans could assemble: Red Tyler (tenor sax), Lee Allen (tenor sax), Frank Fields (bass), Ernest McLean (guitar), Earl Palmer (drums), and an added Huey Smith on the piano.

Little Richard's success became something of an overnight variety and through 1956-57 he cut many frantic rockers: "Long Tall Sally" (SPECIALTY 572), which had been written for the movie *The Thing;* "Rip It Up" (SPECIALTY 579); "Heebie Jeebies" (SPECIALTY 584); "The Girl Can't Help It" (SPECIALTY 591), which was the title track for Jayne Mansfield's movie of the same name, featuring the "3 Chuckles"; "Lucille" (SPECIALTY 598); "Jenny Jenny" (SPECIALTY 606); "Keep It Knockin'" (SPECIALTY 611); "Good Golly Miss Molly" (SPECIALTY 624); "True Fine Mama" (SPECIALTY 633); "Boo Hoo Hoo Hoo" (SPECIALTY 645), and "She Knows How To Rock" (SPECIALTY 652), to a total of eighteen discs, and each one of them a classic in its own way!

In 1956, Little Richard was featured in a Columbia movie, *Don't Knock the Rock,* with co-star Alan Dale and previewed others: "Bill Haley and the Comets," the "Applejacks," and the "Treniers." He also made an appearance in *The Girl Can't Help It.* During Little Richard's peak production period at SPECIALTY label, Joe Lutcher (one of the label's Bluesmen) left to become a minister of the Gospel. This had quite an impact on Little Richard and was demonstrated on his tour of Australia: while sailing down the Hunter River near Sydney on an October day in 1957, he cast four rings (valued at $8,000) into the water as a sign, he said, that God's work comes first. The following January, he enrolled in Oakwood College at Huntsville, Alabama, where he studied theology, psychology, and business administration, and in four years he graduated with his A.B.A., as well as being ordained a minister.

During the late Fifties, Little Richard's group, the "Upsetters," backed Dee Clark, and two of the group (Lee Diamond and Charles Connor) backed James Brown. Little Richard recorded Gospel releases for END,

CORAL, MERCURY and ATLANTIC labels and also "Every Night About This Time/Yes It's Me (I'm In Love Again)" (LITTLE STAR 123), both "Fats" Domino compositions, and in Little Richard's own great R&R style. Then, in a number of comebacks, he made many excellent records: "Bama Lama Bama Loo/Annie's Back (In A Brand New Cadillac)" (SPECIALTY 692), which was also reissued SPECIALTY 697, "I Don't Know What You've Got But It's Got Me" (VEE JAY 698), "I'm Back In Town" (MODERN 1022), "Poor Dog" (OKEH 7251), "The Commandments Of Love" (OKEH 7262), and "Stingy Jenny" (BRUNSWICK 55377), but, unfortunately, he never reached the same heights in record sales.

During his second comeback, in 1970, he made two impressive singles: "Freedom Blues" (REPRISE 0907) and "Greenwood, Mississippi" (REPRISE 0942). He also appeared in the Rock and Roll Festival at the Wembley Stadium in London, England, in 1974. Today, Little Richard lives in Riverside, California.

Discography

LITTLE RICHARD

RCA CAMDEN

4392 TAXI BLUES (1951)/Every Hour
4582 GET RICH QUICK (1952)/Thinkin' About My Mother
4722 AIN'T NOTHING HAPPENING (1952)/Why Did You Leave Me?
5025 I BROUGHT IT ALL ON MYSELF (1952)/Please Have Mercy On Me

WITH "TEMPO TOPPERS" (AND "DEUCES OF RHYTHM")

PEACOCK

1616 FOOL AT THE WHEEL (5-53)/Ain't That Good News

WITH "TEMPO TOPPERS"

1628 RICE, RED BEANS AND TURNIP GREENS (3-54)/Always
1658 LITTLE RICHARD BOOGIE (4-55) [W. Johnny Otis Orch.]/Directly From My Heart
1673 MAYBE I'M RIGHT (5-57) [W. Johnny Otis, piano]/I Love My Baby [Recorded orig. by Larry Darnell, REGAL 3274 (1950)]

LITTLE RICHARD

SPECIALTY

561	TUTTI-FRUTTI (11-55)/I'm Just A Lonely Guy
572	LONG TALL SALLY (3-56)/Slippin' And Slidin'
579	RIP IT UP (6-56)/Ready Teddy
584	SHE'S GOT IT (10-56)/Heebie Jeebies
591	THE GIRL CAN'T HELP IT (12-56)/All Around The World
598	LUCILLE (2-57)/Send Me Some Lovin'
606	JENNY JENNY (6-57)/Miss Ann
611	KEEP A KNOCKIN' (8-57)/Can't Believe You Wanna Leave
624	GOOD GOLLY MISS MOLLY (2-58)/Hey Hey Hey Hey
633	OOH! MY SOUL (5-58)/True, Fine Mama
645	BABY FACE (9-58)/I'll Never Let You Go (Boo Hoo Hoo Hoo)
652	SHE KNOWS HOW TO ROCK (11-58)/Early One Morning
660	BY THE LIGHT OF THE SILVERY MOON (3-59)/Wonderin'
664	KANSAS CITY (4-59)/Lonesome And Blue
670	SHAKE A HAND (6-59)/All Night Long
680	MAYBE I'M RIGHT (12-59)/Whole Lot Of Shakin' Goin' On
681	I GOT IT (12-59)/Baby
686	DIRECTLY FROM MY HEART (4-60)/The Most I Can Offer

END

1057	TROUBLES OF THE WORLD* (1-60)/Save The Lord
1058	MILKY WHITE WAY* (1960)/I've Just Come From The Fountain

CORAL

62366	MILKY WHITE WAY* (1960)/Need Him

MERCURY

71884	HE'S NOT JUST A SOLDIER* (1961)/Joy Joy Joy
71911	DO YOU CARE* (1-62)/Ride On King Jesus
71965	HE GOT WHAT HE WANTED* (5-62)/Why Don't You Change Your Ways

AS (WORLD-FAMOUS) "UPSETTERS"

LITTLE STAR

118	TATER MACHINE (7-62)/Let's Get A Thing Going
123	EVERY NIGHT ABOUT THIS TIME (12-62)/Yes It's Me (I'm In Love Again)
128	VALLEY OF TEARS (7-63)/Freedom Ride

*Gospel releases.

MYSTIC VALLEY

551 YES IT'S ME (1963)/Every Night About This Time

LITTLE RICHARD

WOODMAN

1001 HOLE IN THE WALL (1963)/Crying In The Chapel

ATLANTIC

2181 HOLE IN THE WALL (6-63)/Crying In The Chapel
2192 IT IS NO SECRET (6-63)/Travelling Shoes

"OLDIES 45"

192 BLUEBERRY HILL (5-64)/Lawdy Miss Clawdy

SPECIALTY

692 BAMA LAMA BAMA LOO (5-64)/Annie's Back
[Above record was released April 1970 on SPECIALTY 697.]

VEE JAY

612 WHOLE LOT OF SHAKIN' GOIN' ON (8-64)/Goodnight Irene
625 BLUEBERRY HILL (10-64)/Cherry Red
652 IT AIN'T WHAT YOU DO (1-65)/Cross Over
665 DANCE WHAT YOU WANNA (3-65)/Without Love
698 I DON'T KNOW WHAT YOU'VE GOT, BUT IT'S GOT ME (10-65) [W. Don Covay]/I Don't Know What You've Got, But It's Got Me [Part 2]

MODERN

1018 HOLY MACKEREL (1-66)/Baby, Don't You Want A Man Like Me
1019 DO YOU FEEL IT (1-66)/Do You Feel It [Part 2]
1022 I'M BACK (IN TOWN) (4-66)/Directly From My Heart

OKEH

7251 POOR DOG (WHO CAN'T WAG HIS OWN TAIL) (8-66)/Well

MODERN

1030 SLIPPIN' AND SLIDIN' (11-66)/Bring It Back Home To Me

OKEH

7262 THE COMMANDMENTS OF LOVE (11-66)/I Need Love
7271 I DON'T WANT TO DISCUSS IT (2-67)/Hurry Sundown
7278 DON'T DECEIVE ME (4-67)/Never Gonna Let You Go
7268 A LITTLE BIT OF SOMETHING (7-67)/Money

MODERN

1043 BABY WHAT YOU WANT ME TO DO (11-67) [W. Female Accompaniment]/Baby What You Want Me To Do

BRUNSWICK

55362 SHE'S TOGETHER (2-68)/Try Some Of Mine
55377 STINGY JENNY (GOT WHAT IT TAKES BUT IT BREAKS MY HEART TO GIVE IT AWAY) (5-68)/Baby Don't You Tear My Clothes
55386 CAN I COUNT ON YOU (8-68)/Soul Train

OKEH

7325 WHOLE LOT OF SHAKIN' GOIN' ON (3-69)/Lucille

REPRISE

0907 FREEDOM BLUES (5-70)/Dew Drop Inn
0942 GREENWOOD, MISSISSIPPI (9-70)/I Saw Her Standing There

SPECIALTY

699 POOR BOY PAUL (6-70)/Wonderin'

REPRISE

1005 SHAKE A HAND (4-71)/Somebody Saw You
1062 MONEY IS (1972)/Money Runner

KENT

4568 IN THE NAME (1972)/Don't You Know I

SONET

5001 POOR BOY PAUL (1972)/Wonderin'
5002 KEEP A KNOCKIN' (1973)/Tutti Frutti

BELL

385 GOOD GOLLY MISS MOLLY (8-73)/Good Golly Miss Molly [Part 2]

GREEN MOUNTAIN

413 IN THE MIDDLE OF THE NIGHT (8-73)/Where Will I Find A Place to Sleep This Evening

REPRISE

1130 MOCKINGBIRD SALLY (12-73)/Nuki Suki

MANTICORE

7007 CALL MY NAME (1-76)/Steal Miss Liza

Little Willie John

Real Name: "William Edward John Woods." Born in Camden, Arkansas, on November 15, 1937. Died on May 26, 1968.

When we think of LITTLE WILLIE JOHN in retrospect, one must have a sense of sadness in that not only was he a drug addict but also that he started professionally at much too young an age and thereby forfeited a precious part of childhood. One should also consider the fact of his five-foot stature and, because of it, a conditioned personal inhibition that led him always to carry a gun on stage, which suggested that he might shoot if he lost control or got drunk.

His growing years were rooted in the ghettos of Detroit, where, singing very early at local functions, it soon became evident that Little Willie had natural talent for singing Blues and, in particular, Rhythm and Blues ballads. He began singing with the Paul Williams Orchestra (SAVOY and RAMA labels) and the Duke Ellington and Count Basie bands. At barely seventeen years of age, he then auditioned for Syd Nathan's Cincinnati-based KING label and his debut was the classic "All Around The World" (KING 4818). This was later rearranged and recorded by Little Milton in 1967 under the title "Grits and Groceries." Little Willie's "Need Your Love So Bad" (KING 4841) is in every sense a Rhythm and Blues standard, and, later, in 1975, was done by James Brown as a tribute! His original version of "Fever" (KING 4935), which was written by John Davenport (Otis Blackwell) and Eddie Cooley, became a million-seller and even later—in 1958—was a popular favorite when done by Peggy Lee. His latter version of "Fever" (KING 5591) was released in 1962. Little Willie John, while touring on the black R&B circuit, also tried his hand at songwriting, but we have no definite word of his progress in this direction to date.

After Little Willie John's national hit "Talk To Me, Talk To Me" (KING 5108), written by Joe Seneca and covered in 1963 by "Sunny & the Sunglows," he went on to make many recordings that deserve consideration: "You're A Sweetheart" (KING 5142), "No Regrets" (KING

5170), "Leave My Kitten Alone" (KING 5219), "Heartbreak (It's Hurtin' Me)" (KING 5356), and lastly his biggest all-time Chart hit, "Sleep" (KING 5394). Little Willie's sister, Mabel John, had a successful career recording for STAX label as well as being one of Ray Charles's backup singers in the "Raelets." After his recording of "Take My Love (I Want To Give It To You)" (KING 5516) in 1961, Little Willie John failed to cut a Chart-winning entry. In 1966, he took part in a brawl at a Seattle cafe and was later charged and convicted for the stabbing death of Kendall Rountree, a railroad employee. Little Willie served only three years of his sentence at Washington State Penitentiary in Walla Walla, troubled by a form of claustrophobia, and died there of pneumonic complications on May 26, 1968.

Discography

LITTLE WILLIE JOHN

PRIZE

6900 MOMMY, WHAT HAPPENED TO OUR CHRISTMAS TREE (12-53)/Jingle Bells

THE PAUL WILLIAMS ORCHESTRA

RAMA

167 RING-A-RING (1954) [Feat. Little Willie John]/Don't Teach Me

LITTLE WILLIE JOHN

KING

4818 ALL AROUND THE WORLD (9-55) [Titus Turner '55 song. WING 90006]/Don't Leave Me Dear
4841 NEED YOUR LOVE SO BAD (1-56)/Home at Last
4893 I'M STICKIN' WITH YOU BABY (4-56)/Are You Ever Coming Back
4935 FEVER (6-56)/Letter From My Darling
4960 MY NERVES (9-56)/Do Something For Me
4989 SUFFERING WITH THE BLUES (12-56)/I've Been Around
5003 A LITTLE BIT OF LOVING (2-57)/Will The Sun Shine Tomorrow
5023 LOVE, LIFE AND MONEY (4-57)/You Got To Get Up Early In The Morning

5045 I'VE GOT TO GO CRY (7-57)/Look What You've Done To Me
5066 YOUNG GIRL (9-57)/If I Thought You Needed Me
5083 UH UH BABY (11-57)/Dinner Date
5091 PERSON TO PERSON (1-58)/Until You Do
5108 TALK TO ME, TALK TO ME (3-58)/Spasms
5142 YOU'RE A SWEETHEART (8-58)/Let's Rock While The Rockin's Good
5147 TELL IT LIKE IT IS (10-58)/Don't Be Ashamed To Call My Name
5154 ALL MY LOVE BELONGS TO YOU (12-58)/Why Don't You Haul Off And Love Me
5170 NO REGRETS (3-59)/I'll Carry Your Love Wherever I Go
5219 LEAVE MY KITTEN ALONE (8-59)/Let Nobody Love You
5274 LET THEM TALK (2-60)/Right There
5318 LOVING CARE (4-60)/My Love—Is
5342 COTTAGE FOR SALE (5-60)/I'm Shakin'
5356 HEARTBREAK (IT'S HURTIN' ME) (6-60) [Jon Thomas '60 hit. ABC 10122]/Do You Love Me?
5394 SLEEP (9-60)/There's A Difference
5428 WALK SLOW (11-60)/You Hurt Me
5452 LEAVE MY KITTEN ALONE (1-61)/I'll Never Go Back On My Word
5458 THE VERY THOUGHT OF YOU (3-61)/I'm Sorry
5503 (I'VE GOT) SPRING FEVER (5-61)/Flamingo
5516 TAKE MY LOVE (7-61)/Now You Know
5539 DRIVE ME HOME (9-61)/Need Your Love So Bad
5577 THERE IS SOMEONE IN THE WORLD FOR ME (12-61)/Autumn Leaves
5591 FEVER (2-62)/Bo-Da-Ley Didd-Ley
5602 (I'M AFRAID THE) MASQUERADE IS OVER (3-62)/Katanga
5628 MISTER GLENN (5-62)/Until Again My Love
5641 EVERY BEAT OF MY HEART (6-62) [Gladys Knight and the "Pips" '61 hit. FURY 1050]/I Wish I Could Cry
5667 COME BACK TO ME (8-62)/She Thinks I Still Care
5681 BIG BLUE DIAMONDS (10-62)/Doll Face
5694 HALF A LOVE (12-62)/Without A Friend
5717 HEAVEN ALL AROUND ME (3-63)/Don't Play With Love
5744 MY BABY'S IN LOVE WITH ANOTHER GUY (5-63)/Come On Sugar
5799 LET ME TALK (10-63)/Talk To Me
5818 SO LIVELY (12-63)/Inside Information
5823 PERSON TO PERSON (1-64)/I'm Shakin'
5849 DO SOMETHING FOR ME (2-64)/I'm In Love
5850 BILL BAILEY (2-64)/My Love Will Never Change
5870 ROCK LOVE (4-64)/It Only Hurts A Little While
5886 ALL AROUND THE WORLD (6-64)/All My Love Belongs To You
5949 DO SOMETHING FOR ME (11-64)/Don't You Know I'm In Love
6003 TAKE MY LOVE (7-65)/Talk To Me, Talk To Me
6302 ALL AROUND THE WORLD (6-70)/Need Your Love So Bad

♭ ♯ ♪ ♩ 𝅗𝅥

"Manhattans"

ORIGINAL MEMBERS: Winfred "Blue" Lovett, bass-baritone (born November 16, 1943, Jersey City, New Jersey); Edward "Sonny" Jesse Bivins, Jr. (born January 15, 1942, Macon, Georgia); Kenneth "Wally" Bernard Kelly (born anuary 9, 1943, Jersey City, New Jersey); Richard "Ricky" Taylor (who left to go solo in 1976); George "Smitty" Smith (died in 1970). Gerald Austin (of "Gerald Austin & the New Imperials") replaced Smith as lead singer. The group, originally a quintet, became and remained a quartet after the departure of Richard Taylor.

Hometown: Jersey City, New Jersey.

"MANHATTANS" is synonymous with beautiful ballads and the classical intermixture of individual rapping with rich vocal harmony. There is a sophisticated delivery and disciplined coordination of words and music characteristic of all of their public appearances and recordings. Though recognized as predominantly balladeers, because of tremendous demand, the "Manhattans" have been into Doo-Wopp almost from the very beginning and their recent Pop successes show sensitivity to new grooves and changing moods. From their first New York area hit, "There Goes A Fool" (CARNIVAL 506), to that internationally acclaimed two-million seller "Kiss And Say Goodbye" (COLUMBIA 3-10310) and an ongoing string of national hits with seemingly monotonous ease—excepting their disappointing layoff during 1968-69—the "Manhattans" have proved themselves a group par excellence!

The genesis of the group has to be post-World War II Europe, where Eddie Bivins, Ricky Taylor, and another, unnamed GI met and discussed music as a career after discharge from the U.S. Air Force. Back home again in New York, the veterans teamed up with Buddy Bell and Ethel Samuels, forming the "Dulcets," and "Pork Chops" remains as their first and only recording. Rehearsal hassles and new objectives brought a new name, "The Manhattans" (taken from the borough on the other side of the

Hudson River from Jersey City), and the departure of three group members, leaving only Bivins and Taylor. Winfred "Blue" Lovett, Kenneth "Wally" Kelly and George "Smitty" Smith joined with them and together often crossed the river to 116th Street in the "Big Apple" to that old familiar hang-out corner of the "Harptones," the "Wanderers," and the "Willows"!

The group's first opportunity came in 1964 through a talent show at the Apollo Theater in Harlem, where they not only survived the lusty quips of M.C. Honi Coles, which is a feat in itself, but they carried back third prize to Jersey City. They also endeared themselves to possibly the most lovable and roughest disapproving audience in the world, because, from that time on, "Manhattan" songs began riding high in the hearts and minds of every aspiring singer in the ghettos of America! Only days later, Joe Evans, the president of CARNIVAL RECORDS (a small independent Jersey City label) heard of their enthusiastic reception in Harlem and of their potential style in the footsteps of the "Coasters" and the "Impressions."

The "Manhattans," between 1962 and 1964, had already cut four singles for four different labels, but their first recording for CARNIVAL RECORDS was aptly titled "For The Very First Time" (CARNIVAL 504), released in 1964 to become a Top-Ten New York area success. This was followed by "There Goes A Fool" (CARNIVAL 506), another area hit; "I Wanna Be (Your Everything)" (CARNIVAL 507), a "Blue" Lovett song that became a national hit; "Searching For My Baby" (CARNIVAL 509), again by Lovett and a hit; "Follow Your Heart," (CARNIVAL 512), which sold over half a million, and "Can I" (CARNIVAL 517), a delightful number by George Smith that should have been a much bigger national hit! There were nine other popular singles cut by CARNIVAL RECORDS, including Eddie Bivins's "When You're Made As One" (CARNIVAL 529), ending in June 1968.

That same year, Billy Schiffman (then manager and now owner of the Apollo Theater in Harlem) personally introduced the "Manhattans" to the KING RECORDS complex, a brand-new contract, and an assignment with DELUXE label. Over the next three years, 1969 to 1973, the "Manhattans" made the R&B Charts with regularity and ease but crossed over now and then to score with considerable Pop-action success. During this period we enjoyed, among other releases, "It's Gonna Take A Lot To Bring Me Back" (DELUXE 115), '"From Atlanta To Georgia" (DELUXE 129) a "Wally" Kelly song, "Let Them Talk" (DELUXE 132), a 1960 hit by Little Willie John, "A Million To One" (DELUXE 137), and "Blue" Lovett's lovely song "One Life To Live" (DELUXE 139). 1972, unfortunately, saw the demise of KING RECORDS complex!

On the verge of that heady succession of hits, the "Manhattans" experienced a most discouraging slackening off in their public engagements and recordings during 1968 and 1969. In 1970, they decided to tour the black campuses of the South. On one such occasion, a rather mixed-up one, the "Manhattans" and "Gerald Austin & the New Imperials" showed up for the *same* concert! On that occasion, George Smith invited lead singer Gerald Austin to join the "Manhattans," but without success. Ironically, later that year, George "Smitty" Smith died from brain damage and Gerald Austin came to the "Manhattans"! Gerald Austin became the new lead singer on Eddie Bivins's song "There's No Me Without You" (COLUMBIA 45838), which lifted the "Manhattans" back into the national limelight.

COLUMBIA RECORDS was good for the "Manhattans," and hits came easily and regularly once again. "There's No Me Without You" (COLUMBIA 45838) became solid gold! "Kiss And Say Goodbye" (COLUMBIA 3-10310) went on to international acclaim and over two million in sales! Among the string of other hits were "Don't Take Your Love From Me" (COLUMBIA 3-10045), "I Kinda Miss You" (COLUMBIA 3-10430), "It Feels So Good To Be Loved So Bad" (COLUMBIA 3-10495), and "Here Comes The Hurt Again" (COLUMBIA 3-11024).

Apart from the tragic death of George "Smitty" Smith in 1970 and the departure of Richard "Ricky" Taylor, who decided to go solo in 1976, the "Manhattans" have maintained their original members, except that they are now a quartet rather than the initial quintet! The group, besides being artistic in their sophisticated presentations, are versatile in their creativity. "Blue" Lovett, Eddie Bivins, and Kenneth Kelly have all contributed much to the group's repertoire of song hits. Kelly, a perfectionist, prepares their choreography much as an architect would plan a lofty edifice and is ably and enthusiastically supported throughout by creative input from each and every member of the group. Mike Eichner (vice-president of A&R) had a great deal to do with bringing the "Manhattans" to COLUMBIA RECORDS and with their phenomenal success while there. Bobby Martin made a tremendous contribution in his producing of "Manhattans" recordings throughout their colorful career!

Discography

AS "DULCETS"

Edward "Sonny" Jesse Bivins; Richard "Ricky" Taylor;
unnamed GI; Buddy Bell; Ethel Samuels.

PORK CHOPS

AS "MANHATTANS"

PINEY

107 LIVE IT UP (1962)/Go Baby Go!

CAPITOL

4730 LA-LA-LA (1962)/Sing All The Day

AS "RONNIE & MANHATTANS"

ENJOY

2008 COME ON BACK (1963)

AS "MANHATTANS"

GOLDEN WORLD

14 JUST A LITTLE LOVIN' (1964)/Beautiful Brown Eyes

CARNIVAL

504 FOR THE VERY FIRST TIME (1964)/I've Got Everything But You
506 THERE GOES A FOOL (1964)/Call Somebody Please
507 I WANNA BE (YOUR EVERYTHING) (1-65)/What's It Gonna Be
509 SEARCHING FOR MY BABY (6-65)/I'm The One That Love Forgot
512 FOLLOW YOUR HEART (12-65)/The Boston Monkey
514 BABY I NEED YOU (3-66)/Teach Me (The Philly Dog)
517 CAN I (8-66)/That New Girl
522 I BET'CHA (COULDN'T LOVE ME) (11-66)/Sweet Little Girl
524 IT'S THAT TIME OF THE YEAR (12-66)/Alone On New Year's Eve
526 ALL I NEED IS YOUR LOVE (3-67)/Our Love Will Never Die
529 WHEN YOU'RE MADE AS ONE (7-67)/Baby I'm Sorry
533 I CALL IT LOVE (11-67)/Manhattan Stomp
542 I DON'T WANNA GO (6-69)/Love Is Breaking Out (All Over)

DELUXE

109 THE PICTURE BECAME QUITE CLEAR (1969)/Oh Lord I Wish I Could Sleep
115 IT'S GONNA TAKE A LOT TO BRING ME BACK (1-70)/Give Him Up
122 IF MY HEART COULD SPEAK (6-70)/Loneliness

129	FROM ATLANTA TO GEORGIA (11-70)/Fantastic Journey
132	LET THEM TALK (3-71) [Little Willie John '60 hit. KING 5274]/Let Them Talk [Part 2]
136	I CAN'T STAND FOR YOU TO LEAVE ME (6-71)/Do You Ever
137	A MILLION TO ONE (1-72)/Cry If You Wanna Cry
139	ONE LIFE TO LIVE (9-72)/It's The Only Way
144	BACK UP (1-73)/Fever
146	LONELINESS (1973)/Rainbow Week
152	IF MY HEART COULD SPEAK (1973)/Do You Ever

COLUMBIA

45838	THERE'S NO ME WITHOUT YOU (5-73)/I'm Not A Run Around
45927	YOU BETTER BELIEVE IT (9-73)/Soul Train
45971	WISH THAT YOU WERE MINE (12-73)/It's So Hard Losing You
46081	SUMMERTIME IN THE CITY (8-74)/The Other Side Of Me
3-10045	DON'T TAKE YOUR LOVE FROM ME (1-75)/The Day The Robin Sang To Me
3-10140	HURT (5-75)/Nursery Rhymes
3-10310	KISS AND SAY GOODBYE (4-76)/Wonderful World Of Love
3-10430	I KINDA MISS YOU (11-76)/Gypsy Man
3-10495	IT FEELS SO GOOD TO BE LOVED SO BAD (3-77)/Up On The Street (Where I Live)
3-10586	WE NEVER DANCED TO A LOVE SONG (8-77)/Let's Start It All Over Again
3-10674	AM I LOSING YOU (2-78)/Movin'
3-10766	EVERYBODY HAS A DREAM (6-78)/Happiness
3-10921	HERE COMES THE HURT AGAIN (3-79)/Don't Say Goodbye
3-11024	THE WAY WE WERE/Memories (7-79)/New York City

♭ ♯ ♪ ♩ 𝅗𝅥

Barry Manilow

Born in Brooklyn, New York, on June 17, 1946.

BARRY MANILOW, with his sparse figure and shaggy blond hair, would hardly be recognized as Mr. America, because of his diffident manner, his hesitant way of speaking, and a personal modesty that belies his life-style as one of the truly great show business attractions around today. The transformation takes place as soon as he steps behind the big lights and becomes an all outgoing balladeer and charismatic star! Popular singer, writer, producer and arranger, Barry Manilow got instant action in 1974 with his No. 1 hit, "Mandy" (BELL 45613). His main strength lies in his choice of material and in his warm, appealing vocals, usually ballads, such as "Ready To Take A Chance Again" (ARISTA 0357), a beautiful entry and a perfect example!

Barry Manilow was born in Brooklyn and as a boy learned to avoid the neighborhood bullies in one of the tougher sections of that borough. His parents separated while he was still very young, but his music was assured when young Barry, beginning at the age of seven, studied the accordion for five years. His mother remarried and his stepfather, Willie Murphy, took a personal interest in the talented youngster and exposed him to the jazz concerts of the time, which may have inspired Barry to play the piano. Barry actually dropped a course in marketing and merchandising so that he could enroll at the New York College of Music and Juilliard!

In the late Sixties, Barry Manilow became involved in off-Broadway arranging and enjoyed a series of specials with Ed Sullivan. He also became active recording commercials, of which his best known is McDonald's slogan "You Deserve A Break Today." In 1970, while Barry was working in the mailroom at CBS, one of the directors asked him to be pianist for the New York Continental Baths, and that was where Barry Manilow met Bette Midler! Barry became Bette Midler's musical director on tour, and co-produced her first album, as well as the CBS television series *Call Back.*

With his instant success, "Mandy" (BELL 45613), in 1974, Barry Manilow was assured of stardom, and signed with BELL and later ARIS-

TA to maintain his status by recording many hits: "Could It Be Magic" (ARISTA 0126), "I Write The Songs" (ARISTA 0157), "Weekend In New England" (ARISTA 0212), "Looks Like We Made It" (ARISTA 0244), "Daybreak" (ARISTA 0273), and "Can't Smile Without You" (ARISTA 0305). Barry Manilow and Ron Dante (formerly of the "Archies") produced the '74 Bo Cooper hit "Don't Call It Love" (BELL 45460). His 1978 hit "Copacabana (At The Copa)" (ARISTA 0339) established Barry Manilow on the Disco scene!

Now with all the money he needs, Barry Manilow is quick to remind himself of less affluent stages in his career, such as when he headed the Charts with "Mandy," and how, when still relatively unknown, he was left stranded and broke in Los Angeles by a nightclub owner who let him down, and how he completed a cross-country tour with barely enough cash to get back to New York. Those days are long since gone, and now, Barry Manilow, cool businessman that he is, carefully avoids overexposure on television, on the road, and even in the number of album releases. A prolific writer of songs, having written as high as thirty-eight in one week at his home in Palm Springs, he goes back over them diligently until he is satisfied with ten or twelve of them. Now divorced, Barry Manilow insists on leading a normal and sane life. To ensure this, he keeps a number of independent people around him to jolt him when he shows signs of turning temperamental. Barry Manilow, though not necessarily R&B or R&R, is still our top pop recording star for 1980!

Discography

"FEATHERED" [W. BARRY MANILOW]

BELL

45133	COULD IT BE MAGIC (1970)
971	AMY (11-71)/Morning

BARRY MANILOW

45357	SWEET WATER JONES (1973)/One Of These Days
45422	COULD IT BE MAGIC (1974)/Cloudburst
45443	LET'S TAKE SOME TIME TO SAY GOODBYE (1974)
45613	MANDY (11-74) [Written by Scott English of "Brandy (You're A Fine Girl)" fame]/Something's Comin' Up

ARISTA

11	IT'S JUST ANOTHER NEW YEAR'S EVE (1974)
0108	IT'S A MIRACLE (2-75)/One Of These Days
0126	COULD IT BE MAGIC (6-75)/I Am Your Child
0157	I WRITE THE SONGS (12-75) [Written by Bruce Johnston of "Bruce & Terry"]/A Nice Boy Like Me

FLASHBACK

91	I WRITE THE SONGS (1976)/Could It Be Magic

ARISTA

0172	TRYIN' TO GET THE FEELING AGAIN (4-76)/Beautiful Music
0206	THIS ONE'S FOR YOU (8-76)/Riders To The Stars
0212	WEEKEND IN NEW ENGLAND (11-76)/Say The Words
0244	LOOKS LIKE WE MADE IT (5-77)/New York City Rhythm
0273	DAYBREAK (10-77)/Jump Shout Boogie
0305	CAN'T SMILE WITHOUT YOU (2-78)/Sunrise
0330	EVEN NOW (5-78)/I Was A Fool (To Let You Go)
0339	COPACABANA (AT THE COPA) (6-78) [Long Version]/ Copacabana (At The Copa) [Short Version]
0357	READY TO TAKE A CHANCE AGAIN (9-78)/Sweet Life
0382	SOMEWHERE IN THE NIGHT (12-78)/Leavin' In The Morning
0464	SHIPS (10-79)/They Gave In To The Blues
0481	WHEN I WANTED YOU (12-79)/Bobbie Lee (What's The Difference, I Gotta Live)

♭♯♪♩𝅗𝅥

Van McCoy

Born in Washington, D.C., 1940. Died in hospital at Englewood, New Jersey, on July 6, 1979.

VAN McCOY blossomed late as a recording star, not for lack of performing ability, but simply because of his many other creative drives that had to be expressed. True, he began his star-studded career as a vocalist with a small local group, the "Marylanders," and sang with his own group, the "Starliters" (comprising Norman McCoy—his brother—and three other musical hopefuls), in Washington, D.C., in the mid-Fifties. Three singles were cut for END label during 1959-60, under direction of George Goldner (2) and Richard Barrett (1). Teenager Marvin Gaye performed with the "Starliters" during 1959 but did not participate in the recordings.

1960-61 brought changes when two of the originals left the group, leaving only two (including Norman McCoy, who stuck with Van for a number of years), the group breaking up and Van McCoy deciding to go solo! That first year saw Van McCoy and an uncle setting up their own recording company, ROCK'N label, which released "That's How Much You Mean To Me/I Wantcha Back" (ROCK'N 100) and another. The following year, "Mr. D.J." was cut at SOUND PLUS Studio in Philadelphia (ROCK'N 101); a smooth ballad produced by Doc Bagby (who owned VAL-UE label and recorded "Dumplin'"). This was Van McCoy's own specialty number written for the deejays and it made good nationally via SCEPTER. Van also wrote songs for the "Twylighters" in his recording of "Darling Let's Fall In Love/I'm Gonna Try" (ROCK'N 102). His next and last recording for ROCK'N label, "Girls Are Sentimental/Baby Don't Tease Me" (ROCK'N 1012), was out of New York City, where producer Luther Dixon, seeing great creative potential in Van, personally advised him to do more writing, arranging, and producing. This was justified by the diversified career of Van McCoy!

1961-64 saw Van McCoy at SCEPTER label, getting his basic grounding in the A&R department, where his first sessions with the "Shirelles," scoring with their first Top-Twenty hit, "Stop The Magic," and his producing of "It's Love That Really Counts" brought him into contact with that fabulous combination, Jerry Leiber and Mike Stoller. During this time Van McCoy produced for "Gladys Knight and the Pips," and a smaller hit, "Rat Race," for the "Drifters," then "Keep Lovin' Me" (43415) and "Starlight Starbright" (43495) on COLUMBIA. Van also assumed part ownership of MAXX label with Larry Maxwell, and production of sides for "Jay and the Americans," Bobby Vinton, and others. He also masterminded "I Get The Sweetest Feeling" for Jackie Wilson, "5-10-15-20(25-30 Years Of Love)" for the "Presidents," "Baby I'm Yours" for Barbara Lewis, "Sweet Bitter Love" for Aretha Franklin, and singles for "Ruby and the Romantics," the "Marvelettes," and Ralph Carter. Van also wrote "He's My Guy" for Irma Thomas (IMPERIAL 66080).

Around 1967-68, Mitch Miller (CBS) brought Van McCoy back to COLUMBIA, where we see another side of his creativity. COLUMBIA had suffered the double loss of Nat King Cole (by death) and Johnny Mathis (who had just left for elsewhere) and were anxious to develop another top-ranking mellow-singing artist, possibly in Van McCoy! Van McCoy and COLUMBIA did produce such an album, "Night Is A Mellow Time," but Van McCoy had become involved in other things. He was now tied down at a full-time office-desk role with BLACKWOOD MUSIC and entering into partnership with Dave Kaprilik in their own venture, DAEDALUS PRODUCTIONS (*Daedalus*: a mythical architect/sculptor mentioned by Homer as creating a dance-place in Crete). Kaprilik's involvement with "Sly and the Family Stone" in California forced an early amicable end to this partnership.

1968-70 saw Van McCoy being attracted back to his solo artistry and setting up his own company, VAN McCOY PRODUCTIONS (VMC), and VANDO label (VAN for Van McCoy and DO for Douglas Henderson, his partner). Van McCoy produced for "Little Tony Talent," launched Chris Barkley (before encouraging him to go on to BUDDAH RECORDS and MUSICOR RECORDS). Van McCoy discovered "Faith Hope & Charity" (and, incidentally, the "Presidents"; later "Triology" and "Anacosta"), which he signed for SUSSEX label.

From 1970 Van McCoy had three years of success with "Brenda and the Tabulations," beginning with "And My Heart Sang (Tra La La)," co-written with Joe Cobb, and followed through with "Right On The Tip Of My Tongue," "A Child No One Wanted," and others. Van had not forgotten his loyal fans and had given us releases on LIBERTY, COLUMBIA, EPIC, and SILVER BLUE labels. Around this time, 1972-74, Van produced some sides for "Spice Of Life" that were never released and set about creating his own group, "Choice Four." Again, new challenges came for his many talents.

Hugo (Perretti) and Luigi (Creatore) of AVCO RECORDS brought

Van McCoy over to produce for the "Soft Tones" and the "Stylistics" (after the departure of producer Thommy Bell). Here, we see production of "Let's Put It All Together," "Love Is The Answer" (instrumental), and others. A Van McCoy album was produced with some of the biggest R&B hits of the previous four or five years. Another album, "Disco Baby," by Van McCoy and "The Soul City Symphony" gave us, among other fine numbers, "Hustle" (see also SILVER BLUE 4653), which became one of our leading dance crazes.

Van McCoy's later and most exciting venture had to do with producing "Who Am I," a disco-oriented album heralding return of the great artist David Ruffin. This was a brilliant, highly creative effort of cooperation between producer and artist. This was followed by an album for Melba Moore ("one of the potential superstars of tomorrow") and one of Van McCoy's road trips, which took him into Canada (Montreal) and his nonstop disco music performance there. Gloria Gaynor, "Shirley & Company," "Faith Hope & Charity," and his own "Choice Four" accompanied him on this trip.

Health problems began to develop for this highly talented individual, who insisted on giving so much of himself, in so many ways, to so many people! He entered a hospital in Englewood, New Jersey, and there died of heart arrest on July 6, 1979.

Discography

AS "STARLITERS"

END

1031 THE BIRDLAND (1959)/It's Twelve O'Clock
1049 I CRIED (1959)/You're The One To Blame
1072 A STORY OF LOVE (1960)/Let's Take A Stroll

VAN McCOY

ROCK'N

100 THAT'S HOW MUCH YOU MEAN TO ME (1960)/I Wantcha Back
101 MR. D.J. (1961)/Never Trust A Friend
1012 GIRLS ARE SENTIMENTAL (1961)/Baby Don't Tease Me

LIBERTY

55457 FOLLOW YOUR HEART (5-62)/Lonely

COLUMBIA

43415 KEEP LOVIN' ME (1965)/Butterfly
43495 STARLIGHT STARBRIGHT (1965)/This Is The Way We Fell In Love
43694 THE HOUSE THAT LOVE BUILT (7-66)/I Will Wait For You
43925 PLEDGING MY LOVE (12-66) [Johnny Ace '55 hit. DUKE 136]/I'm Out Of My Mind

AS "VAN McCOY STRINGS"

SHARE

102 SWEET AND EASY/If I Could Make You Mine

VAN McCOY

EPIC

5-10470 I STARTED A JOKE (1969) ["Bee Gees" '68 hit. ATCO 6636]/Tony's Theme

CGC

115 WHERE THERE'S A HEARTACHE (THERE MUST BE A HEART) (8-70)

AS "SHARON RIDLEY & VAN McCOY"

SILVER BLUE

802 I'M IN YOUR CORNER (1973)/To Make A Long Story Short

AS "SOUL CITY SYMPHONY" (VAN McCOY)

AVCO EMBASSY

4639 LOVE IS THE ANSWER (7-74)/Killing Me Softly
4648 RAINY NIGHT IN GEORGIA (1974) [Instr. version of Brook Benton '70 hit. COTILLION 44057]/Boogie Down
4653 THE HUSTLE (4-75)/Hey Girl, Come And Get It
4660 CHANGE WITH THE TIMES (10-75)/Goodnight, Baby
Note: Van McCoy also recorded "IT AIN'T NO BIG THING" on ROCKAWAY label.

VAN McCOY

H&L

2002	RHYTHMS OF THE WORLD (1976)/Soul Chacha

AVCO EMBASSY

4667	NIGHT WALK (5-76)/Love Child
4670	PARTY (6-76)/The Disco Kid
4677	THE SHUFFLE (12-76)/That's The Joint

MCA

40885	MY FAVORITE FANTASY (4-78)/You're So Right For Me
40938	TWO POINTS (8-78)/Trying To Make The Best Of It

♭♯♪♩𝅗𝅥

Clyde McPhatter

Born in Durham, North Carolina, November 15, 1933.
Died in New York City, June 13, 1972.

CLYDE McPHATTER was definitely one of the all-time great Rhythm and Blues singers, with a commanding group light tenor versatility, and a soloist with a unique, smooth velvety styling that distinguished him from most of his contemporaries. He was much like his lifetime idol, Nat King Cole, and when he signed with the MERCURY label he was like another Brook Benton. Clyde McPhatter was reared in Durham, North Carolina, and was one of a religious family comprising three sisters, Gladys, Esther and Bertha, along with three brothers, Leroy, James, and George, Jr. His father, George McPhatter, was a preacher at the Mount Calvary Baptist Church, where his mother, Eva, performed as organist. With this Gospel upbringing, one of the sisters became well known with the "Tears of Joy."

Young Clyde grew up singing in the choir, while also taking an active part in singing Gospel. He attended the local Hillside High School until the age of twelve, when the family moved to New York, where he attended Chelsior High. At fourteen, he formed a Gospel quartet, the "Mount Lebanon Singers," and worked as a clerk up until his first professional singing debut as lead vocal with Billy Ward's "Dominoes." (See FEDERAL label "Dominoes" '50-'53 for his notable lead tenor achievements.) In 1953, Clyde McPhatter formed his own group, the "Drifters," and over one year completed seventeen cuts. (See ATLANTIC label "Drifters" '53-'55) before entering the U.S. Army's Special Services Branch. While there, he recorded three ATLANTIC label solo releases (under manager Irvin Feld); "Everybody's Laughing," a duet with Ruth Brown entitled "I Gotta Have You," followed by a classic hit, "Seven Days." Following his discharge from the service in April 1956, he accomplished a two-million seller hit, "Treasure Of Love," along with a U.S.A. tour (called "The Biggest Rock and Roll Show"), which included Bill Haley. This was followed by another spectacular, "Celebrity of Stars," featuring "Fats" Domino! Clyde became a Rock and Roll celebrity during the Fifties and

Sixties, with guest appearances at the Apollo Theater in New York City, Howard Theater in Washington, D.C., State Theater in Hartford, Connecticut, the Casino Theater in Toronto, Canada, besides making a film debut and numerous television appearances. He appeared in "Mr. Rock 'N'Roll," highlighting the hits "Without Love," "Just To Hold My Hand," and "Rock And Cry." In 1958, Clyde McPhatter scored again with "A Lover's Question," which became a national hit and million-seller. In 1959, he signed with MGM label but with little hit success until a British tour with Bobby Darin and Duane Eddy.

With MERCURY label 1960-1965 Clyde went on to further successes, scoring with "Ta Ta," "Lover Please," "Little Bitty Pretty One," and, lastly, "Deep In The Heart Of Harlem." Following his MERCURY label successes, Clyde McPhatter developed a personal drinking problem and never came back with any major hits. On June 13, 1972, while visiting some friends in upper Manhattan, he suffered a heart attack and died, leaving his wife, Lena, and one child, Patrick.

Discography

THE "DOMINOES"

Clyde McPhatter (lead vocals, replaced in 1953 by Jackie Wilson when Clyde formed original group, the "Drifters"); Bill Brown (bass, replaced in 1952 by David McNeil, a former "Larks" member); William Joe Lamont (baritone); Charlie White (second tenor, replaced in 1952 by James Van Loan, brother of "Ravens" member Joe Van Loan—Charlie later joined the "Clovers"); Billy Ward (piano, arranger, and vocal coach).

AS THE "DOMINOES"

FEDERAL

12001 CHICKEN BLUES (12-50) [Feat. Bill Brown]/Do Something For Me [Feat. Clyde McPhatter]

12010 HARBOUR LIGHTS (1951) [Feat. Clyde McPhatter and Joe Lamont, baritone]/No! Says My Heart [Feat. Clyde McPhatter]

12016 OTHER LIPS, OTHER ARMS (1951)/The Deacon Moves In [With Little Esther (Phillips)]

12022 SIXTY MINUTE MAN* (5-51) [Feat. Bill Brown]/I Can't Escape From You [Feat. Clyde McPhatter and Bill Brown, bass]

---

*Clyde contributed exciting falsetto cries of "Don't Stop," while, interestingly enough, Jackie Wilson backed the group on bass. Record had national success, with 2.5 million sales, yet played only on some R&B stations.

12036 HEART TO HEART (1951) [With Little Esther (Phillips)]/ Looking For A Man
12039 I AM WITH YOU (11-51) [Feat. Clyde McPhatter and Bill Brown, bass]/Weeping Willow Blues
12052 THAT'S WHAT YOU'RE DOING TO ME (4-52) [Feat. Clyde McPhatter and Charlie White]/When The Swallows Come Back To Capistrano [Feat. Clyde McPhatter and Bill Brown]
12068 HAVE MERCY BABY (5-52) [Feat. Clyde McPhatter]/Deep Sea Blues [Feat. Clyde McPhatter]
12072 THAT'S WHAT YOU'RE DOING TO ME (1952) [Feat. Clyde McPhatter and Charlie White]/Love, Love, Love

AS "BILLY WARD & THE DOMINOES"

12105 I'D BE SATISFIED (12-52) [Feat. Clyde McPhatter]/No Room [Feat. David McNeil]
12106 YOURS FOREVER (1952) [Feat. Clyde McPhatter and David McNeil]/I'm Lonely [Feat. David McNeil and Clyde McPhatter, bridge]
12114 THE BELLS (1-53) [Bass intro.—David McNeil and Clyde McPhatter (with Cries)]/Pedal Pushin' Papa [Feat. David McNeil]

AS THE "DOMINOES"

12129 THESE FOOLISH THINGS (REMIND ME OF YOU) (5-53) [Feat. Clyde McPhatter]/Don't Leave Me This Way

AS "CLYDE McPHATTER & THE DRIFTERS"

"Drifters": Clyde McPhatter (lead tenor); Gerhart Thrasher (lead); Andrew Thrasher (baritone); Bill Pinkney (bass); Jimmy Oliver (guitar). ATLANTIC added Sam (The Man) Taylor (sax) and Mickey Baker (guitar).

ATLANTIC

1006 MONEY HONEY (9-53)/The Way I Feel [Feat. Clyde McPhatter]
1019 SUCH A NIGHT (1-54)/Lucille* [Feat. Clyde McPhatter]
1029 HONEY LOVE (5-54)/Warm Your Heart [Feat. Clyde McPhatter]
1043 BIG BAM (10-54) [Feat. Clyde McPhatter]/Someday You'll Want Me To Want You [Feat. Clyde McPhatter and Bill Pinkney, duet]
1055 WHAT'CHA GONNA DO? (2-55)/Gone* [Feat. Clyde McPhatter]

*"Lucille" and "Gone," first session recordings from June 1953.

CLYDE McPHATTER (SOLO EFFORTS)

1070 EVERYBODY'S LAUGHING (9-55)/Hot Ziggity
1077 I GOTTA HAVE YOU (11-55) [With Ruth Brown]/Love Has Joined Us Together
1081 SEVEN DAYS (1-56)/I'm Not Worthy Of You
1092 TREASURE OF LOVE (4-56)/When You're Sincere
1106 THIRTY DAYS (1956)/I'm Lonely Tonight
1117 WITHOUT LOVE (THERE IS NOTHING) (1-57) [Backed by "Cues"]/I Make Believe
1133 JUST TO HOLD MY HAND (4-57) [Backed by "Cues"]/No Matter What
1149 LONG LONELY NIGHTS (8-57) ["Lee Andrews & Hearts" '57 hit. CHESS 1665]/Heartaches
1158 ROCK AND CRY (11-57) [Backed by "Cues"]/You'll Be There
1170 NO LOVE LIKE HER LOVE (1-58)/That's Enough For Me
1185 COME WHAT MAY (5-58)/Let Me Know
1199 A LOVER'S QUESTION (10-58)/I Can't Stand Up Alone
2018 LOVEY DOVEY (4-59)/My Island Of Dreams
2028 SINCE YOU'VE BEEN GONE (6-59) [Backed by "Cues"]/Try Try Baby
2038 YOU WENT BACK ON YOUR WORD (11-59)/There You Go
2049 JUST GIVE ME A RING (3-60)/Don't Dog Me
2060 LET THE BOOGIE WOOGIE ROLL (5-60)/Deep Sea Ball
2082 IF I DIDN'T LOVE YOU LIKE I DID (11-60)/Go! Yes! Go!

MGM

12780 I TOLD MYSELF A LIE (4-59)/(I'm Afraid) The Masquerade Is Over
12816 TWICE AS NICE (8-59)/Where Did I Make A Mistake
12843 LET'S TRY IT AGAIN (12-59)/Bless You
12877 THINK ME A KISS (4-60)/When The Right Time Comes Along
12949 ONE RIGHT AFTER ANOTHER (1-61)/This Is Not Goodbye
12988 GLORY OF LOVE (3-61)/Take A Step

MERCURY

71660 TA TA (7-60)/I Ain't Givin' Up Nothin' (If I Can't Get Somethin' From You)
71692 I JUST WANT TO LOVE YOU (10-60)/You're For Me
71740 BEFORE I FALL IN LOVE AGAIN (12-60)/One More Chance
71783 TOMORROW IS A COMIN' (2-61)/I'll Love You Till The Cows Come Home
71809 YOU'RE MOVING ME (4-61)/Whole Heap Of Love
71841 I NEVER KNEW (7-61)/Happiness
71868 YOUR SECOND CHOICE (10-61)/Same Time, Same Place
71941 LOVER PLEASE (2-62) [Written by 70s star Billy Swan]/Let's Forget About The Past
71987 LITTLE BITTY PRETTY ONE (6-62) [Thurston Harris '57 hit. ALADDIN 3398. Also Bobby Day '57 hit. CLASS 211]/Next To Me
72025 MAYBE (9-62)/I Do Believe

72051 THE BEST MAN CRIED (11-62)/Stop
72166 FROM ONE TO ONE (9-63)/So Close To Being In Love
72220 DEEP IN THE HEART OF HARLEM (1-64)/Happy Good Times
72253 IN MY TENEMENT (3-64)/2nd Window—2nd Floor
72317 LUCILLE (10-64)/Baby Baby
72407 CRYING WON'T HELP YOU NOW (4-65)/I Found My Love

AMY

941 I BELONG TO YOU (12-65)/Everybody's Somebody's Fool
950 LITTLE BIT OF SUNSHINE (3-66)/Everybody Loves A Good Time
968 I'M NOT GOING TO WORK TODAY (11-66)/A Shot Of Rhythm and Blues
975 LAVENDER LACE (2-67)/Sweet And Innocent

DERAM

85032 THANK YOU LOVE (1968)/Only A Fool
85039 BABY YOU'VE GOT IT (2-69)/Baby I Could Be So Good At Lovin' You

DECCA

32719 BOOK OF MEMORIES/I'll Belong To You
32753 WHY CAN'T WE GET TOGETHER (11-70)/Mixed Up Cup

♭ ♯ ♪ ♩ 𝅗𝅥

"Miracles"

ORIGINAL MEMBERS: William "Smokey" Robinson (lead), born February 19, 1940; Claudette (Rogers) Robinson (first tenor), born 1942; Ronnie White (baritone), born April 5, 1939; Bobby Rogers (second tenor), born February 19, 1940; Warren "Pete" Moore (bass), born November 19, 1939; (and Marvin Tapplin on guitar). Claudette (Bobby Rogers's sister) replaced Emerson Rogers (a cousin of Bobby) when he went into the U.S. Army in 1956.

Hometown: Detroit, Michigan.

It can be said that Bill "Smokey" Robinson, through the executives of one of the most influential of recording companies, gave the whole world many unparalleled performances with his "MIRACLES" and his own brilliant compositions, among which "The Tracks Of My Tears" (TAMLA 54118) led another giant entertainer, Bob Dylan, most graciously to describe him as "America's Greatest Living Poet."

Bill Robinson attended Dwyer Elementary School and Northern High School, where, in 1955, he met and sang with Ronnie White, Bobby Rogers, and Pete Moore at school dances. With Bill's extroverted nature he excelled in athletics and socially, but it was his burning desire to record as a group that led to the making of a demo tape with "Nolanstrong and Diablos'" song "Adios, My Desert Love" and the group's own treatment of it, which appealed to Berry Gordy, Jr. (owner of MOTOWN label), and Bill later became, at nineteen years of age, Gordy's first protégé! The group, with Bill's wife, Claudette (Bobby Rogers's sister), made its debut on George Goldner's New York END label with "Got A Job" (END 1016), which was an answer to the "Silhouettes'" "Get A Job" (EMBER 1029). The record did little for the group or Bill Robinson, but it was already noted by the writers (Berry Gordy, Jr.; Tyran Carlo, Jackie Wilson's cousin; and Bill himself) that the beginning of the MOTOWN organization (and its TAMLA label) was in the immediate offing. The "Miracles" had local action with "Bad Girl" (CHESS 1734; also MOTOWN's No. 1).

December of 1960 saw MOTOWN label cut its first Gold record with "Miracles" uptempo "Shop Around" (Subsidiary TAMLA 34034) written and sung by Bill Robinson! Bill also helped out with other MOTOWN group arrangements, the best example being on "Temptations" and their lead vocal David Ruffin's noted "My Girl" (GORDY 7038), a '65 contribution, as well as "I'll Be Doggone" (TAMLA 54112) for Marvin Gaye the same year. The list of "Miracles" recordings during the early Sixties includes "Ain't It, Baby" (TAMLA 54036), "Mighty Good Lovin'" (TAMLA 54044), "Everybody Gotta Pay Some Dues" (TAMLA 54048), and two hits, "What's Good About Goodbye" and the beautifully presented "I'll Try Something New" (TAMLA 54053 and 54059).

One of the principal secrets in the "Miracles'" success lay in how Bill "Smokey" Robinson could, with his humming, blend his remarkable mellow vocals through intricate lyrics and productions. From 1962 the romantic, sorrowful item "You've Really Got A Hold On Me" (TAMLA 54073) and the Holland-Dozier-Holland dance composition "Mickey's Monkey" (TAMLA 54083) highlighted the group's career. It seemed "Smokey" Robinson could be more effective on slower numbers, giving him more impact on a wider range of emotion within a few bars.

His compositions brought Mary Wells to stardom. Her hits "The One Who Really Loves You," "Two Lovers," "What's Easy For Two Is Hard For One," and the ever-popular "My Guy" brought big royalties to Robinson. Other compositions of his put on wax boosted the "Temptations"; "The Way You Do The Things You Do," "It's Growing," "Since I Met My Baby," "Don't Look Back," "I'll Be In Trouble," "Get Ready," and Marvin Gaye's "Ain't That Peculiar," "One More Heartache," and "Take This Heart Of Mine." At the end of the Sixties, Berry Gordy, Jr., made "Smokey" Robinson honorary vice-president of TAMLA-MOTOWN. "Smokey's" wife, Claudette, left the group and they went on to record four of the Top-Twenty discs in 1965: "OOO Baby Baby" (TAMLA 54113), "The Tracks Of My Tears" (TAMLA 54118), the enchanting "My Girl Has Gone" (TAMLA 54123), and the dance hit "Going To A Go-Go" (TAMLA 54127). Bill's writing, in the latter Sixties, had gained more perspective in his "The Love I Saw In You Was Just A Mirage" (TAMLA 54145) and "More Love" (TAMLA 54152), leading to the favorite "I Second That Emotion" (TAMLA 54159). "If You Can Want" (TAMLA 54162) had great response as a follow-up and then the classic soulful entry of 1969, "Baby, Baby Don't Cry" (TAMLA 54178).

It was the dramatic personal style of William "Smokey" Robinson that brought the "Miracles'" combined growing contribution to a memorable climax. "The Tears Of A Clown" (TAMLA 54199), a Stevie

Wonder/Henry Cosby composition, was a million-seller and No. 1 national hit; then "I Don't Blame You At All" (TAMLA 54205) and the lovely "We've Come Too Far To End It Now" (TAMLA 54220) became a musical high for the group and the sad climax, because Bill Robinson was feeling the need to spend more time with his wife and family, and a solo venture was already in sight.

Parting was sweet sorrow, with William Griffin replacing William "Smokey" Robinson, and on January 29, 1972, in Detroit's Elmore Casino, they made a public occasion of it to say bon voyage to Bill. For the record, William Griffin was born in Baltimore on August 15, 1950, and sang with the "Last Dynasty" group until his good friend Damon Harris (member of the "Temptations") brought him to the notice of the "Miracles." In his solo career debut, Bill Robinson paid tribute to his old group, the "Miracles," with "Sweet Harmony (Go Out And Spread Your Joy Round The World)". The "Miracles" continued with intro "Don't Let It End ('Til You Let It Begin)" (TAMLA 54237), the later disc hit of 1975 "Love Machine" (TAMLA 54262), and many others. A series of concerts followed in 1972, at Memorial Hall in Washington, D.C., honoring William "Smokey" Robinson for his wonderful fifteen years with the "Miracles." Both Bill Robinson and the "Miracles" will be long remembered in the volume and quality of their musical contribution to the world!

Discography

AS "MIRACLES"

END

1016 GOT A JOB (3-58)/My Mama Done Told Me
1029 MONEY (8-58) [Also released on END 1084]/I Cry

MOTOWN

1 BAD GIRL (6-59)/I Need You Baby

CHESS

1734 BAD GIRL (6-59)/I Need You Baby
1768 ALL I WANT (IS YOU) (3-60)/I Need A Change

TAMLA

54028 WAY OVER THERE (4-60)/(You Can) Depend On Me

AS "RON (White) AND BILL (Robinson)" [DUET]

ARGO

5350 DON'T SAY BYE BYE (10-60)/It

AS "MIRACLES"

TAMLA

54034 SHOP AROUND (12-60)/Who's Lovin' You
54036 AIN'T IT, BABY (4-61)/The Only One I Love
54044 MIGHTY GOOD LOVIN' (7-61)/Broken Hearted
54048 EVERYBODY GOTTA PAY SOME DUES (11-61)/I Can't Believe
54053 WHAT'S SO GOOD ABOUT GOODBYE (1-62)/I've Been Good To You
54059 I'LL TRY SOMETHING NEW (5-62)/You Never Miss A Good Thing
54069 WAY OVER THERE (9-62)/If Your Mother Only Knew
54073 YOU'VE REALLY GOT A HOLD ON ME (12-62)/Happy Landing
54078 A LOVE SHE CAN COUNT ON (4-63)/I Can Take A Hint
54083 MICKEY'S MONKEY (8-63)/Whatever Makes You Happy
54089 I GOTTA DANCE TO KEEP FROM CRYING (11-63)/Such Is Love Such Is Life
EX009 CHRISTMAS EVERYDAY (12-63)/The Christmas Song
54093 (YOU CAN'T LET THE BOY OVER-POWER) THE MAN IN YOU (2-64)/Heartbreak Road
54098 I LIKE IT LIKE THAT (6-64)/You're So Fine And Sweet
54102 THAT'S WHAT LOVE IS MADE OF (9-64)/Would I Love You
54109 COME ON AND DO THE JERK (12-64)/Baby Don't You Go
54113 OOO BABY BABY (4-65)/All That's Good
54118 THE TRACKS OF MY TEARS (7-65)/A Fork In The Road
54123 MY GIRL HAS GONE (10-65)/Since You Won My Heart
54127 GOING TO A GO-GO (12-65)/Choosey Beggar
54134 WHOLE LOT OF SHAKIN' IN MY HEART (6-66)/Oh Be My Love
54140 (COME ROUND HERE) I'M THE ONE YOU NEED (11-66)/Save Me
54144 I CARE ABOUT DETROIT

"SMOKEY ROBINSON & MIRACLES"

54145 THE LOVE I SAW IN YOU WAS JUST A MIRAGE (3-67)/Come Spy With Me
54152 MORE LOVE (6-67)/Swept For You Baby
54159 I SECOND THAT EMOTION (11-67)/You Must Be Love
54162 IF YOU CAN WANT (3-68)/When The Words From Your Heart Get Caught In Your Throat

54167 YESTER LOVE (6-68)/Much Better Off
54172 SPECIAL OCCASION (8-68)/Give Her Up
54178 BABY BABY DON'T CRY (1-69)/Your Mother's Only Daughter
54183 DOGGONE RIGHT (6-69)/Here I Go Again
54184 ABRAHAM, MARTIN AND JOHN (7-69) ["Dion" '68 hit. LAURIE 3464]/Much Better Off
54189 POINT IT OUT (12-69)/Darling Dear
54194 WHO'S GONNA TAKE THE BLAME (6-70)/I Gotta Thing For You
54199 TEARS OF A CLOWN (10-70)/Promise Me
54205 I DON'T BLAME YOU AT ALL (3-71)/That Girl
54206 CRAZY ABOUT THE LA LA LA (7-71)/Oh Baby—Baby I Love You
54211 SATISFACTION (11-71)/Flower Girl
54220 WE'VE COME TOO FAR TO END IT NOW (6-72)/When Sundown Comes
54225 I CAN'T STAND TO SEE YOU CRY (12-72)/With Your Love Came

"MIRACLES" (WITH BILL GRIFFIN)

54237 DON'T LET IT END ('TIL YOU LET IT BEGIN) (4-73)/Wigs And Lashes

SMOKEY ROBINSON

54233 SWEET HARMONY (7-73)/Wanna Know My Mind
54339 BABY COME CLOSER (11-73)/A Silent Partner In A 3-Way Love Affair

"MIRACLES"

54240 GIVE ME JUST ANOTHER DAY (12-73)/I Wanna Be With You

SMOKEY ROBINSON

54246 IT'S HER TURN TO LIVE (5-74)/Just My Soul Responding

"MIRACLES"

54248 DO IT BABY (8-74)/I Wanna Be With You

SMOKEY ROBINSON

54250 VIRGIN MAN (9-74)/Fulfill Your Need
54251 I AM, I AM, (12-74)/Family Song

"MIRACLES"

54256 DON'T CHA LOVE IT (12-74)/Up Again

SMOKEY ROBINSON

54258 BABY THAT'S BACKATCHA (3-75)/Just Passing Through

"MIRACLES"

54259 GEMINI (4-75)/You Are Love

SMOKEY ROBINSON

54261 THE AGONY AND THE ECSTASY (9-75)/Wedding Song
54265 QUIET STORM (12-75)/A Sleep On My Love

"MIRACLES"

54262 LOVE MACHINE (2-76)/Love Machine [Part 2]

SMOKEY ROBINSON

54267 OPEN (4-76)/Coincidentally

"MIRACLES"

54268 NIGHT LIFE (5-76)/Smog

SMOKEY ROBINSON

54269 WHEN YOU CAME (5-76)/Coincidentally

"MIRACLES"

54276 JUST PASSING THROUGH (10-76)/Old Fashioned Man

COLUMBIA

3-10464 SPY FOR BROTHERHOOD (1-77)/Bird Must Fly Away

SMOKEY ROBINSON

TAMLA

54279 THERE WILL COME A DAY (I'M GONNA HAPPEN TO YOU)/The Humming Song (Lost For Words)

"MIRACLES"

COLUMBIA

3-10517 WOMAN (MAKE THE WORLD GO ROUND) (4-77)/I Can Touch The Sky

SMOKEY ROBINSON

TAMLA

54284 VITAMIN U (6-77)/Holly
54288 THEME FROM "BIG TIME" (9-77)/Theme From "Big Time" [Part 2]
54293 WHY YOU WANNA SEE MY BAD SIDE (3-78)/Daylight & Darkness

"MIRACLES"

COLUMBIA

3-10706 MEAN MACHINE (4-78)/Magic Of Your Eyes

SMOKEY ROBINSON

TAMLA

54296 SHOE SOUL (10-78)/I'm Loving You Softly

DIANA ROSS, MARVIN GAYE, SMOKEY ROBINSON, STEVIE WONDER

MOTOWN

1455 POPS WE LOVE YOU (1-79)/Pops We Love You [Instr.]

SMOKEY ROBINSON

TAMLA

54301 GET READY (6-79) ["Temptations" '66 hit. GORDY 7049]/ Ever Had A Dream
54306 CRUISIN' (9-79)/Ever Had A Dream

♭ ♯ ♪ ♩ 𝅗𝅥

"Moonglows"

ORIGINAL MEMBERS: Harvey Fuqua, piano and lead vocal (born in Louisville, Kentucky, on July 27, 1929); Bobby Lester, first tenor (born in Louisville, Kentucky, on January 13, 1940); Alexander "Pete" Graves, second tenor (born in Cleveland, Ohio, on April 17, 1936); Prentiss Barnes, bass (born in Cleveland, Ohio, in 1921); Billy Johnson, guitar (born in 1924).

"Moonglows" (1959): Harvey Fuqua, lead vocal; Chester Simmons; Reese Palmer; Nolan Lewis; Marvin Gaye; and, later, Bobby Lester.

"Moonglows" (LANA label): Alexander "Pete" Graves; Doc Green; Bearle Ashton; George Thorpe.

"Moonglows" (1972): Harvey Fuqua; Alexander "Pete" Graves; Doc Green; Melvin Lewis.

Hometown: Louisville, Kentucky.

The "MOONGLOWS" will always be fondly remembered for their remarkable Doo-Wopp style, their delightful mood of song and highly sophisticated delivery. Their songs now stand out as a dazzling array of beautifully blended harmony, with each acclaimed a carefully woven masterpiece in its own right. The initial group, called "The Crazy Sounds" came together shortly after Harvey Fuqua came to Cleveland, Ohio, from Louisville, Kentucky, and comprised Alexander "Pete" Graves, Prentiss Barnes (brother of James "Pookie" Hudson of the "Spaniels"), and Harvey himself. In 1951, the group sought a fourth member, and Harvey Fuqua added Bobby Lester, a friend of his from Louisville, who joined them in Cleveland. Lester had already acquired an R&B circuit following and was anxious to form a quartet. Harvey had no professional experience of his own, but show business was in the family through an uncle, Charley Fuqua, being an original with the "Ink Spots"! The group, in 1952, came to the attention of Alan Freed (well-known deejay then at Cleveland's station WJW, who, incidentally, coined the phrase "Rock and Roll") and, after an over-the-phone audition, appeared on the local "Moondogs Show." Freed took over management of the group and suggested a name somewhat like "Moondogs," and that is how "Moonglows" was created!

The "Moonglows" were introduced to the local CHAMPAGNE RECORD COMPANY, and there, in 1952, cut "I Just Can't Tell No Lie" (CHAMPAGNE 7500), a song that was written by "Al Lance," a pseudonym of Alan Freed, but before much else could happen from it the company went out of business. The "Moonglows" were then brought to Chicago and CHANCE RECORDS, where, in June 1953, they cut "Baby Please/Whistle My Love" (CHANCE 1147), with the latter song being co-written by Fuqua and Freed. Several other recordings were made, including "Just A Lonely Christmas" (CHANCE 1150) and "Secret Love" (CHANCE 1152), with the latter riding high on R&B Charts but, again, before the popular new group could capitalize on it the company folded in December of 1954! Somewhat disillusioned after two recording shutouts through no fault of their own, both Harvey Fuqua and Bobby Lester went to work in a coalyard just to keep financially ahead.

The "Moonglows" turned elsewhere, and records were cut at CHESS RECORDS and its subsidiary CHECKER label under the group names "Moonglows" and "Moonlighters," respectively. With Phil Chess's label they cut "Sincerely" (CHESS 1581), which became a monster R&B Top-Twenty hit and proved itself by establishing what was to become the famous "Moonglow Sound": that rich deep harmony with pleading "ooh-wahs" in the background. It was co-written by Harvey Fuqua and Alan Freed. 1955 saw the "Moonglows" score with "Most Of All" (CHESS 1589), "Foolish Me" (CHESS 1598), "In My Diary" (CHESS 1611), and in personal appearances on the Rock concert circuit, as well as in their first movie, *Rock, Rock, Rock.* (Their other films were *Mr. Rock & Roll* and *Go, Johnny, Go.*)

The "Moonglows" continued to hold the public spotlight through 1956 with "We Go Together" (CHESS 1619), "See Saw" (CHESS 1629), "I Knew From The Start/Over And Over Again" (CHESS 1646), and into 1957, when Harvey Fuqua had to take over as lead singer because of internal group problems starting with "(I'm Afraid) The Masquerade Is Over" (CHESS 1651) and "Please Send Me Someone To Love" (CHESS 1661). The group's biggest hit ever and a million-seller, under the credit "Harvey and The Moonglows," was "The Ten Commandments Of Love" (CHESS 1705), but despite its great success it did not prevent the breakup of the "Moonglows"! Harvey Fuqua remained with CHESS RECORDS to record solo and also recorded duet with Etta James, cutting two singles: "If I Can't Have You" (CHESS 1760) and "Spoonful" (CHESS 1771).

In 1960 Harvey Fuqua, in association with Berry Gordy, Jr., formed his own labels, HARVEY and TRI-PHI. His very first release, "That's What Girls Are Made For" (TRI-PHI 1001), with Harvey backed up by the "Spinners," was a major hit. On HARVEY label, backed by the "5 Quails," Harvey Fuqua cut "Been A Long Time" (114), a snappy romantic Doo-Wopp number! Harvey Fuqua and Marvin Gaye (now fast friends and soon to become brothers-in-law of Berry Gordy, Jr., with Harvey marrying his sister Gwen and Marvin marrying sister Anna) recorded several numbers together as "Harv and Marv" for MOTOWN label, but none of these was ever released. Harvey also produced songs for "Johnny and Jackey" (Johnny Bristol and Jackey Beavers), for "Loe-Joe" (Lorre Rudolph and Joe Charles) and Shorty Long, but his greatest success was for Junior Walker with "Cleo's Mood," "How Sweet It Is (To Be Loved By You)," a Holland-Dozier-Holland composition and produced by Harvey Fuqua and Johnny Bristol, "Pucker Up Buttercup," which was written by Fuqua, Bristol, and Danny Coggins and produced by Fuqua and Bristol, and, lastly, Junior Walker's classic "What Does It Take (To Win Your Love)/Brain Washer [Part 1]," both sides written by Fuqua, Bristol, and Vernon Bullock while produced by Fuqua and Bristol. Harvey Fuqua also sang duet with Ann Bogan as "Harvey & Ann." Ann Bogan was with the "Challengers" on TRI-PHI label, then with the "Marvelettes," and finally with the groups "New Birth" and "Love, Peace & Happiness."

In the mid-Sixties, Harvey Fuqua married Gwen Gordy (Berry's sister) and left his singing for production and administration duties with MOTOWN RECORDS. There, with MOTOWN and subsidiary labels, Harvey Fuqua produced "Since I Lost You Girl/Don't Put Off 'Til Tomorrow What You Can Do Today" for the "Monitors," "Just A Closer Walk With Thee" for "Gladys Knight and the Pips," plus a series of excellent discs for Marvin Gaye, all the hits for Tammi Terrell, "25 Miles" for Edwin Starr, "Yester-Me, Yester-You, Yesterday" for Stevie Wonder, "My Whole World Ended (The Day You Left Me)" for David Ruffin, and "Someday We'll Be Together" for "Diana Ross and the Supremes."

Harvey Fuqua left MOTOWN RECORDS in 1969 to create his own music complex in Louisville. He got involved with RCA, producing, arranging and songwriting, and founded his own company, FUQUA III PRODUCTIONS. During the Seventies, Harvey Fuqua reformed and worked with the "Moonglows" and several other groups: "Nite-Liters," "New Birth," and "Love, Peace & Happiness." "Love, Peace & Happiness" comprises Ann Bogan, with Melvin and Leslie Wilson (both members of "New Birth"). The "Nite-Liters" gave us the 1970 instrumental hit "K-Jee" (RCA 74-0461) and are made up of four females (known formerly as the "Mint Juleps") and four males (known formerly as the "Four Guys"). The "New Birth" singers are Londee Loren (lead),

Melvin Wilson, Leslie Wilson, and Alan Frye, who have given us a number of funky and rhythmic numbers, such as "It's Impossible" (RCA 74-0540), "I Can Understand It" (RCA 74-0912), and the intensely inspiring "It's Been A Long Time" (RCA 47-0185). "New Birth" moved over to BUDDAH RECORDS in 1975 and the production talents of James Baker and Melvin Wilson!

Disco superstar Sylvester (Ruby Blue) was with the "Hot Band" when he was discovered by Nancy Pitts, female partner of Harvey Fuqua. Sylvester was rooted in Gospel, Soul and Funk, and it was Harvey Fuqua who produced his two monster discs, "Dance (Disco Heat)" (FANTASY 1160-827) and "You Make Me Feel (Mighty Real)" (FANTASY 1160-846).

Discography

"MOONGLOWS"

CHAMPAGNE

7500 I JUST CAN'T TELL NO LIE (1952) [Feat. Harvey Fuqua]/I've Been Your Dog (Ever Since I've Been Your Man) [Feat. Prentiss Barnes]

CHANCE

1147 BABY PLEASE (6-53) [Feat. Harvey Fuqua]/Whistle My Love [Harvey Fuqua and Bobby Lester, duet]

1150 JUST A LONELY CHRISTMAS (11-53) [Feat. Harvey Fuqua]/Hey Santa Claus [Feat. Prentiss Barnes]

1152 SECRET LOVE (4-54) [Feat. Bobby Lester]/Real Gone Mama [Feat. Harvey Fuqua]

1156 I WAS WRONG (6-54) [Feat. Harvey Fuqua]/Ooh Rocking Daddy [Feat. Bobby Lester]

1161 219 TRAIN (9-54) [H. Fuqua and B. Lester, duet]/My Gal [Feat. H. Fuqua]

"BOBBY LESTER & MOONLIGHTERS"

CHECKER

806 SHOO DOO-BE DOO (MY LOVING BABY) (12-54) [H. Fuqua and B. Lester, duet]/So All Alone [H. Fuqua and B. Lester, duet]

813 HUG AND A KISS (3-55) [H. Fuqua and B. Lester, duet]/New Gal [H. Fuqua and B. Lester, duet]

"MOONGLOWS"

CHESS

1581 SINCERELY (11-54) [Feat. B. Lester]/Tempting [H. Fuqua and B. Lester, duet]

1589 MOST OF ALL (4-55) [Feat. B. Lester]/She's Gone [Feat. A. "Pete" Graves]

1598 FOOLISH ME (6-55) [Feat. B. Lester]/Slow Down [Feat. B. Lester]

1605 STARLITE (8-55) [Feat. B. Lester]/In Love [Feat. B. Lester]

1611 IN MY DIARY (11-55) [Feat. B. Lester]/Lover, Love Me [Feat. B. Lester]

1619 WE GO TOGETHER (3-56) [H. Fuqua and B. Lester]/Chickie Um Bah [All Group]

1629 SEE SAW (9-56) [Feat. H. Fuqua]/When I'm With You [Feat. B. Lester]

1646 I KNEW FROM THE START (1-57) [H. Fuqua and B. Lester, duet]/Over And Over Again [Feat. B. Lester]

1651 (I'M AFRAID) THE MASQUERADE IS OVER (3-57) [Feat. H. Fuqua]/(Please) Don't Say Goodbye [Feat. H. Fuqua]

1661 PLEASE SEND ME SOMEONE TO LOVE (5-57) [Feat. H. Fuqua]/Mr. Engineer (Bring Her Back To Me) [Feat. H. Fuqua]

1669 THE BEATING OF MY HEART (10-57) [H. Fuqua and B. Lester, duet]/Confess It To Your Heart [Feat. B. Lester]

1681 HERE I AM (1-58) [Feat. B. Lester]/Too Late [Feat. H. Fuqua]

1689 IN THE MIDDLE OF THE NIGHT (4-58) [Feat. H. Fuqua]/ Soda Pop [Feat. H. Fuqua]

1701 THIS LOVE (5-58) [Feat. H. Fuqua]/Sweeter Than Words [Feat. H. Fuqua]

"HARVEY & THE MOONGLOWS"

1705 THE TEN COMMANDMENTS OF LOVE (6-58) [H. Fuqua and P. Barnes, duet]/Mean Old Blues [Feat. H. Fuqua]

HARVEY FUQUA (SOLO)

1713 I WANT SOMEBODY (1-59)/Dada Goo Goo

"MOONGLOWS"

1717 I'LL NEVER STOP WANTING YOU (3-59) [Feat. H. Fuqua]/ Love Is A River [Feat. H. Fuqua]

"MOONLIGHTERS"

TARA

100* BROKEN HEART (1959)/Glow Of Love

BOBBY LESTER (SOLO)

CHECKER

921 AM I THE MAN (1959)/Lonely Hearts

HARVEY FUQUA (SOLO)

CHESS

1725 TWELVE MONTHS OF THE YEAR (5-59)/Don't Be Afraid To Love

"MOONGLOWS"

1738 UNEMPLOYMENT (10-59) [Feat. H. Fuqua]/Mama Loocie [Feat. Marvin Gaye]

HARVEY FUQUA (SOLO)

1749 OOH OOH STOP! (TEACHER YOU'RE HURTING ME) (1960)/Blue Skies

ETTA AND HARVEY (ETTA JAMES AND HARVEY FUQUA)

1760 IF I CAN'T HAVE YOU (8-60)/My Heart Cries

"MOONGLOWS"

1770 BEATNIK (12-60) [Feat. H. Fuqua]/Junior [Feat. H. Fuqua]

ETTA AND HARVEY (ETTA JAMES AND HARVEY FUQUA)

1771 SPOONFUL (1-61)/It's A Crying Shame

---

*Also on JOSIE 843.

HARVEY FUQUA (SOLO)

1781 FIRST TIME (1961)/Mama

"SPINNERS"

TRI-PHI

1001 THAT'S WHAT GIRLS ARE MADE FOR (1961) [Feat. H. Fuqua. Marvin Gaye, drums]/Heebie Jeebies [Feat. H. Fuqua]

"5 QUAILS"

HARVEY

114 BEEN A LONG TIME (1961) [Feat. H. Fuqua]/Get To School On Time [Feat. H. Fuqua]

"BOBBY LESTER & THE MOONGLOWS"

CHESS

1811* BLUE VELVET (1-62)/Penny Arcade

"HARVEY & THE SPINNERS"

TRI-PHI

1010 SHE LOVES ME SO (1962)/Whistling About You

"QUAILS"

HARVEY

116 MY LOVE (9-62) [Feat. H. Fuqua]/Never Felt Like This Before [Feat. H. Fuqua]

120 OVER THE HUMP (1963) [Feat. H. Fuqua]/I Thought [Feat. H. Fuqua]

"HARVEY AND ANN" (HARVEY FUQUA & ANN BOGAN)

121 WHAT CAN YOU DO NOW (1963)/Will I Do

*Originally recorded in 1956.

"HARVEY" (HARVEY FUQUA)

TRI-PHI

1024 COME ON AND ANSWER ME (1963)/Memories Of You

"MOONGLOWS"

TIMES SQUARE

30 I'VE GOT THE RIGHT (1-64)/Baby Please

CRIMSON

1003 GEE (1964)/My Imagination

LANA

130 SINCERELY/Time After Time
131 MOST OF ALL/What A Difference A Day Makes
133 SEE SAW/Love Is A River
134 WE GO TOGETHER/Shoo Doo-Bee Doo
135 COMMANDMENTS OF LOVE/Half A Heart

RELIC

1024 I PRAY FOR LOVE/In The Still Of The Night

"BOBBY LESTER"

COLUMBIA

4-45081 HANG UP YOUR HANGUPS (1970)/Sweet Gentle Nighttime

"MOONGLOWS"

MR. P

101 SINCERELY—72 (3-72)/You've Chosen Me

RCA

74-0759 SINCERELY (8-72)/I Was Wrong
74-0839 WHEN I'M WITH YOU (1973)/You've Chosen Me

"NITE-LITERS"

74-0461 K-JEE (6-71)/Tanga Boo Gonu
74-0591 AFRO-STRUT (12-71)/(We've Got To) Pull Together
74-0714 I'VE GOT DREAMS TO REMEMBER (5-72) [Otis Redding '68 hit. ATCO 6612]/Cherish Every Precious Moment
74-0244 SERENADE FOR A JIVE TURKEY (4-74)/Peefoul

"NEW BIRTH"

74-0400 ONE WAY BLUE (1971)/What'll I Do
74-0540 IT'S IMPOSSIBLE (9-71)/Honey Bee
74-0647 TWO KINDS OF PEOPLE (I AM) (4-72)/Unh Song
74-0774 COME BACK INTO MY LIFE (9-72)/Come Back Into My Life [Part 2]
74-0912 I CAN UNDERSTAND IT (3-73)/Oh Baby, I Love The Way
47-0003 UNTIL IT'S TIME FOR YOU TO GO (7-73)/You Are What I'm All About
47-0185 IT'S BEEN A LONG TIME (1973)/Keep On Doin' It
47-9817 PRETTY WORDS DON'T MEAN A THING (LIE TO ME)/ It's You Or No One
10017 I WASH MY HANDS OF THE WHOLE DAMN THING (8-74)/I Wash My Hands Of The Whole Damn Thing [Part 2]
10110 COMIN' FROM ALL ENDS (12-74)/Patiently
10242 DO IT AGAIN (1975)/Pretty Music

BUDDAH

464 GRAND DADDY (4-74)/Grand Daddy [Part 2]
470 DREAM MERCHANT (7-75)/Why Did I

WARNER BROTHERS

8217 THE LONG AND WINDING ROAD (6-76)/Hurry Hurry
8255 FALLIN' IN LOVE (9-76)/Fallin' In Love [Part 2]
8422 DEEPER (9-77)/Deeper [Instr.]
8499 HURRY HURRY (11-77)/Mighty Army
8536 HOW WILL I LIVE (1978)/Squeezing Too Much Living

"LOVE, PEACE & HAPPINESS"

RCA

74-0402 DON'T BLAME THE YOUNG FOLKS (FOR THE DRUG SOCIETY) (12-70)/You've Got To Be The One For Me
74-0468 LOVE IS FAR STRONGER THAN WE (1971)/Message To The Establishment
74-0584 STRIP ME NAKED (12-71)/Unborn Child
74-0740 I DON'T WANT TO DO WRONG (8-72)/Lonely Room

"SYLVESTER"

FANTASY

1160-802	OVER AND OVER (11-77)/Tipsong
1160-827	DANCE (DISCO HEAT) (6-78)/Was It Something That I Said
1160-846	YOU MAKE ME FEEL (MIGHTY REAL) (12-78)/Grateful
1160-855	I (WHO HAVE NOTHING) (3-79) [Ben E. King '63 hit. ATCO 6267]/I Need Somebody To Love Tonight
1160-863	STARS (7-79)/I Need Somebody To Love Tonight

"O'Jays"

MEMBERS: Eddie LeVert (lead vocal), born June 16, 1947; Walter Williams, born August 25, 1942; William Powell (left group in 1976 because of an illness that led to his death, May 26, 1977); Sammy Strain (replacing William Powell), born December 9, 1941 (formerly of "Little Anthony & Imperials"); William Isles (left group August 1966); Robert Massey (left group September 1971).

Hometown: Canton, Ohio.

The group that became the "O'JAYS" was originally a Gospel quintet called the "Triumphs," of which Eddie LeVert and Walter Williams sang in a quartet known as the "LeVert Brothers." They first grouped together while attending McKinley High School, and an interested friend, Andreotti (who wrote songs for a pastime), had the group auditioned with DECCA label, but without success. The group continued to grow in popularity, with a strong hometown following, performing at Canton record hops and the YMCA. Soon, the Cincinnati-based KING label showed interest and had the group, under the name "Mascots," recorded for the prominent R&B label on two Doo-Wopp releases, the second of which, "Lonely Rain" (KING 5435), has now become a favorite Oldies-collectors' item.

A Cleveland, Ohio, disc jockey, Eddie O'Jay, warmly complimented the group and suggested a change of name and the opportunity to manage them. From here on the group became known as the "O'Jays" and went to Detroit, where they recorded "Miracles" (APOLLO 759), produced by Don Davis, who became a noted producer in later years. This record was actually leased to APOLLO label in New York but achieved little success.

H. B. Barnum (a West Coast pianist, producer, and owner of LITTLE STAR label) started working from Los Angeles on the "O'Jays" on what was described as "the fine points of singing." IMPERIAL label signed the "O'Jays," resulting in an instant hit, "Lonely Drifter" (IMPERIAL 5976). At this time the "O'Jays" backed up Lou Rawls and Jimmy Norman, both stars in their own right! After scoring a number of successes with IMPERIAL label, two of which were the "O'Jays'" version of Benny Spellman's New Orleans classic "Lipstick Traces" (IMPERIAL 66307) and that really fine ballad "Stand In For Love" (IMPERIAL 66197), LIBERTY label bought out the IMPERIAL label. This change in destiny, coupled with the departure of Bill Isles and general discouragement at not yet achieving a big national hit, saw the group break up!

In 1967, Leo Frank and Jules Berger reformed the "O'Jays" to perform at Leo's Casino in Cleveland. The "O'Jays" recorded briefly with MINIT label and then local disc jockey Rocky Gee brought the group to BELL label owner Larry Utah, where, under the direction of R&B producer George Kerr (later key figure with the success of ALL PLATINUM/STANG label out of New Jersey), the "O'Jays" recorded "I'll Be Sweeter Tomorrow (Than I Was Today)" (BELL 691), which was written by the Poindexters (Richard and Robert) and Jackie Members. George Kerr possessed a good insight into group harmony, having once sung lead for the "Serenaders" of '51 fame, e.g., "I Wrote A Letter" (CHOCK FULL OF HITS 102). The "O'Jays" now had a national hit and a Top-Ten R&B entry. During a special Christmas show in Cleveland the group was featured with headliner star Chuck Jackson, and during 1968 the "O'Jays" recorded two favorites, "Look Over Your Shoulder" (BELL 704) and "The Choice" (BELL 737).

The "O'Jays" continued as a quartet and, in 1969, signed with the Kenny Gamble-Leon Huff, Philadelphia NEPTUNE label, to record another hit, "One Night Affair" (NEPTUNE 12), which was later covered by Jerry Butler in 1972! Unfortunately, NEPTUNE's CHESS/GRT records ran into financial difficulties and the "O'Jays" allegedly suffered from nonpayment of royalties. Once again, the "O'Jays" returned to Cleveland to create their own SARU label, through which they discovered the soul-talented "Ponderosa Twins + One" for HOROSCOPE label, and it was here that Bobby Massey decided to leave the "O'Jays" to work with that group on production and business matters. In the Seventies, the "O'Jays" started up a Cleveland-based THE SOUNDS OF CLEVELAND label, but it proved an unsuccessful venture.

The "O'Jays," now a funky trio bubbling with excitement, were recalled when Gamble and Huff made a pact with PHILADELPHIA-INTERNATIONAL (COLUMBIA RECORDS) and fitted right in with a distinctive "Philly Sound"! Hits of an astonishing nature resulted for the "O'Jays," with "Back Stabbers" (PHIL-INT. 73517) selling a million, followed by a string of supercharged Disco-oriented classics: "992 Arguments" (PHIL-INT. 73522), "Love Train" (PHIL-INT. 73524), "Time To Get Down" (PHIL-INT. 73531), "Put Your Hands Together" (PHIL-INT. 73535), "For The Love Of Money" (PHIL-INT. 73544), "I Love Music" (PHIL-INT. 8-3577), "Darlin' Darlin' Baby (Sweet, Tender,

Love)" (PHIL-INT. 8-3610), and "Use Ta Be My Girl" (PHIL-INT. 8-3642). It was Kenny Gamble and Leon Huff, with their production techniques, who gave the "O'Jays" sound that message of Brotherly Love for the world to sing and clap along with, and their "Family Reunion" (PHIL-INT. 8-3596) and "Love Train" (PHIL-INT. 73524) provided that message of peace for all!

Discography

AS "MASCOTS"

KING

5377	DO THE WIGGLE (1960)/The Story Of My Heart
5435	LONELY RAIN (1960)/That's The Way I Feel

BLAST

206	ONCE UPON A TIME (1960)/Hey Little Angel

AS "O'JAYS"

APOLLO

759	MIRACLES (1-60)/Can't Take It [Leased from DAYCO]

LITTLE STAR

1401	JUST TO BE WITH YOU (1962)/Now He's Home
124	CRACK UP LAUGHING (2-63)/How Does It Feel
125	JOEY ST. VINCENT (5-63)/Dream Girl

IMPERIAL

5942	CRACK UP LAUGHING (5-63)/How Does It Feel
5976	LONELY DRIFTER (9-63)/That's Enough
66007	THE STORM IS OVER (2-64)/Stand Tall
66025	I'LL NEVER STOP LOVING YOU (5-64)/My Dearest Beloved
66037	LOVELY DEE (7-64)/You're On Top
66076	OH, HOW YOU HURT ME (12-64)/Girl Machine
66102	LIPSTICK TRACES (5-65) [Benny Spellman '62 hit. MINIT 644]/Think It Over, Baby
66121	I'VE CRIED MY LAST TEAR (8-65) [Ernie K-Doe '61 hit. MINIT 634]/Whip It Up Baby
66131	LET IT ALL OUT (10-65)/You're The One
66145	I'LL NEVER LET YOU GO (12-65)/It Won't Hurt
66162	PRETTY WORDS (4-66)/I'll Never Forget You
66177	NO TIME FOR YOU (6-66)/A Blowing Wind

66197 STAND IN FOR LOVE (10-66)/Friday Night
66200 LONELY DRIFTER (11-66)/That's Enough

MINIT

32015 WORKING ON YOUR CASE (1-67)/Hold On

BELL

691 I'LL BE SWEETER TOMORROW (THAN I WAS TODAY) (11-67)/I Dig Your Act

SOUND STAGE 7

2599 LET IT ALL OUT (1968)/Roadside—75

BELL

704 LOOK OVER YOUR SHOULDER (6-78) [Also released 6-73. BELL 1762]/I'm So Glad I Found You
737 THE CHOICE (9-68)/Going Going Gone
749 I MISS YOU (12-68)/Now That I Found You
770 THAT'S ALRIGHT (3-69)/Don't You Know A True Love

NEPTUNE (Distributed by CHESS/GRT)

12 ONE NIGHT AFFAIR (8-69)/There's Someone (Waiting Back Home)
18 BRANDED BAD (10-69)/You're The Best Thing Since Candy
20 (CHRISTMAS AIN'T CHRISTMAS, NEW YEAR'S AIN'T NEW YEAR'S) WITHOUT THE ONE YOU LOVE (12-69)/There's Someone (Waiting Back Home)
22 DEEPER (IN LOVE WITH YOU) (4-70)/I've Got The Groove
31 LOOKY, LOOKY (LOOK AT ME GIRL) (8-70)/Let Me In Your World

PHILADELPHIA-INTERNATIONAL

73517 BACK STABBERS (7-72)/Sunshine
73522 992 ARGUMENTS (11-72)/992 Arguments [Part 2]
73524 LOVE TRAIN (1-73)/Who Am I
73531 TIME TO GET DOWN (5-73)/Shiftless, Shady Jealous Kind Of People

BELL

378 LOOK OVER YOUR SHOULDER (8-73)/Four For The Price Of One

PHILADELPHIA-INTERNATIONAL

73535 PUT YOUR HANDS TOGETHER (12-73)/You Got Your Hooks In Me
73544 FOR THE LOVE OF MONEY (4-74)/People Keep Tellin' Me

ASTROSCOPE

110 PEACE (8-74)/Don't You Know A True Love

ALL PLATINUM

112 PEACE (1974)/Peace [Part 2]

PHILADELPHIA-INTERNATIONAL

8-3558 SUNSHINE (12-74)/Sunshine [Part 2]
8-3565 GIVE THE PEOPLE WHAT THEY WANT (5-75)/What Am I Waiting For
8-3573 LET ME MAKE LOVE TO YOU (8-75)/Survival
8-3577 I LOVE MUSIC (11-75)/I Love Music [Part 2]
8-3581 (CHRISTMAS AIN'T CHRISTMAS, NEW YEAR'S AIN'T NEW YEAR'S) WITHOUT THE ONE YOU LOVE (12-75)/Just Can't Get Enough
8-3587 LIVIN' FOR THE WEEKEND (3-76)/Stairway To Heaven
8-3596 FAMILY REUNION (6-76)/Unity
8-3601 MESSAGE IN OUR MUSIC (8-76)/She's Only A Woman
8-3610 DARLIN' DARLIN' BABY (SWEET, TENDER, LOVE) (11-76)/A Prayer
8-3631 WORK ON ME (7-77)/Let's Spend Some Time Together
8-3642 USE TA BE MY GIRL (4-78)/This Time Baby
8-3652 BRANDY (8-78)/Take Me To The Stars
8-3666 CRY TOGETHER (1-79)/Strokety Stroke
9-3707 SING A HAPPY SONG (8-79)
9-3726 I WANT YOU HERE WITH ME (11-79)
9-3727 FOREVER MINE (11-79)/Get On Out and Party

♭ ♯ ♪ ♩ 𝅗𝅥

Bobby Patterson

Born in Dallas, Texas, on March 13, 1944.

One has to grant the fact that BOBBY PATTERSON was born to entertain! It is said that Bobby, around the age of seven, strummed through his first public appearance on a toylike plastic guitar for the munificent sum of one dollar and fifty cents. With talent from such an early age, he was entertaining professionally around ten years of age and becoming versatile on both the guitar and drums. Bobby Patterson has, undoubtedly, proved himself an all-round talented artist, not only as an accomplished singer/musician, but also as song writer/producer and co-owner of his own label, SOUL POWER, in association with the parent company, JEWEL-PAULA RECORDS, out of Shreveport, Louisiana. Bobby is also a top-notch record promotion man, especially in the Southern states, across which he tours about fifty-two weeks of the year, and, except for the infringing demands of his live performances, he yearns to get back home on weekends to Dallas and his lovely wife, Patty.

Bobby Patterson was born in Dallas, Texas, on March 13, 1944. He attended C. Frazier High School and went on to two years at Arlington State College in Texas. A tireless and well-organized individual, Bobby, at that time, added the mastery of the saxophone and the organ to his accomplishments while attending school early mornings, playing Country and Western afternoons, and rendering Soul evenings! Then, while still in his early teens, Bobby Patterson formed his first group, the "Royal Rockers," with whom he won many local talent contests and "Battle of the Band." In fact, it was one of these events that led to Bobby and his "Royal Rockers" going to California to cut his very first record for LIBERTY, but, unfortunately, it was never released. Bobby Patterson stuck to his schooling but, undiscouraged, maintained an ongoing interest in his first love—music—by appearing at clubs and dances throughout the Dallas area.

The break that came was a local one and it came through one of Bobby's schoolfriends. His father, John Abnak, was owner of ABNAK RECORDS, a local company then beginning to make headway out of

Dallas, and it was ABNAK that signed Bobby Patterson, in 1962, with his recording of "You Just Got To Understand" (ABNAK 117). Though this was far from a success it convinced John Abnak to start a new subsidiary label, JETSTAR, for the growing Soul talent. Switching to JETSTAR saw Bobby Patterson evolve into a highly talented record artist and over a period of six years produce his own sessions and produce his own recordings while continuing his growing solo artist career. Bobby Patterson quickly blossomed into full stature with JETSTAR, giving us "If I Didn't Have You/What's Your Problem, Baby" (JETSTAR 107), "(The Girl I Used To Love) Long Ago/Till You Give In" (JETSTAR 108), and the first of many recordings with the "Mustangs": "Soul Is Our Music/Let Them Talk" (JETSTAR 109), "Broadway Ain't Funky No More" (JETSTAR 111), "T.C.B. Or T.Y.A." (JETSTAR 114), and "The Good O' Days" (JETSTAR 112). This series of hits had one terrific thing in common: Bobby Patterson wrote each one of them, he produced each one of them, he sang each one of them, and he did a bang-up job in the promotion of each of them! Then, in 1969, the JETSTAR label closed down and Bobby was left on his own resources.

Bobby Patterson concentrated on producing an album by himself with his own financial backing and then took the tapings to Los Angeles and New York, where he found various recording companies interested. Still, Bobby had his precious roots in Dallas and on his return home realized only too well that he would be better off and happier with a Southern-based recording outlet. In 1970, Bobby Patterson negotiated an arrangement with Stan Lewis (president of the growing JEWEL-PAULA string of labels) whereby he would be released through PAULA while his co-owned SOUL POWER label became the outlet for his own productions. His first PAULA release, "If You Took A Survey/Right On, Jody" (PAULA 352), was not a smash hit, but Bobby followed through with "How Do You Spell Love" (PAULA 362), which was right on target!

Meantime, SOUL POWER label was successfully on its way with Southern hits by Shay Holliday, and the "African Machine," those studio music-makers who ably supported Bobby himself on "How Do You Spell Love" (PAULA 362). Yet another side of Bobby Patterson, with his many talents, is a very special accomplishment, his pièce de résistance, where he performs on stage by playing the guitar with his teeth—an art he perfected long before Jimi Hendrix even thought about it and by which Bobby rendered readily recognized nursery rhymes and other melodies. All this distinguishes Bobby Patterson as an all-round artistic entertainer, an intelligent, highly creative, most reliable and gentlemanly person who still has a long, long way to go!

Discography

BOBBY PATTERSON

ABNAK

117 YOU JUST GOT TO UNDERSTAND

JETSTAR

107 IF I DIDN'T HAVE YOU (11-66)/What's Your Problem, Baby
108 (THE GIRL I USED TO LOVE) LONG AGO (1967)/Till You Give In

AS "BOBBY PATTERSON AND THE MUSTANGS"

109 LET THEM TALK (1967)/Soul Is Our Music
110 I'M LEROY, I'LL TAKE HER (1977) [Answer to Joe Tex hit "Skinny Legs And All"]/Sock Some Lovin' At Me
111 BROADWAY AIN'T FUNKY NO MORE (1968)/I Met My Match
112 DON'T BE SO MEAN (1968)/Good O' Days
113 SWEET TASTE OF LOVE (11-68)/Busy, Busy Bee
114 T.C.B. OR T.Y.A. (4-69)/What A Wonderful Night For Love
116 MY BABY'S COMING HOME TO ME (1969)/Keep It In The Family
117 GUESS WHO (11-69)
118 TRIAL OF MARY McGUIRE (2-70) Knock Out Power Of Love
119 IF A MAN EVER LOVED A WOMAN/You Taught Me How To Love

BOBBY PATTERSON

121 I'M IN LOVE WITH YOU (10-70)/Married Lady

PAULA

352 IF YOU TOOK A SURVEY (1971)/Right On, Jody
362 HOW DO YOU SPELL LOVE (2-72)/She Don't Have To See You (To See Through You)
379 IT TAKES TWO TO DO WRONG (1972)/Take Time To Know The Truth
386 WHAT GOES AROUND COMES AROUND (1-74)/I Get My Groove From You
388 I'M IN THE WRONG (9-73)/If Love Can't Do It

GRANITE

536 IF HE HADN'T SLIPPED UP AND GOT CAUGHT (4-76)/I Got To Get Over

ALL PLATINUM

2371 RIGHT PLACE, WRONG TIME (9-77)/I Got A Suspicion

♭ ♯ ♪ ♩ 𝅗𝅥

Elvis Presley

Real Name: "Elvis Aron Presley." Born in East Tupelo [Too-pel-o], now called East Heights, Mississippi, on January 8, 1935. Died at his Memphis Graceland Estate on August 16, 1977.

ELVIS PRESLEY was the greatest entertainer and contributor to the Rock and Roll musical phenomenon of the twentieth century. For the millions of his loyal fans he was well named "The King of Rock and Roll," and this was substantiated by his total lifetime record sales of 750 million! He was a unique, one-of-a-kind, much-liked performer who gave everything of himself, both on recording and personal appearances, to make his worldwide fans happy.

Though innately shy by nature because of motherly protection during his early childhood, Elvis Presley had a tremendous personal charisma that lacked anything suggestive of phoniness. A demanding perfectionist from the start, he developed a dynamic sense for phrasing, for imparting mood in song, with impeccable timing. He was a real natural-born ballad singer with a rare individual approach to the uptempo Rock and Roll performance always expected of him. He had great looks and an exciting animated pelvic motion, which fascinated his female fans, besides reflecting something of the Southern gentleman manner so exemplarily masculine to his equally devoted male fans.

Elvis Presley, one of twins, was born into poverty to Vernon and Gladys Presley in East Tupelo (now called East Heights) in Mississippi, on January 8, 1935. His twin brother, who was to be named Jesse *Garon* (to rhyme with Aron), died at birth. From their small two-room house in Tupelo, Elvis, with his parents, attended the First Assembly of God Church, a fundamentalist Baptist denomination, where they all sang in the choir. It was as early as this when Gladys Presley first noted that young Elvis could sing along without losing a note!

It was while Elvis was in fifth grade that his teacher encouraged him to enter the Mississippi-Alabama Fair, where he sang "Old Shep" to win the $5 second prize and free admission to the carnival rides. On his twelfth birthday, Elvis received a most exciting birthday present, a $12.95 folk guitar, from his parents! His Uncle Vester taught young Elvis a few chords, and from then on Elvis would strum and sing along for hours in accompaniment with the songs on the radio. The Presley family then moved to Memphis during September of 1948, and, there, at L. C. Humes High School, Elvis loved to entertain the pupils during lunch break, and earned some money as an usher at Loew's Theatre during the evenings. Elvis, now a spirited lad with some pride in himself, was fired for fighting but soon found new employment with the Marl Metal Products Company.

Things began to look up for this tightly knit family that had struggled so long just to make ends meet. Gladys, the mother Elvis loved so dearly, left her employment at a clothing factory to become a nurse at St. Joseph's Hospital, and Vernon, his father, broke away from sharecropping and truck driving to become a painter for the United Company, and Elvis, on graduation from high school in April 1953, began working for the Crown Electric Company. It was between tours of duty in this company's old Ford pickup truck, during one lunch-hour break, that Elvis went to the SUN Studios and made a $4 demo record of "My Happiness" (an "Inkspots" song) and "That's When Your Heartaches Begin" as a birthday present for his mother! Shortly after, in January 1954, Elvis made yet another demo record, this time of two country ballads: "Casual Love" and "I'll Never Stand In Your Way."

Elvis Presley, now turning eighteen, had fond hopes of becoming part of a vibrant young Gospel group but these hopes suffered a setback when he was turned down by the Gospel quartet the "Song Fellows," and what could have been a crushing blow when head man and DECCA agent Jim Denny told him he should go back to driving a truck! Elvis hung in there, and from his two demo recording sessions came fresh encouragement when SUN's secretary, Marian Keisker, brought "the lad with the sideburns" to the attention of label owner Sam C. Phillips. The Presley family was now living on $38.50 a week in a project called Lauderdale Courts on Winchester Street, but then moved into an apartment on Cypress Street. A specially warm part of Elvis Presley's unfolding dream was to provide his mother with a brand-new home of her very own!

Elvis was now rehearsing with guitarist Scotty Moore and bass fiddle man Bill Black, and it was here that Sam Phillips first heard that "unique sound" of Elvis Presley as the trio relaxed on a session and, amid the enthusiastic slapping of the guitar, sang "That's Alright (Mama)." Dewy Phillips, disc jockey at WHBQ station in Memphis, aired the group effort, "That's Alright (Mama)" (SUN 209), on his "Red, Hot and Blue" show to an overwhelming audience. One side was an old Blues master and the flip-side was Bill Monroe's Bluegrass song "Blue Moon of Kentucky." Elvis was discovering for himself a mixture of Blues, Country, and Rock in what became known as Rockabilly. Several regional hits followed: "Good Rockin' Tonight" (SUN 210), "Milkcow Blues Boogie" (SUN 215), "Baby Let's Play House" (SUN 217), and his own classic version of the Blues standard "Mystery Train" (SUN 223).

Elvis made his first stage-show appearance with Slim Whitman in July 1954 and then he toured the South with Scotty Moore and Bill Black as the "Blue Moon Boys," a group that was managed by Bob Neal and that became regulars on the "Louisiana Hayride." Elvis, around this time, was making commercials for Southern Doughnuts. Then the breakthrough occurred! Elvis appeared on the Country and Western "Hank Snow Jamboree" and in his preliminary performance (preceding Hank Snow) he literally stole the show! Oscar Davis, advance man for Colonel Thomas Andrew Parker (who had previously managed Hank Snow and Eddy Arnold), carried the good news home, and Colonel Parker was interested. The Colonel took over management from Bob Neal and, immediately, with his right-hand man Tom Diskin, headed for New York to seek out a major recording company interested in a contract for Elvis Presley. From bids of $10,000 (MERCURY RECORDS), $15,000 (COLUMBIA RECORDS), and $25,000 (ATLANTIC RECORDS), Colonel Parker turned to one company he had previously done business with as manager for Eddy Arnold. RCA RECORDS, through Larry Kanega (head), Steve Sholes (A&R chief), and Frank Folsom, signed an agreement to purchase SUN RECORDS' contract for $35,000, giving them all rights to previous masters, plus an extra $5,000 bonus for Elvis himself. Elvis Presley and Sam C. Phillips signed the agreement on November 22, 1955, and RCA RECORDS had acquired a bright new rising star!

RCA went to work right away to build effective backup for Elvis Presley recordings and guest appearances by using a barbershop-type singing quartet, the "Jordanaires," a group that remained with Elvis throughout his entire dazzling career and added something peculiarly their own that gave Elvis Presley his unique richer sound. The group's contribution was clearly marked on the first series of million-sellers: "Heartbreak Hotel/I Was The One" (RCA 6520), "I Want You, I Need You, I Love You/My Baby Left Me" (RCA 6540), "Hound Dog/Don't Be Cruel" (RCA 6604), and "Love Me Tender/Anyway You Want Me" (RCA 6643).

With each succeeding release now virtually a Rock and Roll masterpiece it is hard to believe that, barely one year earlier, in New York, Elvis Presley had been rejected for the Arthur Godfrey "Talent Scouts" show and that, earlier still, the knowledgeable head man at DECCA mistook an eager rising young star for a lowly truck driver! If nothing else, this proves that we are all human and have our very own blind spots. On January 28, 1956, Elvis Presley made his television debut on the first of four appearances on the Dorseys' show, singing "Blue Suede Shoes" and "Heartbreak Hotel," backed by the Dorseys' orchestra. This was followed by two appearances on the Milton Berle "Star Theatre," the first of which was on April 3 aboard the aircraft carrier U.S.S. *Enterprise*.

Colonel Tom Parker was proving himself a shrewd and enterprising manager who knew all the intricacies of developing a star performer and making money. The Colonel had Elvis fly to Hollywood and a screen test for Hal Wallis, where, after due consideration, Elvis signed to make at least three movies. These became *Love Me Tender,* 20th Century Fox release in 1956, wherein Elvis co-starred with Debra Paget; *Loving You,* a Paramount release in 1957, co-starring with Lizbeth Scott; *Jailhouse Rock,* a Metro-Goldwyn-Mayer release in 1957, in which Elvis co-starred with Judy Tyler (whose untimely death occurred shortly after completion of the film); and what has to be considered as Elvis Presley's all-time best movie, *King Creole,* a Paramount release in 1958 and co-starring Carolyn Jones.

Then a new Elvis Presley appeared "in tails" on the Steve Allen show, singing "I Want You, I Need You, I Love You," and there he also sang "Hound Dog" to a basset hound. This proved to be the highest-rated program on the NBC network up to that time. Now with money coming in from his movie *Love Me Tender* and other unfolding sources, Elvis Presley satisfied one of his earliest and fondest hopes: he bought his mother her very own home, a $40,000 ranch-style home on Audubon Drive! Then, on September 9, 1956, Elvis Presley made his first of three appearances on Ed Sullivan's *Toast of the Town* show, where he sang "Ready Teddy" and "Love Me Tender" with closeup camera (from waist up) and netted himself $50,000. His gyrating pelvic motions were considered, by some people, to be bordering on the vulgar, but Elvis Presley saw them as part of himself, of his sound, his unique style, his looks, and felt that without them he was "dead."

1957 found Elvis Presley riding high on the Charts and toward million-sellers with "Too Much/Playing For Keeps" (RCA 6800), "All Shook Up/That's When Your Heartaches Begin" (RCA 6870), "(Let Me Be Your) Teddy Bear/Loving You" (RCA 7000), "Jailhouse Rock/Treat Me Nice" (RCA 7035), "Don't/I Beg Of You" (RCA 7150), and so on, all reaching for classic status and million sales. But 1957 brought another change in the life of Elvis Presley, proving itself an eventful year in several ways. That year, he sold the home on Audubon Drive to purchase the Graceland Estate (13.8 acres) for $100,000, saw his family settled there, was honored by his hometome, Tupelo, declaring September 26 "ELVIS PRESLEY DAY," and hearing the call of Uncle Sam to perform more serious duties. Elvis Presley was ready to serve his country, but while waiting he completed a Canadian personal appearance tour in Ottawa, Toronto, and Vancouver. He then entered the U.S. Army as a private of the Second Armored Division, had his hair snipped off at Fort Chafee, Arkansas, and completed his basic training at Fort Hood in Texas.

In the meantime, Gladys Presley, his beloved mother, had developed a serious liver condition, hepatitis, which led to her hospitalization during the summer of 1958. Elvis was granted compassionate leave to see her, just before she died (in her forty-sixth year), on August 14, 1958. There was but little time for sorrow at his loss, for Elvis, on September 22, was aboard U.S.S. *Randall* heading for Bremerhaven for a two-year tour of duty with the U.S. NATO forces in West Germany. He served with some distinction at Frankfurt and reached the rank of Sergeant Specialist (4th Class) and met the second love in his life. She was Priscilla Beaulieu, then only fourteen years of age, daughter of a U.S. Air Force captain. After his discharge and return to his home, Elvis brought Priscilla back to stay at Graceland Mansion and it was there that she completed her schooling.

Elvis was then invited by Frank Sinatra to be a guest on his NBC-TV special and Elvis received an incredible $125,000 for a six-minute performance! The hits continued with the Elvis Presley all-time best-seller "It's Now Or Never" (RCA 7777), which was nominated "Song of the Year." The latest movie, *G.I. Blues,* in which Elvis co-starred with Juliet Prowse and was a Paramount release in 1960, won two Grammies! Colonel Parker then decided that, for Elvis, most of the Sixties would be spent acting and singing in the movies. Elvis Presley made a total of thirty-three movies!

The Elvis Presley hits during the early Sixties included "Are You Lonsome Tonight?/I Gotta Know" (RCA 7810), "Surrender" (RCA 7850), "I Feel So Bad" (RCA 7880), and "(Marie's The Name Of) His Latest Flame/Little Sister" (RCA 7908), with each grossing a million, and Elvis was back again from where he left off! Elvis Presley also raised $52,000 for the Hawaii Death Fund Benefit for Kula Kuiee. Money was more available now and Elvis, who knew what real poverty and lack of money meant, never hesitated in being generous with it. He was generous to his personal bodyguard members, known locally with affection as the "Memphis Mafia," comprising Sonny and Red West, Joe Esposito, Dave Hebler, Alan Fortas, Dick Grob, Jerry Schilling, Charlie Hodge, Ed Parker, and George Klein, among others. Elvis thought nothing of renting the Avon, Memphian, or Crosstown theaters so that he and his bodyguard friends could see the latest movies!

His earnings kept accumulating. Up to 1965 Elvis Presley grossed $135 million from the movies, with another $150 million from record sales.

He owned as many as fourteen different pleasure vehicles at one time, including his most famous 1960 gold Cadillac limousine with the yacht-like interior, tour buses (he even bought one for T. G. Shephard, the Country singer), motorcycles, a $3,000,000 Convair 880 jet aircraft, a Gulfstream twin-engine jet aircraft, a Lockheed Jetstar, a French-constructed Falcon DH-125, and a Boeing 707. Elvis Presley also had part or full ownership in the Elvis Presley Music Company, White Haven Music Company, Gladys Music Company, the Hill & Range Music Company, besides being partners with Colonel Tom Parker in owning BOX CAR label! In the early part of 1967, Elvis bought the 160-acre "Circle G" Ranch ten miles south of the Graceland Estate for $440,100, but sold it a couple of years later to see it turned into a country club.

Elvis Presley married Priscilla Beaulieu, his second great love, on May 1, 1967, and on the following February she presented the proud father with a daughter, Lisa Marie! Elvis Presley returned to the live appearance circuit and his many devoted fans. In 1969, he appeared at the International Hilton in Las Vegas, a return engagement, since he had performed in the New Frontier Hotel, Las Vegas, in 1956. Some of his biggest hits during this period were "If I Could Dream" (RCA 9670), "In The Ghetto" (RCA 9741), "Clean Up Your Own Backyard" (RCA 9747), "Suspicious Minds" (RCA 9764), "Don't Cry, Daddy" (RCA 9768), "Kentucky Rain" (RCA 9791), and "The Wonder Of You" (RCA 9835). Elvis Presley attracted one of the biggest crowds ever to the Houston Astrodome and gave several sell-out performances at Madison Square Garden in New York!

Elvis Presley, now caught up in the great popularity wave of his own making, was then on the road almost continually from here on into the early Seventies and, like many another great entertainment idol before him, it was to bring further heartache to him. Priscilla Presley, his wife, began to feel lost during these three- to four-month intervals of absence, and this, with the continuous presence of a large bodyguard force always around the home on Elvis's return, soon proved too much for her to bear. She finally asked for a divorce, and this was granted as final on October 9, 1973, on grounds of "irreconcilable differences." Elvis was sensitive to it all and deeply hurt.

From then on, Elvis Presley started to put on weight, and was hospitalized many times with a troubled twisted colon. He kept on performing, giving of himself to his demanding fans, to a point of physical and mental exhaustion and the needed support of pep drugs. Elvis Presley was slated to give a grand personal appearance in Portland, Maine, already a sell-out event! The day before this planned event, August 16 (two days after the anniversary of his mother's death on August 14, nineteen years before!), Elvis Presley was found lying face-down on the floor of his private dressing-bath room, at Graceland Estate, by his girlfriend, Ginger. The frantic attempts of bodyguard Joe Esposito and the ambulance staff proved of no avail to revive the stricken Elvis who, later, at Memphis Baptist Hospital, was pronounced dead from an apparent heart attack.

Discography

With Corresponding Backup Personnel

ELVIS PRESLEY

SUN

209 THAT'S ALL RIGHT (MAMA) (8-54) [Arthur "Big Boy" Crudup '50 tune. RCA 130-284]/Blue Moon Of Kentucky

210 GOOD ROCKIN' TONIGHT (10-54) [Wynonie Harris '49 tune. KING 4218]/I Don't Care If The Sun Don't Shine

215 MILKCOW BLUES BOOGIE (1-55) [Kokomo Arnold '35 tune. DECCA 7029]/You're A Heartbreaker
The above recordings were backed by Scotty Moore (lead guitar) and a stand-up bass played by Bill Black, with a slapping on bass, for there was no drummer!

217 I'M LEFT, YOU'RE RIGHT, SHE'S GONE (5-55)/Baby, Let's Play House [An Arthur Gunter '54 tune. EXCELLO 2047]

223 MYSTERY TRAIN (8-55) [Little Junior Parker and "Blue Flames" '53 tune. SUN 192]/I Forgot To Remember To Forget
The above singles were backed by Scotty Moore (lead guitar), Bill Black (bass), Elvis (rhythm guitar), and D. J. Fontana (drums).

RCA

6357 MYSTERY TRAIN (11-55)/I Forgot To Remember To Forget

6380 THAT'S ALL RIGHT (MAMA) (11-55)/Blue Moon Of Kentucky

6381 GOOD ROCKIN' TONIGHT (11-55)/I Don't Care If The Sun Don't Shine

6382 MILKCOW BLUES BOOGIE (11-55)/You're A Heartbreaker

6385 I'M LEFT, YOU'RE RIGHT, SHE'S GONE (11-55)/Baby, Let's Play House
Above were released SUN MASTERS by RCA.

6420 HEARTBREAK HOTEL (1-56) [Written by Mae Boren Axton, mother of singer Hoyt Axton]/I Was The One
The above sides were backed by musicians chosen by Chet Atkins: Scotty Moore (lead guitar), Bill Black (bass), Floyd Cramer (piano), Elvis (rhythm guitar), Chet Atkins (rhythm guitar), D. J. Fontana (drums) with backup vocalists, Gordon Stoker (one of the "Jordanaires"), Ben Speer, and Brock Speer.

6540 I WANT YOU, I NEED YOU, I LOVE YOU (5-56)/My Baby Left Me

The recording of "I Want You, I Need You, I Love You" was backed by the same musicians as for "Heartbreak Hotel," except that Marvin Hughes was on the piano (instead of Floyd Cramer); on "My Baby Left Me" there was only Scotty Moore, Bill Black, D. J. Fontana, Elvis, and Shorty Long (who had a respectable career as soloist for RCA, KING, TRI PHI, and SOUL labels).

6604 HOUND DOG (7-56) [Willie Mae (Mama) Thornton '53 tune. PEACOCK 1612]/Don't Be Cruel

The above sides were backed by Scotty Moore (lead guitar), Bill Black (bass), Elvis (rhythm guitar), Shorty Long (piano), D. J. Fontana (drums), with the "Jordanaires" featured, that is, Gordon Stoker, Neil Matthews, Jr., Hoyt Hawkins, and Hugh Jarrett.

6636 BLUE SUEDE SHOES (9-56) [Carl Perkins '56 hit. SUN 234]/ Tutti Frutti

6637 I'M COUNTING ON YOU (9-56)/I Got A Woman

6638 I'LL NEVER LET YOU GO (9-56)/I'm Gonna Sit Right Down And Cry Over You

6639 TRYIN' TO GET TO YOU (9-56) ["Eagles" '54 tune. MERCURY 70391]/I Love You Because

6640 BLUE MOON (9-56) [Lynn Hope '51 tune. ALADDIN 3095]/ Just Because

6641 MONEY HONEY (9-56) [Clyde McPhatter and "Drifters" '53 hit. ATLANTIC 1006]/One-Sided Love Affair

6642 SHAKE, RATTLE AND ROLL (9-56) [Joe Turner's '54 hit. ATLANTIC 1026]/Lawdy Miss Clawdy

The above seven singles were taken from earlier sessions and released for Rhythm and Blues impact and to create a black buying market for Elvis' style!

6643 LOVE ME TENDER (10-56)/Anyway You Want Me

The recording of "Love Me Tender" was backed by the "Ken Darby Trio"; "Anyway You Want Me" was backed by Scotty Moore (lead guitar), Bill Black (bass), Elvis (rhythm guitar), D. J. Fontana (drums), Shorty Long (piano), and the "Jordanaires."

6800 TOO MUCH (1-57) [Bernard Hardison '54 hit. REPUBLIC 7111]/Playing For Keeps

On the above sides the backup musicians were the same as on "Anyway You Want Me," except that it is unknown who played piano.

6870 ALL SHOOK UP (3-57)/That's When Your Heartaches Begin

7000 (LET ME BE YOUR) TEDDY BEAR (6-57)/Loving You

7035 JAILHOUSE ROCK (10-57)/Treat Me Nice

The above three singles were backed by Scotty Moore (lead guitar), Bill Black (bass), Elvis (rhythm guitar), D. J. Fontana (drums), and the "Jordanaires." On #6870 Dudley Brooks played piano; on #7000 no piano was used; and on #7035 Mike Stoller played piano. "All Shook Up" had Elvis tapping on his guitar.

7150 DON'T (1-58)/I Beg Of You

"Don't" was backed by Scotty Moore (lead guitar), Bill Black (bass), Elvis (rhythm guitar), Dudley Brooks (piano), D. J. Fontana (drums), Millie Kirkham (vocals), and the "Jordanaires"; "I Beg Of You" had the same musicians and the "Jordanaires," but without Millie Kirkham!

7240 WEAR MY RING AROUND YOUR NECK (4-58)/Doncha' Think It's Time
The above sides were backed by Scotty Moore (lead guitar), Bill Black (bass), Elvis (rhythm guitar), H. J. Timbrell (guitar), Dudley Brooks (piano), D. J. Fontana (drums), and the "Jordanaires."

7280 HARD-HEADED WOMAN (6-58)/Don't Ask Me Why
The above sides were backed by Scotty Moore (lead guitar), Bill Black (bass), Elvis (rhythm guitar), D. J. Fontana (drums), and the "Jordanaires."

7410 I GOT STUNG (11-58)/One Night
"I Got Stung" was backed by Hank Garland (lead guitar), Chet Atkins (rhythm guitar), Elvis (rhythm guitar), Bob Moore (bass), Floyd Cramer (piano), D. J. Fontana (drums), Murrey Harman (bongos), and the "Jordanaires"; "One Night" was backed by Scotty Moore (lead guitar), Bill Black (bass), Elvis (rhythm guitar), Dudley Brooks (piano), D. J. Fontana (drums), and the "Jordanaires."

7506 A FOOL SUCH AS I (3-59) [Tommy Edwards '53 hit. MGM 11395]/I Need Your Love Tonight
The above sides were backed by the same musicians and vocal accompaniment as on "I Got Stung."

7600 A BIG HUNK O' LOVE (7-59)/My Wish Came True
"A Big Hunk O' Love" was backed by the same musicians and accompaniment as was used on "I Got Stung"; "My Wish Came True" was backed by the same musicians and vocal accompaniment as was used on RCA 7240 sides. [*In 1959, Bill Black formed his own combo, the "Bill Black Combo," which recorded instrumental hits, "Smokie" and "White Silver Sands." Bill died of a brain tumor on October 21, 1965.*]

7740 STUCK ON YOU (4-60)/Fame And Fortune
The above sides were backed by Scotty Moore (lead guitar), Bob Moore (bass), Elvis (rhythm guitar), Hank Garland (bass), Floyd Cramer (piano), D. J. Fontana (drums), Murrey Harman (drums), and the "Jordanaires."

7777 IT'S NOW OR NEVER (7-60)/A Mess Of Blues
"It's Now Or Never" was backed by the same musicians and vocal accompaniment as was used on RCA 7740 and included Boots Randolph (tenor sax); "A Mess Of Blues" was recorded earlier on the RCA 7740 session!

7810 ARE YOU LONESOME TONIGHT? (11-60) [Blue Baron and "Blue Notes" '51 hillbilly tune on MGM]/I Gotta Know
The above sides were backed by the same musicians and vocal accompaniment as were used on "It's Now Or Never."

7850 SURRENDER (2-61)/Lonely Man

7865 WOODEN HEART (4-61)/Shoppin' Around
Above singles with the "Jordanaires."

7880 I FEEL SO BAD (5-61) [Chuck Willis '54 tune. OKEH 7026]/ Wild In The Country
"I Feel So Bad" was backed by Hank Garland (lead guitar), Boots Randolph (tenor sax), Floyd Cramer (piano) and the "Jordanaires"; "Wild In The Country" is by Elvis and the "Jordanaires."

7908 (MARIE'S THE NAME OF) HIS LATEST FLAME (8-61)/ Little Sister
7968 CAN'T HELP FALLING IN LOVE (12-61)/Rock-A-Hula Baby
7992 GOOD LUCK CHARM (3-62)/Anything That's Part Of You
8041 SHE'S NOT YOU (8-62)/Just Tell Her Jim Said Hello

The singles above were with vocal accompaniment of the "Jordanaires."

8100 RETURN TO THE SENDER (10-62)/Where Do You Come From?

The above sides were with vocal accompaniment of the "Jordanaires" and the "Amigos."

8134 ONE BROKEN HEART FOR SALE (2-63)/They Remind Me Too Much Of You

The above sides were with vocal accompaniment of the "Mello Men."

8188 (YOU'RE THE) DEVIL IN DISGUISE (6-63)/Please Don't Drag That String Around

The above sides were with vocal accompaniment of the "Jordanaires."

8243 BOSSA NOVA BABY (10-63)/Witchcraft
8307 KISSIN' COUSINS (2-64)/It Hurts Me
0639 KISS ME QUICK (5-64)/Suspicion [Terry Stafford '64 hit. CRUSADER 101]

"Bossa Nova Baby" was with vocal accompaniment of the "Jordanaires" and the "Amigos"; other above sides were backed by the "Jordanaires."

8360 VIVA LAS VEGAS (5-64)/What'd I Say

The above sides were with vocal accompaniment of the "Jordanaires," the "Carol Lombard Quartet," and the "Jubilee Four."

8400 SUCH A NIGHT (7-64) [Clyde McPhatter & "Drifters" '54 hit. ATLANTIC 1019]/Never Ending

"Such A Night" was recorded in 1960 with backup musicians Hank Garland (lead guitar), Scotty Moore (lead guitar), Elvis (rhythm guitar), Bob Moore (bass), Floyd Cramer (piano), Boots Randolph (tenor sax), D. J. Fontana (drums), Murrey Harman (drums), and the "Jordanaires; "Never Ending" was recorded in 1963 with vocal accompaniment of the "Jordanaires."

8440 AIN'T THAT LOVING YOU, BABY (10-64) [Jimmy Reed '55 hit. VEE JAY 169]/Ask Me

"Ain't That Loving You, Baby" was recorded in 1958 with backup musicians Hank Garland (lead guitar), Chet Atkins (rhythm guitar), Elvis (rhythm guitar), Bob Moore (bass), Floyd Cramer (piano), D. J. Fontana (drums), Murrey Harman (bongos), and the "Jordanaires"; "Ask Me" was recorded early in 1964 with the vocal accompaniment of the "Jordanaires."

0720 BLUE CHRISTMAS (11-64)/Wooden Heart [Joe Dowell '61 hit. SMASH 1708]

"Blue Christmas" was recorded in 1957 with backup musicians Scotty Moore (lead guitar), Elvis (rhythm guitar), Bill Black (bass), Dudley Brooks (piano), D. J. Fontana (drums), and vocal accompaniment of the "Jordanaires"; "Wooden Heart" was recorded in 1960 with vocal accompaniment of the "Jordanaires."

8500 DO THE CLAM (2-65)/You'll Be Gone
"Do The Clam" was recorded in 1964 with the vocal accompaniment of the "Jordanaires," the "Carol Lombard Trio," and the "Jubilee Four"; "You'll Be Gone" was recorded in 1962 with the "Jordanaires."

0643 CRYING IN THE CHAPEL (4-65) ["Orioles" '53 hit. JUBILEE 5122]/I Believe In The Man In The Sky
The above sides were recorded in 1960 with the vocal accompaniment of the "Jordanaires."

8585 (SUCH AN) EASY QUESTION (6-65)/It Feels So Right
"Easy Question" was recorded in 1962 with the "Jordanaires"; "It Feels So Right" was recorded in 1960 with the same backup musicians and vocal accompaniment as used on RCA 7740.

8657 I'M YOURS (8-65)/(It's A) Long Lonely Highway
"I'm Yours" was recorded in 1961 with the same vocal accompaniment of the "Jordanaires" (as used on RCA 7908); "Long Lonely Highway" was recorded in 1963 with the same vocal accompaniment of the "Jordanaires" (as used on RCA 8188).

0650 PUPPET ON A STRING (11-65)/Wooden Heart
"Puppet On A String" was recorded in 1964 with the vocal accompaniment of the "Jordanaires," the "Carol Lombard Trio," and the "Jubilee Four." For "Wooden Heart" see RCA 0720.

0647 BLUE CHRISTMAS (12-65)/Santa Claus Is Back In Town
The above sides were recorded in 1957. See RCA 0720 and "Blue Christmas" for backup information.

8740 TELL ME WHY (1-66)/Blue River
"Tell Me Why" was recorded in 1957 with backup musicians and vocal accompaniment as used on RCA 6870; "Blue River" was recorded in 1963 with the "Jordanaires."

0651 JOSHUA FIT THE BATTLE (2-66)/Known Only To Him

0652 MILKY WHITE WAY (2-66)/Swing Down, Sweet Chariot
The above Gospel recordings were made in 1960 with the "Jordanaires."

8780 FRANKIE AND JOHNNY (3-66) [Brook Benton '61 hit. MERCURY 71859]/Please Don't Stop Loving Me
The above sides were backed by UNITED ARTISTS recording studio musicians in Hollywood, 1965, with vocals by the "Jordanaires."

8870 LOVE LETTERS (7-66) [Ketty Lester '62 hit. ERA 3068]/Come What May
The above sides were backed by Scotty Moore (lead guitar); Chip Young and Harold Bradley (guitars); Bob Moore (bass); Floyd Cramer (piano); David Briggs and Henry Slaughter (organ); Charlie McCoy (bass and harmonica); Murrey Harman and D. J. Fontana (drums); Millie Kirkham (steel guitar); with vocal accompaniment from the "Jordanaires" and the "Imperial Quartet" (Jake Hess, Jim Murray, Garry McSpadden, and Amond Morales).

8941 SPINOUT (10-66)/All That I Am
The above sides were backed by James Burton (lead guitar); Bob Moore (bass); Floyd Cramer (piano); Murrey Harman (drums); and the "Jordanaires."

8950 IF EVERY DAY WAS LIKE CHRISTMAS (12-66)/How Would You Like To Be
"If Every Day Was Like Christmas" was backed by the same musicians and vocal accompaniment as was used on RCA 8870. "How Would You Like To Be" was recorded in 1962 with vocal accompaniment from the "Mello Men" (same session as RCA 8134).

9056 INDESCRIBABLY BLUE (1-67)/Fools Fall In Love ["Drifters" '57 hit. ATLANTIC 1123]
The above sides were backed by the same musicians and vocal accompaniment as used on RCA 8870.

9115 LONG-LEGGED GIRL (WITH THE SHORT DRESS ON) (5-67)/That's Someone You Never Forget
"Long-Legged Girl" was backed by the "Jordanaires." "That's Someone You Never Forget" was recorded in 1961 and backed by the "Jordanaires" (same session as RCA 7908).

9287 THERE'S ALWAYS ME (8-67)/Judy
The above sides were recorded in 1961 and backed by the same musicians and vocal accompaniment as used on "I Feel So Bad" (RCA 7880).

9341 BIG BOSS MAN (10-67) [Jimmy Reed '60 hit. VEE JAY 380]/ You Don't Know Me
"Big Boss Man" was backed by Scotty Moore (lead guitar); Grady Martin (rhythm guitar); Bob Moore (bass); Pete Drake (steel guitar); Charlie McCoy (harmonica); Floyd Cramer (piano); Murrey Harman (drums); with vocal accompaniment from the "Jordanaires" and Millie Kirkham. "You Don't Know Me" was backed by Grady Martin and Harold Bradley (guitars); Bob Moore (bass); Pete Drake (steel guitar); Floyd Cramer (piano); Murrey Harman (drums); vocal accompaniment by the "Jordanaires" and Millie Kirkham.

9425 GUITAR MAN (1-68)/High-Heel Sneakers
The above sides were backed by the same musicians and vocal accompaniment as were used on "Big Boss Man" (RCA 9341), except that Jerry Reed was featured here on guitar.

9465 U.S. MALE (3-68)/Stay Away, Joe
"U.S. Male" was backed by the same musicians and vocal accompaniment as were used on "Big Boss Man" (RCA 9341). "Stay Away, Joe" was with the "Jordanaires."

9600 YOU'LL NEVER WALK ALONE (4-68) [Roy Hamilton '54 hit. EPIC 5-9015]/We Call On Him
The above sides were backed by the same musicians and vocal accompaniment as were used on "Big Boss Man (RCA 9341).

9541 LET YOURSELF GO (6-68)/Your Time Hasn't Come Yet, Baby
"Let Yourself Go" was backed by Scotty Moore (lead guitar); Elvis and Charlie Hodge (guitars); and D. J. Fontana (drums). "Your Time Hasn't Come Yet, Baby" was recorded in 1967 with the "Jordanaires."

9610 A LITTLE LESS CONVERSATION (10-68)/Almost In Love
Above sides from the movie Live a Little, Love a Little.

9670 IF I CAN DREAM (11-68)/Edge Of Reality
"If I Can Dream" was backed by Tommy Tedesco (lead guitar); Mike Deasy (rhythm guitar); Larry Knectal (bass); Don Randi (piano, organ); Hal Blaine (drums); and the NBC Orchestra. Female accompaniment from the "Blossoms" (Darlene Love, Jean King, and Fanita Jones). "Edge Of Reality" came from the same soundtrack as RCA 9610.

9731 MEMORIES (3-69)/Charro!
"Memories" was backed by the same musicians as used on RCA 9547. "Charro!" was backed with the "Jordanaires."

0130 HOW GREAT THOU ART (4-69)/His Hand In Mine
"How Great Thou Art" was recorded in 1966 and backed by the same musicians and vocal accompaniment as used on RCA 8870. "His Hand In Mine" was recorded in 1960 with the "Jordanaires" (along with 1966 releases RCA 0651 and RCA 0652).

9741 IN THE GHETTO (5-69)/Any Day Now [Chuck Jackson '62 hit. WAND 122]
The above sides were backed by Reggie Young (guitar and electric sitar); Tommy Cogbill (guitar and bass); Mike Leech (bass); Bobby Emmons (piano); Glen Spreen (organ); Gene Chrisman (drums); with vocal accompaniment from Jeannie Green, Mary, and Ginger Holladay; also Wayne Jackson, Bob Taylor, and Ed Logan (on horns, with the "Memphis Strings").

9747 CLEAN UP YOUR OWN BACKYARD (7-69)/The Fair's Moving On
"Clean Up Your Own Backyard" was backed by the "Jordanaires." "The Fair's Moving On" was backed by the same musicians and vocal accompaniment as used on RCA 9741, except that here Sandy Posey was singing.

9764 SUSPICIOUS MINDS (9-69)/You'll Think Of Me
The above sides were backed by the same musicians and vocal accompaniment used on RCA 9741.

9768 DON'T CRY, DADDY (11-69)/Rubberneckin'

9791 KENTUCKY RAIN (1-70)/My Little Friend
"Don't Cry, Daddy" is a duet with Elvis Presley singing with Ronnie Milsap. All the above sides were backed by the same musicians and vocal accompaniment as used on RCA 9741.

9835 THE WONDER OF YOU (5-70) [Ray Peterson '64 hit. RCA 47-8333]/Mama Liked The Roses
"The Wonder Of You" was backed by James Burton (lead guitar); John Wilkinson (rhythm guitar); Charlie Hodge (guitar and vocal); Glenn D. Hardin (piano); Jerry Scheff (bass); Ronnie Tutt (drums); with Joe Guercio Orchestra and vocal accompaniment from Millie Kirkham, the "Sweet Inspirations," and the "Imperial Quartet." "Mama Liked The Roses" was backed by the same musicians and vocal accompaniment used on RCA 9741. Ronnie Tutt and Jerry Scheff originally backed "Delaney and Bonnie."

9873 I'VE LOST YOU (7-70)/The Next Step Is Love

9916 YOU DON'T HAVE TO SAY YOU LOVE ME (10-70) [Dusty Springfield '66 hit. PHILIPS 40371]/Patch It Up

9960 I REALLY DON'T WANT TO KNOW (12-70) [Tommy Edwards '60 hit. MGM 12891]/There Goes My Everything
The above recordings were backed by James Burton (lead guitar); Chip Young (guitar); Norbert Putnam (bass); Charlie McCoy (harmonica); David Briggs (piano); Jerry Carrigan (drums); vocal accompaniment from the "Jordanaires," Mary and Ginger Holladay, the "Imperial Quartet," and the "Nashville Edition."

9980 WHERE DID THEY GO, LORD? (3-71)/Rags To Riches
The above sides were backed by Edward Hinton (lead guitar); Chip Young (guitar); Norbert Putnam (bass); Charlie McCoy (organ); David Briggs (piano); Jerry Carrigan (drums); and vocal accompaniment from the "Jordanaires" and Jeannie Green.

9985 ONLY BELIEVE (5-71)/Life
The above sides were backed by the same musicians and vocal accompaniment used on RCA 9873, 9916, and 9960.

9998 I'M LEAVIN' (7-71)/Heart Of Rome
"I'm Leavin'" was backed by James Burton (lead guitar); Chip Young (guitar); Norbert Putnam (bass); Charlie McCoy (harmonica); David Briggs (piano); Jerry Carrigan (drums); with vocal accompaniment from the "Imperial Quartet," Temple Riser, Millie Kirkham, and Ginger Holladay. "Heart Of Rome" was recorded by the same musicians and vocal accompaniment used on RCA 9873, 9916, and 9960.

48-1017 IT'S ONLY LOVE (10-71)/The Sound Of The City
"It's Only Love" was backed by the same musicians and vocal accompaniment used on "I'm Leavin'" (RCA 9998). "The Sound Of The City" was recorded in 1970 and backed by the same musicians and vocal accompaniment used on RCA 9873, 9916, and 9960.

74-0572 MERRY CHRISTMAS, BABY (12-71)/Oh Come, All Ye Faithful

74-0619 UNTIL IT'S TIME FOR YOU TO GO (1-72) [Written by Buffe Ste. Marie]/We Can Make The Morning
The above recordings were backed by the same musicians and vocal accompaniment used on "I'm Leavin'" (RCA 9998).

74-0651 THE BOSOM OF ABRAHAM (3-72)/He Touched Me
"The Bosom Of Abraham" was backed by James Burton (lead guitar); Chip Young (guitar); Norbert Putnam (bass); Charlie McCoy (harmonica); David Briggs (piano); Glen Spreen (organ); Jerry Carrigan and Ken Buttrey (drums); with vocal accompaniment from the "Imperial Quartet," Millie Kirkham, June Page, and Sonja Montgomery. "He Touched Me" was recorded in 1971 and backed by same musicians and accompaniments as "I'm Leavin'" (RCA 9998).

74-0672 AN AMERICAN TRILOGY (5-72)/The First Time Ever I Saw Your Face
"An American Trilogy" was backed by James Burton (lead guitar); John Wilkinson (guitar); Charlie Hodge (guitar and vocal); Jerry Scheff (bass); Glenn D. Hardin (piano); Ronnie Tutt (drums); with vocal accompaniment from the "Sweet Inspirations," Kathy Westmoreland, and J. D. Sumner and the "Stamps"; also the Joe Guercio Orchestra. "The First Time Ever I Saw Your

Face" was recorded in 1971 with the same backup musicians and vocal accompaniment used on RCA 9873, 9916, and 9960, but with the addition of Millie Kirkham and Jeannie Green on vocals.

74-0769 BURNING LOVE (8-72)/It's A Matter Of Time

74-0815 SEPARATE WAYS (12-72)/Always On My Mind

The above recordings were backed by James Burton (lead guitar); John Wilkinson (guitar); Emory Gordy (bass); Glenn D. Hardin (piano); Ronnie Tutt (drums); with vocal accompaniment from "J. D. Sumner and the Stamps."

74-0910 STEAMROLLER BLUES (4-73)/Fool

"Steamroller Blues" was recorded in 1973 with the same musicians and vocal accompaniment that were used on "American Trilogy" (RCA 74-0672), excluding Ronnie Tutt. "Fool" was recorded in 1972 and backed by the same musicians and vocal accompaniment that were used on RCA 74-0769 and 74-0815.

0088 RAISED ON ROCK (9-73)/For Ol' Times Sake

0196 I'VE GOT A THING ABOUT YOU, BABY (2-74)/Take Good Care Of Her

The above recordings were backed by James Burton (lead guitar); Reggie Young (guitar); Johnny Christopher (guitar); Tommy Cogbill (bass); Bobby Wood (piano); Ronnie Tutt and Jerry Carrigan (drums); with vocal accompaniment from "J. D. Sumner and the Stamps," Mary and Ginger Holladay.

0280 IF YOU TALK IN YOUR SLEEP (6-74)/Help Me

10074 PROMISED LAND (10-74) [Chuck Berry '64 hit, CHESS 1916]/It's Midnight

10191 MY BOY (1-75)/Thinking About You

The above recordings were backed by James Burton (lead guitar); Johnny Christopher (guitar); Norbert Putnam (bass); David Briggs (piano and organ); Pete Hullin (piano); Ronnie Tutt (drums); with vocal accompaniment from "J. D. Sumner and the Stamps," Mary Holladay, Jeannie Green, and Susan Pilkington.

10278 T-R-O-U-B-L-E (5-75)/Mr. Songman

"T-R-O-U-B-L-E" was backed by James Burton (lead guitar); Charlie McCoy (harmonica); John Wilkinson and Charlie Hodge (guitars); Duke Bardwell (bass); David Briggs (clarinet); Ronnie Tutt (drums); with vocal accompaniment from Mary and Ginger Holladay. "Mr. Songman" was recorded in 1973 and backed by the same musicians and vocal accompaniment used on RCA 0280, 10074, and 10191.

10401 BRINGING IT BACK (11-75)/Pieces Of My Life

The above sides were backed by the same musicians and vocal accompaniment used on "T-R-O-U-B-L-E" (RCA 10278).

10601 HURT (3-76)/For The Heart

10857 MOODY BLUE (11-76)/She Thinks I Still Care

The above recordings were backed by James Burton (lead guitar); John Wilkinson and Charlie Hodge (guitars); Jerry Scheff (bass); David Briggs (electric piano); Glenn D. Hardin (piano); and Ronnie Tutt (drums).

10998 WAY DOWN (6-77)/Pledging My Love
"Way Down" was backed by James Burton (lead guitar); John Wilkinson, Charlie Hodge and Jerry Stembridge (guitars); Jerry Scheff (bass); David Briggs (electric piano); Ronnie Tutt (drums); with vocal accompaniment from J. D. Sumner (one of the great bass voices!), the "Sweet Inspirations," Gary Buckles, Kathy Westmoreland, Ed Enoch ("Stamps"), Sherril Nielsen, and Ed Hill.

RELEASED AFTER THE DEATH OF ELVIS PRESLEY (AUGUST 16, 1977)

ON *RED* WAX

RCA

11165 MY WAY (11-77) [Previously recorded by Frank Sinatra in 1969. REPRISE 0817]/America
"My Way" was recorded in 1973 with the same musicians and vocal accompaniment used on "Way Down" (RCA 10998).

ON *WHITE* WAX

11212 UNCHAINED MELODY (3-78) [Roy Hamilton '55 hit. EPIC 5-9102]/Softly, As I Leave You
"Unchained Melody" was backed by the same musicians and vocal accompaniment used for "Way Down" (RCA 10998).

ON *GREEN* WAX

11320 (LET ME BE YOUR) TEDDY BEAR (11-78)/Puppet On A String

ON *YELLOW* WAX

50476 LITTLE DARLIN' (11-78) ["Diamonds" '57 hit. MERCURY 71060]/I'm Movin' In
"Little Darlin'" was backed by the same musicians and vocal accompaniment used for "Way Down" (RCA 10998).

COLLECTOR SERIES (ALL ON *BLACK* WAX) RELEASED IN 1978

2694 ALL SHOOK UP/Heartbreak Hotel
2695 JAILHOUSE ROCK/Treat Me Nice
2696 I GOT STUNG/One Night

2697 A FOOL SUCH AS I/I Need Your Love Tonight
2698 IT'S NOW OR NEVER/Make Me Know It
2699 ARE YOU LONESOME TONIGHT?/I Gotta Know
2700 WOODEN HEART/Tonight Is So Right For Love
2701 SURRENDER/Lonely Man
2702 HIS LATEST FLAME/Little Sister
2703 ROCK-A-HULA BABY/Can't Help Falling In Love
2704 GOOD LUCK CHARM/Anything That's Part Of You
2705 SHE'S NOT YOU/Just Tell Her Jim Said Hello
2706 RETURN TO SENDER/Where Do You Come From?
2707 (YOU'RE THE) DEVIL IN DISGUISE/Please Don't Drag That String Around
2708 CRYING IN THE CHAPEL/I Believe In The Man In The Sky
2709 THE WONDER OF YOU/Mama Liked The Roses
2710 HOUND DOG/Don't Be Cruel
2711 BLUE CHRISTMAS/Santa Claus Is Back In Town
2712 SUSPICIOUS MINDS/You'll Think Of Me
2713 BURNING LOVE/Steamroller Blues
2714 HOW GREAT THOU ART/Amazing Grace
2715 BLUE SUEDE SHOES/Tutti Frutti
2716 DANNY BOY/The Last Farewell
2717 BLUE HAWAII/Hawaiian Wedding Song
2718 MOODY BLUE/Way Down
2719 YOU GAVE ME A MOUNTAIN/The Impossible Dream
2720 LOVE ME TENDER/One Night

ON *BEIGE* WAX

11533 ARE YOU SINCERE (4-79) [Unreleased Version]/Solitaire

ON *PINK* WAX (ELVIS PRESLEY with "SCOTTY AND BILL")

SUN

600 TWEEDLEE DEE (released 1978) [LaVern Baker '55 hit. ATLANTIC 1047]/Louisiana Hayride Interview [W. Elvis]

ALL ON *BLACK* WAX (CONT.)

227 HEARTBREAK HOTEL (released 1978)/Shake, Rattle And Roll

SIESTA

101 GENTLE ON MY MIND (recorded June 1970, released 1978)/Faded Love [Long Version]

SUN

520	TIGER MAN ('78)/Harbour Lights
521	BLUE SUEDE SHOES ('78)/My Baby's Gone
522	MONEY HONEY ('78)/Blue Moon
523	TUTTI FRUTTI ('78)
524	I GOT A WOMAN ('78)
525	TWEEDLEE DEE ('78)/Lawdy Miss Clawdy

SOUNDTRACKS: PREVIOUSLY UNRELEASED OUTTAKES AND ALTERNATE TAKES FROM ELVIS'S MOVIES:

101	(ELVIS and ANN-MARGRET)—THE LADY LOVES ME ('78)
102	(ELVIS)—JAILHOUSE ROCK ('78)
103	(ELVIS)—LET'S HAVE A PARTY ('78)
104	(ELVIS)—MEAN WOMAN BLUES ('78)

RCA

11679	I GOT A FEELIN' IN MY BODY (7-79)/There's A Honky Tonk Angel (Who Will Take Me Back In)

♭♯♪♩𝅗𝅥

Lloyd Price

Born in New Orleans, Louisiana, on March 9, 1935.

LLOYD PRICE, a husky New Orleans type of Rhythm and Blues singer, distinguished musician, arranger and composer, will be best remembered for the fact that his "Lawdy Miss Clawdy" was the first R&B record to sell a million! Lloyd, in 1959 and at the age of twenty-four, was voted "Top Rhythm and Blues Singer" on the Cashbox D.J. Poll and headed the cast of "Caravan of the Stars," Dick Clark's coast-to-coast musical show, which included such talent as the "Coasters," and "Drifters," Lavern Baker, and Phil Phillips. The same year, he gained international recognition with his "Stagger Lee," which gave him his second gold disc. Around that time, Lloyd also packed Combo Hall in Detroit with twelve thousand excited fans, more than came to enjoy Cassius Clay, the "Falcons," or Bobby Comstock!

Lloyd Price is not only a highly accomplished singer, musician, and producer of three million sales in records; he is also, with laudable distinction, a generous human being who has contributed much of his income to charity and educational scholarships for underprivileged ghetto students. He is one of the great shouters of the Fifties and early Sixties who gave us that sound with the tremendous heavy beat accompanied by a shrieking female chorus and massed brass backup. Now in near oblivion, following the recording career pattern of "Fats" Domino (and the late Elvis Presley in the Pop field), Lloyd now seems to prefer to rest on the laurels of the finest concentrated contribution ever made by any R&B artist.

Lloyd Price was born the seventh child of Louis and Beatrice Price, one of a very large and musical family comprising seven brothers and three sisters. His father, Leo, was a professional guitarist who became a minister of the Gospel. His mother, Beatrice, played the piano and sang traditional Gospel. His brother, Leo, not only got his start with Lloyd's youthful five-piece combo but was co-author (with John Marascalco) of many classic R&R songs, such as "Send Me Some Lovin'" and "Can't

Believe You Wanna Leave." Each member of the family could play at least one musical instrument, and Lloyd, at fourteen, was proficient at the piano and was leading his small band of junior music-makers at various social gatherings throughout the state. Lloyd, in retrospect and ever with an eye for talent, often compared their young soloist, Carmen, to Ella Fitzgerald!

Lloyd Price, while in high school at Kenner, took up the trumpet, which was something entirely different from what the rest of the family did. His youthful group became competent enough to appear in regular broadcasts on WBOK in New Orleans and it was while he was there that Lloyd caught the imagination of the public. He created "Lawdy Miss Clawdy" for a station-break commercial; it brought a flood of listener interest for more of the same and, eventually, became Lloyd Price's first recording in 1951 and his first million-seller! This has also been recorded by many other artists and remains one of the few Rock and Roll classics that became a standard. It was also Lloyd Price's first recording for Art Rupe's SPECIALTY label, one of fifteen very successful releases.

In 1957, Lloyd Price answered the draft and reported for duty to Special Branches Section, U.S.A.F., where he maintained his growing musical identity in performances before the armed forces in Japan, Okinawa, Korea, and elsewhere, often in cooperation with other topflight entertainers. During this time, Lloyd made quite a number of his own compositions, which became future smash recordings, often reflecting some of his personal experiences. On his discharge as sergeant, with honors, Lloyd returned to Washington, D.C., where he joined two former acquaintances, Bill Haskent and Harold Logan, to form their own recording company, K.R.C. Productions (Kent Recording Company) and the KRC label, which, in due time, lead to other labels: DOUBLE-L, TURNTABLE, and so on. Their first releases, "The Chicken & The Bop" (KRC 301), "How Many Times" (KRC 305), and "Hello Little Girl" (KRC 303), all suffered from limited distribution inherent to any small new company, but Lloyd Price soon corrected this by making arrangements with ABC-Paramount for future distribution on a national scale! The next release, "Just Because" (ABC 9792), was so big in sales that Harold Logan decided to devote all of his time and energy to managing Lloyd's increasing personal appearance demands and sold out his share interests to Bill Haskent.

1959 saw Lloyd Price achieve international recognition through "Stagger Lee" (ABC 9972). It topped the Charts everywhere and proved to be his second gold record. Then came his third million-seller, "Personality" (ABC 10018), and yet another, "I'm Gonna Get Married" (ABC 10032). Around this time, Lloyd appeared on the Ed Sullivan

TV show and the Dick Clark show, besides making personal appearances across the nation, all of which made Lloyd Price a household name!

Lloyd Price, from the very beginning of his career, had an appreciative eye for new talent and had much to do with the discovery or development of Larry Williams, John Patton, and Leon Blue, who all saw service as pianists with him. Lloyd also produced, for Howard Tate, "My Soul's Got A Hole In It." Two of his DOUBLE-L label smash R&B releases were "If You Need Me" and "It's Too Late" featuring Wilson Pickett. He also produced for the "Spaniels" on CALLA label in 1970 and gave us fresh talent in Wilbert Harrison, Pookie Hudson, Buddy Lamp, and ex-"Coaster" Billy Guy.

Lloyd Price also gave us something else creative of himself in "Pistol Packin' Mama" (DOUBLE-L 714), "This Is My Band," and Earl Garner's standard "Misty," which made the thirties in "HOT 100." We must also mention "Lady Luck/Never Let Me Go" and "Question/If I Look A Little Blue" (both ABC releases, 10075 and 10123). Lloyd also highlighted Johnny Nash on his JAD label.

In 1964, Lloyd Price signed with MONUMENT label and gave us several releases, such as "I Love You/Don't Cry" (MONUMENT 856), a cover version of "Amen," and "Woman/Oh Lady Luck" (MONUMENT 877). Lloyd, in 1966, also gave us another fine release on REPRISE label, "The Man Who Took The Valise (Off The Floor Of The Grand Central Station At Noon)/I Wont Cry Anymore" (REPRISE 0499), and, in 1969, he gave us "The Will To Sing For You/I Understand" (TURNTABLE 501) and "Bad Conditions/The Truth" (TURNTABLE 506). On the GSF label, Lloyd enjoyed several fine releases, including "Trying To Slip (Away)/They Get Down" (GSF 1208-6904), written and produced by Frederick Knight.

Lloyd Price is happily married to Emma Meredith and enjoying their two children, Lloyd and Lori, at home in Philly. From his office in New York, Lloyd conducts several of his prospering business enterprises, some label productions, personal appearances, and he can be seen twice weekly with his band at his Turntable spot (the old Birdland Club) on Broadway. And, as we said before, Lloyd Price seems to be resting rather profitably on his well-earned laurels!

Discography

LLOYD PRICE

SPECIALTY

428	LAWDY MISS CLAWDY (5-52)/Mailman Blues
440	OOOH—OOOH—OOH (10-52)/Restless Heart

452	AIN'T IT A SHAME (1-53)/Tell Me Pretty Baby
457	WHAT'S THE MATTER NOW (1953)/So Long
463	WHERE YOU AT? (1953)/Baby Don't Turn Your Back On Me
471	I WISH YOUR PICTURE WAS YOU (1953)/Frog Legs
483	LET ME COME HOME, BABY (1954)/Too Late For Tears
494	WALKIN' THE TRACK (1954)/Jimmie Lee
535	CHEE-KOO BABY (1954)/Oo Ee Baby
540	LORD, LORD, AMEN! (1954)/Trying To Find Someone To Love
571	I YI YI GOMEN-A-SAI (I'M SORRY) (3-56)/Woe Ho Ho
578	ROCK'N'DANCE (6-56)/Country Boy Rock
582	FORGIVE ME, CLAWDY (9-56)/I'm Glad, Glad
602	BABY PLEASE COME HOME (5-57)/Breaking My Heart (All Over Again)
661	LAWDY, MISS CLAWDY (4-59)/Mailman Blues

ABC

9792*	JUST BECAUSE (2-57)/Why

KRC (KENT RECORD COMPANY)

301	LONELY CHAIR (7-57)/The Chicken & The Bop
303	GEORGIANNA/Hello Little Girl
305	HOW MANY TIMES/To Love And Be Loved
5000	NO LIMIT TO LOVE/Such A Mess
5002	GONNA LET YOU COME BACK/Down By The River

ABC

9972	STAGGER LEE (12-58)/You Need Love
9997	WHERE WERE YOU (ON OUR WEDDING DAY) (3-59)/Is It Really You
10018	PERSONALITY (5-59)/Have You Ever Had The Blues
10032	I'M GONNA GET MARRIED (8-59)/Three Little Pigs
10062	COME INTO MY HEART (11-59)/Won't Cha Come Home
10075	LADY LUCK (2-60)/Never Let Me Go
10102	NO IFS—NO ANDS (5-60)/For Love
10123	QUESTION (7-60)/If I Look A Little Blue
10139	JUST CALL ME (AND I'LL UNDERSTAND) (9-60)/Who Coulda' Told You (They Lied)
10162	(YOU BETTER) KNOW WHAT YOU'RE DOIN' (12-60)/That's Why Tears Come And Go
10168	THE LEGEND OF NIGGER CHARLIE/In The Eyes Of God
10177	I MADE YOU CRY (3-61)/Boo Hoo
10197	SAY I'M THE ONE/One Hundred Percent
10206	CHANTILLY LACE/Strings Of Pearls
10221	I AIN'T GIVIN' UP NOTHIN' (8-61)/Mary And Man—O
10229	I COVER THE WATERFRONT/Talk To Me
10288	BE A LEADER/'Nother Fairy Tale
10299	TWISTIN' THE BLUES/Popeye's Irresistible You

*Also on KENT 300.

10342 COUNTERFEIT FRIENDS (7-62)/Your Picture
10372 UNDER YOUR SPELL AGAIN (11-62)/Happy Birthday Mama
10412 WHO'S SORRY NOW (1963)/Hello Bill

DOUBLE-L

714 TENNESSEE WALTZ/Pistol Packin' Mama
722 MISTY (10-63)/Cry On
728 MERRY CHRISTMAS MAMA (12-64)/Auld Lang Syne
729 BILLIE BOY (1-64)/Try A Little Tenderness
730 I'LL BE A FOOL FOR YOU/You're Nobody Till Somebody Loves You
736 GO ON LITTLE GIRL (10-65)/You're Reading Me
739 PEEPING AND HIDING (11-66)/Every Night
740 SEND ME SOME LOVIN'/Somewhere Along
READY FOR BETTY/Beat In Trinidad

MONUMENT

856 I LOVE YOU (9-64)/Don't Cry
865 AMEN (1-65)/I'd Fight The World

HURD

82 SATURDAY NIGHT (1966)/Misty

MONUMENT

877 WOMAN (4-65)/Oh, Lady Luck
887 TWO FOR LOVE (7-65)/If I Had My Life To Live Over

REPRISE

0499 THE MAN WHO TOOK THE VALISE (OFF THE FLOOR OF GRAND CENTRAL STATION AT NOON) (8-66)/I Won't Cry Anymore

LUDIX PRODUCTIONS

4747 CUPID'S BANDWAGON (1968)/Feelin' Good

JAD

208 TAKE ALL (1969)/Luv, Luv, Luv

TURNTABLE

501 THE WILL TO SING FOR YOU (1969)/I Understand
506 BAD CONDITIONS (10-69)/The Truth
LAWDY, MISS CLAWDY (1970)/Little Volcano

SCEPTER

12310 HOOKED ON A FEELING (3-71)/If You Really Love Him
12327 NATURAL SINNER (7-71)/Mr & Mrs Untrue

GSF

1208-6882	SING A SONG (1972)
1208-6894	LOVE MUSIC (2-73)/Just For Baby
1208-6904	TRYING TO SLIP (AWAY) (8-73)/They Get Down

CURIO

7039	COME ON ME/Misery

SIMTONE

2002	GLITTER QUEEN (1974)/Glitter Graphics

LPG

111	WHAT DID YOU DO WITH MY LOVE (8-76)/Love Music

OLDE WORLD

1104	FOR NO REASON (7-78)

Otis Redding

Born in Dawson, Georgia, on September 9, 1941. Died (near Madison, Wisconsin) on December 10, 1967, when his private twin-engine Beechcraft crashed into Lake Monona. Killed with him were four of his backup band, the "Bar-Kays."

OTIS REDDING was a big, shy country boy who became the major force behind the success and acclaim of the Memphis Sound! On stage, he took after his idol Little Richard and by his raw aggressiveness and nonstop emotionalism quickly whipped the audience into a frenzy. Otis Redding not only created his own songs while playing his guitar but founded his own publishing company, Redwal Music, and later his own label, JOTIS, which introduced his protégé, Arthur Conley, with whom Otis produced and showed great promise in Conley's top-selling smash "Sweet Soul Music" (ATCO 6423) in 1967.

Otis Redding was brought up in Macon, Georgia, and was one of six children to the Reverend Otis Redding, Sr., and his wife, Fanny. He had four sisters (Louise, Christine, Deborah, and Darlene) and one brother, Luther (who worked with Clarence Carter). Otis, like so many other talented black youngsters before him, sang in the church choir and developed the habit of winning talent shows. After leaving Ballard Hudson High School with a ninth-grade education, he worked at well drilling and, in 1961, married Zelma Atwood. Otis Redding was already proving to be a friend to everyone around him.

Otis Redding made his debut on Denver's FINER ARTS label in 1959 and with the "Shooters" group cut "Tuff Enuff" (FINER ARTS 2016), but this was not released until 1966. During the early Sixties, Otis played piano and toured with Johnny Jenkins and the "Pinetoppers" between Macon and Memphis. It was STAX owner Jimmy Stewart who signed Otis Redding for his subsidiary label, VOLT. Earlier, in 1960, Otis Redding was featured with the "Pinetoppers" in "Shout Bamalama" (CONFEDERATE 135), an uptempo wild rocker that has become a classic and that was revived by Mickey Murray (S.S.S. INTERNATIONAL

715) in 1967. In 1962, Duane Allman was featured at the guitar and Otis Redding at the piano on the catchy instrumental "Love Twist" (ATLANTIC 2144). Shortly afterward, Joe Galkin discovered Otis Redding and brought him to Phil Walden (later CAPRICORN label owner), who became his manager.

"These Arms Of Mine" (VOLT 103) became Otis Redding's first Rhythm and Blues national hit, with Johnny Jenkins at the guitar. "Pain In My Heart" (VOLT 112) was recorded at the Apollo Theater, in New York City and was followed by "Security" (VOLT 117), which became a hit when revived by Etta James (CADET 5594) in 1968. Otis Redding then built a large ranch of three hundred acres called the "Big O" for his family. Other exciting and stimulating recordings followed: "Mr. Pitiful/That's How Strong My Love Is" (VOLT 124) and the beautiful "I've Been Loving You Too Long" (VOLT 126), which was written with Jerry Butler. Then Otis Redding recorded two of his favorites: "Respect" (VOLT 128), which was revived by Aretha Franklin for a 1967 smash hit (ATLANTIC 2043), and "I Can't Turn You Loose" (VOLT 130), which also became a hit for the Chambers Brothers (COLUMBIA 44679) in 1968.

With the "Rolling Stones" then doing cover versions of "Pain In My Heart" and "That's How Strong My Love Is," Otis Redding soon reacted with his own renditions of "Satisfaction" (VOLT 132) and "My Lover's Prayer" (VOLT 136), which reached Top-Ten R&B Chart appeal. Then two all-time Otis Redding standards followed: "Fa-Fa-Fa-Fa-Fa (Sad Song)" (VOLT 138) and "Try A Little Tenderness" (VOLT 141). After a very successful British and European live guest singing appearance, Otis Redding returned to the U.S. for the 1967 Monterey Festival. No matter how great his career or the tremendous public demand Otis Redding never neglected that most special interest of all, his wife and family (he now had three sons); his recording "I Love You More Than Words Can Say" (VOLT 146) was dedicated to his wife! This was followed by his first "Otis & Carla" (THOMAS) record, "Tramp" (STAX 216), their most successful together.

With 1967 edging to a close came his two Oldie revivals: "Shake" (VOLT 149), in a personal tribute to one of Otis Redding's inspirations, Sam Cooke, and "The Glory Of Love" (VOLT 152), that grand group standard. That same year Otis, already owning a Piper Cub plane, secured for his increased workload a Beechcraft, which carried him and his group from New Jersey through Memphis and back north to Cleveland. It was on the fateful December 10, 1967, that Otis Redding, with Jimmy King (18), Ron Caldwell (19), Phalin Jones (18), and Carl Cunningham (18) (all members of his "Bar-Kays"), and their pilot died when their plane crashed into Lake Monona, near Madison, Wisconsin.

Discography

AS "PINETOPPERS" (Feat. OTIS REDDING)

CONFEDERATE

135 SHOUT BAMALAMA (5-60)/Fat Gal
[Also on KING 6149 and BETHLEHEM 3083]

ALSHIVE

5082 GETTIN' HIP/Gamma Lama

GALE

102 IT'S LOVE AND IT'S REAL

ATLANTIC

2144 LOVE TWIST (5-62)/Pinetop
[Also on GERALD 1001]

AS "SHOOTERS" (Feat. OTIS REDDING)

FINER ARTS

2016 TUFF ENUFF (11-66)/She's Alright

OTIS REDDING

VOLT

103 THESE ARMS OF MINE (3-63)/Hey Hey Baby
109 MARY'S LITTLE LAMB (9-63)/That's What My Heart Needs
112 PAIN IN MY HEART (11-63)/Something Is Worrying Me
116 COME TO ME (3-64)/Don't Leave Me This Way
117 SECURITY (4-64)/I Want To Thank You
121 YOUR ONE AND ONLY MAN (10-64)/Chained And Bound
124 MR PITIFUL (2-65)/That's How Strong My Love Is
126 I'VE BEEN LOVING YOU TOO LONG (5-65)/I'm Depending On You
128 RESPECT (9-65)/Ole Man Trouble
130 I CAN'T TURN YOU LOOSE (12-65)/Just One More Day
132 SATISFACTION (3-66) ["Rolling Stones" '65 hit. LONDON 9766]/Any Ole Way
136 MY LOVER'S PRAYER (6-66)/Don't Mess With Cupid
138 FA-FA-FA-FA-FA (SAD SONG) (10-66)/Good To Me

141 TRY A LITTLE TENDERNESS (12-66) [Edited Version]/I'm Sick Y'all

146 I LOVE YOU MORE THAN WORDS CAN SAY (4-67)/Let Me Come On Home

AS "OTIS & CARLA"

STAX

216 TRAMP (5-67)/Tell It Like It Is

OTIS REDDING

VOLT

149 SHAKE (6-67) [Sam Cooke '65 hit. RCA 47-8486]/You Don't Miss Your Water

152 GLORY OF LOVE (8-67)/I'm Coming Home

AS "OTIS & CARLA"

STAX

228 KNOCK ON WOOD (9-67) [Eddie Floyd '66 hit. STAX 194]/ Let Me Be Good To You

OTIS REDDING

VOLT

157 (SITTIN' ON) THE DOCK OF THE BAY (2-68)/Sweet Lorene

AS "OTIS & CARLA"

STAX

244 LOVEY DOVEY (3-68) [Clyde McPhatter '59 hit. ATLANTIC 2018]/New Year's Resolution

OTIS REDDING

VOLT

163 THE HAPPY SONG (DUM DUM DE DE DE DUM DUM) (5-68)/Open The Door

AS "THE SOUL CLAN"

Ben E. King; Otis Redding; Johnnie Taylor;
Arthur Conley; Percy Sledge.

ATLANTIC

2530 SOUL MEETING (7-68)/That's How It Feels

OTIS REDDING

ATCO

6592 AMEN (7-68) ["Impressions" '64 hit. ABC 10602]/Hard To Handle
6612 I'VE GOT DREAMS TO REMEMBER (10-68)/(It's) Nobody's Fault But Mine
6631 WHITE CHRISTMAS (12-68)/Merry Christmas Baby
6636 PAPA'S GOT A BRAND NEW BAG (12-68) [Edited Edition] [James Brown '65 hit. KING 5999]/Direct Me
6654 A LOVER'S QUESTION (3-69) [Clyde McPhatter '58 hit. ATLANTIC 1199]/You Made A Man Out Of Me

AS "OTIS & CARLA"

6665 WHEN SOMETHING IS WRONG WITH MY BABY (4-69) [Sam & Dave '67 hit. STAX 210]/Ooh Carla Ooh Otis

OTIS REDDING

6677 LOVE MAN (5-69)/I Can't Turn You Loose
6700 FREE ME (8-69)/Higher and Higher
6723 LOOK AT THE GIRL (1969)/That's A Good Idea
6742 JOHNNY'S HEARTBREAK (1970)/Demonstration
6766 GIVE AWAY NONE OF MY LOVE (7-70)/Snatch A Little Piece
6802 I'VE BEEN LOVING YOU TOO MUCH (1971)/Try A Little Tenderness
6907 MY GIRL (11-72) ["Temptations" '65 hit. GORDY 7038]/Good To Me

♭♯♬♩♩

"Sam and Dave"

Samuel David Moore was born in Miami, Florida, on October 12, 1935. David Prater (Praeter) was born in Ocilla, Georgia, on May 9, 1937.

"SAM AND DAVE" remain the dual personification of that highly emotive "give-it-all-you've-got" rhythmic pulsation that is truly Rhythm and Blues! They're an explosion of human energy, with big band backup, which lifts all those present to even greater heights and which was best described by an admiring New York reporter: "Nobody steams up the place like 'Sam and Dave.' Weaving and dancing (as they sing) they gyrate enough acrobatics to wear out more than one hundred costumes a year."

Samuel David Moore and David Prater (Praeter) both evolved as Gospel shouters, first singing in their church choirs and then touring with Gospel groups. During the early Sixties, they met in Miami, Florida, where they formed their famous duo with their own backup band and performed professionally at "The King of Hearts" nightclub while building their animated presentation and becoming well known as "Double Dynamite." They auditioned successfully, as "Sam and Dave," for Morris Levy of ROULETTE label of New York City and released, among others, "I Need Love" (4419), "No More Pain" (4445), "It Feels So Nice" (4461), "It Was So Nice While It Lasted" (4480) and "I Found Out" (4533), but with only regional success!

Steve Alaimo "discovered" "Sam and Dave" and the duo signed with STAX RECORDS (out of Memphis), where most of their material was written by Isaac Hayes and David Porter, who, with Jimmy Stewart, handled production. With STAX, "Sam and Dave" recorded the fantastic "I Take What I Want" (175), which, surprisingly, did not take off, but it was followed by a big hit single, "You Don't Know Like I Know" (180), which earned them the nomination for the award "MOST PROMISING MALE DUO OF THE YEAR."

"Hold On! I'm Comin' " (STAX 189) introduced the higher-voiced Sam Moore while featuring session guitarist Steve Cropper and, later, was a hit for Chuck Jackson and Maxine Brown in 1967! Other hits followed for "Sam and Dave": "Said I Wasn't Gonna Tell Nobody" (STAX 198), "You Got Me Hummin'" (STAX 204), which was also done by the group the "Hassles" (which featured Billy Joel), and "When Something Is Wrong With My Baby" (STAX 210), an Otis Redding hit in 1969. Success on wax sparked public demand and the duo was soon booked in clubs and theaters throughout the R&B circuit, including the famed Apollo Theater in New York City!

1967 saw "Sam and Dave" abroad and winning plaudits in major United Kingdom cities and on the Continent, along with release of their biggest hit, "Soul Man/May I Baby" (STAX 231), a double-sided smash hit that reached No. 1 on both U.S. and European Charts. Incidentally, "Soul Man" resurfaced again ten years later as a hit for the "Soul Brothers." "Sam and Dave" added further to their laurels in 1968 with "I Thank You/Wrap It Up" (STAX 242), another Top-Ten Chart single! Some of the arrangements used by "Sam and Dave" were later developed inimitably by the "Staple Singers" and the "Sweet Inspirations."

GULF & WESTERN bought out STAX RECORDS in 1969 and "Sam and Dave" moved over to ATLANTIC label, retaining their Gospel shouting style of rhythmically throwing phrases back and forth in Eddie Floyd's "You Don't Know What You Mean To Me" (2517), but they went on to more closely knit vocals and drumming on the Horner Bank/Raymond Jackson composition "Can't You Find Another Way (Of Doing It)" (2540) in the Joe Tex manner! A real winner! Then came the million-seller "Soul Sister, Brown Sugar/Come On In" (2590), reflecting the new spirit in black America. The duo recorded "Ooh Ooh Ooh" (2668) (which was written by Donnie Fritts/John Reid and produced by Tom Dowd and Jerry Wexler) at Muscle Shoals, Alabama, and this was a gem! The lone early-Seventies hit for "Sam and Dave" at ATLANTIC RECORDS may have been attributable to the fact that Isaac Hayes, co-author and part-producer of much of their work, had now embarked on a brand-new solo career!

"Sam and Dave" will always be remembered and admired not only for their highly animated style but for their artistry, ranking alongside those of "Arthur and Booker" of the Fifties, James and Bobby Purify of the Sixties, and "McFadden and Whitehead" today, all in that great Soul Tradition!

Discography

AS "SAM AND DAVE"

ROULETTE

4419	I NEED LOVE (4-62)/Keep A Walkin'
4445	NO MORE PAIN (9-62)/My Love Belongs To You
4461	IT FEELS SO NICE (12-62)/She's Alright
4480	AIN'T NO BIG THING BABY (1963)/It Was So Nice While It Lasted
4508	IF SHE'LL STILL HAVE ME (1963)/Listening For My Name
4533	I FOUND OUT (1964)/I Got A Thing Going On
4671	IT FEELS SO NICE (9-65)/It Was So Nice While It Lasted

STAX

168	A PLACE NOBODY CAN FIND (8-65)/Goodnight Baby
175	I TAKE WHAT I WANT (10-65)/Sweet Home
180	YOU DON'T KNOW LIKE I KNOW (1-66)/Blame Me (Don't Blame My Heart)
189	HOLD ON! I'M COMIN' (4-66)/I Got Everything I Need
198	SAID I WASN'T GONNA TELL NOBODY (9-66)/If You Got The Loving (I Got The Time)
204	YOU GOT ME HUMMIN' (12-66)/Sleep Good Tonight
210	WHEN SOMETHING IS WRONG WITH MY BABY (2-67)/Small Portion Of Your Love
218	SOOTHE ME (6-67)/I Can't Stand Up For Falling Down
231	SOUL MAN (9-67)/May I Baby
242	I THANK YOU (1-68)/Wrap It Up

ATLANTIC

2517	YOU DON'T KNOW WHAT YOU MEAN TO ME (5-68)/This Is Your World
2540	CAN'T YOU FIND ANOTHER WAY (OF DOING IT) (8-68)/Still Is The Night
2568	EVERYBODY GOT TO BELIEVE IN SOMEBODY (11-68)/If I Didn't Have A Girl Like You
2590	SOUL SISTER, BROWN SUGAR (12-68)/Come On In
2608	BORN AGAIN (3-69)/Get It
2668	OOH OOH OOH (9-69)/Holdin' On
2714	BABY, BABY, DON'T STOP NOW (12-70)/I'm Not An Indian Giver
2728	ONE PART LOVE, TWO PARTS PAIN (3-70)/When You Steal From Me
2733	KNOCK IT OUT IN THE PARK (6-70) [W. "Dixie Flyers"]/You Easily Excite Me

SAM MOORE [SOLO]

2762	TENNESSEE WALTZ (11-70) [Bobby Comstock's '59 hit. BLAZE 349]/Give You Plenty Lovin'
2791	STOP (4-71) [Howard Tate '68 hit. VERVE 10525]/Keep On Sockin' It To Me

DAVE PRATER [SOLO]

ALSTON (ATLANTIC Subsidiary)

4596 KEEP MY FINGERS CROSSED (7-71)/Love Business

SAM MOORE [SOLO]

ATLANTIC

2814 IF I SHOULD LOSE YOUR LOVE (9-71)/Shop Around

AS "SAM AND DAVE"

2839 DON'T PULL YOUR LOVE (11-71)/Jody Ryder Got Killed

UNITED ARTISTS

438 A LITTLE BIT OF GOOD (CURES A WHOLE LOT OF BAD) (6-74)/Blinded By Love

531 UNDER THE BOARDWALK (9-75) ["Drifters" '64 hit. ATLANTIC 2237]/Give It What You Can

CONTEMPO

7004 WE CAN WORK IT OUT (3-77)/Why Did You Do It

♭ ♯ ♪ ♩ 𝅗𝅥

Neil Sedaka

Born in Brooklyn, New York, on March 13, 1939.

NEIL SEDAKA was a very talented youngster of Turkish descent who grew up in Brooklyn with the fond hope of one day becoming a concert pianist. It was in 1954, when he was only fifteen years of age and attending Abraham Lincoln High School, that his interest turned seriously to modern music and he formed a group, the "Tokens," from his mathematics class. This was the group that later recorded "Tonight I Fell In Love" and "The Lion Sleeps Tonight." It was because of his conscientious attitude in directing pupils at summer camps and at school productions, besides his own Pop-oriented songwriting, that Neil Sedaka won a scholarship to the famous Juilliard School of Music.

In 1956, Morty Craft had Neil render the chimes when the black group the "Willows" recorded "Church Bells May Ring" (MELBA 102) on the same label that, later in 1957, featured Neil Sedaka and the "Tokens" on "While I Dream" (MELBA 104). Neil's initial talents were brought to bear in 1956 when, preparing a classical programme for teenagers over station WQXR in New York City, he proved himself successfully under the cordial guidance of Classical pianist Arthur Rubinstein. That same year, Neil Sedaka wrote "Passing Time" (ATLANTIC 1084), and this record received very good exposure!

Neil Sedaka contributed many delightful songwriting numbers to such notables as Carole King/husband Gerry Goffin, Jack Keller, Barry Mann/Cynthia Weil and, of course, his own main man, Howard Greenfield. Among Neil Sedaka's hits for others were "Stupid Cupid," "My Heart Has A Mind Of Its Own," and "Fallin'," sung by Connie Francis; "Crying In The Rain" by the Everly Brothers; "Venus In Blue Jeans" by Jimmy Clanton; "Puppet Man" by "5th Dimension"; "Love Will Keep Us Together" by Captain & Tennille, along with many other hits. This assures Neil Sedaka the signal honor of being one of the all-time greats because of his contributions that became part of the backbone of Rock and Roll!

Discography

NEIL SEDAKA

DECCA

30520 LAURA LEE (1957)/Snowtime

AS "TOKENS" FEATURING NEIL SEDAKA

MELBA

104 WHILE I DREAM (1957)/I Love My Baby

NEIL SEDAKA

GUYDEN

2004 RING-A-ROCKIN' (1958) [Also released on LEGION 133]/ Fly Fly Don't Fly On Me
Note: Neil Sedaka was signed to a long-term contract by Steve Sholes of RCA RECORDS.

RCA

7408 THE DIARY (12-58)/No Vacancy
7473 I GO APE (3-59)/Moon Of Gold
7530 YOU GOTTA LEARN YOUR RHYTHM'N'BLUES (6-59)/ Crying My Heart Out For You
7595 OH! CAROL* (10-59)/One Way Ticket (To The Blues)
7709 STAIRWAY TO HEAVEN (4-60)/40 Winks Away
7781 YOU MEAN EVERYTHING TO ME (8-60)/Run Samson Run
7829 CALENDAR GIRL (12-60)/The Same Old Fool
7874 LITTLE DEVIL (5-61)/I Must Be Dreaming
7922 SWEET LITTLE YOU (9-61)/I Found My World In You
7957 HAPPY BIRTHDAY, SWEET SIXTEEN (11-61)/Don't Lead Me On
8007 KING OF CLOWNS (3-62)/Walk With Me
8046 BREAKING UP IS HARD TO DO (6-62)/As Long As I Live

AS "MARVELS AND NEIL SEDAKA"

PYRAMID

623 OH DELILAH (1962)/Neil's Twist [Instr. by the "Marvels"]

---

*This song was written for Carole King, who was a schoolgirl chum of both Neil Sedaka and Howard Greenfield in Brooklyn.

NEIL SEDAKA

RCA

8086 NEXT DOOR TO AN ANGEL (10-62)/I Belong To You
8137 ALICE IN WONDERLAND (2-63)/Circulate
Note: In 1956, Neil Sedaka, an accomplished Classical pianist, tried to present a piano recital in the USSR but was turned down, possibly because of his Rock affiliations.
8169 LET'S GO STEADY AGAIN (4-63)/Waiting For Never
8209 THE DREAMER (7-63)/Look Inside Your Heart
8254 BAD GIRL (11-63)/Wait 'Till You See My Baby
8341 THE CLOSEST THING TO HEAVEN (3-64)/Without A Song
8382 SUNNY (7-64)/She'll Never Be You
8453 TOO LATE (10-64)/I Hope He Breaks Your Heart
8511 LET THE PEOPLE TALK (3-65)/In The Chapel With You
8637 THE WORLD THROUGH A TEAR (8-65)/High On The Mountain
8737 (YOU'RE) THE ANSWER TO MY PRAYER (2-66)/Blue Boy
8844 THE ANSWER LIES WITHIN (6-66)/Grown-Up Games
9004 WE CAN MAKE IT IF WE TRY (1-67)/Too Late

SGC

005 STAR CROSSED LOVERS (1-69)/We Had A Good Thing Goin'
008 RAINY JANE (5-69)/Jeannine

KIRSHNER

63-5017 I'M A SONG (1-72)/Silent Movies
63-5020 SUPERBIRD (4-72)/Rosemary Blue
63-5024 BEAUTIFUL YOU (9-72)/Anywhere You're Gonna Be
Note: Neil Sedaka recorded an LP, "Solitaire," backed by the group "10 C.C.," in Britain.

RCA

40313 LAUGHTER IN THE RAIN (10-74)/Kiddio

POLYDOR

2058-561 THE IMMIGRANT* (3-75)/Hey Mr. Sunshine [Also RCA 40,370]
2058-615 THAT'S WHEN THE MUSIC TAKES ME (6-75)/Standing On The Inside [Also RCA 40,426]
2058-641 BAD BLOOD (9-75) [W. Elton John]/Your Favourite Entertainer [Also RCA 40,460]
2058-669 BREAKING UP IS HARD TO DO (12-75)/Nana's Song [Also RCA 40,500]

---

*Referring to John Lennon.

MGM

14564	STANDING ON THE INSIDE/Let Daddy Know
14661	ALONE IN NEW YORK (IN THE RAIN) (12-75)/Suspicions

POLYDOR

2058-717	LOVE IN THE SHADOWS (4-76)/Baby, Don't Let It Miss Your Mind [Also RCA 40,543]
2058-746	STEPPIN' OUT (6-76)/I Let You Walk Away [Also RCA 40,582]
2058-786	YOU GOTTA MAKE YOUR OWN SUNSHINE (9-76)/Perfect Strangers [Also RCA 40,619]

ELEKTRA

45406	AMARILLO (5-77) [Tony Christie '72 song. KAPP 2161. Also released on MCA 40749]/The Leaving Game

POLYDOR

2058-918	ALONE AT LAST (9-77)/Sleazy Love [Also on ELEKTRA 45421]

DARA SEDAKA (NEIL'S DAUGHTER)

RSO RECORDS

892	MY GUY (4-78) [Mary Wells '64 hit. MOTOWN 1056]/ Beautiful You

NEIL SEDAKA

ELEKTRA

45525	ALL YOU NEED IS THE MUSIC (10-78)/Sad, Sad Story
45525	SAD, SAD STORY (10-78)/Candy Kisses
46017	SAD, SAD STORY (2-79)/Tillie The Twirler

Bunny Sigler

Real Name: "Walter Sigler." Born in Philadelphia, Pennsylvania, on March 27, 1941.

BUNNY SIGLER has to be considered one of the most exciting and versatile of musicians/entertainers in the entire business, excelling, as he does, at the piano, organ, guitar, trumpet, trombone, and bass. He is certainly a funky, gritty party-hearty performer who has established himself from the very beginning as a top writer, producer, and singer, besides proving himself an inspiration to many other aspiring artists, such as Ike Perkins (APT label), "Cruisers" (V-TONE label), Len Barry (DECCA label), "Chambers Brothers" (COLUMBIA label), through to Wilson Pickett (ATLANTIC label). In the Seventies, while working at SIGMA Studios, Bunny Sigler helped "Archie Bell & Drells," the "O'Jays," Billy Paul, Phil Hurtt, Lou Rawls, Joe Simon, and, again, many others. His particular protégés were the "T.N.J.s," James Carmichael, "Instant Funk" (Bunny's backup group during the Seventies, who gave us that 1978 disco funk hit, "I Got My Mind Made Up"), and also the "John Brothers," who, incidentally, are the sons of Little Willie John. Bunny Sigler won his first national acclaim in 1967 when, with John Madara's CAMEO/PARKWAY label, he recorded the hit "Let The Good Times Roll & Feel So Good" (PARKWAY 153).

Born Walter Sigler on March 27, 1941, in Philadelphia, Pennsylvania, Bunny first sang at Emmanuel Baptist Church. The popular tag-name "Bunny" came naturally to him because he was born just two days before Easter of that year, and later injured his leg while playing baseball and was inclined to dance around like a bunny, hence the name "Bunny"! With his brother, Jimmy, and Ritchie Rome (of the Seventies disco "Ritchie Family") and Jack Faith, Bunny Sigler formed a Doo-Wopp group called the "Opals." Bunny himself became a nightclub performer on his own at the local Music City club, Skiolo's, and Columbo's."

Bunny Sigler was discovered by a disc jockey called "Cannonball," who prompted his first release as "Mr. Emotions" Sigler with the Jr. Parker song "Come On Home" (CRAIG 501). During the Sixties, Bunny sang under the performing names of "O'Sigler," "De Siglio," and "Sliglowitz." As Bunny Sigler, he signed with DECCA label in 1965 and it was while there that he had the fortunate experience of working with Leon Huff and Kenny Gamble, both of whom became owners of major NEPTUNE label and PHILADELPHIA-INTERNATIONAL label, which, eventually, provided the outlet for many of Bunny Sigler's forthcoming hit records.

Some of Bunny Sigler's more prominent and interesting releases were "Where Do The Lonely Go" (NEPTUNE 25), "Tossin'n'Turnin'" (PHIL-INT. 3523), "That's How Long I'll Be Loving You" (PHIL-INT. 3536), and "Love Train" (PHIL-INT. 3545). With SALSOUL/GOLD MIND label, Bunny Sigler had good results with "Let Me Party With You" (GOLD MIND 7-4008), which was inspired from the Marvin Gaye smash of 1977, "Got To Give It Up" (TAMLA 54280). This was followed up, in 1978, by Bunny Sigler's (known as "Bundino Sigalucci") three fabulous discs, "It's Time To Twist" (GOLD MIND 7-4010), the beautiful "Don't Even Try (Give It Up)" (GOLD MIND 7-4014), and, with Loleatta Holloway, "Only You" (GOLD MIND 7-4012). Bunny Sigler continues today as a very fine and influential disco creator!

Discography

BUNNY SIGLER

HI LO (An ABC Subsidiary)

102 PROMISE ME (1959) [W. "Cruisers"]/Jazzy Little Mama

BUNNY SIGLER (WITH "CARDELLS")

BEE

1113 SQUARE FROM NOWHERE

AS "BUNNY 'MR. EMOTIONS' SIGLER"

CRAIG

501 COME ON HOME [Jr. Parker Song]/I Won't Cry

BUNNY SIGLER

DECCA

31880 EVERYTHING'S GONNA BE ALRIGHT (1965)/For Cryin' Out Loud

31947 WILL YOU LOVE ME TOMORROW (1966)/Comparatively Speaking

PARKWAY

153 LET THE GOOD TIMES ROLL & FEEL SO GOOD (7-67)/ There's No One Left

DECCA

32183 LET THEM TALK (9-67)/Will You Love Me Tomorrow

PARKWAY

6000 LOVEY DOVEY & YOU'RE SO FINE (10-67)/Sunny Sunday
6001 FOLLOW YOUR HEART (12-67)/Can You Dig It

NEPTUNE

14 GREAT BIG LIAR (8-69)/Where Do The Lonely Go

BUNNY SIGLER (WITH CINDY SCOTT)

15 SURE DON'T TAKE LONG (FOR THE NEWS TO GET AROUND) (9-69)/We're Only Human

AS "BUNNY SIGLER AND CINDY SCOTT"

24 WE'RE ONLY HUMAN (4-70)/Conquer The World Together

BUNNY SIGLER

25 WHERE DO THE LONELY GO (5-70)/Don't Stop What You're Doing

PHILADELPHIA-INTERNATIONAL—CBS

3505 EVERYBODY NEEDS GOOD LOVIN' (2-71)/Everybody Needs Good Lovin' [Part 2]

BUNNY SIGLER & DEE DEE SHARP

3512 WE GOT A GOOD THING GOING ON (11-71)/Conquer The World Together

BUNNY SIGLER

3519 REGINA (9-72)/Theme For Five Fingers Of Death
3523 TOSSIN'N'TURNIN' (12-72)/Picture Us
3532 THEME FOR FIVE FINGERS OF DEATH (6-73)/Regina

BUNNY SIGLER & DEE DEE SHARP

3536 HEAVEN KNOWS I'VE CHANGED (1973)/That's How Long I'll Be Loving You

BUNNY SIGLER

3545 LOVE TRAIN (6-74)/Love Train [Part 2]
3554 KEEP SMILIN' (11-74)/Somebody Free
3560 SHAKE YOUR BOOTY/Your Love Is Good
3575 THAT'S HOW LONG I'LL BE LOVING YOU (9-75)/Somebody Free
3582 JINGLE BELLS (12-75)/Jingle Bells [Part 2]
3597 MY MUSIC (7-76)/Can't Believe That You Love Me
3608 SOMEBODY LOVES YOU (12-76)/Woman, Woman

BUNNY SIGLER & BARBARA MASON

CURTOM

689 LOVE SONG

GOLD MIND

7-4008 LET ME PARTY WITH YOU (2-78)/Let Me Party With You [Part 2]
7-4010 I GOT WHAT YOU NEED (5-78)/It's Time To Twist

AS "BUNNY SIGLER & LOLEATTA HOLLOWAY"

7-4012 ONLY YOU (8-78)/Good, Good Feelings

BUNNY SIGLER

7-4014 DON'T EVEN TRY (GIVE IT UP) (10-78)/I'm A Fool
7-4018 BY THE WAY YOU DANCE (I KNEW IT WAS YOU) (3-79)/Glad To Be Your Love
7-4020 GLAD TO BE YOUR LOVER (7-79)/I'm Funking You Tonight With My Music

♭♯♪♩𝅗𝅥

"Simon and Garfunkel"

Paul Frederick Simon was born in Newark, New Jersey, on November 5, 1941. Arthur Garfunkel was born in New York City on October 13, 1942.

The soft rhythmic words and music of "SIMON AND GARFUNKEL" touched the pulse of an entire self-despairing young generation. From their own midteens of great expectations and broken dreams to the heights of international acclaim these Rock-Folk balladeers proved themselves possibly the most articulate, scholarly, listened-to, and appreciated stars in the fickle firmament of sophisticated entertainment. These one-time Bebop kids, Rock and Roll swingers, and folk singers recognized the quizzical smile of Dame Fortune in the chance selection of a Boston deejay and the electronic-dubbing wizardry of COLUMBIA's engineer, Tom Wilson, which actually launched them upon a meteoric career. Two richly endowed perfectionists with a multicolored goal, "Simon and Garfunkel" learned early to labor joyfully weeks into months to polish brighter still each artistic offering, and their musical heritage reflects homework faithfully done and assignments masterfully completed. With many fabulous hits to their credit, they can now smile indulgently upon any criticism comparing their gentle touch in music with that of the dynamic Bob Dylan as we acknowledge their "Bridge Over Troubled Water" (COLUMBIA 45079) as one of the two best-sellers of all time, with over two million sales at home and nine million around the world!

Paul and Art were buddies at P.S. 164 in Queens, where they both played in *Alice in Wonderland,* with Paul as the Rabbit and Art as the Cheshire Cat, roles that now, humorously, reflect their now-public ones! Prank-earned detention was used to practice harmony and arrangement, and with talent and enterprise they early combined in their midteens as "Tom and Jerry" (Art as "Tom Graph" and Paul as "Jerry Landis") in cutting a demo at SAUNDERS STUDIO in New York, which became "Hey! Schoolgirl (In The Second Row)" (BIG 613) making the Top-Forty on U.S. Charts. At that time, they also made some public appearances, one of them on the Dick Clark TV *American Bandstand* with Jerry Lee Lewis.

Nothing else happened and the disappointing lull impelled "Simon and Garfunkel" toward higher education, Paul seeking a major in English Literature at Queens College, and Art seeking his M.A. at Columbia University. That late Sixties period saw Paul playing his guitar, bass, alongside Carole (Klein) King on the piano and drums (that same Carole King who eventually rode the Charts with hits from her "Tapestry" album to equal sales of "Bridge Over Troubled Water"), making demos for Burt Bacharach (noted music composer of the 1960s with lyricist Hal David). From these demos came "Jackie Brown" (ERA 1063) by the black group the "Passions," "Just To Be With You" (AUDICON 102), and "I Only Want You" (AUDICON 105) by the white Doo-Wopp group the "Passions," "Hushabye" (LAURIE 3028), and "Don't Take The Stars" (LAURIE 3038) by another white Doo-Wopp group, the "Mystics." Paul also composed and recorded as "Jerry Landis" and with "Tico and the Triumphs" but most of his earlier songs had to await the electronic backup era.

Paul Simon then went to England, where he, writing and recording, became influenced by the intellectual "underground" and was joined there by Garfunkel between semesters. Then came their big break! Tom Wilson (who had signed the boys for COLUMBIA) had recorded their album "Wednesday Morning—3 A.M.," which went nowhere. A Boston deejay aired "The Sounds Of Silence" (a song he liked from the year-old album) and was hit by replay demands from various university campuses. Tom Wilson listened to the studio recording and decided on more instrumental backup, but, with Paul abroad and Art at school, he went ahead and overdubbed, and released "Sounds Of Silence" (COLUMBIA 43396) as a single and launched "Simon and Garfunkel" on their way!

The good news brought Paul and Art back together again, and in December 1965 they began work on a new album, "Sounds Of Silence," which included the overdubbed title song itself. Other smash hits followed and among many others were "Homeward Bound" (COLUMBIA 43511), "I Am A Rock" (COLUMBIA 43617), "The Dangling Conversation" (COLUMBIA 43728), "A Hazy Shade Of Winter" (COLUMBIA 43873), "Fakin' It" (COLUMBIA 44232), and "Scarborough Fair" (COLUMBIA 44465), Garfunkel's own song, in March 1968. Both got involved in the soundtrack of *The Graduate* (Oscar for Best Film of 1968), which gave us another hit single, "Mrs. Robinson" (COLUMBIA 44511). During 1968, while this single was No. 1, the LPs "The Graduate," "Bookends," and "Parsley, Sage, Rosemary And Thyme" were 1-2-3 on the U.S. Charts! 1969-70 saw "The Boxer" (COLUMBIA 44785), "Cecilia" (COLUMBIA 45133), "El Conda Pasa (COLUMBIA 45237), and the greatest of them all, "Bridge Over Troubled Water" (COLUMBIA 45079), released.

With superstardom came interlocking career problems, surfacing when Garfunkel was involved in the filming of *Catch 22* and held up recording of "Bridge Over Troubled Water." Unfortunately the problems persisted, and, in 1971, Paul Simon and Arthur Garfunkel decided to go their separate ways. Paul's debut release, "Mother And Child Reunion" (COLUMBIA 45547), was on the Charts for most of 1972. That same year saw his first album, "Paul Simon." We then had two Gold albums, "Me And Julio Down By The Schoolyard" and "There Goes Rhymin' Simon," and a string of top singles: "American Tune" (COLUMBIA 4-45900), "(She) Loves Me Like A Rock" (COLUMBIA 45907), a Gospel Rock that unusually blended Dixieland-Reggae, "Take Me To The Mardi Gras" (COLUMBIA 3-10197), and, in 1976, "Still Crazy After All These Years" (COLUMBIA 3-10332). He also recorded "Gone At Last" (COLUMBIA 10197) with Phoebe Snow and the "Jesse Dixon Singers," and Paul's gem "50 Ways To Leave Your Lover" (COLUMBIA 3-10270).

Arthur Garfunkel completed his films *Catch 22* and *Carnal Knowledge,* besides the releases, among other singles, "All I Know" (COLUMBIA 45926), "I Only Have Eyes For You" (COLUMBIA 3-10190), "Crying In My Sleep" (COLUMBIA 10608), "In A Little While (I'll Be On My Way)" (COLUMBIA 3-10933), and, in 1979, "Bright Eyes" (COLUMBIA 111050). He also released "Angel Clare," a very successful album! Occasionally, Paul Simon and Arthur Garfunkel got together to give us "My Little Town" with "Rag Doll (Art Garfunkel)/You're Kind (Paul Simon)" (COLUMBIA 3-10230) and "(What A) Wonderful World" (COLUMBIA 3-10676), a "Simon-Garfunkel" combination with James Taylor. Art Garfunkel also gave us the hit "Since I Don't Have You" (COLUMBIA 3-10999), with a beautiful blending of organ.

Discography

AS "TOM AND JERRY"

BIG

613 HEY! SCHOOLGIRL (IN THE SECOND ROW) (12-57)/ Dancin' Wild [Also KING 5167]

AS "TRUE TAYLOR" (PAUL SIMON)

614 TRUE OR FALSE (1958)/Teenage Fool

AS "TOM AND JERRY"

616	OUR SONG (1958)/Two Teenagers
618	THAT'S MY STORY (1958)/Don't Say Goodbye [Also on HUNT 319]
629	BABY TALK (1959)/Two Teenagers

AS "JERRY LANDIS" (PAUL SIMON)

MGM

12822	ANNA BELLE (1959)/Loneliness

WARWICK

552	JUST A BOY (1959)/Shy
588	JUST A BOY (1960)/I'd Like To Be
619	PLAY ME A SAD SONG (1960)/It Means A Lot To Them

AS "TOM AND JERRY"

EMBER

1094	I'M LONESOME (1960)/Looking At You

MERCURY

71753	SOUTH (1961)/Golden Wildwood Flower

ABC

10363	SURRENDER, PLEASE SURRENDER (1962)/Fightin' Mad

AS "JERRY LANDIS" (PAUL SIMON)

CANADIAN-AMERICAN

130	I WISH WE WEREN'T IN LOVE (1961)/I'm Lonely

AS "ARTIE GARR" (ART GARFUNKEL)

OCTAVIA

8002	PRIVATE WORLD (1961)/Forgive Me
515	BEAT LOVE (1962)/Dream Alone

AS "TICO & THE TRIUMPHS" [Feat. PAUL SIMON]

MADISON

169 MOTORCYCLE (1961)/I Don't Believe Them

AMY (BELL Subsidiary)

835 MOTORCYCLE (11-61)/I Don't Believe Them
845 WILD FLOWER (1962)/Express Train
860 CRY, LITTLE BOY, CRY (1962)/Get Up And Do The Wobble

AS "JERRY LANDIS" (PAUL SIMON)

875 LONE TEEN RANGER (1-63)/Lise

AS "TICO & THE TRIUMPHS" [Feat. PAUL SIMON]

876 CARDS OF LOVE (1963)/Noise

AS "PAUL KANE" (PAUL SIMON)

TRIBUTE

128 CARLOS DOMINGUEZ (1964)/He Was My Brother

"SIMON AND GARFUNKEL"

COLUMBIA

43396 SOUNDS OF SILENCE (11-65)/We've Got A Groovy Thing Goin'
43511 HOMEWARD BOUND (2-66)/Leaves That Are Green (Turn To Brown)

ABC

10788 THAT'S MY STORY (3-66)/Tijuana Blues

COLUMBIA

43617 I AM A ROCK (5-66)/Flowers Never Bend With Rainfall
43728 THE DANGLING CONVERSATION (8-66)/Big Bright Green Pleasure Machine
43873 A HAZY SHADE OF WINTER (11-66)/For Emily (Wherever I May Find Her)

44046 AT THE ZOO (3-67)/The 59th Street Bridge Song (Feelin' Groovy)
44232 FAKIN' IT (7-67)/You Don't Know Where Your Interest Lies
Note: Paul Simon backed up Dana Valery during 1967 on "Having You Around" (COLUMBIA 44004).
44465 SCARBOROUGH FAIR (3-68)/April, Come She Will
44511 MRS. ROBINSON (4-68) [Theme from *The Graduate*]/Old Friends
44785 THE BOXER (4-69)/Baby Driver
45079 BRIDGE OVER TROUBLED WATER (2-70)/Keep The Customer Satisfied
45133 CECILIA (4-70)/The Only Living Boy In New York City
45237 EL CONDOR PASA (9-70)/Why Don't You Write Me

PAUL SIMON

45547 MOTHER AND CHILD REUNION (2-72)/Paranoia Blues
45585 ME AND JULIO DOWN BY THE SCHOOLYARD (4-72)/Congratulations
45638 DUNCAN (7-72)/Run That Body Down

"SIMON AND GARFUNKEL"

45663 AMERICA (5-73)/For Emily (Wherever I May Find Her)

PAUL SIMON

45859 KODACHROME (5-73)/Tenderness
45907 (SHE) LOVES ME LIKE A ROCK (8-73) [W. "Dixie Hummingbirds"]/Learn How To Fall

ART GARFUNKEL

45926 ALL I KNOW (9-73)/Mary Was Only A Child

PAUL SIMON

4-45900 AMERICAN TUNE (12-73)/One Man's Ceiling Is Another Man's Floor

AS "GARFUNKEL" (ART GARFUNKEL)

4-45983 I SHALL SING (12-73)/Feuilles—Oh/Do Space Men Pass Dead Souls On The Way To The Moon?
4-46030 TRAVELING BOY (4-74)/Old Man

PAUL SIMON

4-46038 SOUNDS OF SILENCE (5-74)/Mother And Child Reunion

AS "GARFUNKEL" (ART GARFUNKEL)

3-10020 SECOND AVENUE (9-74)/Woyaya
3-10190 I ONLY HAVE EYES FOR YOU (8-75) ["Flamingos" '59 hit. END 1046]/Looking For The Right One

PAUL SIMON AND PHOEBE SNOW

3-10197 GONE AT LAST (8-75) [W. "Jesse Dixon Singers"]/Take Me To The Mardi Gras

"SIMON AND GARFUNKEL"

3-10230 MY LITTLE TOWN (10-75)/Rag Doll (Art Garfunkel)/You're Kind (Paul Simon)

PAUL SIMON

3-10270 50 WAYS TO LEAVE YOUR LOVER (12-75)/Some Folks' Lives Roll Easy

ART GARFUNKEL

3-10273 BREAK AWAY (1-76)/Disney Girls

PAUL SIMON

3-10332 STILL CRAZY AFTER ALL THESE YEARS (5-76)/I Do It For Your Love

ART GARFUNKEL

3-10608 CRYING IN MY SLEEP (10-77)/Mr Shuck'N'Jive

PAUL SIMON

3-10630 SLIP SLIDIN' AWAY (10-77)/Something So Right

ART GARFUNKEL WITH JAMES TAYLOR AND PAUL SIMON

3-10676 (WHAT A) WONDERFUL WORLD (1-78) [Sam Cooke '60 hit. KEEN 8-2112]/Wooden Planes (by Art Garfunkel)

PAUL SIMON

3-10711 STRANDED IN A LIMOUSINE (4-78)/Have A Good Time

ART GARFUNKEL

3-10933 IN A LITTLE WHILE (I'LL BE ON MY WAY) (3-79)/And I Know

3-10999 SINCE I DON'T HAVE YOU (5-79) ["Skyliners" '59 hit. CALICO 103]/When Someone Doesn't Want You

111050 BRIGHT EYES (8-79)/Sail On A Rainbow [from movie *Watership Down*]

♭♯♪♩𝅗𝅥

Johnnie Taylor

Real Name: "Johnnie Harrison Taylor." Born in Crawfordsville, Arkansas, near West Memphis, Crittenden County, on May 5, 1938.

JOHNNIE TAYLOR, the "Soul Philosopher," or, to his STAX colleagues "Taylor the Wailer," became the label's top hit-maker. His father was pastor of a local congregation, and Johnnie saw his first singing as a boy in the choir. Growing up in the Blues Delta, which produced Jr. Parker and Howlin' Wolf, Johnnie received his early education at West Memphis College and went on to major in metaphysics in Kansas City. He worked in a Cleveland chemical plant. His first public appearance was with the group the "Five Echoes" at a local church. Johnnie joined the group after the 1953 release of "Lonely Mood" (SABRE 102) and the departure of Tommy Hunt (later "Flamingos" member). He stayed for only three singles, "So Lonesome" (SABRE 105), "If You Don't Love Me" (SABRE 106), and "Why Oh Why" (SABRE 111), on Art Sheridan's label, with only regional success. He also sang with the "Highway QC's" (which had earlier featured Sam Cooke) and the "Melody Masters." About this time, Sam Cooke left the notable Gospel group the "Soul Stirrers," and Johnnie Taylor was asked to be his replacement. His most impressive leads were on "The Love Of God" (SPECIALTY 908) and "Stand By Me, Father" (SAR 101).

It was Sam Cooke, owner of SAR label, who asked Johnnie Taylor to sing Rhythm and Blues for his label and also for DERBY label, which was owned by Sam's manager, J. W. Alexander. The most interesting among these releases were the hand-clapping uptempo number "Dance What You Wanna" (DERBY 101) and that beautiful rendition of Ed Townsend's composition "Never Never" (SAR 151). It was the latter recording that actually launched Johnnie Taylor's career! Johnnie scored a minor hit with Sam Cooke's composition "Baby, We've Got Love" (DERBY 1006), and he toured with Sam Cooke right up to Sam's death on December 11, 1964.

In 1965, Johnnie signed with Memphis STAX label and, backed by

Booker T. Jones, he recorded that intense Blues ballad "I Had A Dream" (186). Success continued with the bluesy "Little Blue Bird" (202) on through "Somebody's Sleeping In My Bed" (235). It was with the addition of ex-Detroit producer Don Davis that Johnnie gained a Motor City recording sophistication. He came into his own with the three-million seller "Who's Making Love (With Your Old Lady)" (0009), written by Homer Banks, Betty Crutcher, Don Davis, and Raymond Jackson. Then came "Take Care Of Your Homework" (0023), to be followed by Johnnie's rendition of the "Parliaments" (Detroit) oldie "Testify (I Wonna)" (0033).

In 1969, many of the prominent STAX artists—Johnnie Taylor, William Bell, Eddie Floyd, Isaac Hayes with Carla Thomas and the "Staple Singers," Pervis, Mavis and Cleotha joined together on "Soul-A-Lujah" (0040). It was Johnnie Taylor's Black Pop message of "I Could Never Be President" (0046) and follow-up "Love Bones (0055) with which he warned James Brown, Wilson Pickett, and Tyrone Davis to check out their soulful love pleas. It was at this point in his career that Johnnie departed from the Wilson Pickett shouting style of delivery.

Johnnie's 1971 two-million seller "Jody Got Your Girl And Gone" (0085) gave clear evidence that he was now entering a gentler approach, with brilliant phrasing and a pronounced rhythmic styling. "Doing My Own Thing" (0122) and "Stop Doggin' Me" (0142) brought us Johnnie's own personal treatment with a blending of strings and guitar. In 1973, "I Believe In You (You Believe In Me)" (0161) was a hit and received "honorable mention" on the Pop Charts, and "Cheaper To Keep Her" (0176), a Mack Rice (formerly with the Detroit group the "Falcons") composition, became a Taylor "trademark," with an added humorous touch, as in his follow-up, "I've Been Born Again" (0208). His "It's September" (0026) and "Try Me Tonight" (0241) brought to a close not only his years with STAX, but a departure from his, up to that time, total Rhythm and Blues idiom.

With COLUMBIA, Johnnie Taylor became an important part of the disco scene with his monster seller "Disco Lady" (3-10281). Other disco releases were "Somebody's Gettin' It" (3-10334), "Love Is Better In The A.M." (3-10478), "Your Love Is Rated X" (3-10541) and "Disco 9000' (3-10610).

Discography

"FIVE ECHOES"

Count Sims, lead vocal; Johnnie Taylor, second lead;
Earl Lewis, first tenor; Herbert Lewis, baritone;
Fred Marshall, bass.

AS "FIVE ECHOES"

SABRE

105 SO LONESOME (1954)/Broke
106 IF YOU DON'T LOVE ME (1954)/The Hurt
111 WHY OH WHY (1954)/That's My Baby

WITH "SOUL STIRRERS"

SPECIALTY

908 THE LOVE OF GOD (1958) [Feat. Johnnie Taylor]/Out On A Hill [Feat. Johnnie Taylor]
911 LOVED ONES ARE WAITING (1958) [Feat. Paul Foster]/Until Then [Feat. Johnnie Taylor]
918 WHEN THE GATES SWING OPEN (1959)/The Lord Laid His Hand On Me

SAR

101 STAND BY ME, FATHER (1959) [Feat. Johnnie Taylor]/He's Been A—Shelter For Me [Feat. Jessie J. Farley]
103 HE CARES (1959) [Feat. Johnnie Taylor]/Wade In The Water [Feat. Paul Foster]
Note: Johnny Taylor also sang lead of the "Soul Stirrers"—"God Is Standing By" (SAR 124).

JOHNNIE TAYLOR

114 A WHOLE LOTTA WOMAN (6-61)/Why Why Why
131 ROME (WASN'T BUILT IN A DAY) (1962)/Never Never
151 NEVER NEVER (1963)/Rome (Wasn't Built In A Day)
156 OH HOW I LOVE YOU (1964)/Run But You Can't Hide

DERBY

101 DANCE WHAT YOU WANNA (1961)/Shine Shine Shine
106 BABY, WE'VE GOT LOVE (11-63)/(I'll Always Be) In Love With You
1010 GETTING MARRIED SOON (1964)/I Need Lots Of Love

LOOK

103 CHOCOLATE CAKE (1962)/Some Of Your Time

FIRE

106 CRAZY MIXED UP RHYTHM AND BLUES (1962)/Sad Sad Saturday Night

STAX

186 I HAD A DREAM (3-66)/Changes
193 I GOT TO LOVE SOMEBODY'S BABY (8-66)/Just The One I've Been Looking For
202 LITTLE BLUEBIRD (11-66)/Toe Hold
209 AIN'T THAT LOVING YOU (FOR MORE REASONS THAN ONE) (2-67)/Outside Love
226 YOU CAN'T GET AWAY FROM IT (8-67)/If I Had It To Do Over
235 SOMEBODY'S SLEEPING IN MY BED (12-67)/Strange Things (Happening in My Heart)
247 NEXT TIME (4-68)/Sundown
253 I AIN'T PARTICULAR (6-68)/Where There's Smoke There's Fire
0009 WHO'S MAKING LOVE (10-68)/I'm Tryin'
0023 TAKE CARE OF YOUR HOMEWORK (1-69)/Hold On This Time
0033 TESTIFY (I WONNA) (5-69) [Parliament's '67 hit. REVELOT 207]/I Had A Fight With Love
0040 SOUL-A-LUJAH (1969)/Soul-a-Lujah [Instr.]

JOHNNIE TAYLOR AND CARLA THOMAS

0042 JUST KEEP ON LOVING ME (1969)/My Life

JOHNNIE TAYLOR

0046 I COULD NEVER BE PRESIDENT (8-69)/It's Amazing
0055 LOVE BONES (12-69)/Mr. Nobody Is Somebody
0068 STEAL AWAY (6-70) (Jimmy Hughes '64 hit. FAME 6401)/ Friday Night
0078 I AM SOMEBODY (10-70)/I Am Somebody [Part 2]
0085 JODY GOT YOUR GIRL AND GONE (1-71)/Fool Like Me

0089	I DON'T WANNA LOSE YOU (5-71) [Steve Mancha '66 hit. GROOVESVILLE 1002]/Party Life
0096	HIJACKIN' LOVE (8-71)/Love In The Streets (Ain't Good As The Love At Home)
0114	STANDING IN FOR JODY (1-72)/Shackin' In
0122	DOING MY OWN THING (4-72)/Doing My Own Thing [Part 2]
0142	STOP DOGGIN' ME (9-72)/Stop Teasin' Me
0155	DON'T YOU FOOL WITH MY SOUL (3-73)/Don't You Fool With My Soul [Part 2]
0161	I BELIEVE IN YOU (YOU BELIEVE IN ME) (6-73)/Love Depression
0176	CHEAPER TO KEEP HER (10-73)/I Can Read Between The Lines
0208	I'VE BEEN BORN AGAIN (6-74)/At Night (My Pillow Tells A Tale on Me)
0226	IT'S SEPTEMBER (10-74)/Just One Moment
0241	TRY ME TONIGHT (7-75)/Free

COLUMBIA

3-10281	DISCO LADY (2-76)/You're The Best In The World
3-10334	SOMEBODY'S GETTIN' IT (5-76)/Please Don't Stop (That Song From Playing)
3-10478	LOVE IS BETTER IN THE A.M. (2-77)/Love Is Better In The A.M. [Part 2]
3-10541	YOUR LOVE IS RATED X (5-77)/Here I Go (Through These Changes Again)
3-10610	DISCO 9000 (9-77)/Right Now

RCA

11137	HEAVEN BLESS THIS HOME (10-77)/I Want You Back Again

COLUMBIA

3-10709	KEEP ON DANCING (4-78)/I Love To Make Love When It's Raining
3-10776	EVER READY (6-78)/Give Me My Baby
1-11084	(OOH-WEE) SHE'S KILLING ME (10-79)/Play Something Pretty

♭♯♪♩𝅗𝅥

Ted Taylor

Born just outside Tulsa, in Farm Town, Okmulgee, Oklahoma, on February 16, 1937.

TED TAYLOR is a remarkably talented Soul singer who hits you with a sweet sophisticated delivery and then can turn it on with his high-pitched falsetto shrills. He sings Spirituals, Blues, R&B ballads, up-tempo Soul Rockers and even exceptional Disco. It now appears that Ted Taylor, though now with a solid quarter century professional background, has not been given the credit he deserves. If one would listen to any of his recordings on labels EBB, DUKE, TOP RANK, GOLD EAGLE, JEWEL, SONCRAFT, DADE, OKEH, EPIC, ATCO, RON, or even ALARM, one must agree, without any doubt, that his singles are top-notch caliber and accept Ted Taylor to be one of the finest Soul singers of all time.

It was during the early Fifties, while Ted Taylor was still in his teens and singing with a Gospel quartet called the "Glory Bound Travellers," that a Los Angeles businessman, Henry Wilson, heard him and prompted him to go to Los Angeles. On completion of high school, Ted Taylor moved to the West Coast and there joined the "Mighty Clouds of Joy" (not to be confused with Little Johnny Taylor's group of the same name) and sang with them for a year and a half.

In 1954, Ted Taylor formed his own Spiritual group, calling it the "Santa Monica Soul Seekers," who became known, separately, as the "Jacks" and the "Cadets"—two groups with different names but comprising the same members: Willie Davis (lead, second tenor); Aaron Collins (lead, second brother of "Teen Queens' " Betty and Rosie Collins, who recorded "Eddie My Love" in 1956—RPM 453); Will "Dub" Jones (bass, and later a member of the "Coasters"); Ted Taylor (bass, str. tenor); and Lloyd McGraw (baritone and manager). The "Jacks" recorded "Why Don't You Write Me" (RPM 428), which was originally a 1954 tune by the "Feathers" (SHOWTIME 1105). The "Cadets" recorded, initially, "Don't Be Angry" (Modern 956), a group version of Nappy Brown's 1955 classic (SAVOY 1155), but their big success hit proved to be "Stranded In The Jungle" (MODERN 994), which was recorded in 1956.

Ted Taylor won a talent show that was put on by Johnny Otis and, besides his taking of the first prize, he gained the more substantial opportunity of recording for EBB label (owned by Lee Rupe, wife of Art Rupe, SPECIALTY RECORDS). After only local action with the Bluesy "Days Are Dark" (EBB 113) and "Keep Walking On" (EBB 132), Ted Taylor traveled with the "Fullbright Band" and went on to Houston, Texas. Don Robey, of DUKE RECORDS, took an interest in his possibilities and backed Ted Taylor with the "El Torros" and the recording of "Be Ever Wonderful" (DUKE 304), which went on to sell over a million discs!

During the early Sixties, Ted Taylor formed his own combo, comprising Wiley Terry, guitar; Richard Lovelace; Roland Mitchell; Arthur Porter; and Mr. Graham. His most outstanding hits of the early Sixties, recorded on TOP RANK INTERNATIONAL label, were "Has My Love Grown Cold" (TRI 2048), "Look Out" (TRI 2076), and, on GOLD EAGLE label, "No Matter What You Do" (GE 1812), on SONCRAFT label "Anytime, Anyplace, Anywhere" (S 400), and on DADE label "I Lost The Best Things I Ever Had" (Dade 5000), and on OKEH label "I Can't Take No More (OKEH 7165), "Somebody's Always Trying" (OKEH 7198), "Don't Deceive Me" (OKEH 7206), and his mid-Sixties Chart-maker "Stay Away From My Baby" (OKEH 7231).

Following his 1967 success "Feed The Flame" (ATCO 6481), Ted Taylor got back with Stan Lewis and his RONN label. Here he recorded, among others, several beautiful sides: "I Need Your Love So Bad" (RONN 21), "It's Too Late/The Road Of Love" (RONN 34), "Only The Lonely Knows" (RONN 57), "I'm Just A Crumb In Your Bread Box Of Love" (RONN 63), "I Want To Be A Part Of You Girl" (RONN 65), and then that favorite entry "For All The Days Of My Life" (RONN 82). With ALARM label, Ted Taylor recorded disco-oriented tracks, with his most notable "Stick By Me" (ALARM 114) proving a standout. Ted Taylor now performs with his own band, called "Gene Franklin & The House Rockers."

Discography

TED TAYLOR WITH "JACKS"

RPM

428 WHY DON'T YOU WRITE ME (4-55) [Feat. Willie Davis]/My Darling [Feat. Ted Taylor]

TED TAYLOR WITH "CADETS"

MODERN

956 DON'T BE ANGRY (4-55) [Feat. Aaron Collins]/I Cried [Feat. Ted Taylor]
963 I CRIED (7-55) [Feat. Ted Taylor]/Fine Lookin' Woman [Feat. Willie Davis]
971 DO YOU WANNA ROCK (10-55) [Feat. Ted Taylor]/If It Is Wrong [Feat. Aaron Collins]
Note: Besides the above-mentioned, the "Jacks"/"Cadets" recorded twenty more singles, but *not* with Ted Taylor singing lead vocal.

TED TAYLOR (SOLO)

EBB

113 DAYS ARE DARK (57)/Everywhere I Go
132 KEEP WALKING ON (58)/If I Don't See You Again

JEWEL (Bought Out EBB)

135 STRANGE THINGS HAPPENING EVERY DAY (58)/Little Boy (How Old Are You?)
151 WRAPPED UP IN A DREAM (58)/Very Truly Yours

MELOTONE (Early Item)

1003 I'M LEAVING YOU

DUKE

304 BE EVER WONDERFUL (6-59)/Since You're Home
308 COUNT THE STARS (10-59)/Hold Me Tight

TOP RANK INTERNATIONAL

2010 FALLIN' IN LOVE (10-59)/Jimmy Jum Jum
2011 I'M SAVING MY LOVE (10-59)/Chanta—Lula
2048 HAS MY LOVE GROWN COLD (7-60)/I Need You So
2076 LOOK OUT (10-60)/Darling Take Me Back
3001 SOMEDAY (I Know, I Know) (2-61)/You Know I Do
(Above also on WARWICK 628 from June 1961)

AS "AUSTIN TAYLOR"

LAURIE

3067 A HEART THAT'S TRUE (60)/Push Push

TED TAYLOR

3076 YOU'VE BEEN CRYING (1-61)/Close Your Eyes
(Above also on Jewel 759)

AS "AUSTIN TAYLOR"

3082 LOVIN' HANDS (61)/I Don't Want To Love You

TED TAYLOR

GOLD EAGLE

1805 MY DARLING (61)/She's A Winner
1810 THAT HAPPY DAY (61)/I Don't Care
1812 NO MATTER WHAT YOU DO (62)/Never In My Life

As "TED TAYLOR COMBO" [Feat. WILEY TERRY]

1808 ROCKIN' HOSS (61) [Instr.]/Bandstand Drag [Instr.]

SONCRAFT

400 ANYTIME, ANYPLACE, ANYWHERE (62)/I Lost The Best Things I Ever Had

DADE (Distributed by ATLANTIC)

5000 I LOST THE BEST THINGS I EVER HAD (62)/Darling If You Must Leave

APT

25063 LITTLE THINGS MEAN A LOT/My Days And Nights Are So Blue

OKEH (COLUMBIA Subsidiary)

7154 DON'T LIE TO ME (9-62)/Pretending Love
7159 YOU MUST HAVE BEEN MEANT FOR ME (11-62)/Time Has A Way
7165 I CAN'T TAKE NO MORE (1-63)/I'll Release You (Answer to Esther Phillip's "Release Me")
7171 BE EVER WONDERFUL (4-63)/That's Life I Guess
7176 HIM INSTEAD OF ME (7-63)/You Gave Me Nothin' (To Go On)
7179 I'LL MAKE IT UP TO YOU (9-63)/It Ain't Like That No More
7190 SO HARD (3-64)/Need You Home

7198 SOMEBODY'S ALWAYS TRYING (7-64)/Top Of The World
7206 DON'T DECEIVE ME (10-64)/If It Wasn't For You
7214 SO LONG, BYE BYE (2-65)/I Love You Yes I Do
7222 I'M SO SATISFIED (5-65)/(Love Is Like A) Ramblin' Rose
7231 STAY AWAY FROM MY BABY (11-65)/Walking Out Of My Life
7240 DADDY'S BABY (3-66)/Mercy Have Pity
7252 BIG WHEEL (7-66)/No One But You

EPIC

2241 BE EVER WONDERFUL/Ramblin' Rose
2249 STAY AWAY FROM MY BABY/Daddy's Baby

JEWEL

748 DAYS ARE DARK/Very Truly Yours
759 YOU'VE BEEN CRYING/Close Your Eyes
774 KEEP WALKING ON/Everywhere I Go

ATCO

6388 DANCING ANNIE (65)/Try Me Again
6408 RIVER'S INVITATION (66) [Percy Mayfield '63 hit. TANGERINE 931]/Long Distance Love
6434 THANK YOU FOR HELPING ME SEE THE LIGHT (66)/Help The Bear
6481 FEED THE FLAME (6-67)/Baby Come Back To Me

RONN (JEWEL Subsidiary)

15 MISS YOU SO (67)/I'm Gonna Get Tough
21 I NEED YOUR LOVE SO BAD (68) [Little Willie John '56 hit. KING 4841]/Ollie Mae
25 WITHOUT A WOMAN (68)/Honey Love
29 YOU GOT TO FEEL IT (69)/Strangest Feeling (Somebody Sleepin' In My Bed)
33 LONG AGO (69)/I'm Gonna Send You Back to Oklahoma
34 IT'S TOO LATE (8-69) [Chuck Willis '56 hit. ATLANTIC 1098]/The Road of Love
37 I'M LONELY TONIGHT (12-69)/If I Thought You Needed Me
40 I FEEL A CHILL (4-70)/Loving Physician
44 SOMETHING STRANGE IS GOIN' ON IN MY HOUSE (7-70)/Funky Thing
46 IT'S A FUNKY SITUATION (11-70)/I'm Glad You're Home
49 CAN'T TAKE NO MORE (3-71)/Singing Man
52 HOW'S YOUR LOVE LIFE BABY (8-71)/This Is A Troubled World
57 ONLY THE LONELY KNOWS (2-72)/How Do You Walk Away From Fear
63 I'M JUST A CRUMB IN YOUR BREAD BOX OF LOVE (6-72)/Houston Town

65 I WANT TO BE A PART OF YOU GIRL (10-72)/Going In A Hole
72 WHAT A FOOL (8-73)/Make Up For Lost Time
74 BREAK OF DAY (10-73)/Fair Weather Woman

TED TAYLOR & LITTLE JOHNNY TAYLOR

75 CRY IT OUT BABY (1-74)/Walking The Floor

TED TAYLOR

77 SHE LOVES TO DO IT AS WELL AS YOU (6-74)/Ready For The Heartbreak
82 FOR ALL THE DAYS OF MY LIFE (11-74)/I've Got To Find Somebody New

ALARM

110 EVERYBODY'S STEALING LOVE THAT YOU DON'T LOCK UP/Caught Up In A Good Woman's Love
112 STEAL AWAY (6-76)/Somebody's Gettting It
114 I'M GONNA HATE MYSELF IN THE MORNING/Stick By Me
117 GHETTO DISCO/You Can Make It If You Try

LITTLE JOHNNY TAYLOR AND TED TAYLOR

RONN

89 PRETENDING LOVE (9-77)/Funky Ghetto

TED TAYLOR

MCA

40937 KEEPIN' MY HEAD ABOVE WATER (8-78)/I Can't Fake It Anymore
40977 DOUBLE MY MONEY BAG (11-78)/Chase The World Away

"Temptations"

MEMBERS: *Eddie James Kendricks* (falsetto bass), born December 7, 1939, in Birmingham, Alabama, left in 1971 [replacement Ricky Owens, formerly of "Vibrations," staying only a short time; replacement Damon Harris, formerly of "Vandalls," left in 1975; replacement Glen Leonard, formerly of "Uniifics," "Chancellors," "Instant Groove," and "Reflections"]; *Paul Williams* (baritone, guitar, and piano), born July 2, 1939, in Birmingham, Alabama, left in 1971 [replacement Richard Street, former "Monitors" lead and initially with Paul Williams and Melvin Franklin in 1958]; *Melvin Franklin* (bass), real name David English, born October 12, 1942, in Montgomery, Alabama; *Otis Williams* (baritone), real name Otis Miles, born October 30, 1941, in Texarkana, Texas; *Eldridge Bryant* (tenor), real name Al Jackson, left in 1963 [replacement David Ruffin (baritone), formerly of "Dixie Nightingales," born January 8, 1941, leaving in 1948; replacement Dennis Edwards, formerly of "Contours," born February 3, 1943, in Birmingham, Alabama, left in 1977; replacement Louis Price, who sang lead vocals on ATLANTIC sides].

Hometown: Detroit, Michigan.

The "TEMPTATIONS," that famous MOTOWN recording quintet, have a most popular and unique style, with a combined talent capable of turning to anything and everything in music. Here is a group celebrated for its dazzling nightclub appearances, in which the identity of each artist is subordinated into a professionally carved public image. The durability of the group has become evident over the years through the interchanging combination of Eddie Kendricks's plaintive high tenor and David Ruffin's range from a winning softness to a throaty passionate shouting, but most of all in its adaptability to survive after the loss of David Ruffin, Eddie Kendricks, and Paul Williams!

It all started back where Eddie Kendricks and Paul Williams formed the "Primes" while in a Birmingham, Alabama, high school during the mid-Fifties. Being fans of the "Cadillacs" and "Frankie Lymon & Teenagers," they patterned their sound after them. On graduation the group broke up, leaving the two originals, still aspiring to a singing career, heading for Detroit, where they joined Otis Williams and Melvin Franklin to reform the "Primes" and for a period the "Elgins" as a quartet, until Eldridge Bryant joined them to make it a quintet. As the "Primes" the group had sung with a female group calling themselves the "Primettes," which, later, became the famous "Supremes"!

In 1960, the group assumed the name "Temptations" and should not be confused with the "Temptations" (on KING) or the white group the "Temptations" from New York who recorded "Barbara" (GOLDISC 3001). After Berry Gordy, Jr., signed the "Temptations" to the small independent MIRACLE label (Detroit), the group sang Doo-Wopp and Gospel-inspired entries, "Oh Mother Of Mine" and "Check Yourself," which had a good reception in the Detroit area. In 1962, Berry Gordy, Jr. (owner of TAMLA label), formed his GORDY label and signed the "Temptations." Their first release, written and produced by Berry Gordy, Jr., was the beautiful and charming "Dream Come True" (GORDY 7001), which reached No. 22 on the R&B Charts.

The "Temptations'" second release, "Paradise/Slow Down Heart" (GORDY 7010), proved to be a disappointment, but led to two significant events in their career. Eldridge Bryant left the group and was replaced by David Ruffin (who had been trying for a solo career, with small success, on MIRACLE label), and the group teamed up with Smokey Robinson! Success was not to be immediate, because neither Smokey's "I Want A Love I Can See" (GORDY 7015) nor Gordy's "Farewell My Love" (GORDY 7020) did anything exciting. It broke loose just before Christmas 1963 when Smokey Robinson and the "Temptations" used MOTOWN's little four-track studio to record "The Way You Do The Things You Do" (GORDY 7028), featuring Eddie Kendricks's delicate high tenor, to become No. 11 on the R&B Charts and the first of many hits.

1964 saw the impact of the lead voice of David Ruffin in "My Girl" (GORDY 7038), which becamc No. 1 smash hit on both R&B and Pop Charts and the beginning of the big time for the "Temptations"! Here the group versatility comes alive in the switch back and forth of the smooth tender lead of Eddie Kendricks and the commanding raw throaty lead of David Ruffin. Following this, the "Temptations" entered a period of involved and beautifully presented hits: "Ain't Too Proud To Beg" (GORDY 7054), "Beauty Is Only Skin Deep" (GORDY 7055), "(I Know) I'm Losing You" (GORDY 7057), "All I Need" (GORDY 7061), "You're My Everything" (GORDY 7063), "(Loneliness Made Me Realize) It's You That I Need" (GORDY 7065), "I Wish It Would Rain" (GORDY 7068), "I Could Never Love Another (After Loving

You)" (GORDY 7072), and "Please Return Your Love For Me" (GORDY 7074).

Then the bombshell came. Lead singer David Ruffin decided to go solo in 1968! That the idol to so many fans should be leaving the "Temptations" brought about a general disillusionment and uncertainty, because everyone believed "no one could replace David Ruffin." Incidentally, Rod Stewart considers David Ruffin to be one of the best Rock and Roll singers of all time. Still—Dennis Edwards (gravel-voiced lead singer of the "Contours") did more than fill the gap, because the "Temptations" as led by David Ruffin and as led by Dennis Edwards sounded so different as to be almost accepted as two different groups. David Ruffin had become prominent through the songs and production of Smokey Robinson, and Dennis Edwards starred on material virtually all supplied by Norman Whitfield and Barrett Strong. David Ruffin waxed extremely romantic, tender, passionate, and affectionate, but Dennis Edwards brought with him a new psychedelic Soul!

The "Temptations" changed direction totally with "Cloud Nine" (GORDY 7081), a change that was to continue with "Runaway Child, Running Wild" (GORDY 7084), "Don't Let The Joneses Get You Down" (GORDY 7086), "I Can't Get Next To You" (GORDY 7093), "Psychedelic Shack" (GORDY 7096), and "Ball Of Confusion (That's What The World Is Today)" (GORDY 7099). This helped to change the entire music scene. The "Temptations" best exemplified this powerful change, signaling the coming of disco!

The "Temptations" faced drastic personnel changes through the first half of the Seventies. In 1971, the group lost the two original members, Eddie Kendricks and Paul Williams, who went on in their own separate ways. Eddie Kendricks recorded several Chart hits: "If You Let Me" (TAMLA 54222), "Keep On Truckin'" (TAMLA 54238), "Boogie Down" (TAMLA 54243), and his Disco-oriented favorite "One Tear" (TAMLA 54255). Paul Williams, who had left the group because of failing health, attempted a solo career, but with no success and ended his life, tragically, with a gun. David Ruffin, launched on his solo career, gave us the hits "My Whole World Ended (The Moment You Left Me)" (MOTOWN 1140), "I'm So Glad I Fell For You" (MOTOWN 1158), "Me And Rock'n'Roll (Are Here To Stay)" (MOTOWN 1327), and that double-sided smash that is a disco classic, "Walk Away From Love/ Love Can Be Hazardous To Your Health" (MOTOWN 1376).

The "Temptations'" early-Seventies hits were "Ungena Za Ulimwengu (Unite The World)" (GORDY 7102), "Just My Imagination (Running Away With Me)" (GORDY 7105), "Superstar (Remember How You Got Where You Are)" (GORDY 7111), and "Papa Was A Rolling Stone" (GORDY 7121), which won two Grammys in 1972. Eddie

Kendricks wrote "Evil/Are You Ready" (JANUS 133) for "Group Posse." Ricky Owens (former member of the "Vibrations") had replaced Eddie Kendricks with the "Temptations," but stayed only a short time. He was replaced by Damon Harris (formerly with the "Vandalls"), who brought a pure falsetto, very similar to Eddie Kendricks, to the group. Richard Street (former member of the "Monitors") had replaced Paul Williams.

One song that deserves honorable mention is the "Temptations' " 1978 entry "That's When You Need Love," which is done in great Disco fashion. Looking now at the "Temptations," with personnel changes such as Damon Harris leaving for a solo career, new member Glen Leonard and lead vocalist Louis Price, it is difficult to foresee just what tomorrow will bring for the "Temptations," but, judging from their adaptability for survival in the past, one must expect still greater things. They have always been one of the finest and most popular of the Soul-oriented groups and, as a supergroup, became a model for so many groups to admire and follow. With their common roots as "Primes" and "Primettes" and their separate rise to glittering success as the "Temptations" and the "Supremes," it seemed only natural that we could enjoy some joint effort of their talents, such as "I'm Gonna Make You Love Me/A Place In The Sun" (MOTOWN 1137) and "The Weight/For Better Or Worse" (MOTOWN 1153).

Discography

AS "TEMPTATIONS"

MIRACLE

5 MOTHER OF MINE (8-61)/Romance Without Finance
12 YOUR WONDERFUL LOVE (2-62) Check Yourself

AS "PIRATES"

MEL-O-DY

105 MIND OVER MATTER (I'M GONNA MAKE YOU MINE) (1962)/I'll Love You Till I Die

AS "TEMPTATIONS"

GORDY

7001 DREAM COME TRUE (4-62)/Isn't She Pretty
7010 PARADISE (1-63)/Slow Down Heart
7015 I WANT A LOVE I CAN SEE (3-63) [Feat. Paul Williams]/ The Further You Look, The Less You See
7020 FAREWELL MY LOVE (6-63)/May I Have This Dance
7028 THE WAY YOU DO THE THINGS YOU DO (1-64)/Just Let Me Know

AS "TEMPTATIONS" [LIZ LANDS &]

7030 KEEP ME (4-64)/Midnight Johnny

AS "TEMPTATIONS"

7032 THE GIRL'S ALRIGHT WITH ME (4-64)/I'll Be In Trouble
7035 GIRL (WHY YOU WANNA MAKE ME BLUE) (8-64)/ Baby, Baby I Need You
7038 MY GIRL (12-64)/(Talkin' About) Nobody But My Baby
7040 IT'S GROWING (3-65)/What Love Has Joined Together
7043 SINCE I LOST MY BABY (6-65)/You've Got To Earn It
7047 MY BABY (9-65)/Don't Look Back
7049 GET READY (2-66)/Fading Away
7054 AIN'T TOO PROUD TO BEG (5-66)/You'll Lose A Precious Love
7055 BEAUTY IS ONLY SKIN DEEP (8-66)/You're Not An Ordinary Girl
7057 (I KNOW) I'M LOSING YOU (11-66)/I Couldn't Cry If I Wanted To
7061 ALL I NEED (4-67)/Sorry Is A Sorry Word
7063 YOU'RE MY EVERYTHING (6-67)/I've Been Good To You
7065 (LONELINESS MADE ME REALIZE) IT'S YOU THAT I NEED (9-67)/Don't Send Me Away
7068 I WISH IT WOULD RAIN (12-67)/I Truly Truly Believe
7072 I COULD NEVER LOVE ANOTHER (AFTER LOVING YOU) (4-68)/Gonna Give Her All The Love I've Got
7074 PLEASE RETURN YOUR LOVE TO ME (7-68)/How Can I Forget
7081 CLOUD NINE (11-68)/Why Did She Have To Leave Me

AS "SUPREMES" AND "TEMPTATIONS"

MOTOWN

1137 I'M GONNA MAKE YOU LOVE ME (2-68) [Orig. Madeline Bell '68 hit. PHILIPS 40517]/A Place In The Sun

AS "TEMPTATIONS"

GORDY

7082 RUNAWAY CHILD, RUNNING WILD (2-69)/I Need Your Lovin'

AS "SUPREMES" AND "TEMPTATIONS"

MOTOWN

1142 I'LL TRY SOMETHING NEW (3-69) ["Miracles" '62 hit. TAMLA 54059]/The Way You Do The Things You Do

AS "TEMPTATIONS"

GORDY

7086 DON'T LET THE JONESES GET YOU DOWN (5-69)/Since I Lost You

7093 I CAN'T GET NEXT TO YOU (8-69)/Running Away Won't Help You

AS "SUPREMES" AND "TEMPTATIONS"

MOTOWN

1153 THE WEIGHT (9-69) ["Band" '68 hit. CAPITOL 2269]/For Better or Worse

AS "TEMPTATIONS"

GORDY

7096 PSYCHEDELIC SHACK (1-70)/That's The Way Love Is

7099 BALL OF CONFUSION (THAT'S WHAT THE WORLD IS TODAY) (5-70)/It's Summer

7102 UNGENA ZA ULIMWENGU (UNITE THE WORLD) (9-70)/Hum Along And Dance

7105 JUST MY IMAGINATION (RUNNING AWAY WITH ME) (2-71)/Paradise

7109 IT'S SUMMER (7-71)/I'm The Exception To The Rule

7111 SUPERSTAR (REMEMBER HOW YOU GOT WHERE YOU ARE) (11-71)/Gonna Keep On Trying Till I Win Your Love

7115 TAKE A LOOK AROUND (3-72)/Smooth Sailing (From Now On)

7119 FUNKY MUSIC SHO NUFF TURNS ME ON (7-72)/Mother Nature

7121 PAPA WAS A ROLLING STONE (10-72)/Papa Was A Rolling Stone [Instr.]
7126 MASTERPIECE (2-73)/Masterpiece [Instr.]
7129 PLASTIC MAN (6-73)/Hurry Tomorrow
7131 HEY GIRL I LIKE YOUR STYLE (8-73)/Ma
7135 HEAVENLY (3-74)/Zoom
7136 YOU'VE GOT MY SOUL ON FIRE (6-74)/I Need You
7138 HAPPY PEOPLE (12-74)/Happy People [Instr.]
7142 SHAKY GROUND (3-75)/I'm A Bachelor
7144 GLASSHOUSE (7-75)/The Prophet
7146 KEEP HOLDING ON (1-76)/What You Need Most (I Do Best Of All)
7150 UP THE CREEK (WITHOUT A PADDLE) (6-76)/Darling, Stand By Me (Song For My Woman)
7152 WHO ARE YOU (10-76)/Let Me Count The Ways (I Love You)

ATLANTIC

3436 IN A LIFETIME (11-77)/I Could Never Stop Loving You
3461 THINK FOR YOURSELF (3-78)/Let's Live In Peace
3517 BARE BACK (9-78)
3538 EVER READY LOVE (11-78)

DAMON HARRIS [Solo; he left "Temptations" in 1975]

FANTASY

839 SILK (11-78)/Funday

AS "TEMPTATIONS"

ATLANTIC

3567 I JUST DON'T KNOW HOW TO LET YOU GO (4-79)

DAVID RUFFIN
PRE-"TEMPTATIONS"

ANNA

1127 I'M IN LOVE (1-61)/One Of These Days

CHECK-MATE

1003 ACTION SPEAKS LOUDER THAN WORDS (1961)/You Can Get What I Got
1010 KNOCK YOU OUT (WITH LOVE) (1962)/Mr. Bus Driver—Hurry!

POST-"TEMPTATIONS": DAVID'S HIT SOLO PERIOD

MOTOWN

1140 MY WHOLE WORLD ENDED (THE MOMENT YOU LEFT ME) (2-69)/I've Got To Find Myself A Brand New Baby
1149 I'VE LOST EVERYTHING I'VE EVER LOVED (6-69)/We'll Have A Good Thing Going On
1158 I'M SO GLAD I FELL FOR YOU (12-69)/I Pray Every Day You Won't Regret Loving Me

AS "RUFFIN BROTHERS" [DAVID & JIMMY]

SOUL

35076 STAND BY ME (10-70)/Your Love Was Worth Waiting For

DAVID RUFFIN

MOTOWN

1178 DON'T STOP LOVING ME (2-71)/Each Day Is A Lifetime

AS "RUFFIN BROTHERS" [DAVID & JIMMY]

SOUL

35082 WHEN MY LOVE HAND COMES DOWN (4-71)/Steppin' On A Dream

DAVID RUFFIN

MOTOWN

1204 A LITTLE MORE TRUST (7-72)/A Day In The Life Of A Working Man
1223 BLOOD DONORS NEEDED (GIVE ALL YOU CAN) (4-73)/Go On With Your Bad Self
1259 COMMON MAN (8-73)/I'm Just A Mortal Man
1327 ME AND ROCK'N'ROLL (ARE HERE TO STAY) (11-74)/Smiling Faces Sometimes
1336 SUPERSTAR (REMEMBER HOW YOU GOT WHERE YOU ARE) (1975) ["Temptations" '71 hit. GORDY 7111]/No Matter What
1376 WALK AWAY FROM LOVE (11-75)/Love Can Be Hazardous To Your Health
1388 HEAVY LOVE (3-76)/Love Can Be Hazardous To Your Health
1393 EVERYTHING'S COMING UP LOVE (6-76)/No Matter Where
1405 ON AND OFF (10-76)/Statue Of A Fool

1420 JUST LET ME HOLD YOU FOR A NIGHT (7-77)/Rode By The Place Where We Used To Stay
1435 YOU'RE MY PEACE OF MIND (2-78)/Rode By The Place Where We Used To Stay

WARNER BROTHERS

49030 BREAK MY HEART (8-79)/Sexy Dancer
49123 I GET EXCITED (11-79)/Chain On The Brain

EDDIE KENDRICKS

TAMLA

54203 IT'S SO HARD FOR ME TO SAY GOODBYE (5-71)/This Used To Be The Home Of Johnnie Mae
54210 I DID IT ALL FOR YOU (9-71)/Can I
54218 LET ME RUN INTO YOUR LONELY HEART (1-72)/Eddie's Love
54222 IF YOU LET ME (9-72)/Just Memories
54230 GIRL, YOU NEED A CHANGE OF MIND (2-73)/Girl, You Need A Change Of Mind [Part 2]
54236 DARLING COME BACK HOME (7-73)/Loving You The Second Time Around
54238 KEEP ON TRUCKIN' (8-73)/Keep On Truckin' [Part 2]
54243 BOOGIE DOWN (1-74)/Can't Help What I Am
54247 SON OF SAGITTARIUS (5-74)/Trust Your Heart
54249 TELL HER LOVE HAS FELT THE NEED (8-74)/Loving You The Second Time Around
54255 ONE TEAR (12-74)/The Thin Man
54257 SHOESHINE BOY (2-75)/Hooked On Your Love
54260 GET THE CREAM OFF THE TOP (7-75)/Honeybrown
54263 HAPPY (10-75)/Deep And Quiet Love
54266 HE'S A FRIEND (1-76)/All Of My Love
54270 NEVER GONNA LEAVE YOU (6-76)/Get It While It's Hot
54277 GOIN' UP IN SMOKE (10-76)/Thanks For The Memories
54285 BORN AGAIN (6-77)/Date With The Rain
54290 INTIMATE FRIENDS (2-78)/Baby

ARISTA

325 AIN'T NO SMOKE WITHOUT FIRE (4-78)/Love Love Love
346 THE BEST OF STRANGERS (8-78)/Don't Underestimate The Power Of Love
466 I JUST WANT TO BE THE ONE IN YOUR LIFE (10-79)

♭♯♪♩♩

"Tymes"

Original "Tymes": George Williams, lead singer; Donald Banks, bass; Norman Burnett, baritone; Albert "Caesar" Berry, first tenor; George Hilliard, piano (left group 1974).
1976 "Tymes": George Williams, lead singer; Albert Berry, first tenor; Norman Burnett, second tenor and baritone; Wade Davis, baritone; Jerry Ferguson, tenor; Donald Banks, bass. Also featured were female singers, Terri Gonzales, soprano, and Melanie Moore, second soprano.

Hometown: Philadelphia, Pennsylvania.

The "TYMES" have to be seen as one of those naturally talented quintets who really try their utmost to make their audience happy. An example is the case when, in 1963, everyone could be heard whistling along with the group's million-seller "So Much In Love" (PARKWAY 871C). This number conveyed a typical cheerful and pleasant message to the public and was written by group member George Williams (along with his two friends, Billy Jackson and Roy Straigis), and was produced by Billy Jackson.

It was shortly after George Hilliard and Norman Burnett met at a summer camp in 1956 that they started to sing together, and were joined that same year by Donald Banks, Albert Berry, and George Williams. They performed at various local dances and amateur shows, as the "Latineers."

In April 1963, the group appeared as the "Tymes" on "The Wads Talent Show" (radio-sponsored) in a Philadelphia night spot, and it was there that a PHILLY-PARKWAY executive spotted them. That same year, the "Tymes" made several recordings with PARKWAY label, the second of which, "So Much In Love" (PARKWAY 871C), that song that had such happy audience appeal, went right to the top of the Charts. It was followed immediately by another great favorite, "Wonderful! Wonderful!" (PARKWAY 884), and early the next year by "Somewhere (My Love Waits For Me)" (PARKWAY 891) and the classic "To Each His Own" (PARKWAY 908).

The "Tymes" have always taken great professional pride in their singing expertise and their rapport with their enthusiastic listeners. They proved themselves most successful with their smash disco-oriented hits, "You Little Trustmaker" (RCA 10022) in 1974 and "Ms. Grace" (RCA 10128) early in 1975.

Discography

AS "TYMES"

PARKWAY

871A	SO IN LOVE (6-63) [First Pressing]/Roscoe James McClain
871C	SO MUCH IN LOVE (6-63) [Second Pressing]/Roscoe James McClain
884	WONDERFUL! WONDERFUL! (8-63) [Johnny Mathis '57 hit. COLUMBIA 40784]/Come With Me To The Sea
891	SOMEWHERE (MY LOVE WAITS FOR ME) (12-63)/View From My Window
908	TO EACH HIS OWN (3-64) ["Inkspots" tune, "Platters" '60 hit. MERCURY 71697]/Wonderland Of Love
919	THE MAGIC OF OUR SUMMER LOVE (6-64)/With All My Heart
924	HERE SHE COMES (11-64)/Malibu
933	ISLE OF LOVE (1965)/Twelfth Of Never
7039-45	ISLE OF LOVE/I'm Always Chasing Rainbows

WINCHESTER (Owned by Leon Huff. Distributed by CAMEO)

1002	THESE FOOLISH THINGS (1965)/This Time It's Love

MGM

13631	TOUCH OF BABY (11-66)/What Would I Do
13536	PRETEND (5-66)/Street Talk

AS "SWEET TYMES"

EPIC

10227	I THINK I KNOW HER (1967)/You Ought To Belong To Me

AS "MAGIC TYMES"

MALA

541	HAPPY FEET NIGHT (1967)/When You're Sitting All Alone

AS "TYMES"

COLUMBIA

44630	PEOPLE (11-68) [From Broadway show *Funny Girl*]/For The Love Of Ivy
44799	GOD BLESS THE CHILD (3-69)/Love That You're Looking For
44917	IF YOU LOVE ME BABY (8-69)/Find My Way
45078	MY MOST BEAUTIFUL MARRIED LADY (2-70)/Love Child
45336	SHE'S GONE (4-71)/Someone To Watch Over Me

RCA

10022	YOU LITTLE TRUSTMAKER (8-74)/The North Hills
10128	MS. GRACE (1-75)/The Crutch
10244	SOMEWAY, SOMEHOW I'M KEEPING YOU (5-75)/Inter-loop!
10422	GOD'S GONNA PUNISH YOU (11-75)/If I Can't Make You Smile
10561	IT'S COOL (2-76)/Good Morning Dear Lord
10713	ONLY YOUR LOVE (7-76)/Goin' Through The Motions
10862	SAVANNAH SUNNAY SUNDAY (1976)
11136	HOW I KNOW (1977)/I'll Take You There

♭♯♪♩♩

Johnny Guitar Watson

Born in Houston, Texas, February 3, 1935.

JOHNNY WATSON looms as a slick, funky individual of genial and modest character who is better known among the musicians' elite than with the general public. He gained his understanding of the music business during the Fifties and Sixties, recording for several small personal labels for which he readily showed a preference. Johnny was raised in Houston, Texas, where his grandfather, a local preacher, taught him to play the piano. In 1950, when he was only fifteen, his family moved to Los Angeles, where he attended Jefferson High School, during which time he appeared in and won numerous talent shows. Johnny Otis discovered Johnny Watson while Hunter Hancock, a local disc jockey, arranged for audition of his first recordings. As "Young John Watson," he played piano and sang "Highway-60" and "Half-Pint Whiskey" (both produced by Maxwell Davis), while his "Space Guitar" had effects that would emerge as the guitar style to follow by Jimi Hendrix in the Sixties.

The creative Johnny Watson wrote "Try It, You'll Like It" for Betty Everett and "Don't Change Horses (In The Middle Of The Stream)" for the group "Tower of Power," but it was not until 1975, in his Chart hit "I Don't Want To Be A Lone Ranger" (FANTASY 739), that Johnny gained the freedom to produce his own songs. Dick James, who discovered Elton John and guided Elton's career for five years, took a main interest in Johnny Watson and signed him to D.J.M. label with the group the "Watsonian Institute." Here, Johnny recorded two certified Gold albums from which came the singles "Ain't That A Bitch" (D.J.M. 1238-1020) and "A Real Mother For Ya" (D.J.M. 1238-1024). His "Love That Will Not Die" (D.J.M. 1238-1034) had much of that same winning appeal!

Johnny Watson dropped his playing of the piano for the guitar during the early Fifties, inspired by early Texas Blues influences of Clarence "Gate Mouth" Brown, Lowell Fulsom, Aaron "T-Bone" Walker, and others, and inserted "Guitar" between his Christian name and his surname! His first hit came with "Those Lonely Lonely Nights" (R.P.M. 436), and it was during the Fifties that he recorded many classics, excellent Blues/R&B discs, "Hot Little Mama," a great guitar number with splendid vocals, "Too Tired," "Oh Baby," and "She Moves Me," besides writing "Give Me Love" and doing session work, vocally and instrumentally, for Eugene Church and the West Coast groups the "Olympics" and the "Shields."

His "Johnny Guitar" (ARVEE 5016), another exceptional disc, denotes Johnny Watson's desire (on wax) to sing in *your* hometown! He, then, made his memorable KING classics, "The Eagle Is Back," "Broke And Lonely," "Sweet Lovin' Mama (What You Do To Me)" and his unique "Gangster Of Love," popularized by the Steve Miller Band. It was Johnny Otis, being the A&R man for KING, who after watching Johnny Watson's development on several small personal labels, inspired him toward future success on the big labels!

In 1966, Johnny got together with Soul singer Larry Williams as a duet and recorded the R&B hits "Mercy, Mercy, Mercy," "Two For The Price Of One," "Nobody," and "I Can't Love You Baby." Later, Johnny recorded fine entries for MAGNUM, BELL, HIGHLAND, and VULTURE.

Discography

AS "YOUNG JOHN WATSON"

FEDERAL

12120	HIGHWAY-60 (1953) [with "Amos Milburn Band"]/Motor Head Baby
12131	SAD FOOL (1953) [with "Lamplites"]/Motor Head Baby
12143	I GOT EYES (1954)/Walkin' To My Baby
12175	HALF-PINT WHISKEY (1954)/Space Guitar
12183	YOU CAN'T TAKE IT WITH YOU (1954)/Gettin' Drunk

AS "JOHNNY WATSON"

R.P.M.

423	HOT LITTLE MAMA (1955)/I Love To Love You
431	TOO TIRED (1955)/Don't Touch Me
436	THOSE LONELY, LONELY NIGHTS (1955)/Someone Cares For Me
447	OH BABY (1955)/Give A Little
455	THREE HOURS PAST MIDNIGHT (1956)/Reuben
471	SHE MOVES ME (1956)/Love Me Baby

JOHNNY WATSON (& HIS "NIGHT OWLS")

CACTUS

118 LET'S ROCK (R-A-B)/I'm Not Crazy

JOHNNY WATSON

KEEN

4003* ONE ROOM COUNTRY SHACK (1957)/Gangster of Love
4023 HONEY (1958)/Deana Baby

MARGARET

996 JOHNNY'S JIVE/Kitty O
997 WHAT IN THE WORLD/Can't Be Still

JOWAT

118 BABY DON'T LEAVE/Ain't Gonna Move

CLASS

246 ONE MORE KISS (1959)/The Bear

JOHNNY "GUITAR" WATSON

GOTH

101 RAT NOW/Falling In Love

ARVEE

5016 JOHNNY GUITAR (1960)/The Untouchables

ESCORT

116 THE EAGLE IS BACK (1961)/Looking Back

KING

5536 EMBRACEABLE YOU (7-61)/Posin'
5579 CUTTIN' IN (3-62)/Broke and Lonely
5607 I JUST WANTS ME SOME LOVE (4-62)/The Nearness Of You
5666 SWEET LOVIN' MAMA (8-62)/That's The Chance You've Got To Take

*Also on KEEN 4005.

5716 THAT'S THE CHANCE YOU'VE GOT TO TAKE (3-63)/ Cold, Cold Heart
5774 GANGSTER OF LOVE (8-63)/In The Evening
5833 I SAY, I LOVE YOU (1964)/You Better Love Me

OKEH

7263 KEEP ON LOVIN' YOU (1966)/South Like West
7270 HOLD ON I'M COMIN' (1967)/Wolfman

AS "LARRY WILLIAMS & JOHNNY WATSON"

7274 MERCY, MERCY, MERCY (3-67)/A Quitter Never Wins
7281 TWO FOR THE PRICE OF ONE (6-67)/Too Late

AS "JOHNNY WATSON"

7290 SOUL FOOD (8-67)/I'd Rather Be Your Baby

AS "LARRY WILLIAMS & JOHNNY WATSON"

7300 NOBODY (1-68)/Find Yourself Somebody To Love

AS "JOHNNY WATSON"

7302 SHE'LL BLOW YOUR MIND (2-68)/Crazy About You

AS "LARRY WILLIAMS & JOHNNY WATSON"

BELL

813 I CAN'T LOVE YOU BABY/Can't Find No Substitute For You

JOHNNY "GUITAR" WATSON

MAGNUM

726 BIG BAD WOLF/You Can Stay

HIGHLAND

1151 WAIT A MINUTE BABY/Oh So Fine

VULTURE (A LIZARD Subsidiary)

5003 THERE'S A RECESSION GOING ON (9-71)/Mama

FANTASY

721	TREAT ME LIKE I'M YOUR MAN (5-74)/You Bring Love
739	I DON'T WANT TO BE A LONE RANGER (6-75)/You Can Stay But The Noise Must Go
752	IT'S WAY TOO LATE (12-75)/Tripping

D.J.M.

1238-1013	I NEED IT (7-76)/Since I Met You Baby
1238-1019	SUPERMAN LOVER (11-76)/We're No Exception
1238-1020	AIN'T THAT A BITCH (2-77)/Won't You Forgive Me Baby
1238-1024	A REAL MOTHER FOR YA (6-77)/Nothing Left To Be Desired
1238-1029	LOVER JONES (10-77)/Tarzan
1238-1034	LOVE THAT WILL NOT DIE (1-78)/It's A Damn Shame

BIG TOWN

714	THOSE LONELY, LONELY NIGHTS (1978)/Oh Babe
718	TOO TIRED TO COME (1978)/Hot Little Mama

D.J.M.

1238-1101	GANGSTER OF LOVE (11-78)
1238-1106	WHAT THE HELL IS THIS (6-79)

♭♯♪♩𝅗𝅥

Barry White

Born in Galveston, Texas, on September 12, 1944.

BARRY WHITE spent much of his early life in Los Angeles, where he sang as a choirboy and later directed the choir. He joined the R&B group the "Upfronts" on "It Took Time" (LUMMTONE 103). He worked in the studios with Jack Stern during the early Sixties, where he played the keyboards and, learning to produce, produced a national hit, "Harlem Shuffle" (MARC 104), for Bob and Earl. Earl went solo under Jackie Lee, and Barry White was his road manager at the time of "The Duck" (MIRWOOD 5502) in 1965. Barry White, alias "Barry Lee," recorded an R&B item, "Man Ain't Nothing" (DOWNEY 134), and then he joined MUSTANG/BRONCO, as A&R man, where he released "All In The Run Of A Day" (BRONCO 2056), besides writing "I Feel Love Comin' On" for Felice Taylor.

With his heavy breathing and growling in song, Barry White created a motivation mood for longing and sexual adoration. Barry is one of the most articulate and stimulating of the performers, producers, and directors to emerge from the Seventies. It was in 1969 that he met the three women who were to become "Love Unlimited" and that a most successful decade unfolded for Barry White. Barry, in charge of Sa-vette Music and Barry White Inc., put a lot into the creation of his female protégées and his backup group "Love Unlimited," featuring his wife, Glodean James, her sister Linda and Diane Taylor, and, of course, the "Love Unlimited Orchestra."

"Love Unlimited" had its debut in 1972 with a Barry White composition, "Walkin' In The Rain (With The One I Love)," and Barry himself struck it big in 1973 with a series of soulful Chart hits: "I'm Gonna Love You Just A Little More" (20th CEN. 2018), "I've Got So Much To Give" (20th CEN. 2042), and "Never, Never Gonna Give Ya Up" (20th CEN. 2058). 1974 proved to be another fabulous year for Barry White, with "Honey Please Can't You See" (20th CEN. 2077), "Can't Get Enough Of Your Love, Babe" (20th CEN. 2120), "You're The First, The Last, My Everything" (20th CEN. 2133), and his exciting treatment of "I'll Do For You Anything You Want Me To" (20th CEN. 2208). His updated Chart disc of 1977, "It's Ecstasy When You Lay Down Next To Me" (20th CEN. 2350), had great success impact.

Discography

"ATLANTICS" (WITH BARRY WHITE)

FARO

613 TRACY (1964)/Flame Of Love

AS "BARRY LEE"

DOWNEY

134 MAN AIN'T NOTHING/I Don't Need It

VEEP

1201 MAKE IT (1-65)/Things Gotta Change

BARRY WHITE

BRONCO

2056 ALL IN THE RUN OF A DAY (5-67)/Don't Take Your Love From Me

20th CENTURY

2018 I'M GONNA LOVE YOU JUST A LITTLE MORE (4-73)/Just A Little More Baby
2042 I'VE GOT SO MUCH TO GIVE (9-73)/I've Got So Much To Give [Part 2]
2058 NEVER, NEVER GONNA GIVE YA UP (10-73)/Never, Never Gonna Give Ya Up [Instr.]
2077 HONEY PLEASE CAN'T YOU SEE (2-74)/Honey Please Can't You See [Instr.]
2120 CAN'T GET ENOUGH OF YOUR LOVE, BABE (8-74)/Just Not Enough
2133 YOU'RE THE FIRST, THE LAST, MY EVERYTHING (11-74)/More Than Anything, You're My Everything
2177 WHAT AM I GONNA DO WITH YOU (3-75)/What Am I Gonna Do With You Baby

2208 I'LL DO FOR YOU ANYTHING YOU WANT ME TO (5-75)/ Anything You Want Me To
2265 LET THE MUSIC PLAY (1-76)/Let The Music Play [Instr.]
2277 YOU SEE THE TROUBLE WITH ME (3-76)/I'm So Blue and You Are Too
2298 BABY, WE BETTER TRY TO GET IT TOGETHER (7-76)/ If You Know, Won't You Tell Me
2309 DON'T MAKE ME WAIT TOO LONG (11-76)/Can't You See It's Only You I Want
2328 I'M QUALIFIED TO SATISFY YOU (2-77)/I'm Qualified To Satisfy You [Instr.]
2350 IT'S ECSTASY WHEN YOU LAY DOWN NEXT TO ME (8-77)/I Never Thought I'd Fall In Love With You
2361 PLAYING YOUR GAME, BABY (1-78)/Of All The Guys In The World
2365 OH WHAT A NIGHT FOR DANCING (4-78)/You're So Good You're Bad
2380 YOUR SWEETNESS IS MY WEAKNESS (9-78)/It's Only Love Doing It's Thing
2395 JUST THE WAY YOU ARE (1-79)/Now I'm Gonna Make Love To You

UNLIMITED GOLD

8-1401 ANY FOOL COULD SEE (YOU WERE MEANT FOR ME) (3-79)/You're The One I Need
8-1404 IT AIN'T LOVE, BABY (UNTIL YOU GIVE IT) (6-79)/It Ain't Love, Baby (Until You Give It) [Part 2]

20th CENTURY

2416 I LOVE TO SING THE SONG I SING (8-79)
2433 HOW DID YOU KNOW IT WAS ME? (11-79)/Oh Me, Oh My

UNLIMITED GOLD

9-1411 LOVE AIN'T EASY (12-79)/I Found Love

"LOVE UNLIMITED"

UNI

55319* WALKIN' IN THE RAIN (WITH THE ONE I LOVE) (3-72)/ I Should Have Known
55342* IS IT REALLY TRUE BOY—IS IT REALLY ME (8-72)/ Another Chance

20th CENTURY

2062* IT MAY BE WINTER OUTSIDE (BUT IN MY HEART IT'S SPRING (12-73)/It's Winter Again

*Written by Barry White.

2082* UNDER THE INFLUENCE OF LOVE (3-74)/Under The Influence Of Love
2110* PEOPLE OF TOMORROW ARE THE CHILDREN OF TODAY (8-74)/So Nice To Hear
2141* I BELONG TO YOU (11-74)/And Only You
2183 SHARE A LITTLE LOVE IN YOUR HEART (4-75)/I Love You So, Never Gonna Let You Go

MCA

40009 I'LL BE YOURS FOREVER MORE/Fragile—Handle With Care

"LOVE UNLIMITED ORCHESTRA"

20th CENTURY

2069* LOVE'S THEME (12-73)/Sweet Moments
2090 RHAPSODY IN WHITE (4-74)/Barry's Theme
2107 TOGETHER BROTHER (7-74) [MOVIE]/Find The Man, Brother
2145 BABY BLUES (11-74)/What A Groove
2162 SATIN SOUL (2-75)/Just Living It Up
2197 FOREVER IN LOVE (1975)/Only You Can Make Me Blue
2301 MY SWEET SUMMER SUITE (9-76)/Just Living It Up
2325 THEME FROM KING KONG (1-77)/Theme From King Kong [Part 2]
2348 BRAZILIAN LOVE SONG (9-77)/My Sweet Summer Suite
2364 HEY LOOK AT ME, I'M IN LOVE (4-78)/Whisper Softly
2367 DON'T YOU KNOW HOW MUCH I LOVE YOU (10-78)/ Hey Look At Me, I'm In Love
2281 MIDNIGHT GROOVE (1976)/It's Only What I Feel

"LOVE UNLIMITED"

UNLIMITED GOLD

91409 HIGH STEPPIN', HIP DRESSIN' FELLA (You Got It To Get Her) (9-79)

---

*Written by Barry White.

♭♯♪♩𝅗𝅥

Jackie Wilson

Born in Detroit, Michigan, on June 9, 1934.

JACKIE WILSON, "Mr. Excitement," became Brunswick label's top hit-maker. He grew up in the Motor City ghetto. When he was about ten, he won an amateur show by singing "Danny Boy," recorded on Dizzy Gillespie's DG label. Jackie also, under the pseudonym "Little Mr. Midnite," recorded for REGAL label.

At sixteen, during his Highland Park High School years, Jackie became a "Golden Gloves" welterweight champion, but his mother discouraged any future hopes in this direction, and as a result he made singing his life. Jackie was originally with the "Ever Ready Gospel Singers" and the "Thrillers" (comprising Hank Ballard, Freddie Pride, Tommy Davis, Sonny Woods, and Lawson Smith, several of whom formed the Fifties black group the "Royals," which later became "Hank Ballard & the Midnighters").

At a local talent show in 1951, Jackie was "discovered" by the "Godfather of Rhythm and Blues," Johnny Otis. He sang in local nightclubs around Detroit until his first big break in 1953, when he became lead singer with Billy Ward and the "Dominoes," on the departure of Clyde McPhatter to form the original "Drifters." His highlight here was "Christmas In Heaven" (KING 1281). After that, Nat Tarnopol, a Detroit music publisher and owner of BRUNSWICK label, became Jackie's manager. "Reet Petite" (BRUNSWICK 55024) was Jackie Wilson's first solo effort, in 1957.

Eddie Holland, who became a MOTOWN early Sixties hit-maker, developed a style similar to Jackie Wilson's and, interestingly enough, made demos of "Reet Petite," "Lonely Teardrops," and "That's Why" out of the composition by Berry Gordy, Jr., and Tyran Carlo.

Jackie Wilson sang from his heart some of the most beautiful love ballads in semioperatic fashion, such as "As Long As I Live" (BRUNSWICK 55070) and "Night" (BRUNSWICK 55166). He also reached a high-standard self-styled vocal range in Rhythm and Blues uptempo recordings such as "Reet Petite (The Finest Girl You'll Ever Want to

Meet)," "Lonely Teardrops" (BRUNSWICK 55105), "That's Why" (BRUNSWICK 55121), "Am I The Man" (BRUNSWICK 55170), "What Good Am I Without You" (BRUNSWICK 55236), "Baby Workout" (BRUNSWICK 55239), and finally his most successful Sixties hit, "Higher And Higher" (BRUNSWICK 55336). Jackie Wilson appeared in two films, *Go Johnny Go* and *Teenage Millionaire.* He became known as "Mr. Excitement" because he was a most exciting entertainer to watch and to listen to. He combined the dancing ability and showmanship of James Brown with the singing attributes of Mario Lanza. In 1961, Jackie Wilson was shot, allegedly by a female fan.

The Sixties saw a widening development in Jackie, and his teaming up with Linda Hopkins on three occasions, with emphasis on "I Found Love" (BRUNSWICK 55224), and once with Lavern Baker on "Think Twice" (BRUNSWICK 55287). Other outstanding contributions of the Sixties have to be "No Pity (In the Naked City)" (BRUNSWICK 55280), "Whispers (Gettin' Louder)" (BRUNSWICK 55300), "(Your Love Keeps Lifting Me) Higher And Higher" (BRUNSWICK 55336), "I Get The Sweetest Feeling" (BRUNSWICK 55381), "For Once In My Life" (BRUNSWICK 55392) and "I Still Love You" (BRUNSWICK 55402). The only significant hits of the Seventies remain "Let This Be A Letter (To My Baby)" (BRUNSWICK 55435) and "(I Can Feel Those Vibrations) "This Love Is Real" (BRUNSWICK 55443).

Tragedy struck Jackie Wilson suddenly in the most unfortunate circumstances during his singing of "Lonely Teardrops" at a performance in the Latin Casino in Cherry Hill, New Jersey, on the evening of September 27, 1975. It was then and there that Jackie suffered a heart attack, suddenly collapsed, and struck his head on the stage, thus immediately stopping his breathing and shutting off air to his brain. Although he finally emerged from a three-and-a-half-month-long coma, and is no longer dependent on artificial respiration, he is now functioning at "brainstem level" or, as most commonly known, in "a chronic vegetative state."

Discography

AS "LITTLE MR. MIDNITE"

REGAL

3287 GOT A BRAND NEW BABY (1953)/Four O'Clock Blues

AS "THE DOMINOES"

FEDERAL

12139 WHERE NOW, LITTLE HEART (53) [Feat. James Van Loan]/ You Can't Keep A Good Man Down [Feat. Jackie Wilson]

12162 UNTIL THE REAL THING COMES ALONG (1-54) [Feat. Jackie Wilson (W. James Van Loan on bridge)]/My Baby's 3-D [Feat. Clifford Givens]

12178 TOOTSIE ROLL (4-54) [Feat. Clifford Givens]/(I'm Gonna Move To) The Outskirts of Town [Feat. Jackie Wilson]

12193 ABOVE JACOB'S LADDER* (8-54) [Feat. Jackie Wilson and Clifford Givens]/Little Black Train [Feat. Clifford Givens]

12209 IF I NEVER GET TO HEAVEN (2-55)/I Can't Do Sixty No More [Feat. Clifford Givens]

12218 LOVE ME NOW OR LET ME GO (4-55) [Feat. Jackie Wilson and Clifford Givens]/Cave Man [Feat. Clifford Givens]

12263 BOBBY SOX BABY (7-56)/How Long, How Long Blues

12301 ONE MOMENT WITH YOU (7-57) [Feat. Jackie Wilson]/St. Louis Blues [Feat. Jackie Wilson and James Van Loan]

KING

1280 RAGS TO RICHES (11-53) [Feat. Jackie Wilson]/Don't Thank Me [Feat. James Van Loan]

1281 CHRISTMAS IN HEAVEN (12-53) [Feat. Jackie Wilson]/ Ringing In A Brand New Year [Feat. James Van Loan]

1342 TENDERLY (54) [Feat. Jackie Wilson]/A Little Lie [Feat. Jackie Wilson]

1364 THREE COINS IN THE FOUNTAIN (54) [Feat. Jackie Wilson]/Lonesome Road [Feat. Clifford Givens]

1368 LITTLE THINGS MEAN A LOT (54) [Feat. Jackie Wilson]/ I Really Don't Want To Know [Feat. Clifford Givens]

1492 MAY I NEVER LOVE AGAIN (55) [Feat. Milton Merle]/ Learnin' The Blues [Feat. Jackie Wilson]

1502 OVER THE RAINBOW (55) [Feat. Milton Merle]/Give Me You [Feat. Jackie Wilson and Clifford Givens]

Note: Jackie Wilson was with the group for two JUBILEE recordings and six DECCA recordings, but the above are his most popular group contributions.

5463 LAY IT ON THE LINE (1961) [Feat. Monroe Powell]/That's When You Know You're Growing Old [Feat. Jackie Wilson]

JACKIE WILSON

BRUNSWICK

55024 REET PETITE (10-57)/By The Light Of The Silvery Moon
55052 TO BE LOVED (4-58)/Come Back To Me
55070 AS LONG AS I LIVE (6-58)/I'm Wanderin'
55086 SINGING A SONG (9-58)/We Have Love
55105 LONELY TEARDROPS (11-58)/In The Blue Of The Evening
55121 THAT'S WHY (3-59)/Love Is All
55136 I'LL BE SATISFIED (6-59)/Ask
55149 YOU BETTER KNOW IT (9-59)/Never Go Away

*A Gospel release.

55165 TALK THAT TALK (11-59)/Only You And Only Me
55166 NIGHT (3-60)/Doggin' Around
55167 ALL MY LOVE (7-60)/A Woman, A Lover, A Friend
55170 ALONE AT LAST (10-60) [Based on Tchaikovsky's First Piano Concerto]/Am I The Man
55201 MY EMPTY ARMS (1-61)/Tear Of The Year
55208 PLEASE TELL ME WHY (3-61)/Your One And Only Love
55216 I'M COMIN' ON BACK TO YOU (6-61)/Lonely Life
55219 YEARS FROM NOW (8-61)/You Don't Know What It Means
55220 THE WAY I AM (10-61)/My Heart Belongs To Only You
55221 THE GREATEST LOVE (1-62)/There'll Be No Next Time
55224 I FOUND LOVE (4-62) [W. Linda Hopkins]/There's Nothing Like Love
55225 HEARTS (4-62)/Sing
55229 I JUST CAN'T HELP IT (7-62)/My Tale Of Woe
55233 FOREVER AND A DAY (9-62)/Baby That's All
55236 A GIRL NAMED TAMIKO (12-62)/What Good Am I Without You
55239 BABY WORKOUT (3-63)/I'm Going Crazy (Gotta Get You Off My Mind)
55243 SHAKE A HAND (5-63) [W. Linda Hopkins]/Say I Do
55246 SHAKE! SHAKE! SHAKE! (7-63)/He's A Fool
55250 BABY GET IT (And Don't Quit It) (9-63)/The New Breed
55254 SILENT NIGHT (12-63)/O Holy Night
55260 HAUNTED HOUSE (3-64)/I'm Travelin' On
55266 BIG BOSS LINE (5-64)/Be My Girl
55269 SQUEEZE HER—TEASE HER (8-64)/Give Me Back My Heart
55277 DANNY BOY (2-65)/Soul Time
55278 YES INDEED (3-65) [W. Linda Hopkins]/When The Saints Go Marching In
55280 NO PITY (In The Naked City) (7-65)/I'm So Lonely
55283 I BELIEVE I'LL LOVE ON (10-65)/Lonely Teardrops
55287 THINK TWICE (1-66) [W. Lavern Baker]/Please Don't Hurt Me
55289 3 DAYS, 1 HOUR, 30 MINUTES (3-66)/I've Got To Get Back (Country Boy)
55290 BRAND NEW THING (4-66)/Soul Galore
55294 I BELIEVE (7-66)/Be My Love
55300 WHISPERS (Gettin' Louder) (10-66)/The Fairest Of Them All
55309 I DON'T WANT TO LOSE YOU (2-67)/Just Be Sincere
55321 I'VE LOST YOU (5-67)/Those Heartaches
55336 HIGHER AND HIGHER (8-67) [Written by Carl Smith, noted black composer, for Fontella Bass]/I'm The One To Do It
55354 SINCE YOU SHOWED ME HOW TO BE HAPPY (11-67)/The Who Who Song
55365 FOR YOUR PRECIOUS LOVE (2-68) [W. Count Basie] [Jerry Butler and "Impressions" '58 hit. ABNER 1013]/Uptight
55373 CHAIN GANG (4-68) [W. Count Basie] [Sam Cooke '60 hit. RCA 47-7783]/Funky Broadway
55381 I GET THE SWEETEST FEELING (7-68)/Nothing But Heartaches (Keep Haunting Me)
55392 FOR ONCE IN MY LIFE (11-68) [Stevie Wonder '68 hit. TAMLA 54174]/You Brought About A Change In Me

55402 I STILL LOVE YOU (4-69)/Hum De Dum De Do
55418 HELPLESS (9-69)/Do It The Right Way
55423 WITH THESE HANDS (11-69)/Why Don't You
55435 LET THIS BE A LETTER (To My Baby) (5-70)/Forever And A Day
55443 (I Can Feel Those Vibrations) THIS LOVE IS REAL (12-70)/ Love Uprising [Otis Leavill song]
55449 THIS GUY'S IN LOVE WITH YOU (5-71) [Herb Alpert '68 hit. A&M 929]/Say You Will
55461 LOVE IS FUNNY THAT WAY (11-71)/Try It Again
55467 YOU GOT ME WALKING (2-72)/The Fountain
55490 BEAUTIFUL DAY (2-73)/What'cha Gonna Do About Me
55495 BECAUSE OF YOU (4-73)/Go Away
55499 SEND A LITTLE SONG (8-73)/No More Goodbyes
55504 IT'S ALL OVER (11-73)/Shake A Leg
55522 DON'T BURN NO BRIDGES (12-75) [W. the "Chi-Lites"]/ Don't Burn No Bridges [Instr.]

♭♯♪♩♩

Bobby Womack

Born in Cleveland, Ohio, on March 4, 1944.

BOBBY WOMACK had his roots in Gospel and in singing R&B with his brothers, then known as the "Womack Brothers" or the "Valentinos." He was inspired by his father, Friendly Womack, Sr. (on guitar), along with his brothers, Friendly, Jr., Curtis, Harry and Cecil, making his debut performance at Friendship Baptist Church with the "Soul Stirrers." Opportunity came suddenly and in a big way when, in 1960, Roscoe Robinson (lead singer of the "Ohio Blind Boys"), a friend, contacted Sam Cooke, inquiring if he remembered the "Womack Brothers" appearing at local church concerts, and Sam, having remembered, suggested a joint meeting in Chicago. The result was the SAR label signing of the Womacks as the "Womack Brothers," recording a couple of Gospel tunes. With a name change to the "Valentinos" (and the "Lovers"), they switched to Rhythm and Blues. "Lookin' For A Love" (SAR 132) was recorded in Chicago with a regional action group club apperance in Los Angeles. Later, looking for a potential hit, they contacted Sam Cooke's manager, J. W. Alexander, and recorded a song written by Bobby himself, "It's All Over Now" (SAR 152), which became a hit and also achieved further fame when recorded by the "Rolling Stones" in 1964. Incidentally, the Womacks were all outstanding left-handed guitarists!

Bobby Womack toured with Sam Cooke, and it was Sam's keen interest in him that kept Bobby writing and singing. This influence was to continue after Sam Cooke's sudden and tragic death when Bobby Womack married Barbara Campbell, Sam's widow. Then, Bobby went on to write "I'm In Love" and "People Make The World" for Wilson Pickett and accompanied him on their recording. Through the latter Sixties, Bobby Womack recorded for several labels: HIM, CHECKER, ATLANTIC, and KEYMEN, but with little success until MINIT/LIBERTY label had Bobby record his own arrangement of the Pop entries "Fly Me To The Moon" (MINIT 32048), "California Dreamin' " (MINIT 32055), and "I Left My Heart In San Francisco" (MINIT 32059).

It was during the Seventies that Bobby Womack, now known as "The Preacher" really excelled, with his recordings of "More Than I Can Stand" (MINIT 32093), "That's the Way I Feel About Cha" (UNITED ARTISTS 50847), "Harry Hippy" (UNITED ARTISTS 50946), and the "Valentinos'" "I Can Understand It" (CLEAN 60005). Bobby Womack always kept his brothers around him in party style, with happiness, fun, and singing hopes and it came as quite a shock when Harry was stabbed to death by a girlfriend, in Bobby's apartment, on March 9, 1974.

Bobby Womack's major releases during the Seventies were "I'm Through Trying To Prove My Love To You" (UNITED ARTISTS 255), "Lookin' For A Love" (UNITED ARTISTS 375), which earned Bobby a million-selling disc, and "I Don't Know" (UNITED ARTISTS 561). Bobby Womack has a naturally dynamic singing voice, which was best exemplified in the following winning releases: "Check It Out" (UNITED ARTISTS 621), "Daylight" (UNITED ARTISTS 763), a great tune that was covered by Vicki Sue Robinson, and the fabulous "Home Is Where The Heart Is" (COLUMBIA 3-10437). Bobby Womack has become a legend in his own lifetime and one of the most expressive and creative of individuals. Some of his other excellent recordings are "Trust Your Heart" (COLUMBIA 3-10672), "Wind It Up" (COLUMBIA 3-10732), and "How Could You Break My Heart" (ARISTA 421). Truly a fascinating career for one of the most talented Soul masters, who, in 1979, celebrated twenty-five years in show business!

Discography

AS "WOMACK BROTHERS"

SAR

118 SOMEBODY'S WRONG (8-61) [Feat. Curtis Womack]/Yield Not To Temptation

AS "VALENTINOS"

132 LOOKIN' FOR A LOVE (7-62) [Feat. Bobby Womack]/ Somewhere There's A Girl [Also on ASTRO Label 1026]

IMPERIAL

5804 WHAT ABOUT ME (1962)

AS "LOVERS"

SAR

137 I'LL MAKE IT ALRIGHT (1-63)/Darling Come Back Home

AS "VALENTINOS"

144 SHE'S SO GOOD TO ME (1963)/Baby Lots Of Luck
152 IT'S ALL OVER NOW (6-64) [Feat. Bobby Womack]/Tired Of Living In The Country [Written by Sam Cooke]
155 EVERYBODY WANTS TO FALL IN LOVE (1964)/Bitter Dreams

BOBBY WOMACK

HIM

100 NOTHING YOU CAN DO (1965)

CHECKER

1122 A LONESOME MAN (1965)/I Found A True Love

AS "VALENTINOS"

CHESS

1952 DO IT RIGHT (1965)/What About Me
1977 LET'S GET TOGETHER (11-66)/Sweeter Than The Day Before

BOBBY WOMACK

ATLANTIC

2388 FIND ME SOMEBODY (3-67)/How Does It Feel

MINIT

32024 BABY I CAN'T STAND IT (7-67)/Trust Me
32030 BROADWAY WALK (11-67)/Someone Special
32037 WHAT IS THIS (3-68)/(When Your Love Is Gone) What You Gonna Do
32048 FLY ME TO THE MOON (8-68)/Take Me [Written by Big Dee Irwin]

AS "VALENTINOS"

JUBILEE

5636 TIRED OF BEING NOBODY (11-68)/The Death Of Love
5650 TWO LOVER'S HISTORY (3-69)/You Got That Kind Of Love That's Real

BOBBY WOMACK

MINIT

32055 CALIFORNIA DREAMIN' (12-68)/Baby! You Oughta Think It Over
32059 I LEFT MY HEART IN SAN FRANCISCO (4-69)/Love, The Time Is Now
32071 IT'S GONNA RAIN (8-69)/Thank You
32081 HOW I MISS YOU BABY (11-69)/Tried And Convicted
32093 MORE THAN I CAN STAND (4-70)/Arkansas State Prison

LIBERTY

56186 I'M GONNA FORGET ABOUT YOU (8-70)/Don't Look Back
56206 EVERYBODY'S TALKING (11-70)/Something

UNITED ARTISTS (MINIT Parent Label)

50773 THE PREACHER (4-71)/The Preacher/More Than I Can Stand
50816 COMMUNICATION (10-71) [Backed by Sly Stone, Delaney & Bonnie, and Ike Turner]/Communication [Part 2]

SZABO GABOR AND BOBBY WOMACK

BLUE THUMB

200 BREEZIN' (10-71)/Azure Blue

BOBBY WOMACK

UNITED ARTISTS

50847 THAT'S THE WAY I FEEL ABOUT CHA (12-71)/Come L'Amore

AS "LOVE & THE BROTHERHOOD" ("VALENTINOS")

CHESS

2126 WHAT ABOUT ME (1972)

BOBBY WOMACK

UNITED ARTISTS

50902 WOMAN'S GOTTA HAVE IT (5-72)/(If You Don't Want My Love) Give It Back
50946 HARRY HIPPY (12-72)/Sweet Carolina [Came out August 1972]
196 ACROSS 110th STREET (3-73)/Hang On In There
255 NOBODY WANTS YOU WHEN YOU'RE DOWN AND OUT (6-73)/I'm Through Trying To Prove My Love To You

AS "VALENTINOS"

CLEAN

60005 I CAN UNDERSTAND IT (1973) [Feat. Curtis Womack] ["New Birth" '73 hit. RCA 74-0912]/I Can Understand It [Part 2]

BOBBY WOMACK

UNITED ARTISTS

375 LOOKIN' FOR A LOVE (2-74)/Let It Hang Out
439 YOU'RE WELCOME, STOP ON BY (7-74)/I Don't Want To Be Hurt
561 I DON'T KNOW (9-74)/Yes Jesus Loves Me
621 CHECK IT OUT (6-75)/Interlude #2
674 IT'S ALL OVER NOW (8-75) [W. Bill Withers]/Git It
763 DAYLIGHT (2-76)/Trust Me

CURTIS WOMACK (BOBBY'S BROTHER)

PLAYBOY

6071 BOOGIE WOOGIE JONES (7-76)/Last Date

BOBBY WOMACK

UNITED ARTISTS

804 I FEEL A GROOVE COMIN' ON (8-76) [W. Herbie Hancock, piano]/Trust Me

AS "BOBBY WOMACK & BROTHERHOOD"

COLUMBIA

3-10437	HOME IS WHERE THE HEART IS (11-76)/We've Only Just Begun
3-10493	STANDING IN THE SAFETY ZONE (3-77)/A Change Is Gonna Come
3-10672	TRUST YOUR HEART (2-78) [W. David Ruffin]/When Love Begins Friendship Ends
3-10732	WIND IT UP (5-78)/Stop Before We Start

BOBBY WOMACK

ARISTA

421	HOW COULD YOU BREAK MY HEART (5-79)
446	THE ROADS OF LIFE (8-79)

Stevie Wonder

Real Name: "Stevland Judkins." Born in Saginaw, Michigan, on May 13, 1950.

STEVIE WONDER was not only born black and poor, he was born blind—*and* he was born to conquer! A genuine, exuberant star, he never became disenchanted with either his initial lowly position in life or with his grave physical handicap. "Blindness," he said, "was not a handicap unless you decided to make it so." Music came naturally and early to little Stevie, but it was only by tremendous enthusiasm and unrelenting hard work that it was squeezed out of his tender young frame. He was born the third oldest of six children, four brothers (Timothy, Calvin, Milton, and Larry) and one sister (Renee), to Mama Lulu Judkins. His father (Judkins) left when Stevie was very young, and the family moved to Detroit. There, the family name was to change twice with two stepfathers, "Morris" and "Hardaway." Stevie's introduction to the joys of musical instrumentation was through the gift of a four-hole key-chain harmonica from an uncle, and in his fascination with the variety of sounds he could make as he played it almost continuously. From the very beginning, he dreamed of becoming another Ray Charles.

In Detroit, he attended public school classes for the blind and, later, the School for the Blind in Lansing, Michigan, where he got a good grounding in piano and Classical music. Stevie also became junior deacon and played the bongos at Whitestone Fundamentalist Baptist Church while, over the same period, becoming proficient with the harmonica, piano, drums, clarinet, and the organ! From the age of ten, young Stevie became a familiar figure around Studio A at HITSVILLE, U.S.A. (which became Detroit's MOTOWN) where "the little wonder boy," as he became known, enjoyed the activity, sounds, and music of actual recording while mingling with the performers. Stevie's first big break came through John Glover, his school chum and a friend of a younger brother of Ronnie White (of the famous "Miracles"), when Ronnie heard young Stevie entertaining the family in that home. An immediate audition was arranged with the TAMLA-MOTOWN label, where Brian Holland (of Holland-Dozier-Holland songwriting fame, which characterized the Detroit Sound), studio A&R man, and Berry Gordy, Jr., the chief, liked what they heard. That was 1960, when, only ten years old, Stevie was not only put under contract but under the wonderful influence and skilled guidance of Clarence Paul, MOTOWN engineer-arranger-producer, the man who gave him the title "Little Stevie Wonder" and whom, years later, Stevie was to describe as like a father or older brother.

Stevie Wonder did some backup Gospel sessions and wrote "Lonely Boy." His first release came in 1962 with his harmonica-rocking "I Call It Pretty Music (But The Old People Call It The Blues)" (TAMLA 54061), which was followed by Lamont Dozier's moderately successful "Contract On Love" (TAMLA 54074). Two initial problems faced Berry Gordy, Jr., in that he could not financially afford heavy backup support for his budding star and Stevie was not old enough for nightclub exposure, but Gordy solved both by the inspired use of the Apollo Theater in Harlem and recording Little Stevie Wonder in concert! Then came the harmonica-wailing classic "Fingertips [Part 2]," which was written by Stevie, followed by the single as well as the album "That 12-Year Old Genius," which reached No. 1 on the U.S. Charts. The impact of Little Stevie Wonder was phenomenal, with songs by Henry Cosby, Clarence Paul, Brian Holland, his own, and some co-written with Clarence Paul and his mother, now Lulu Hardaway. Sometimes the enthusiastic Little Stevie Wonder had to be removed from the crowded platforms after a performance: "I used to pick him up and carry him off, until he got too heavy," Clarence Paul loves to remind us.

Stevie enjoyed priority bookings over the "Temptations" and "Martha and the Vandellas" when he toured on "The Little Stevie Wonder Show," with audiences becoming hysterical as he blew wild harmonica solos punctuated by brass support. Attempts were made to curb and shape the excess enthusiasm and bubbling talent of Little Stevie Wonder, but he proved himself to be a junior-sized James Brown who was at his best when unrestrained by convention or conditions. "Hey, Harmonica Man" (TAMLA 54096) led the three last releases as Little Stevie Wonder, and plans were made to broaden his material outside his actual age (he was fifteen). This was done with his first "Stevie Wonder" release, "High Heel Sneakers" (TAMLA 54119), in August 1965. He was now acquiring something of the "Genius Magic" of his idol Ray Charles, and MOTOWN soon borrowed the "genius" tag and used it on the Stevie Wonder album "Tribute To Ray Charles." A steady stream of Top-Forty hits poured from Stevie Wonder before he reached seventeen, such as "Uptight (Everything's Alright/Purple Raindrops" (TAMLA 54124), "Blowin' In The Wind" (TAMLA 54136), "A Place In The Sun" (TAMLA 54139), and his own uptempo top-winning "I Was Made To Love Her" (TAMLA

54151). These were followed by "Shoo-Be-Doo-Be-Doo-Da-Day" (TAMLA 54165), "For Once In My Life" (TAMLA 54174), "My Cherie Amour" (TAMLA 54180), "Yester-Me, Yester-You, Yesterday" (TAMLA 54188), and a release under the pseudonym "Eivets Rednow" ("Stevie Wonder" spelled backward) for GORDY label. Stevie Wonder became a sensation, appearing at places like the Kiel Opera House in St. Louis, the Regal in Chicago, and the New Graystone in Detroit, besides gyrating wildly on the *American Bandstand* show!

A youthful Stevie Wonder was most fortunate in such early relationships with MOTOWN personnel, because it was highly unlikely that any other such group would have even listened, let alone give him a working opportunity. MOTOWN (then HITSVILLE, U.S.A.) at that time was a small-time black recording company that acted paternally to most of its young, black, usually uneducated, aspirants right off the streets with little hope of securing expensive legal counsel. A mutual contract, in the artist's best interest, was drawn up, covering bookings, staging, recording, and even the copyrighting of his songs. Stevie Wonder's royalties were all kept in trust for him, with a guardian appointed by the state, until he was twenty-one years of age. The fact of Stevie's not being old enough to enter the nightclub circuit or make legal decisions on his own behalf, and that of his continuing education, created problems for Berry Gordy, Jr., who patiently resolved them one at a time, particularly the hassle with the Detroit Board of Education, which permitted Stevie to finish his schooling at Lansing, Michigan.

Stevie Wonder married Syreeta Wright on September 14, 1970. Syreeta, who was talented and had her sights on a career of her own, was already one of Stevie's co-authors and had been backup singer on his "Talk of the Town" album. Stevie wrote most of the material and produced Syreeta's first album, entitled simply "Syreeta" ano, though he hoped it would not be accepted as a Stevie Wonder supported package but star Syreeta's first album, entitled simply "Syreeta" and, though he hoped lesser Diana Ross style with something of the passion of Dionne Warwick, paled in the support wizardry of Stevie Wonder, and their union of talent proved as unsatisfactory as their marriage, which ended after only eighteen months. Syreeta remained a secondary part of Stevie Wonder's musical career by appearing in his staged "Wonderlove," which also presented Lanie Grooves and Linda (who became Lynda Lawrence of the "Supremes"), and they insisted on remaining good friends. Stevie had, by then, moved out of the family home and set himself up in New York and completed his album "Where I'm Coming From."

The highly versatile Stevie Wonder, now described by Berry Gordy, Jr., as "The Prince Regent of Soul," had become a master showman, toured with the "Rolling Stones" in 1972, did the production of Minnie Ripperton's "Perfect Angel" under the pseudonym "El Toro Negro" in 1974, and wrote "Tell Me Something Good," which was recorded by the funky group "Rufus" (ABC 11427) the same year, as well as providing Moog synthesizer backup on sessions for Jeff Beck, Eric Clapton, Steve Stills, and James Taylor! A renowned producer of the Seventies, Stevie now entered upon a new musical innovation, bringing his religious ideals and a blending of Rock to Boogie and Reggae. "Superstition" (TAMLA 54226) intimated an acceptance of astrological signs, a funky song that became a No. 1 hit. The follow-up, "You Are The Sunshine Of My Life" (TAMLA 54232), proved to be Stevie's most recorded song by other artists, and as a beautiful ballad it ranked top of the Charts.

The happy climax in his life came with Yolanda Simmons, one-time secretary at MOTOWN whom Stevie Wonder met again when she sought employment with his BLACK BULL Music Company. Yolanda, his beloved "Londie," became his wife and devoted aide both at home and on the road, and bore him a daughter, Aisha Zakia (meaning "Strength and Intelligence"), of whom Stevie boastfully sang in his song "Isn't She Wonderful."

But with joy sometimes comes tragedy! On August 6, 1973, a freak accident almost brought to an end a brilliant career. While Stevie was riding in the front seat on his way to a concert engagement, the car, which was being driven by John Harris (his cousin), was being edged past a heavily loaded truck of logs in North Carolina when a log slipped loose and rammed through the windshield of the Wonder car, leaving Stevie close to death in a coma, in the hospital, for ten days! There, according to Ira Tucker, a concerned group of friends gathered around his bed reciting lyrics from his "Higher Ground," when suddenly Stevie's fingers began to move in rhythm and he showed signs of recovery.

On September 25, less than eight weeks afterward, Stevie Wonder was back on a jam session with Elton John in "Honky-Tonk Woman." He had refused cosmetic surgical treatment and bears the scars, above his right eye and on the lower right side of his face, to this day. Stevie Wonder, philosophically, accepted the whole ghastly experience as an admonition from God "to slow down and live." "I came out of it believing that life is really beautiful," he later said, "more lovely than I had ever imagined."

Something needs to be said about the charitable side of this musical colossus, who, besides being recipient of the Human Kindness Day Award in Los Angeles in 1974, gave a total charity benefit appearance in Washington, D.C., before fifty thousand enthusiastic fans. The proceeds of his 1975 concert tour, which was a smashing success, all went to charity, and he even planned on going to Africa to raise money and help finance medical restoration of sight for those blinded by an alien fungus attacking the cornea of the eye. Heavy commitments frustrated this fond hope, but he did set up several homes for the blind. Another benevolent side to Stevie Wonder is his grateful loyalty to those who labored with him, and this was shown during the period immediately after his near-fatal mishap, when he was unable to perform in any way, by his retaining all his personnel on payroll.

Stevie Wonder, between 1974 and 1977, collected many Grammys and earned the title "The Ellington of the Seventies." His hits continued with "Don't You Worry 'Bout A Thing" (TAMLA 54245), "You Haven't Done Nothin' Yet" (TAMLA 54252), "Boogie On Reggae Woman" (TAMLA 54254), "I Wish" (TAMLA 54274), and his ever-popular "Sir Duke" (TAMLA 54281), his tribute to Duke Ellington. On April 16, 1977, Yolanda presented Stevie Wonder with a son, Keita Sawandi (meaning "Worshiper, Founder"). Since 1973, Stevie Wonder has ruled as the Superstar's Superstar, with records selling like hotcakes, and has toured the greatest of the stadiums, with each performance drawing the jammed fans on to the stage just to touch him. This ongoing euphoria was only temporarily interrupted by his accident and his stay in the hospital. All of this has to be topped by the fact of the release of his album "Songs To The Key Of Life," a release that was prolonged because of his renegotiation of contract with MOTOWN, a deal that would eventually bring him $13,000,000 over the next seven years—the biggest ever in the history of recording!

Discography

AS "LITTLE STEVIE WONDER"

TAMLA (Subsidiary of MOTOWN)

54061	I CALL IT PRETTY MUSIC (BUT THE OLD PEOPLE CALL IT THE BLUES) (1962)/I Call It Pretty Music (But The Old People Call It The Blues) [Part 2]
54070	LITTLE WATER BOY (10-62)/La La La La La
54074	CONTRACT ON LOVE (12-62)/Sunset
54080	FINGERTIPS (6-63)/Fingertips [Part 2]
54086	WORKOUT STEVIE, WORKOUT (10-63)/Monkey Talk
54090	CASTLES IN THE SAND (2-64)/To Thank You
54096	HEY HARMONICA MAN (6-64)/This Little Girl
54103	SAD BOY (9-64)/Happy Street
54114	KISS ME BABY (2-65)/Tears In Vain

AS "STEVIE WONDER"

TAMLA

54119 HIGH HEEL SNEAKERS (8-65) [Tommy Tucker '64 hit. CHECKER 1067]/Music Talk
54124 UPTIGHT (EVERYTHING'S ALRIGHT) (12-65)/Purple Raindrops
54130 NOTHING'S TOO GOOD FOR MY BABY (4-66)/With A Child's Heart
54136 BLOWIN' IN THE WIND (7-66) [W. Clarence Paul]/Ain't That Asking For Trouble
54139 A PLACE IN THE SUN (11-66)/Sylvia
54142 SOME DAY AT CHRISTMAS (12-66)/The Miracles Of Christmas
54147 TRAVELIN' MAN (3-67)/Hey Love
54151 I WAS MADE TO LOVE HER (6-67)/Hold Me
54157 I'M WONDERING (10-67)/Every Time I See You I Go Wild
54165 SHOO-BE-DOO-BE-DOO-DA-DAY (4-68)/Why Don't You Lead Me To Love
54168 YOU MET YOUR MATCH (7-68)/My Girl

AS "EIVETS REDNOW"

GORDY

7076 ALFIE (10-68)/More Than A Dream

AS "STEVIE WONDER"

TAMLA

54174 FOR ONCE IN MY LIFE (11-68) [Jackie Wilson '68 hit. BRUNSWICK 55392]/Angie Girl
54180 MY CHERIE AMOUR (5-69)/I Don't Know Why (I Love You) (2-69)
54188 YESTER-ME, YESTER-YOU, YESTERDAY (10-69)/I'd Be A Fool Right Now
54191 NEVER HAD A DREAM COME TRUE (2-70)/Somebody Knows, Somebody Cares
54196 SIGNED, SEALED, DELIVERED I'M YOURS (6-70)/I'm More Than Happy (I'm Satisfied)
54200 HEAVEN HELP US ALL (10-70)/I Gotta Have A Song
54202 WE CAN WORK IT OUT (3-71) Never Dreamed You'd Leave In Summer
54208 IF YOU REALLY LOVE ME (8-71)/Think Of Me As Your Soldier
54216 SUPER WOMAN (WHERE WERE YOU WHEN I NEEDED YOU) (5-72)/I Love Every Little Thing About You
54226 SUPERSTITION (11-72)/You've Got It Bad

54232 YOU ARE THE SUNSHINE OF MY LIFE (3-73)/Tuesday Heartbreak
54235 HIGHER GROUND (8-73)/Too High
54242 LIVING FOR THE CITY (11-73)/Visions
54245 DON'T YOU WORRY 'BOUT A THING (4-74) [W. Yolanda murmuring audibly]/Blame It On The Sun
54252 YOU HAVEN'T DONE NOTHIN' YET (8-74)/Big Brother
54254 BOOGIE ON REGGAE WOMAN (11-74)/Seems So Long
54274 I WISH (11-76)/You And I
54281 SIR DUKE* (4-77)/He's Misstra Know-It-All
54303 SEND ONE YOUR LOVE (11-79)/Send One Your Love [Instr.]
54286 ANOTHER STAR (8-77)/Creepin'
54291 AS (11-77)/Contusion

AS "STEVIE WONDER" (WITH DIANA ROSS, MARVIN GAYE, AND SMOKEY ROBINSON)

MOTOWN

1455 POPS WE LOVE YOU [Vocal] (1-79)/Pops We Love You [Instr.]

---

*Featured brass backup: Hank Redd (sax); Ray and Steve Madaio (trumpets); Trevor Lawrence (tenor sax).